Football
Coaching

Football Coaching

Compiled by
**The American
Football Coaches Association**

Edited by **Dick Herbert**

Charles Scribner's Sons • New York

This book owes its existence to many coaches who have sustained the great game of football and who have shared their knowledge freely. To them, and especially to the late DeOrmond (Tuss) McLaughry and to William D. Murray, executive directors whose astute guidance has made the American Football Coaches Association a strong force for the good in football, this book is dedicated.

—D. H.

Chapter 48, "The Football Coach and Liability" by Eugene P. O'Connor: Excerpts in this chapter from the Trial magazine article "Responsibility is Also Part of the Game" by Samuel Langerman and Noel Fidel are reprinted by permission from Trial magazine, January 1977, The Association of Trial Lawyers of America.

Chapters 1 to 50 previously appeared in the Proceedings and Summer Manuals of the AFCA. Chapter 51, A Coach's Guide to Safe Football, is reprinted from a pamphlet prepared and distributed by the AFCA.

Library of Congress Cataloging in Publication Data
Main entry under title:

Football coaching.

1. Football coaching—Addresses, essays, lectures. I. American Football Coaches Association.
GV956.6.F66   796.332'07'7   81-9056
ISBN 0-684-17149-X   AACR2

Printed in the United States of America

Contents

Editor's Note

Coaching is a profession of change. A number of contributors to this book, as of its publication date, no longer have the position ascribed to them in the chapter bylines. The changes are as follows:

CHAPTER
1 Woody Hayes. Retired from coaching.
3 Shirley Majors. Deceased.
5 Jim Young. Head coach, Purdue University.
7 John McKay. Head coach, Tampa Bay, NFL.
10 Larry Smith. Head coach, University of Arizona.
12 Darrell Royal. Assistant to the president, University of Texas.
15 Jimmye Laycock. Head coach, College of William and Mary.
19 Bill Walsh. Head coach, San Francisco, NFL.
20 Homer Rice. Athletic director, Georgia Tech.
22 Homer Smith. Offensive coordinator, UCLA.
23 Roger Theder. Head coach, California, Berkeley.
25 Mike Mikolayunas. Deceased.
26 Pepper Rodgers. Out of coaching.
27 Jim Hoggatt. Out of coaching.
28 Bill Bryant. Assistant coach, Weber State.
30 Esco Sarkkinen. Out of coaching.
32 Bill Oliver. Head coach, Tennessee, Chattanooga.
   Paul Crane. Out of coaching.
35 Ben Martin. Out of coaching.
37 Frank Maloney. Out of coaching.
38 George Hill. Assistant coach, Philadelphia, NFL.
43 Lee Corso. Head coach, Indiana University.
49 Chuck Mills. Athletic director/head coach, Southern Oregon State.

Preface

Football is very simple in its basic principles, but it is amazingly complex in its preparation and execution. No other team sport requires so many participants with individual skills that must mesh into a smooth team execution.

Those who teach the sport are constantly seeking the best ways to produce a team superior to those it plays. Yet it has been a tradition of the American Football Coaches Association since its founding in 1922 to share freely with other members of the association the "secrets" of their methods.

At the annual convention of the AFCA, there are three days of football lectures by the leading coaches of the season just concluded. These lectures are printed in the AFCA's *Proceedings*. In addition, the association annually publishes its *Summer Manual,* which contains clinical articles on coaching.

Until now, these articles and lectures were available only to the members of the AFCA. That organization, however, has regularly received requests for a book for public sale that would contain expert coaching methods for every phase of the sport. How could there be a better book on coaching than one made up of lectures and articles from past AFCA publications?

This has been done in *Football Coaching.* The most difficult problem was confining the book to only what is between these covers. The final selection omits many articles of value. The scope of the book, however, imposed limits on how much each section could include.

Dr. Dave Hutter, athletic director at Bethany College, West Virginia, was especially helpful in getting the project moving. Many coaches contributed, each subscribing to the AFCA tradition of considering it an honor to share his knowledge with his colleagues and competitors.

From the publishing end, Louise B. Ketz, managing editor at Charles Scribner's Sons, has guided the project with expertise. Even before being confronted with the sometimes strange language of football coaches, she could talk intelligently with anyone about the sport.

In the original production of these articles the work of Marty Pierson of Durham, N.C., a former coach, on most of the diagrams and of David Bryant of Creative Printers, Chapel Hill, N.C., in the printing of the *Proceedings* and *Summer Manuals* greatly eased the burden of the editor.

This book was conceived with the basic purpose of providing one volume to which a young person with a consuming urge to someday be called "Coach" could turn and find much of what it takes. From it the experienced coach can add to his knowledge. The football fan will find some of the technical articles somewhat baffling, but there is much he can understand easily that should make him an all-star Monday quarterback.

Dick Herbert, Editor

Part One
The Philosophy of Coaching

1

Ohio State Philosophy of Football

(From 1970 Proceedings of the AFCA)

WOODY HAYES Head Coach, Ohio State University

I shall start with some insights into the coaching profession that are taken from a book published in 1969. The author* has graciously given me permission to read from it. The name of it is *Hot Line to Victory.*

1. One of the most important characteristics of a successful coach is be yourself. It was Socrates who said, "Know thyself"; but it is up to the coach to be himself. Often a young coach will imitate one of his former coaches. It is excellent to emulate a former coach, but do not imitate him.

2. There are two qualities that a coach must have to a far greater degree than any other member of the teaching staff: First, the coach must have an intense and continuing interest in the welfare and in the all-around development of each player. With little reflection, the coach will realize that his own success is dependent on the attitude and the effort of those players. If he is successful, he certainly owes much to those players, and his continual interest and help to those young men become important and worthwhile.

Second, the coach must have an extremely strong desire to win. However, it must be a "we" win attitude, not an "I" win attitude. He is the leader of the team, but he is also a member of the team. When he is confronted with defeat, he must never use the sick alibis, "if that pass hadn't been intercepted" or "if our end had caught the ball in the end zone." Such excuses are a reflection on the individual player and will be construed as an attempt by the coach to remove himself from the blame of losing. In time of victory there are enough plaudits for everyone, but in time of defeat, the responsibility must be taken by the most mature and most responsible man involved—the head coach.

* Mr. Hayes himself is the author of *Hot Line to Victory.*

3. There is one luxury the coach cannot afford—it is the luxury of self-pity. When the coach resorts to this psychological mechanism, his days in the profession are numbered.

4. The coach must assume a positive attitude toward his job. If he enjoys coaching, as a good coach will, he must realize that he gets paid for the headaches involved in the coaching profession. Headaches—such as morale problems, training problems, undue pressure—all of these are things tied in with the profession, and the coach must recognize them for what they are. He must anticipate these problems; he must say not, "If they happen," but, "**When** they happen"; and then he must take all precautions to keep them from happening.

5. The coach must win. There is a Roman expression, *"Res nolunt diu male administrari,"* which purportedly means, "Things refuse to be mismanaged long." In the coaching profession there is no adequate substitute for winning.

6. Criticism must be regarded as impersonal, for it is an occupational hazard. Usually the critic is vocal only because the team lost, and this cannot be regarded as a personal criticism. This critic may not even know the coach, but he does know that the coach is the leader of the team that lost. Quite often this type of criticism is hardest on the coach who returns to his own college or to his own community. He must realize that the same person who patted him on the back as a player can change his aim and figuratively beat him over the head as a coach. The coach and his family who are not prepared for this will have bad times.

7. In high school the coach is hired for one thing and fired for another. One of the true anomalies in the high school coaching profession is the fact that the coach receives a small percent of his salary for coach-

ing and the large percent of it for his classroom teaching and other duties. However, he will rarely be dismissed for his failure as a classroom teacher.

8. The head coach's job security lies in three areas:

First, he must rely on his own abilities and resources.

Second, he must believe absolutely in the players and his coaches. This does not mean that the discerning coach does not recognize the weaknesses of each player and coach, but at the same time he must recognize in them and in himself the opportunity for team victory. He must realize that you win with people, the right people, properly led.

Third, the football coach must cooperate with his administration. Coach Bear Bryant, one of the truly great college coaches of all time, would second this 100 percent. He goes further to say that a coach should always have a long-term contract. This cooperation with the administration is obviously a two-way street. Most administrators see in the coach and the athletic team a positive force for good attitude and good discipline in the school system.

9. The training of the coach must be an extremely broadening experience. In general, coaches feel that the most important coaching preparation is, first, actual coaching experience after graduation; second, undergraduate athletic experience; and third, coaching schools and coaching clinics after graduation. Undergraduate work in physical education, psychology, education, and practice teaching are regarded by coaches as having relatively little value in preparation for coaching. With this in mind it would appear that the coach upon graduation should make a strong effort to get on a good high school coaching staff or stay at his university, or some other university, for graduate work. Even though he works for "peanuts," it will be worth his while to be able to work on a good college coaching staff for a year or two. When a coach becomes a head coach he must have a sound knowledge of all of the phases of football. For this reason a young coach must be a fast and eager learner. Although we often say that there are things more important than drawing circles and x's, this is only partly true; for the young coach's first contact with the player is as an individual coach, and he must prove himself to be a good technician with a good knowledge of intricate football. He must be able to captivate the player mentally and to build within the player the desire to compete and to improve. The first impression the player must have is, "Here's a man who really knows the game and knows how to put it across." Considering first things first, the young coach must be a good technician.

10. Moving into college coaching, we find that almost always a successful high school coach has aspirations of moving into college coaching. Although there are many reasons for this, some of the most important seem to be:

First, to find the answer to the question, "How good a coach am I?"

Second, the college coach gets to spend more time on actual coaching and less time on other duties.

Third, the college coach gets more recognition, and, for this reason, to move into college is an advancement. The high school coach has seen his own players move into college ranks, and he has the desire to follow them there and to work with more mature athletes.

Fourth, he has the desire to excel and he believes he can achieve this better on the college level.

Fifth, higher pay standards are also a factor, although this is not always the case.

11. Much has been written and discussed about the coach and public relations. Certainly his most important qualification in this area is to live up to all the fine things for which football stands.

In this area he must be like no one but himself. In dealing with the press he should tell the truth, or say nothing. To mislead the press is neither ethical nor sensible. Most of these men are interested in sports and want to portray sports in a positive sense, and very often a coach can give them information that will help them do this. On the other hand, the coach has no right to expect these men to write exactly as the coach sees it.

One caution: The public relations image can be grossly exaggerated; for the coach who is spending much of his time associating with different groups is making a mistake. The alumni, the boosters, and your own close friends never win games; but a well-trained and minutely coached group of young men will win.

In educational circles very often the word "win" is given an evil connotation, because it is often implied that winning means breaking some rules, but this is certainly not true. On the contrary, winning means the bringing together in a common effort all the physical and mental resources of the football squad and its coaches, which in no way warrants an apology.

12. If a football coach is successful, he will usually move up by changing positions some five or six times during his career. At each of these moves his interview with the selection committee is a very important step in his success. The job interview is rarely discussed, but it will suffice to say that the coach should go into this interview as well prepared as he can possibly be, having anticipated every exigency that will probably arise, for his future depends on his selling himself at this crucial moment.

13. Coaching is not a profession that offers great

security; a coach almost always gives up active coaching before he is ready to retire. This phenomenon is equally true in high school and college and must be taken into consideration in the coach's life preparation.

As a head coach, here are some suggestions you may wish to consider in organizing and leading a football staff. For the assistant coach it may be well for you to know what your head coach is thinking.

1. In coaching, select each of your associates first on character, second on personality traits and work habits, and third on technical competence. If he rates "4.0" in the first two, he can be taught anything else he needs to know.

2. As you add this man to your staff, be sure to show him that he belongs. When you interview him, have other members of your staff also interview him. When he is hired, remind him that he impressed not only you but the other members of the staff as well, or he would not have been hired.

3. If you feel it is necessary to have any rules of discipline for your coaches, make them explicit. However, as among the players, we feel that attitudes are much more important than rules.

4. Treat your associates with the respect they deserve. The best way to do this is by asking their opinions—unless the answers are too readily forthcoming.

5. Set up definite work areas and assignments for each coach. By doing this you can avoid the overlapping of responsibility.

6. Be explicit in showing your coaches what to do, but do not show them how to do it. The "how" must be a part of their ingenuity and coaching personality.

7. Develop a system of follow-up procedures, for some coaches assume responsibility much better than others. It may be necessary for you to check on certain coaches in the area of paperwork and correspondence.

8. Always keep the lines of communication open. Keep the coaches up-to-date on any changes you anticipate and explain **why** these are being considered.

9. In staff meetings avoid a heated hassle unless it absolutely cannot be avoided.

10. In order to get independent opinions from each of your coaches, take secret votes on many issues. The vote should always include the question "Why?" We use this technique often. In asking our coaches, "After your film study what will be our best running plays for this week?" It is amazing in these secret votes how unified the thinking is rather than how differentiated.

11. In making decisions, avoid favoritism.

12. Never make a decision to placate a subordinate. When Coach Lou Holtz left us to assume the head football coaching position at the College of William and Mary, his parting advice was, "The assistant coach must always work to please the head coach, never the reverse of this."

13. When we go on the field we must be in complete accord as to our plans. There must never be any gesture that might lead the players to believe otherwise. On the field the "umpire on the mound is supreme."

14. Back up your coaches.

15. Never stand in the way of a coach's promotion. His responsibility to his family and to his future should govern his decision rather than advice from the head coach.

16. Since each coach will always want to know, "How am I doing?," it is the responsibility of the head coach to let him know. Be specific in your praise and also specific in any criticism so that the coach knows exactly the fault that must be corrected. If a coach continues to make the same mistake, then use a different method of correction, for it is obvious that the first method did not work. One that is used here is if a mistake continues, be sure to give that coach all of the nasty little jobs for a week without actually making mention of it, and he will get the word. If this doesn't work, then it is the responsibility of the head coach to have a very serious talk with him.

17. When a coach comes to you with a criticism, be sure to listen rather than to think about the rebuttal you are going to make. It has been this coach's experience over the years that anyone who has the courage to come to the head coach with a criticism deserves to be heard, for quite often that man is right.

18. After spring practice and after fall practice request each coach to write an informal critique immediately. In this critique the coach should stress both the good and the bad and emphasize even more the changes in plans that he recommends for the following year. Two things are important about this critique. First, it must be written immediately after the end of practice while the thoughts are fresh in each coach's mind, and, second, the head coach must be sure to study these critiques and discuss them with each coach in staff meetings.

19. Last, and most important, **the head coach must be a man of his word.**

I would like to spend a few minutes talking about the coach-player relationship. We feel that the single most important consideration is that the football player must be at college to get an education and that nothing short of a degree is considered a complete education. The help and encouragement that the coach can give the player is extremely important, particularly during the first year that the player is on campus.

So many youngsters at this time will neither be properly guided nor motivated, and since the coach has the closest contact with these players, he is in an ideal position to render real help. The coach who is intelligent enough to coach and teach in a university must be intelligent enough to sit down with a student and tutor and help him over his rough spots. Any college coach who is not capable or willing to do this should not be on a college staff.

In our program we believe the only way that we can repay a player for his efforts is to make sure that we do everything within our college rules that we can to help this man get an education. Only in this way can we make sure that the college athlete is not being cheated. This is the basis of the coach-player relationship at Ohio State University.

At Ohio State we are aware of the enormous educational value of football. It has never been our intention to overemphasize football, but perhaps at some time we have done so. However, the longer a coach stays in college football, the greater weight he gives to the educational value of the sport. As he studies former football players in their varied careers, he realizes that a large part of the useful education that they take from the campus is directly or indirectly tied in with football.

To play football is to respect rules, for the game of football could not exist without rules. Rules may not be absolutes, but they are absolute necessities for group achievement. The football player must not only have great respect for rules, he must also have an equal respect for the necessity of a rule change when a rule is outmoded or fails to fulfill its intended purpose. The absolute should be orderly change. This implies the democratic process, a process that has recently been flouted on many campuses, but a process that in comparison to all other methods of change, stands out as the best. If this sounds like indoctrination, that is exactly what it is meant to be.

A good football squad is controlled better by attitudes than by rules. Attitude includes many things: First, the desire to improve individually, to warrant membership on a team; second, the desire to win as

translated into team conduct; and third, to develop a high respect for the rights and privileges of others on the squad. On our squad there are two rules:

First, there is no place on the football squad for haters, either white or black. Second, each player has a right to approach any coach off the field without fear of recrimination if the player feels he has a legitimate complaint. We feel that this is a necessary safety valve.

Standards for football players must, of necessity, vary from those of other students. His conduct must always be considered in light of the effect it has on other members of the football squad. In matters of dress, punctuality, and living habits, the football player leads a much more disciplined life and must realize that for the team to succeed, this is a necessity.

Another area in which the coach can be of great help to the player is in the player's selection of his college associates. We tell him when he starts to run around with some new acquaintance he should always ask himself, "Would this man (or woman) be welcome at my home for the weekend?" This may sound rather cornball, but we have found it quite effective.

With college students we are continually stressing the importance of such things as appearance and associates, but we know that these students do not like to be harped at and, although we are always aiming at the same objectives, we like to change our approach. So, in closing I would like to recite a little poem through which we like to stress the importance of college associates. It goes like this:

*It was sometime in November, in a town I
    can't remember.*
I was carrying home a jag with maudlin pride,
*When my feet began to stutter, and I fell
        down in the gutter, and a pig came up
        and lay down by my side.*
*As I lay there in the gutter, thinking thoughts
        I dared not utter,*
*A lady passing by was heard to say, "You can
        tell a man who boozes by the company he
        chooses."*
And the pig got up and slowly walked away.

2
Football Philosophy I Believe In

(From 1978 Proceedings of AFCA)

LOU HOLTZ Head Coach, University of Arkansas

I would like to talk about some things that I believe are really important in coaching. I am not going to try to say that they are absolute or proper, but these are things I believe in very strongly.

You Must Have Goals

First of all, you have to have goals. Goals are as important to success as scoring more points than your opponent is to victory. I think everybody needs to re-evaluate his goals and where he wants to go. When I was sixteen years of age, I would ask my father for the car and he would say, "Where are you going?" I would reply, "I don't know. I am just going riding for a while." He would say, "How do you know where you are going until you get there?"

The following will verify areas where you need to set goals in order to be a complete person:
1. Spiritually—What type of Christian do you wish to be?
2. Father and husband?
3. Personality—What type of personality and values do you wish to project?

I think it is also important to believe in yourself, assistant coaches, and athletes. The greatest mistake you can make is to undersell yourself, your children, or your athletes. Concerning our opponents, we never worry about them. Coach Woody Hayes has said on many occasions, "Only be concerned with those items you can control." So many people lose a football game prior to the start of it because deep down inside they don't believe they can win. One of the biggest problems we had going into the Oklahoma game in 1977 was that we were playing without four starters on offense and we were eighteen-point underdogs prior to the start of the game. Consequently, our biggest pur-

pose was to convince our players that we could win. I feel that the one game we lost was not because of our execution or theory, but primarily because our players deep down inside did not believe they could win.

Good Coaches Mandatory

I think it is far more important to have good coaches than it is to have great athletes. You cannot win without athletes, but you can lose with them. Our philosophy from spring practice to the end of the season is that you win with coaching, and from the end of the season to the start of spring practice, we believe you win with athletes.

I don't care how much you pay a poor assistant—it is too much. And I don't care how much you pay a good one—it is not enough! We expect the following things from our coaches and our players:

1. *To be loyal.* This is an area that I did not emphasize enough in 1977, but I will never make that mistake again. There is no way that your football team can ever be disrupted by outside forces if you remain strong within. The greatest organization is in serious jeopardy if it is not extremely strong from within.

2. *Hard work.* I don't believe in busy work, but I do believe in doing what you have to do in order to achieve your goals.

3. *Work well with people.* There is no way you can get along with people if you don't like them. It is impossible to dislike somebody who sincerely likes you.

4. *An individual whose philosophy will coincide with mine.* I always give them a book, prior to hiring them. It explains what I expect from them and what they can expect from me. My first purpose is not squad morale, but staff morale. It is impossible to have squad morale without staff morale. I have never had

a problem with a coach or a player if they are both there for the same purpose as I am. You might have differences of opinion but never a problem. I think it is extremely important to get players and coaches who cannot live with losing. Everybody wants to win, but the main question is, can you live with losing?

I think the basis of our football program is that it can be done. You must create a positive environment that leaves little doubt in anybody's mind that you will succeed. It is strictly a question of when. You can do absolutely anything in this world you want to if you believe you can. You are not born winners and you are not born losers. You are exactly what you think you are—nothing more and nothing less.

5. *Facilities.* I think you have an obligation as football coach to put your players in the best possible facilities that you can. That does not mean that you have to spend a lot of money to do that. A coat of paint will work wonders.

6. *Morale.* The more honesty and respect on the team, the greater the team. We never talk about winning or losing because that will take care of itself. Playing a game so that people will respect you is important. Players gain their teammates' respect by their performance on the practice field, not on the game field. It is impossible to have a winning football team without your seniors playing the best football of their career. Not everybody can be All-America, All-Conference, or even first team; but every man can hustle to the best of his abilities, show physical courage in all his assignments, and care for and love his teammates. There is no place in football or life for hatred or prejudice. You never get ahead of anybody as long as you are trying to get even. I think it is very difficult to have squad morale if anybody can walk off the street and be a member of your football team without paying a severe price to be a part of it.

I don't want anyone around—coach or player—who can live with losing. If they cannot live with losing, they will do the things that are necessary to win. This means that they will conduct themselves off the field in a manner that will reflect the pride and self-discipline it takes to succeed. On the field, they will work to the maximum of their abilities. You are going to have problems from time to time, but when the problem arises, you only have three alternatives: (a) You have to change the individual until he accepts your philosophy and beliefs; (b) If you cannot change him, then you will have to learn to live with him; (c) If you cannot change him and you cannot live with him, then you must divorce yourself from him. This is a drastic step to take.

7. *Discipline.* There is a very thin line between discipline and harassment. Discipline breeds success—harassment breeds contempt. We ask three questions:

Will it make him a better student, a better athlete, and a better man? If the answers are yes, we will compromise. You never lose a football game because an athlete doesn't play. You win because of the manner in which those who do play perform.

8. *Appearance.* We have very few rules, but the rule we have is what is now famously referred to as the "Do Right Rule." Individuals know what is right and what is wrong. I personally believe that we have a well-disciplined squad. I am not a disciplinarian. A disciplinarian is somebody who turns over rocks to find things that are wrong. I will not turn my back, though, on something that I think is wrong and detrimental to our future. They are not obstacles, but only opportunities. We do have a hair rule during the season. They are to have no facial hair below the bottom lip unless it presents a hardship on them.

Give Substitutes a Boost

At the Orange Bowl game in 1978, we were minus twenty-two football players whom we had lost during the year with injuries. We never talk about injuries, but we sure try to pump up the substitute. We have to depend on so many players who are not physically good enough to play to come through and perform in an outstanding manner when called upon. We try to put a lot of players into a game. In the first half of the Orange Bowl, we used fifty-one players. We try to be fair and firm and honest.

The toughest thing to do is to discipline a player. The year 1977 was only the third time in my coaching career that I had to do so. Every time, it has been a star. It is easy to discipline the third-string player, but you really receive a tremendous amount of pressure when you do it to a starter.

Confidence Building

I have four signs posted on my desk. My favorite is "Make me feel good and I will produce." We try to coach in a positive environment. We work more on fundamentals than any other single item. Morale comes about when you feel you are improving toward a worthwhile goal. Morale is not being happy—it is believing you are achieving something. It is amazing what you accomplish when no one cares who gets the credit. Not everybody can win. When things go wrong, here are some of the factors to consider:

F — Frustration
A — Aggressiveness
I — Insecurity
L — Loneliness
U — Uncertainty
R — Resentment
E — Empathy

Consequently, failure leads to more failure unless the player understands what has happened and what to do to come back. We then try to build their confidence when things are going wrong.

There are many other items I would like to discuss with you, but I will leave you with this last item. You, as a football coach, should not be paid when things are going well. You earn your salary when adversity strikes. There isn't a coach in the profession who will not have at least three crises on his team or in his personal life. A crisis is not bad if you react favorably and take a strong, positive approach to it. Self-pity is self-destruction. Never feel sorry for yourself or your team.

There can only be one person's philosophy on a football team. All of the coaches and players must blend their efforts to make this philosophy successful. Everybody wants to help you make your decisions when things are going well.

When you are faced with adversities, then you must show more courage and be more positive than ever. If you have built the football program on a good, firm foundation, you will never have to worry about problems from within. If you remain strong within, then you will stand all other outside pressures and alternatives. You will achieve your goals and when you do, you will suddenly realize it was not so much what you achieved as what you had to overcome to achieve them.

3
Advice to Young Coaches

(From 1973 Summer Manual of the AFCA)

SHIRLEY MAJORS Head Coach, University of the South

Be creative, be yourself, and don't be afraid of hard work that does not allow for the counting of hours and energy expended.

You are the only football coach in the world with your specific job, material, and schedule; and you are the only one who has your personality, your brain, and your opportunity.

You are in your particular post because those who hired you feel that you can get the job done better than anyone else. It's up to you to prove them right—but if you are going to try to be another Mac Somebody, then your school had just as well have hired Mac.

You must be ambitious; but be ambitious to do a top job where you are. You aren't going to get anywhere in the long run by having half of your mind on doing your present job and the other half—or two-thirds—busy trying to determine what better job you can get at what school.

There is a very trite but very true old adage that says, "Build a better mousetrap and the world will beat a path to your door." You are in the position of creating a product, namely an effective football team. If you create a product that elicits the envy of other schools, they'll call you. You won't have to be reading the sports pages to see what schools are looking for coaches.

If you're going into coaching for the money, forget it. There are a number of other careers that pay more. Besides, pay is not the most important thing in coaching football. The most important thing is to get the job done well. If you do that, other things will work out as they should, or at least as well as you deserve.

Long Days, Short Nights

If you plan to succeed in coaching, you must be willing to make a sacrifice in the form of long days and short nights; and some of the nights are as sleepless as they are short. There is no other way you can be a dedicated and successful gridiron mentor.

You can use a stopwatch and a calendar where the speeds of players and the number of days and weeks of play and practice are concerned; but you can't use either a stopwatch or a calendar when it comes to you and your coaching staff. You and your assistants must do whatever is necessary to produce a good team. Fatigue and time don't count.

You must believe in your own system and procedures. If you don't believe in your offense and your defense, I assure you nobody else will—not even your players. Belief or nonbelief in what you are using will be transmitted to your players, for good or ill.

In that regard, it is well to repeat the admonition to be creative and to be yourself. You can't coach like any other coach because you are not any other coach. You are you. Don't fight that fact; capitalize on it. Coach the way you want to coach. If you don't, you'll find that you don't really know what you should do at any given time.

Communicate Properly

A head coach, whether young or old, isn't a mechanic or a tactician in the overall scheme of coaching. He is, or should be, a communicator and a handler of young men.

I would say that this is the critical area in the performance of a head coach. You should check yourself every day and every hour to be certain that you are communicating in a positive and beneficial way. You'll be communicating something, in some way. It's what and how you are communicating that is vital.

There may be times when you think and feel that you aren't getting any messages through, but you may find after checking it out that you have communicated more than you thought. However, check that area of your coaching thoroughly and constantly.

It is just as important in coaching to know what not to do as it is to know what to do. Many times, knowing what to omit is even more vital than to know what to include.

Don't be stubborn enough to coach all teams and all players alike. They are not alike, which means that if you try to coach as if they were, you can be in a lot of trouble.

Some teams and some players require more work than others, some require much less. Some individuals will get timing, execution, and precision down to a fine point much more quickly than will others.

Don't Overcoach

Be careful not to overcoach and wear out some capable teams and individuals before they get to real combat. Take an inventory after each day's practice and determine what is necessary and what is unnecessary. A team undercoached will perform better than a team overcoached.

At the University of the South in 1963, we had two linebackers to whom I gave virtually no coaching at all, and I gave them very little work on the practice field. When we held a scrimmage, I put those linebackers in action just long enough to get in one good lick apiece, then they came out. They were key players in carving out an undefeated and untied season.

It is important to extend your players so that they will become what they can and should be instead of what they are. At the same time, you must be careful to estimate the unique ability of each individual and refrain from asking him to do something that is beyond his capacity.

You must exercise your very best judgment in that area. It is just as important to know what a player or a team cannot do as to know what he or it can do.

You must show maturity. You are a coach now, not a player. You must be realistic, sincere, and, most important, truthful.

Be Yourself

Don't dare be a phony. Your players will recognize it in a hurry, for you are dealing with very intelligent and perceptive young men. Remove all doubt as

to your sincerity as early as you can. Never bluff in any manner or degree, because the only person you will delude will be yourself.

Don't have a large number of "little" training rules. Actually, training rules are necessary only when principles are violated. If you are mature in your attitudes and directions, most of your players will indicate maturity and won't need picky training regulations. What you really want is to keep your players in condition and dedicated and determined. When one is not any or all of these things, then disciplinary action must be made to fit the individual and the circumstances anyway.

As a coach you must have vitality, strength, and youthful enthusiasm, no matter what your chronological age. It isn't the calendar that is important; it is you. You must not, however, let your pep, power, and gung-ho cause you to get carried away. The qualities should be channeled throughout your overall program, not into only one particular facet or phase.

Be Loyal to School

This may not seem modern and enlightened to some, but you should be loyal to the school for which you are coaching and to its administration.

If you aren't loyal to the school, how can you expect the players to be? If they are not loyal, how can you expect to field an effective football team?

There are many intangibles in coaching per se. There are many more of them when it comes to your relationship to the school and its administration.

By loyalty to the school and its administration, I don't mean complete blindness. Don't be blind to facts and situations when things aren't going well, but don't discuss such matters, or complain about them, in the presence of your players. If you do, they may be disenchanted even after the situation about which you spoke has been straightened out.

You can be alert to weak points in the athletic system and its relationship to the institution and help to strengthen or eradicate them. Do, however, be loyal!

Always remember that football is an extracurricular activity. You aren't teaching football in college; it isn't a course. You are teaching how to play football.

Coaches have more influence in shaping the lives of boys who play under them than they realize. Some of your players may go into professional football, but there won't be such a large number of them going into the pro ranks as to justify your neglecting to give all your players some perspective on football, education, and life. Even if you are coaching for one of the many schools that give football grants-in-aid, you don't dare lead a boy to believe that football is the only thing in life.

Be Decisive

Avoid indecision at any and all times. Don't be wary of making a decision for fear of being wrong. Being wrong is just as much a part of football coaching as it is a part of life.

Make a decision quickly and firmly when it is called for. When your decision turns out to be wrong, be quick to admit that it was wrong. Everybody will know it anyway.

You should make your attitude, your interest, your concern, and your knowledge of what you are doing apparent enough that your players will seek you out for counsel and direction, not always just in the area of football. Impart to your players the impression that you know what you are doing in football and in life. Religious conviction and principles won't hurt, and they may help both you and your players a lot.

It is your responsibility as a head coach to teach a quarterback how to call plays during practice sessions and in private conferences with him. Having done both, let the youngster use his imagination on the field. If it isn't adequate under fire, then you must determine how good a job you did teaching the young man. But let your quarterback call them; that's one of the reasons for his being in that position on the field.

At the beginning of each season, create a mental picture of where you are going and select the route you want to travel. You won't accomplish anything you can't first conceive. After you have picked your destination and your route, you may need to stop some weeks, or each week, to be sure you haven't departed from the route you picked, or maybe whether you need to reroute your football vehicle in order to reach your destination. Don't be afraid to ask directions, either.

They'll Find You

Let me repeat: Do be ambitious, but don't try to advance by contacting other schools for jobs when you have been where you are for a year or two. That really isn't the best way to advance anyhow.

Many of the most successful football coaches in America have never applied for a job anywhere. They have done such outstanding jobs wherever they have been, and with whatever they had for material, that other schools have continually contacted them, as have professional teams.

You can be certain that if you do your job well enough where you are, the fact will be noticed—and somebody will be contacting you.

You're a football coach. Do the job well where you are and we'll be seeing you up the ladder soon. Don't call them; they'll call you.

Part Two
Organization

4

About Everything—Except Offense, Defense, and Kicking

(From 1976 Proceedings of the AFCA)

BO SCHEMBECHLER Head Coach, University of Michigan

I have often wondered, and I am sure you have, too, about what is the first thing that a coach does when he meets his squad in the fall. I have coached with Woody Hayes, Ara Parseghian, and people like that, so I have some idea of what they do in their initial meeting; but, I have often wondered what Bear Bryant or other coaches like him do when they assemble their squad for the first time and lay the groundwork for the season. What are the important things that they go over?

Our Opening Lecture

I'd like to give to you the opening lecture that I gave this past year. Of course, we modify it from year to year, but the first thing we do is welcome our squad back for the new season. I then talk about the meetings and how important they are and how much time we will spend in meetings. And when we meet, the purpose of our meeting is to eliminate, there in the classroom, possible mistakes. We will have promptness at all times. You might as well lay the groundwork now for the discipline of football and that is why we want everybody there—on time and no excuses, because if you accept an excuse from someone, you may give him an opportunity to tell you an untruth about why he is late for the meeting. So, I accept no excuses—you are there promptly, on time, ready to go.

I want the players sitting up in their seats; I want them alert. I want their feet on the floor, and I don't want any hats on their heads; and I think if we have those things, then the chances are we are going to get a guy to pay some attention. You can waste ability, I tell them. You will if you are a player who is poor in the classroom, not just in terms of gaining eligibility up on the campus, but in learning all that is necessary to know about your position and about our football. I

have seen some great football players who are very talented who didn't play because they couldn't learn well enough in the classroom.

Next I want them to understand that the meeting attitude always will be evaluated because I think there are great practice players and there are some lousy guys in the classroom and so we want to evaluate that as well. Then I introduce all of our coaches because you have got to understand that in collegiate football today there are usually thirty to thirty-five youngsters who really do not know all the coaches or the positions they coach. So we introduce our coaches, our graduate assistants, and our senior managers. Then I have each of the freshmen stand up and give his name, where he is from, and the position he plays. I want all the other guys, the eighty or so football players who were with us in the spring, to have an opportunity to see these guys. Some they know, some they are seeing for the first time.

The next thing I talk about is our football building. In the case of some of you, that would be your locker room. I want them to understand there will be 115 guys using the building. At Michigan we are fortunate because we have a football building that is for football alone. We have no other sports in there. It is a beautiful building, with fine locker rooms, training rooms, equipment rooms, air-conditioned classrooms, sauna baths, and a $150,000 weight room that has everything. So I want to talk to the players about how to take care of that building, because I don't want it abused, and how they should keep the area in front of their locker clean, including putting the tape in the barrel so that we don't have to have people around there always policing the area. I talk to them about their valuables. I've had morale on the team destroyed when there has been thievery in the locker room and around our campus, and I am sure that as soon as the team comes back, every hood in town knows it and they know that we all meet together and practice together. They hit our locker room, they hit our dormitories, and you know that can cause an awful lot of problems on your team. So we talk about their valuables and how we don't want to leave them loose, to lock them up in their lockers.

We talk about where they should park their cars if they have them. I ask them if they are going to meet people to meet them somewhere else besides our locker room. I want that to be private. If they have people picking them up, they should do it outside. I don't want outsiders in our locker room. It is strictly for football personnel and no one else.

Then I talk to the players about policing the area and taking care of their locker room. Next I talk about the dormitory and the dining room. You are living in a dormitory, you're eating on the training table meal—that's the way we do it at Michigan—and they are all living together, and I talk to them about being courteous. If they have any complaints, I have a coach on my staff who is responsible for that. If they don't like the food or where they are living, there is a coach they can go to talk to about it. I want them to understand that if they get any parking tickets up around that dorm, I am not going to take care of it. That is their responsibility. I do not want them to change rooms. When we assign them a roommate, they stay in that room—they do not change.

Every night I have two varsity coaches and two graduate assistants in that dormitory. Players are not to lock their door at night until a coach checks them in. There is a purpose for that because you and I know that with two-a-day sessions there aren't too many guys who are ready to run around and party at night; otherwise you were not doing much on the field. But I do want coaches to check to see if anyone is hurt or sick, because there are problems that can arise at night, as you know, during those two-a-day sessions, and we want that coach to be checking players in the evening before they go to bed. We want them to keep their rooms neat. We want them to be in proper dress. I like a player to wear shoes and a shirt when he goes into the dining hall to eat, and I think that is important. I want him to be courteous in the chow line, and they have to bus their own trays. I don't want any hats on in the dining room any more than in the meeting room. They must not leave their doors unlocked while at practice because, as I said before, people like to come in at that time knowing we are out on the field. Players must lock their doors or they are going to lose radios and other things.

They have to be in their own rooms at ten P.M. during two-a-day sessions. They must keep the volume on their radios and stereos down low.

One rule I have that I think is a very important rule—no football player, regardless of his class in school, will ever go to the head of the chow line, because you and I know that when that happens, you can have trouble with morale on your squad. No one is allowed to cut into the chow line!

Now these rules may sound like insignificant things, but I think all of them are important to go over. If we have some specific problems that arose the year before, I add them to the following year's list and make sure I go over them.

Next thing we talk about is the training room. I require all football players, regardless of the type of practice, to have their ankles wrapped or taped. I don't want anyone out there who doesn't have his ankles wrapped or taped. I want the specialists—kickers, passers, receivers—to go to the head of the line so that they get taped first and get on the field for our specialty period. I encourage them to have prompt treatment of all injuries. I tell them I want them to be tough, but I don't want them to be stupid. If you have an injury, no matter how minor, get it treated now so that it won't cost you practice time, hurt your chances, and hurt our chances for having a good team.

Insist that players take care of their feet. That is fundamental! So many players end up with blisters, bad toes, and so forth that force them out of practice. I will not accept time in the training room as an excuse for being late on the field. I also remind them that the players with a low threshold of pain have a tough time playing football.

We talk about water and salt on hot days because we want to take no chances. I know back in the old days we weren't allowed water—how foolish that was! We have water behind every drill so that any time a player wants a drink he has an opportunity to get one.

We have a weight training program in the fall. I believe sometimes we make a mistake in our off-season program. We build strength and stability, then we fail to work on it during the season. We encourage our guys on Mondays and Thursdays to participate in the weight program that is conducted by our coaches.

I then introduce our trainer and let him go over training room procedures. Next thing we talk about is the equipment room. I don't want football players going up and demanding things from equipment men. Every guy that we have hired at Michigan—the trainer, the equipment man—every one of them believes strongly in our program, has a great desire to win, likes to work with youngsters, and is going to be cooperative. But we are not going to treat them impolitely. I ask players not to steal anything. We talk about the headgear and how important it is that headgear fits properly and for that reason our equipment man will fit each guy individually. You and I know it is the most important single piece of equipment that players have. As for extra shoes, we have every conceivable kind of shoe there is. Some are good when the surface is wet and some are good when it is dry. Usually each of our players ends up with six or eight pairs of shoes. We went to the Orange Bowl in 1976 and used our entire budget of $10,000 to buy shoes because we had never played on polyturf surface before.

I want the shoulder pads fitted properly, because at one time we had a raft of shoulder separations. I require all football players to wear hip pads, and you and I know some of those wide receivers like to get away with little or nothing around their hips and end up with hip pointers that keep them out of action. I impress on them that the equipment must protect them. Loss of time in practice is going to hurt their chances of making our team and perhaps ruin our chances for the entire year if it is a serious injury.

We require that chin straps be fastened and mouth guards used all the time in practice. We harp on it. We don't like headgear being taken off and the chain straps loosened all the time because when we do tighten them up, they aren't secure enough to keep that helmet on the head. Then we weigh each player once a week, particularly when they report back in, because we have a certain weight that we want them to come in at.

Next we talk about the training table. We want the same kind of behavior once our training table starts in the fall, and when we break up and go to our respective dormitories or housing we want to make sure we continue to act properly and like gentlemen.

Next Topic: Academics

Academic standing is vitally important not just from an eligibility standpoint, but for my situation at the University of Michigan. It is imperative that we do everything we can to see that every player who comes in there has every opportunity possible to graduate, because at our school the administration is probably more concerned with our percentage of graduates than they are with the number of games we win. So we stress that an awful lot.

We tell our players about the difficulty of switching departments or from one school on our campus to another without good grades. We impress on them that we will help them in every way—tutoring, counseling, whatever it may be—but we will not do their work for them. I try to stress the importance of class attendance because, as you and I know, those who get in trouble academically are usually the ones who have not attended classes regularly. I do not want any subjects dropped unless our academic counselor knows about it, because players must have a minimum load of twelve hours and must make progress toward a degree. You just can't be maintaining eligibility. Then I give them a little lesson on how to compute a grade-point average. I have never seen so many football players, smart kids, who can't even compute their grade-point average.

Next I talk to the players about professional football and the importance of a degree. We all talk about it a lot. There have been some fine examples at Michigan of great football players, guys who have been All-Americas who have gone to professional ball and failed to make it. But if our players have their degree, it isn't really that important whether they make it in professional football or not. I think it is important that you discuss that with them. I think it is important for high school coaches to discuss academics with their team. Many of those youngsters want to go on to college and many of them may be good enough football players to be heavily recruited by colleges. High school coaches should stress how important it is that they do the job academically so that they can qualify. The same thing applies in the collegiate ranks. If you have the degree, it really doesn't make a lot of difference if you make it in professional football or not.

I also talk to players about our study table. I would guess that it might be important for some high school coaches to consider a study table of their own for guys who are not doing the job, because if you can put them on a study table, encourage them to study, help them, and get them motivated academically, then their chances of succeeding in college are much better as are their chances of being recruited by college coaches. I think that would be a worthwhile thing to do. Players must know everything about academic eligibility, and to stress that point I read off the names of those I want to talk to after the meeting who are not doing well academically.

Then, in front of the varsity squad, I discuss some of the things that are important for freshmen to know because we're now playing freshmen regularly on our varsity squad, and there are some things that I think they should understand—how to approach coaches, things of that nature. So I do talk to the freshmen in front of the rest of them. We got involved in the redshirt rule a few years ago, and I've had players who don't understand what it means, and so I explain the redshirt rule to them and assure them that no football player on our team is now under consideration to be redshirted. That is determined on the basis of how things go, and at no time are we going to even consider redshirting until we get midway through our season and a youngster has not yet had an opportunity to play in a game.

Next Topic: Pro Football

Next we talk about professional football, pro scouts, pro agents, and gambling. I make it a point to let every football player know that we cooperate with the professionals and the professional scouts at all times, but we do not determine when and how players are drafted. The same thing is true in high school. I've seen so many coaches come under heavy criticism because they didn't get a youngster a grant-in-aid in college. You've got to make it clear that that isn't your responsibility and that you do not determine whether they're going to be offered grant-in-aids by colleges or that they're going to be drafted in a certain round by the professionals just because you're going to have something to say about it. And I want all my players to understand this.

I talk to them about agents, because I'm not very fond of them. I tell them not to make agreement on contracts while they are still eligible because if they do they become ineligible and we would have to forfeit games. Then we talk about gambling, because it can happen. There'd be a lot of gamblers who would like to know the situation of our football team just prior to our game with Ohio State—the magnitude of the game and so forth. We've got to be very careful who we coaches deal with, who we talk to, and how we discuss the situation; and I think it's important that players know that as well.

Seniors Provide Leadership

Then I talk to my seniors. I've been a great believer in senior leadership because since 1969 we have had a great senior class every year. I want our seniors to understand that they are primarily responsible for the leadership of our team, that we depend on them, and that every single one of them must play their greatest year of football. That's true of every one of them, whether they're a regular, a substitute, or the head of one of our demonstration teams. They must give us their greatest year of football. If they do that, then they've demonstrated leadership to everyone else involved. I also make a great effort to let the seniors know how important they are. When we travel to an away game in a chartered airplane, I make sure that all the first-class seats are filled by the senior members of our team. My athletic director, my board of regents, and the president of the university, if he wants to go, will sit in the back of the plane because the players come first on this trip because that's what the game is all about. We want senior players to understand how important they are and how their leadership is going to determine the success or failure of our team.

Then I go back and demonstrate to them some of the things that great senior classes have done for us in the past and how important it is for them to do likewise. Next we talk about a coach-and-player relationship, and I know this is always a ticklish subject and coaches don't always know exactly how to approach it. First thing I say to them is if they have a problem,

I want them to go through their position coach first. Then, if they can't get satisfaction there or if it's a personal problem that they want to discuss with me, that's something else. If they are talking about football, I would appreciate if they would go through their position coach first. I let them understand that our football staff is always available to a football player. I think that is fundamental. I will not be interrupted at a staff meeting by anyone other than my wife, the athletic director, or a player—and that's it! I think it is important that they know they can come to me. There is nothing worse than having a football player muster up the courage to come into your office to talk with you and when he gets to the secretary, finds out that you're busy and can't be seen then and he has to turn around and walk back. That player will think twice about going to the coach again. I don't want that to happen! I want him to come to my office and know that if it is important that he see me, he will see me. I want him to understand that I listen to only our assistant coaches in terms of who plays and how we play and what we do. No alumni, no newspapers, no parents, or anyone else is going to determine any decisions that I make. I am only influenced by the coaches on my staff, no one else! I don't want players to worry about pressure on me to play a guy at quarterback or someone else at another position. I don't want them to think that is going to happen. I want them to understand we coach aggressively and we play that way too, because it's that kind of a game.

When you coach aggressively, players have got to understand that they should not take what happens on that field in a personal nature. The enthusiasm of coaches is to get the job done and make sure players understand what they are trying to get across. This is because we do coach aggressively—every member of my staff does.

Then we talk about alibis, including "Old Alibi Ike," the guy who didn't make it, the coach that was always against him, the personality conflicts, and all of that. I don't want those guys around. If they want to make the alibis, I would rather that they just leave, because, as you know, that can have a bad effect on the squad.

I want mutual trust and mutual understanding, and the only way I know how to get that with a player is to tell him the truth from the time I recruit him. I never offer them anything that I can't deliver; I never promise a guy he will play; I never promise a guy he will get something more than anyone else because he is that much better a prospect. They all come in on the same grant-in-aid and they are all going to be treated alike. I want each player to understand that when I tell him something, that's the way it is and that I'm not going to lie to him. And by the same token, I sure don't want him lying to me! You will never be successful with any football player who will not look you in the eye and tell you the truth. If he is going to lie to you consistently, you might as well get rid of him since he is either going to beat you or he is going to make costly mistakes in the game because he is not a guy of sound character. So I just want him to tell the truth. I'm going to tell them the truth, I want them to tell me the truth! I want them to understand that no player or coach is indispensable to our program. None. As a matter of fact, when I was recovering from a heart attack, it was the greatest year of recruiting we ever had. I wasn't available.

It's a Family Affair

What goes on in our meetings and in our football practice is a family affair. I don't want players running to their girlfriends, mommies and daddies, their roommates, or the people up on campus to tell them every thing that happens on our practice field or in our classrooms. It is none of their business. It is a family affair. We want to keep it that way, on our campus or in your school or anywhere else, the student newspapers and everybody else would just love to get some juicy story about what happened on the practice field. We want to keep that stuff private, and so we talk about that being family business and we don't discuss it with other people. We want to be closed-mouthed about our team. We don't want to brag about it and we don't want to discredit it.

I tell players to be careful with the press. I don't mind telling them. A lot of press people are my best friends, and I'd trust them implicitly, but there are also some I wouldn't turn my back on for two seconds. It's difficult to tell the good ones from the bad ones, especially for a player. Nowadays reporters want a sensational story. They don't want to know something that is interesting and good that has happened—they want to know something that is sensational and bad—so I tell players to be very careful with the press; not that I keep them from the press, but I want them to be careful with them.

I want them to know that I am not influenced by outsiders. I think it is important that they know that. I want them to know that they are judged on the basis of their performance and their attitude only. Nothing else! How you perform and the attitude that you have is how you are going to be judged.

Then we talk about the relationships with each other. I want players to get to know their teammates, especially the freshmen. I don't want a lot of cliques on the team. They have to understand they can live together and win or live separately as fools and lose. It is as simple as that. That is why it is important that we have good player-player relationships. Players and coaches must have respect for everyone and under

stand that everyone is different. And you know that gripers cling together—misery loves company. You ought to tell players about it because then they think twice about doing it.

Our training rules aren't any different than anybody else's. I like to see a neat, clean team, but I'm not nearly as strict as I used to be in that regard. I do think it is important that they have a proper diet and get proper rest. It is also important that you make sure they understand you don't like drinking and smoking. Not that I'm naive enough to think that no football player at Michigan has ever done it, but I've never seen them, and that's why I want them to be darn discreet about what they do and when they do it. We also talk about drugs on our campuses and in our high schools and the embarrassment that it can cause a team and a player or his family. Ann Arbor, Michigan, has a five-dollar pot fine—can you imagine that? Five dollars. And there are guys who go through there and pay that fine; nobody knows who they are until one Michigan football player does it—one, and then everybody in the United States of America will know—it is as simple as that. And that's why they have to be very careful in what they do, who they associate with, what parties they go to, and things like that because players sometimes don't think of the possible consequences of their actions.

I'll never prostitute the discipline on our team for anyone. I don't care how great he is. If he has to go or if he has to be disciplined, he is going to get it. It has to be that way. We want relentless pursuit of our goals. We are a goal-seeking team, and we don't want anything to stand in our way, and misconduct of this kind can certainly do it. That's why we talk about it and make sure we don't have any of it.

Goals Are Important

We also talk about goals. We think it is important that a football player has goals today. We hand out a goals notebook before we ever hand out our football notebook. On the first page of the notebook we write down what the team goals are going to be for the year. I want them to be realistic. We have been through spring practice; they know how good they are; they know what potential we have; and I want them to put it down in the notebook on the basis of what we decide to go after. Invariably it is the Big Ten championship, the Rose Bowl, the things like that. In 1971 the national championship was our primary goal. Some years we wanted to go for an undefeated season and we would put that goal down. I caution them that whatever goals they put down, they better be willing to pay the price to achieve them, because it is easy to write them down in a notebook, but it is hard to achieve them. It takes a lot of extra work and effort to do that.

The second page of that notebook is where we put our offensive and defensive goals, and they are determined from year to year. I can give you an example of an offensive goal. (I think you can achieve anything in football if you make up your mind to do it.) In 1972 we failed to go undefeated by one game. We were down inside our opponent's 5-yard line on two occasions and were stopped on the 1-foot line and lost the game 14 to 11. Up to that time we had usually been a very good, strong goal-line offensive team. Our number one goal in the following season was that we would never be stopped inside the 10-yard line. Never. And we weren't because we worked on it. We talked about it, we put it in the goal notebook, we made sure that players understood that, and we were successful in achieving a touchdown every single time we got the ball inside the 10 the following year. That is the type of goal we think is important from that standpoint.

On the third page of the notebook, we take time out to put down our individual goals. Although football is a team game and everything that we do is primarily for the team, every individual must have some goals for himself, no matter what they may be, but they must be realistic. I am sure there have been guys on my team who wanted to be All-America or Big Ten champs and some who wanted just to make the first string, just our traveling squad, or just wanted to get in the game and make a contribution to a championship team. Whatever that goal may be, I think they should put it down in their notebook. When they have completed that notebook we lock it in their individual lockers. When things start to go bad in the middle of the season (and there isn't a guy who doesn't run into the old "midseason slump," when they don't like to practice and things aren't going very well), we tell them to go back and look at that goal notebook and come back out the next day ready to do a better job than what they have done the previous day. You know we are a defensively oriented team; we believe in defense. We think you can never win championships without a strong defense. In our conference you must be able to defense the run. If you can't defense the run, you cannot win the championship, because we are a very run-oriented league. For the first six years we were at Michigan, we led the nation in the fewest turnovers and defense against the score. During that same period of time we were the winningest football team in the country. We must work to keep our defense in good field position and eliminate our turnovers.

In the past we were a very conservative football team that didn't make mistakes. In 1975 in twelve games we turned it over thirty-three times, 2.75 times per game, and had the worst record we've had in seven years, and those turnovers were very instrumental. Our defense, because of turnovers, went from 7.8 points per game over a six-year period to this past year, when 10.8 points per game were scored against us. I feel very strongly that our football team should know that. When we decide what our offensive and defensive goals are going to be, we want to make some changes and make sure that we're not turning that ball over and that we do not put our defense in bad position. Therefore we have an opportunity to win more games.

We then hand out our football notebook and impress upon the player its importance—how valuable it is, that we don't want to lose it, that we want to make sure that they take good care of it, and that no one leaves the squad until he turns it in. All seniors are allowed to keep their notebooks.

Then we go over our schedule. In our schedule we talk about red-letter games. We feel there are only so many games on our schedule that we can have the truly great maximum effort, and we pick out those three or four that we are shooting for, that we have to win. We mark them in red letters. Our coaching staff selects those games because we know more about our opponents than our players do. We then impress upon them why we put those teams in the red letters, why we are going to make such a concentrated effort to beat them.

Victors' Club Works

We always review our motivational set-up—the things that we try to do to stimulate players to greater performances. We have what we call a Victors' Club. Jim Young was the guy who originated it. When a guy is in the Victors' Club, he's entitled to have his name on a beautiful plaque in front of our locker room and the Victors' Club emblem on his practice jersey. At the end of the year if he makes it eight out of eleven games, he'll receive a trophy, and those are the only trophies that we give other than the most valuable player. For admission to the club, you have to have 100 percent hustle and second effort in practices and games at all times. You must know all your assignments; you must be hard-nosed in practice and in the game; you must have a willingness to come out early and stay late during our specialty period; and you must be present at all practices and meetings, without exception. If you are injured, you're off, and we can't help that. Week-to-week admission is all of the above and then personally being responsible for a key play leading to victory, such as being a member of an offensive unit that scores thirty points or a defensive team that holds an opponent to one touchdown.

You lose membership in the Victors' Club by being responsible for a fumble, a pass interception, or a penalty, missed tackle, or a missed assignment that is the turning point of a game. Lack of 100 percent hustle at all times in practice or games, loss of temper, unsportsmanlike conduct, missing a game or three days of practice due to any reason during the regular season. A poor performance for an entire game also eliminates a player from the Victors' Club. We put a Wolverine decal on the back of their headgear if they achieve the following things: on offense, if they have an outstanding block, catch, or run, a touchdown pass or run of over twenty-five yards, an outstanding second effort, four crossfield blocks in one game, a touchdown-saving tackle on punt return, scoring a touchdown with a first down between the 10- and 8-yard line, making a first down from starting inside your 2, a scout player doing the best job against the defense, downing a punt inside the 10-yard line, a kickoff return beyond the opponent's 30-yard line, a ball carrier gaining 100 yards, and a linesman who blocks with 80 percent efficiency.

The decal is awarded to a defensive player if he intercepts a pass or blocks a kick or kickoff tackle inside the 20-yard line, causes a fumble or interception, recovers a fumble, or stops a team inside the 10-yard line. When the defense scores a touchdown, everyone gets a decal.

And then we have our Champions of the Week on offense, defense, and on our scout team, and our kicking champion or special team champion. They get a certificate and a plaque and a small trophy each week, which we award during our film sessions. At the end of the year we give the Champion of the Year trophy, and there's only one trophy bigger than that for Champion of the Year, and that's for the Most Valuable Player.

The guys who have been the Champion of the Year are the senior guys who've been out there for four years, who have done the best job on our demonstration teams, and we've had some great candidates and some great kids. Chuck Randolph, a player from Cincinnati, won it in 1976. For four years he wasn't good enough to play for us; he was a great leader and a great demonstrations player playing defense against our offensive team.

We're Lucky to Be Coaches

I talk about some of the success stories and also about some of the great talented guys who have never made it, but that is the great joy of coaching football. I think all of us are lucky to have an opportunity to be a coach, to work with young people, and to see the things that can happen. There are a lot of kids who want to play football, if we just encourage them to come out and stay with it. But sometimes we coaches are too obsessed with getting another job, advancing,

or going somewhere else that we don't do a good job at what we've got at hand—that we don't take care of the kids we've got and that we don't work with them, especially some of them who aren't very good.

I take great pride in trying the best I can to treat every one of them alike, because if I do that, then I know I'm not slighting any of them. To me the most important single thing that you can do in coaching is to be interested in and give your time to the guys who play for you.

The next thing you do is be honest with them. The worst problem we have with young people today is that they lie right through their teeth and get away with it. But you know what? There are a lot of coaches who are lying to players, and how are they ever going to learn the right way to do it if we don't level with them. If I think a guy isn't any good I'm going to tell him he isn't any good. When I recruit a player I'm sure not going to tell him he's going to play as a freshman if I don't believe down in my heart that he can do it.

You must be honest. I'll tell you this, you'll never get fired in coaching if your players don't want you fired. This doesn't mean you have to treat them nice; all you have to do is treat them fair. That's what I guarantee them in that first meeting—I'll treat you fair, you treat me fair; you tell me the truth and I'll tell you the truth; you level with me and I'll level with you; and we can get along together. You may hate my guts because you think you're something that I don't think you are as a player, but at least you are going to know where you stand, and if you have any doubts about where you stand on our football team, you know where my office is and I'll tell you.

I think all of us are lucky that we are in this profession. I don't care how much money you make or what you're doing, you're lucky to have an opportunity to work with these young kids, and the greatest friends you have are the kids who have played for you and left and come back.

I'm not an old coach, I haven't coached very long, but I now have kids that are coming back. And I'm so proud of them. I've had failures—and you'll have failures, too, of guys who didn't believe what you said and did things that they ought not to have done and ended up in trouble.

If we run the program right, if we're enthusiastic, if we believe in what we are doing, and above all, if we treat kids fairly, just fairly, not nice, but fairly, then all of it is worth it, every single bit of it. That is my philosophy. I want them to understand it, and if they understand it in that first meeting, our chances of success are a lot better.

5
Arizona Game-Week Preparation

(From 1976 Summer Manual of the AFCA)

JIM YOUNG Head Coach, University of Arizona

Our weekly preparation in terms of the players is based on the idea that the football player is a student-athlete. It is important to us that the mental approach to the game be handled completely and efficiently. Efficiency is most important in that we do not want to meet "just to meet," but want to organize our week to develop the proper mental aspect of our players in the minimum amount of time.

Our first area of concern is getting our players (and ourselves) to forget the previous game fast. This may seem to be a rather insignificant point, but until a staff, team, or individual forgets the success achieved in the previous game, the other points are moot in that proper mental preparation can only begin after one has totally recognized the task before him. We probably have all participated in great emotional victories at one time or another, and it seems paradoxical to me that, unless those wins closed out the season, we (players and coaches) usually have less than twenty-four hours to enjoy them.

One of our strongest beliefs is that any material pertaining to the game should be in the hands of the players as early in the week as possible. Naturally, the coaches must formulate their own thoughts and determine a game plan before it is delivered to the team. Therefore, our preparation as a staff is done almost entirely in the first three days of the week, with little or no changes after Tuesday's practice.

Sunday

Our staff's first objective is to view and grade the films from the previous day's game. In past years, we used a numerical grading system with a percentage grade, but we now have abandoned a numerical grade

and replaced it with a performance rating of (−) unsatisfactory; (0) adequate, but will need improvement; and (+) satisfactory. In addition to the performance rating, the individual players receive a card with strong and weak points noted for their own benefit.

Performance sheets are passed out at the Sunday meeting for all members to see how individual positions have been rated. (See Diagram 1.)

Diagram 1

OFFENSIVE PERFORMANCE SHEET   GAME   Pacific

Bear Down Club:	Piper, Segal, Hodgeson, Windisch, Howard, Baker, Randolph
Champion - Line:	Hodgeson
Champion - Backs:	Baker
Champion - Scout:	McClanahan
Outstanding Plays:	Baker - run Randolph - run

UNIT PERFORMANCE

Turnovers:	+	1 fumble
Kicking Game:	o	dropped snap - field goal
Conditioning:	−	
Critical Situations:	−	not scoring enough in score zone

POSITION PERFORMANCE

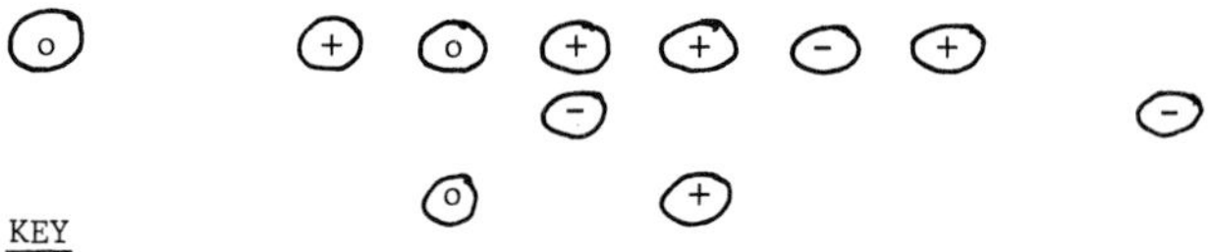

ⓞ   ⊕ ⊙ ⊕ ⊕ ⊖ ⊕   ⊖
      ⊖
   ⊙ ⊕

KEY

+ Championship
o Adequate, need improvement
− Not good enough

22

Grading is completed by noon on Sunday and the entire afternoon is spent watching as many films as possible of the opponent, with each coach making his own notes about the other team. Little or no discussion concerning the game plan goes on during Sunday afternoon. At 5:30 we like to break completely from the films and all the coaches have dinner together. The dinner hour is meant to give each of us some time to relax, get some fresh air, and prepare any materials for the team meeting at 7:00.

We meet with our players only one night a week during the season—that being Sunday evening. In that meeting, it is important that we start to forget the previous game. We meet for approximately two hours, spending one hour on the previous game and one hour on the upcoming game.

The actual team meeting lasts only fifteen minutes, and during that time I review the previous game, present awards to outstanding players as selected by the staff, and give a general personnel scouting report on the upcoming opponent. Immediately following this short meeting, our team breaks up into groups for film study.

Each position coach takes his players to separate areas and meets with them for the rest of the evening. They quickly go through the previous week's game films, making specific comments relative to their position performance in the game. We went to group meeting for the first time this year and felt that it helped a great deal. Our graduate assistants have all our film cut into offensive and defensive copies by our evening meetings and, by swapping halves of the game between coaches, we find that we can utilize all of our film at one time. The advantages to us seem to be that it is easier to criticize—constructively or otherwise—within a group that meets and works together most of the time. Additionally, players of one position are not held up reviewing a film while another position is being "coached" from the film. By using this group method, we have found that we can adequately review a film with our players in less than an hour.

Once the film review has ended, all our scout team players (generally those not on our traveling team) go with the graduate assistant coaches and watch the films of our upcoming opponent so that they can most effectively give us the proper practice look during the week. We stress to those individuals their importance and ask them to study and assume an individual opponent's role as much as possible. Two of our six weekly awards in the early team meeting go to the members of the scout teams who most effectively simulated the opponent's offense and defense during the previous week.

After the scout team has left for its film study, our position groups begin their film study of the opponent.

Each position coach generally spends about forty-five minutes looking at portions of two to three films. Our main concern is to get the players thinking about the next game and, to that end, emphasis is placed on a player's studying his individual opponent. In other words, we stress the one-on-one challenge of the game. In various ways we try to challenge the player to get himself ready to be successful against whatever type of player he is going to meet, be he good or great. Few comments are made concerning new plays, defenses, or adjustments because they are generally not finalized until Monday morning.

After the player meetings, our staff again turns its attention to films we have not been able to see yet. As soon as the last film is finished, we start on our game plan. At this time, each coach is expected to present his own views about how we should play the next game. In general, our thoughts run along the same paths; however, the particulars can cause lengthy discussion. We base the entire game plan on four things: (1) What are the strengths and weaknesses of the opponent; (2) what do we already have in our offense/ defense to combat their strengths and take advantage of their weaknesses; (3) what, if anything, must we do differently to win the game; and (4) any changes must be simple enough to teach and learn that we can execute them successfully after one week's practice. Sunday usually ends about midnight with half of the game plan tentatively set.

Monday

Monday begins at 7:00 A.M. by completing the game plan, reviewing selected films that present the opponent's attack in a diversified manner, and refining any changes that need to be made. We feel Monday is a great day for our players to "learn by doing" at practice rather than merely loosening up. Each position coach will prepare one or two sheets of adjustments (these include any changes or new techniques to be used) and present it prior to practice to his players.

It is important in our organization that all game plans—notwithstanding some minor adjustments—be completed by 3:00 P.M. Monday. For that reason, our staff meets throughout the day on Monday. Our players are encouraged, at their convenience, to come in during the day for more individual film study on their own. We make offices available for them for this. We find that players oftentimes will study an opponent better when a coach is not there to lead him through the film.

At 3:00, players again meet with their position coaches. During that meeting, the coaches go over portions of the scouting report as it applies specifically to their position. In the past, we delivered detailed scouting reports to all players. We found, however, that the reports, as the season went along, became so voluminous that they tended to lose importance to the player. We now only cover material specific to a particular position. For example, defensive backs never see the interior blocking patterns of the offense, and the defensive line never sees the pass patterns of the opponent.

Once the scouting report has been covered, the position coaches go over the particular adjustments of the game. Actually, the bulk of the meeting is spent in these adjustments and applying them to the situations we expect to see. Our offensive linemen meet in a large room and walk through any new adjustments or problem defenses for the week. At the same time, our graduate assistant coaches take the scout team players and work on timing up the opponent's offenses and defenses.

Actual practice on Monday lasts only one hour and fifteen minutes and is conducted in shorts. The bulk of the practice is spent on the adjustments and problems covered in the earlier meeting. We write a script (Diagram 2) for the Monday practice with an extensive full team period to show our units an overall picture of what to expect.

We can get some running done and, at the same time, check preliminary assignments. The dummy session during practice gives the player a real experience with which to compare and visualize himself against the opponent.

I do not want to digress from the topic, but I would be remiss if I had not taken some space to emphasize our use of visualization. Everything we do with our team in preparation for a game centers around providing successful experiences to the players and having them visualize continued successes versus the opponent. If it is true that the mind cannot tell the difference between a real and imagined experience, then every block or tackle our team visualizes during the week can only help to prepare us for Saturday.

Immediately after practice and a hurried shower, we again meet in position groups to view the opponent's film for about one hour. In that meeting, players are encouraged to shift attention from individual film study to recognition of plays and/or defenses. As we look at the film, we will freeze the film and have players apply their adjustments orally to what they see in the film. Aside from keeping their attention and making them think quickly and decisively, we feel it also strongly reinforces in another way what they have learned in the earlier meeting and practice.

The meeting usually breaks up around 6:30 and all players are then free unless required to attend study table. After dinner, our staff continues work on the game plan.

Diagram 2

FULL TEAM

LEFT HASH

	FORMATION	PLAY	DEFENSE
1.	S-Red	46	70 Dog
2.	Red Spread	54	T 30 Corner
3.	Red Spread	35	53 Swap Dog
4.	S-Pro	116	70 Dog
5.	Red Spread	39	70 Stunt Dog
6.	S-Pro	22	30 Gap Dog
7.	Red Spread	47	T 30 Corner
8.	S-Pro	116	53 Swap Dog
9.	S-Red	54	T 30 Corner
10.	S-Red	46	T 30 Corner

RIGHT HASH

	FORMATION	PLAY	DEFENSE
1.	S-Con	117	30 Gap Dog
2.	White	34	52 Swap Dog
3.	S-White	47	70 Dog
4.	S-Con	117	43 Swap Dog
5.	Red Spread	35	70 Stunt Dog
6.	Red Spread	47	70 Stunt Dog
7.	Red Spread	39	52 Dog
8.	S-Con	117	70 Dog
9.	White	46	70 Dog
10.	S-White	47	52 Dog

Tuesday and Wednesday

Tuesday morning is spent finalizing the game plan. Less than 10 percent of the game plan will change after noon on Tuesday. Once again we write a script for practice to ensure that our players are seeing exactly from our scout teams those things we feel are the most important for our preparation. Tuesday's and Wednesday's schedules are similar for the players. Each coach again meets with his players at a free time in his schedule. The player's class schedule takes precedence over any staff meetings or responsibilities. Most players are free at 2:00, and we like to meet them at that time because we feel it is best to meet and go straight to practice to cover the materials of the meeting.

All final adjustments are reviewed in this meeting and again the bulk of the meeting is spent applying those adjustments to the opponent's film. Generally, we meet for one hour and practice, in pads, for two hours on Tuesday and Wednesday. There are no night meetings on these days except for our quarterbacks, who meet for an hour after practice.

We film our Tuesday-Wednesday practice and that film is cut up in sections to be used in the group meetings on Wednesday and Thursday. We have found this to be one of our best teaching aids since the camera angle is behind the unit that is filmed, and this gives our players a better picture of what they will see on the weekend. It also helps us considerably in our evaluations of our adjustments and the technique performances of our players.

Thursday

By Thursday we have eliminated the mistakes of Tuesday and Wednesday, and our approach turns again to the opponent—what we can expect from them and what we must expect of ourselves in order to win the game. During Wednesday and Thursday, the staff is preparing game-day charts, writing scripts for the practice schedules, and using film study with the players to correct mistakes and promote visualization.

On Thursday, our offensive and defensive signal callers will "play a game" by use of visualization, with one coach giving down-and-distance situations and the signal caller giving appropriate calls to be made. Every imaginable situation is presented to allow the caller an opportunity to make the correct calls in practice. Even if the game situations do not match those of the practice games, the feeling of having made a tough call earlier lends confidence to the coach.

We again meet with our players in position groups for a short time before practice to review practice film and go over any special play or defense adjustments. We practice for one hour in pads but do not have any contact. Immediately after practice, we meet as a team and discuss again the challenges of the team we are playing on Saturday. We then break into position group meetings again and look at portions of several films. During this session we run through as much film as possible, stopping only to point out a special situation or to answer a question raised by a player. The players are dismissed after about thirty minutes. Some, however, stay on their own without coaches and study again the individual he will be playing in the game.

Friday

This is a travel day or class day depending on the schedule. We like to work out in the stadium at nearly as close to game time as possible and set our schedule around the workout. Relaxation and rest are important to all of us, and we want our coaches and players to act appropriately. Our signal callers rehearse their play-calling sometime during the day.

We do not see our players on Friday until 5:45, at which time they report and go to a local hotel as a team. Following a team dinner, we all return to the stadium for a light-sweats workout of about fifteen minutes. We like to rehearse our game-day procedures on Friday so we all know where to go. After the workout, we return to the hotel and relax until an 11:00 P.M. lights-out check by coaches. Generally, around 10:00 P.M., the position coaches visit the players in their rooms and give them a written test or review the points of the game as it applies to that position.

Saturday

We have an 8:30 wakeup on Saturday morning followed by a 9:00 buffet breakfast. After breakfast, we walk to our Student Union Theater for a movie with our team. We rent all our films—whether at home or on the road—to ensure that we have a "good" movie for our squad. A group of players makes the tentative selections early in the fall, subject to change by the coach in charge of ordering the films. I realize that much has been said about the type of movie a player should see before a game (light versus heavy, war versus drama, sex or no sex). Let me just say that we have never lost after viewing *The Magnificent Seven, Kelly's Heroes,* or a Clint Eastwood movie; but we did lose after seeing *Pretty Maids All in a Row.*

After the movie, we return to the hotel. The players are left alone at this time to relax, sleep, or watch the TV game. We eat our pregame meal at 3:00 and leave for the stadium at 5:15. From the pregame meal on, we want all thoughts on the game.

Our schedule on road games is basically the same, altered only by traveling connections to the game site. If we play away in the afternoon, we simply change the schedule to accommodate the earlier time on Saturday.

Essentially, our approach on Friday and Saturday up to game time is for the players to clear their minds and relax. We talk about and hope that beginning Friday evening the players will begin to think and visualize themselves being successful in the game Saturday night. We hope through our efforts and theirs that the process will continue and develop to bring them to a proper mental pitch for the Saturday kickoff.

6
Limited Staff—
Limited Budget

(From 1978 Summer Manual of the AFCA)

HARPER DAVIS Head Coach, Millsaps College

Millsaps College is a liberal arts college located in Jackson, Mississippi, and supporting a campus enrollment of approximately 1,000 students. We are a member of the NCAA Division III, and our football coaching staff consists of two coaches, including myself. We operate on a football budget of $18,000 per year, and this budget includes everything connected with football except the salaries of the two coaches.

Now please don't jump to conclusions and say that here is a coach who is going to cry about his staff and budget, because I'm not. This is what the college can afford, and it has worked out pretty well for the football program over the years. I'm sure that I will hear from coaches who operate on even less than this. However, I don't think that there are many, if any, schools in Division III that have to travel as far as we do in a season in order to get a competitive schedule with not only Division III schools, but with NAIA colleges as well. We have only one opponent that is under two hundred miles from our campus and another that is 225 miles away, but all the others range from 425 to 680 miles away. We make all trips by bus the day before the game and return right after the game, whether it is a day or a night game. Several years ago, we could travel by commercial airlines, but this has gone out of our reach.

Try to Find Bargains

Needless to say, most of my budget is eaten up by travel expenses as we fill a forty-six-passenger bus to capacity with thirty-nine football players, three managers, a cameraman, a statistician, and two coaches. We shop around for motel rooms and sleep four to a room. Coaches from opposing teams usually can tell us where we will receive the best rates for motel rooms, and we eat in cafeterias as much as possible. When doing this, we limit each man to a certain amount, and anything over this, the player pays for.

One of our next biggest expense items is the preseason training table. Since Division III has discontinued spring football, we are forced to bring our players back to school as early as possible in order to evaluate the personnel. Previously, we started practice when school started and this didn't cost us anything since the players eat on the boarding plan. We don't provide any training table or athletic dormitory as is the case with most Division III schools. At any rate, preseason meals are taking a $2,500 hunk out of our budget.

The next biggest item is equipment. We recondition as much as possible and, by limiting the squad to approximately forty-five players or less, we don't have to equip as large a squad as many teams do. We buy the best that is available and try not to hold anything back in regard to the safety of the players.

The rest of my budget is made up of expenses for game officials, 800 feet of film for each game, recruiting, and medical expenses, which can sometimes entail hospital bills. We spend very little to recruit in the way of travel to different high schools and none to bring an athlete to our campus. This is furnished by the recruit himself. We write a lot of letters and process about 350 potential players per year with the use of film and recommendations from coaches, players, and alumni. Out of this many prospects, we concentrate and make an honest effort to recruit about sixty of these for our team next season. On the average, about twenty-five of these show up at the start of fall practice each year. The usual attrition because of graduation, failures in school, not playing, hot weather, and other reasons, round our squad out to about forty-five players each season. This is about all that a small staff can work with anyway.

Hospital Care Costly

One area that concerns me is expenses because of injuries. This is not to say that I'm not concerned by the injuries themselves, because I am. But since we are talking about expenses at this time, I want to confine myself to that area. We have some fine team doctors who forfeit their fees to take care of our players, but we still must pay for X rays and the like, such as the emergency room after practice or games. Any time we send a player to the emergency room, it will cost us $50 just to walk in the door, so to speak. This can add up in a hurry and we certainly don't hold back when an injury occurs.

I think that players, and maybe we coaches too, are more injury prone than in the "old days," and I have been in football for thirty-five years. I'm certainly not saying that there is anything wrong with being concerned with injuries, but I think that the response to injuries was different twenty years ago. As coaches, we know that there will be major injuries that will involve operating rooms, hospital expenses, and doctors' bills that can add up to quite a sum of money. In cases such as this, we ask the parents of the player to allow their insurance to pay for as much of this as possible, and the college pays the balance. Occasionally the player will not have insurance and the college foots the whole bill in this case. As you well know, this can reduce a small budget in a hurry. I haven't found an easy solution and I have asked several coaches for their opinions on this, and many of them handle it the same as we do.

As to our coaching staff, we operate with Assistant Coach Tommy Ranager, a member of the staff for the same length of time as myself, fourteen years. Actually, "assistant coach" is a misnomer since we operate almost as two head coaches. Only in about four of these years have we had a student to volunteer his services. Maybe we just don't work hard enough to recruit student assistants, but we haven't been fortunate enough in this regard. We don't have a graduate school, so perhaps this accounts for this deficiency.

Our duties, other than football, account for six hours of teaching load during the fall and twelve hours during the spring semester. In the fall, I teach one activity class and one academic class in theory of high school coaching, while Coach Ranager has one activity and one class in hygiene. He also coaches baseball in the spring. Besides football and baseball, Millsaps College supports intercollegiate sports in girls and boys basketball, tennis, and golf. None of our five-man coaching staff overlaps in any one sport.

Practice Schedule

In writing this article, I was asked to outline the practice schedule of a two-man coaching staff with forty or more football players. We have had winning seasons in ten of the fourteen years that we have coached at Millsaps College. Three of the four losing seasons came in the first four years of our tenure. Our record for the past ten years has been fifty-five wins, thirty-three losses, and one tie. Not sensational by any means, but fairly solid, and one season we did make it to the Division III playoffs where we won our first game against a strong single-wing team—Colorado College—and lost the semifinal game to the eventual national champion, Wittenberg University. This experience was the highlight of my coaching career and something that benefited our program a great deal. We can at least say that we have been there and it gives us something to work toward in the future. The point I'm trying to make is that maybe we do something that's right and can come up with a win here and there.

We've had to reevaluate our thinking as far as fall practice goes since Division III discontinued spring football. Previously, we used this period to experiment with players in different positions, try new offenses and defenses, and generally toughen up our players. We feel that we can have too much contact work in the fall with such a small squad. We did have more contact during the past two seasons, although we didn't want to. The consequence is that we had more injuries and went with a new lineup into virtually every game that we played.

Our preseason fall schedule is pretty much set, as I'm sure that most of yours are. We do about the same sequence every year in preseason and during the season itself. Maybe some of you would be interested in our daily and weekly schedule, especially if you, too, work with a small staff.

One thing that we do every session is a prepractice routine that is repetitious and can, I suppose, become boring to the players, but we feel is important. Our passers and receivers, as well as every player, are asked to be on the field at least twenty minutes before the whistle blows to start the formal part of practice. During this time, the passers start off with look-in routes to each receiver from the left and right side. We ask our receivers to run all patterns at nine-tenths speed on all routes and with proper cuts to familiarize the quarterbacks with game patterns.

After this we run sidelines of 10 yards with a coach standing in a position 45 degrees behind the center to be sure that our quarterbacks, if need be, are sprinting out at an angle deep enough to turn into the line of scrimmage. The receivers must make a 90-degree cut. Next we throw deep post routes and again the receivers must run nine-tenths speed in order to acclimate catching the football under game conditions. Since we run a lot of motion routes, we go to this pattern next and again the quarterbacks must get depth on this sprint route.

We then work on pass defense with two-man routes and occasionally one-on-one routes. Every once in a while, we tackle during this period because we have found that the defenders will tend to soften up and not play through the receivers unless we stress this phase of the drill.

Our next prepractice drill is to run through the option attack with the ends forcing the quarterbacks to pitch or keep. We run four different option plays from the I formation and let our quarterbacks run each one of them three times. We have never worked more than three quarterbacks in a season. We stress staying on the line of scrimmage, fullback-tailback alignment, depth of the execution, and position in relation to the quarterback. One thing that comes out of this drill is the occasional fumble, and we stress a fanatical recovery by all players involved with the offense. If anyone fails to go after the fumble, we institute a fumble drill on the spot and this usually takes care of that problem.

To mention our offensive formation briefly, we use the I formation with a pro and slot set both left and right. I'm sure that everyone has his own ideas of why they use such and such a formation, but we think that the I will let us adjust to the material that we recruit each year more readily than other formations. The Houston veer and wishbone coaches will, I'm sure, say the same thing about those formations. Also, we don't throw any drop-back passes since we feel the blocking is different from sprint action and we don't have the time to teach both techniques.

The prepractice schedule for the line is also a repetition each day. Coach Ranager works with these men, and they practice form blocking on the boards and also work under the cage. The linebackers are practicing other drills and proper form tackling. They also go over blocking rules against the different defenses, especially the ones that we are likely to encounter that particular week. Occasionally we have contact during this period with two-on-one blocking, rushing the passer, and the like.

Our practice starts with stretching exercises during two-a-days. We follow the exercises set up in "A Coach's Guide to Safe Football" (see Chapter 51) published by the American Football Coaches Association. They take longer to do than the conventional exercises, but they are well worth the time. We find that players who have no flexibility at first, improve 100 percent within two weeks. We think these exercises have helped solve the pulled muscle problem that seems to plague us during the first two weeks. After we get into the season, we go to reaction exercises because we feel we don't have time to continue with the stretching drills, although we could continue them if we worked with only offensive and defensive teams entirely.

Our next station is for the entire team to go to the seven-man sled. We feel that this helps in many respects, including gaining confidence in the shoulder pads, agility, and proper blocking and tackling stances to take when executing these maneuvers. We first go through hand shivers with the feet squared and moving with chopping steps. Then the forearm shiver is executed by the entire team and again the body is squared with the sled and proper arm and shoulder technique is stressed. We next go to the "pianola" drill with each contact a full-speed shot and a spinout on all fours before squaring up and hitting every other pad. We find that new players are a bit timid with this drill, but are really popping it by midseason. After this drill, we have the team divided up into groups of six, and we drive the sled in a 360-degree turn with the stress on chopping the feet and staying square with the block.

Besides planning each practice before we go on the field, I make a chart of what we have done during each practice and how much time we spent with each phase of the practice schedule. I put anything down on these cards that I think is significant during practice and I keep them on file for each year. I like to go back and review these cards to see if we are doing anything different or if we should be doing something that we have done in past years. They are good to review each year to get in the swing of the practice schedule for each day during that particular phase of the practice season.

Once we start the season, we do pretty much the same thing on every day's practice. A week's practice schedule goes like this:

Monday

3:30 Exercises.

3:35 Sled.

3:40 Fumble Gauntlet—Any player who fumbles in the previous game runs the gauntlet through the entire team six times.

3:45 Live extra points and field goals from each hash mark.

3:55 Live punting from the end zone and from each hash mark.

4:10 Punt returns—Three to each side and three punt blocks.

4:20 Opponent's plays drawn up on cards against first-team defense.

4:40 Two offensive teams passing against opponent's defenses.

4:55 Two offensive teams using running plays against blocking dummies.

5:15 Three hundreds with kickers, holders, centers, and receivers practicing on their specialties after hundreds.

Tuesday

3:30 Exercises.

3:35 Sled.

3:40 Three S drill from the 10-yard line. Stance. Starts. Strike. This is a half-line scrimmage with two offensive teams going against opponent's defenses. Five minutes to each side.

3:50 Our passes against defensive team using opponent's defenses. Two teams.

4:10 Opponent's play on cards against our defensive team. Second defense five minutes.

4:30 Drills. Backs and ends handoff drill, gauntlet, figure eights, crossovers, fight for the ball, intercept over dummies. Line on reaction drills, quickness drills, form tackles and cage.

4:45 Backs running plays through dummy gauntlet. Line running plays against dummies.

4:55 Two offensive teams running plays against dummies using opponent's defenses.

5:15 Five hundreds. Specialists after hundreds.

Wednesday

3:30 Exercises.

3:35 Sled.

3:40 Two offensive teams passing against four-deep defenses.

4:05 Opponent's plays against our defenses. Second defense 5 minutes.

4:25 Drills. Same as described during Tuesday's practice.

4:40 Backs running plays through dummy gauntlet. Line on running plays against dummies.

4:50 Pass defense. Two teams running our plays against defensive backfield.

5:00 Two teams running offense against dummies using opponent's defenses.

5:20 Five hundreds. Specialists stay out after hundreds.

Thursday

3:30 Exercises led by game captains.

3:35 Defensive team working opponent's offense from left hash mark.

3:42 Same from right hash mark.

3:49 Same from middle of the field.

3:56 Prevent defense.

4:00 Goal line defense against opponent's offense, from 5-yard line.

4:10 Our goal line passing attack from the 5-yard line against defense.

4:25 Our goal line running plays from 5-yard line. Two offensive teams.

4:40 Sprint off field to film room.

Friday

3:30 Exercises led by game captains. Team in sweats.

3:35 Kickoff team. Kick and cover four times.

3:40 Kickoff receiving team. Returns left, right, and middle.

3:45 Punting team. Four punts and cover.

3:50 Punt receiving team. Returns left, right, middle. Block.

3:55 Field goal and extra-point team. Two each.

4:00 Goal line defensive team. Opponent's favorite goal line plays.

4:05 Two offensive teams work from 20-yard line against defensive team using opponent's defenses.

4:15 Sprint off field to film room.

7
Football at the University of Southern California

(From 1973 Proceedings of the AFCA)

JOHN McKAY Head Coach, University of Southern California

First, I'd like to say that in all the clinics that I have attended over the years, the big thing is that when someone wins anything, everybody comes and takes the diagrams he puts up and says "That's it." The last couple of years, as you know, it's been the wishbone.

We don't use the wishbone, but just to get in the swing of things, we changed the name of our offense from the I to the I Bone. The offense is the same, and just the name is changed.

I'll tell you about our philosophy. For years, we wanted to run right at you with the blast play and find out where you are, and establish the fact that we are as strong, physically, as you are. Then, after we established the blast, we went to our pitch play, or, as it's also called, "student body left or right."

This year, we started with the pitch and ran it until you stopped it, and then we'd go to the blast. This way, we can say we are continually changing.

We really are pretty simple. We run the pitch for awhile, then go to the blast, and back to the pitch. The big thing we changed this year was our uniforms.

Defensively, in 1971 we were beaten by a wishbone team and were told by some of their people that you could not use a 50 defense to stop the wishbone. I said that I could stop anything if you gave me the right people. So, I went out and got the right people!

Our idea there was to get smaller people to play on the outside and be sure they were very quick. We wouldn't let anybody play outside linebacker unless he could run 4.6 or better.

Inside, we didn't think players had to be as fast, but we did want our inside linebackers to run 4.7. That we figured was a pretty good idea, and those are our theories.

Before I draw up any plays, let me tell you this:

Over the years, we have found out that **players** win, plays have never won anything.

Two Basic Plays

I will give you our two basic plays, and then show you our basic defense set, along with why we use it and why we think we can stop most offenses with it.

First of all, offensively, our attack is based on multiple sets, using motion and shifting. We start out with sixteen different sets, and by using motion and shifting, we can add greatly to the number of things we do. I think it is pretty complicated for the opponent, but it's simple to us, and out of it comes our two basic plays, the pitch and blast.

As I told you before, we are going to start by running the pitch play, until you put so many people outside that we can make our inside offense go.

We start every offensive set to run the ball outside. If we go outside to the tight end side, we ask the tight end to block the outside man on the line. We don't care where you line him up, we feel we can block him. We ask him to block the defensive man high up in his face, and his main job is to keep the defender on the line, and, if possible, hook the man. If the defender fights to the outside fast, then we ask him to drive him to the sideline, but stay up on him and keep him on the line.

We tell our tackle to hook the tackle, to stay up, never go to your knees. Stay up and block him as high as you can, keep pushing on him. If the defensive man slants inside, our tackle just goes on to the linebacker.

The center's job is to reach to the onside, unless he is covered, and then take that man.

We tell the guard to block the onside linebacker. We ask him to pull around the tight end for the linebacker. If, as the guard starts his pull, the linebacker shoots, he just stops and takes him, so it is imperative that the guard keeps his eyes on the linebacker all the time.

We tell the offside guard to pull and go through the first opening he can find. The offside tackle's assignment is the same as the guard's.

Our quarterbacks, at times, lead this play. If we ask them to lead, assuming we're going to the right, they should step right with their right foot, and then reverse pivot. Don't reverse pivot first; if he does, he will be behind the play. Then, he just leads around the end and looks inside. We ask him to just fall at the feet of the defender. We don't want him to body block him or get tough like these other people do. Our quarterbacks make a lot of good blocks that way.

We tell our fullback to take a slight step forward, and then go parallel to the line and annihilate the cornerback. We don't want him to body block—just run right over him.

That is how our interior people block the play.

Diagram 1a

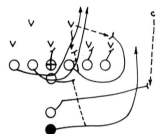

Diagram 1b

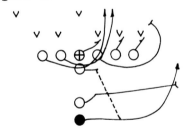

Our Z-back's (flanker's) job changes, depending on where he is set. If he is set wide, we ask him to crack back on the first man inside, usually the strong safety. If he is set in the Power I position, then he leads outside the tight end, and helps him with the defensive end. If our tight end has his man, then Z leads straight up for the safety man.

Our tailback's job is to open step toward the sideline, catch the pitch from the quarterback, and run as fast as he can for the outside, always keeping his eyes up the field. If he can get all the way outside, then we want him to run off the fullback's block on the corner.

If there is a funnel there, we tell him to turn up the field and go. (See Diagram 2.)

Diagram 2

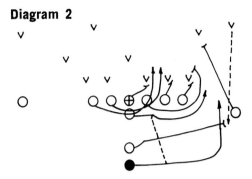

If the defensive end, or rover (R in the diagrams), ever gets up the field or outside too fast, then our tailback will cut up inside and pick up the blocks of our backside pullers. (See Diagrams 3 and 4.)

Diagram 3

Diagram 4

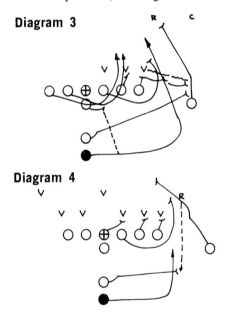

If people are overplaying this play with an unbalanced defense, we will shift, or motion, our Z-back to balance up or take advantage of the defense.

This year, for example, we faced a rover defense, which put two men on the line outside our tight end or Z-back.

We put the rover here:

Diagram 5

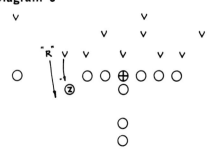

and then put our Z-back in motion through the backfield, and ran the pitch away from the rover.

Diagram 6

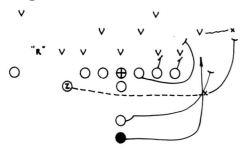

Now, getting to the blast play, most people run it—some maybe run it better than we do. Our coaching point on it is extremely important. We want our backs to stay deep. Where you line up is as important as where you wind up. If you want to crowd up, it means you're too slow to play in the backfield.

It's highly important that the fullback is at least $4\frac{1}{2}$ to 5 yards, and the tailback be 6 to $6\frac{1}{2}$ yards, so that they can option run versus all the potential stunts we may see.

It's impossible for an offensive tackle or guard to keep a defender lined up head on him, from going inside. If you're stubborn enough to say you're going to run the ball through any one hole, then certain stunts will wipe this play out.

So, it's important that they stay back. We ask them to key the first defensive lineman to the onside. As they approach the hole, they will run away from the direction the lineman slants.

If the defensive lineman slants in, it's obvious the linebacker is coming to the outside. Our tackle will just block the defensive tackle the way he wants to go, and our fullback will "kick out" the linebacker the

Diagram 7

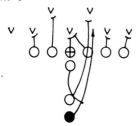

Diagram 8

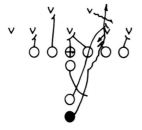

way he is going. If the tailback stays back away from the fullback, there's an alley between those blocks that he can hit.

The rest of the blocking is pretty simple. Again, the big coaching point is keeping your back deep. Someone made the comment to me the other day that they were amazed that we kept our tailback at 7 yards during the entire game against Ohio State in the Rose Bowl. I said "Yep, that's what we want when the defense stunts on us." We want him back where he can see.

The other important point is that the quarterback gives the tailback the ball as deep as possible. I do not believe you can run as hard when you get the ball close to the line of scrimmage. The first thing any back thinks of is possession, possession first. I must have the ball, then I can think about the other things. So, we ask our quarterback to reverse pivot and get the ball deep.

This play can be a great goal-line play, provided the back is willing to go "over the top" versus the gap defenses. If we face a goal line or gap set, we tell our tailback to be ready to dive over the line. Again, he must line up deep to have time to secure the ball and then get "up in the air." He takes off about a yard back and a good diver can go about five or six yards. Now, what you have got to do is convince the diver. We never practice this play. People say, how do you practice this play? We don't. We tell the diver this: They will probably catch you, and that's the best thing that can happen to you. Now, if we block well, you'll hit the ground, and that's the worst thing that can happen to you, because you're going to hit approximately right on your head.

I'll give you a little stat—and this is a true one—and it's going to be more, but including the first six games this year and the last two games, thirty-seven times, on short yardage or on the goal-line situation, we either made it or scored on all but one time. The thing about it is that we know how to block the play, that the quarterback must give the ball back deep.

Our Basic Defense

We have used a lot of defenses over the years, and whenever we were any good, we just stayed in the 50 defense.

Every time we went to a clinic, we came back with a new, pro defense. We had so many pass coverages, it took us a week to break the huddle.

So, we went back to what we did the best, a 50 defense with a few simple coverages. We are going to run one defense until you can prove to us you can beat it. We are not going to change to confuse you. We went through that routine, and the only people we confused was ourselves.

As I said, we are the best when we are in a straight 50 defense. We don't stunt much, and when we do, it's because we can't hold up playing straight.

We only have three down linemen. Our nose man generally plays straight; he is responsible for the counters, and so forth. Our tackles play on the outside shoulders and play pretty well. Those are the only linemen we have; the rest are trained as linebackers.

We have four linebackers, and each is trained for specific spots.

Diagram 9

Our LIZ linebacker always went to the weak side (split side). We did not care how big he was. The young man who played there, Jim Sims, is 5 feet, 11 inches and weighs 192 pounds. He also runs 4.6, and he is some kind of football player. He is the best pass rusher we have ever had, and we've had some good ones. If you think any 260-pound tackle can keep him from rushing the passer, you're wrong; he is too fast.

The other three linebackers play in pretty much traditional fashion. We teach them like all 50 defensive teams teach their men. In selecting personnel for these spots, speed was the prime requirement. We are willing to give up a little size for speed.

Our basic pass defense is built around a three-man rush and eight men coming off the line into the coverage. Our pass defense philosophy is defend, defend. We want to make you throw into eight people.

Can we rush three men? Yes, if we go with the right three people. We had two very tall youngsters in our rush.

Now, we can also bring in any one or more of these four linebackers. They are brought in by the coverage call or by their names. If we called "50 SAM," SAM would rush. If we said "50 LIZ," LIZ would rush. That's our defense, gentlemen.

Why did we go to this? Basically, because of the wishbone. It is an excellent offensive theory and very difficult to stop outside unless you can match the offense's speed with your outside people.

So, we went to outside linebackers with defensive back speed and agility. If you'll just think about it a minute, you very seldom see a defensive halfback knocked down. He moves his feet; he moves out of the way; he jumps; he just does a better job of staying alive in an open area. We felt that the bigger the man, the less successful he was against the wishbone's lead blocker. We just didn't want to get caught playing the wishbone with some 6-foot, 3-inch, 230-pound guy we'd picked because he could rush the passer.

This season, against the wishbone, our outside people were much more successful against the lead block. In fact, we were pretty good against any option-type team.

Our problems this year came from the bigger teams like Notre Dame. They pulled guards on our outside kids, and this bothered us for awhile. They did a good job of moving the ball on us. Their offensive ideas against us were excellent.

We will stay with our theory. We want to outrun you outside, then we'll worry about the strength problem.

As I said, I don't think theories win; players win. Down through the years, we haven't changed much. The things we do best are those things we know best and have taught for years.

8
Two-Minute Offense and Defense

(From 1975 Summer Manual of the AFCA)

TONY KNAP Head Coach, Boise State University

To begin with, everyone agrees that each team should be prepared to move the ball quickly while conserving time when needed. This statement presumes that each team has varying degrees of strength and skill, as represented by its personnel and its formations. The wise selection of plays used in a two-minute offense must fit these strengths and skills. Everyone agrees, too, that it is foolish to go to a style of play that does not use the skills and personnel strengths of the team simply to conserve time, that is, a power or option team going to the pure passing game without having developed the skills necessary to make that kind of play effective simply because every incomplete pass stops the clock.

At Boise State, our entire offensive thinking has developed from the desire to be a great "catch-up" team when necessary. We wanted to avoid that very uncomfortable situation of being behind and being unable to strike upfield quickly at a minimum cost in time. The players at Boise State who have been recruited here were, and are, people who possessed the skills we needed; we decided on the formations to be used as they contributed to this philosophy. Finally, we spend the necessary time in practice to develop these skills and strengths. Our two-minute offense not only fits into the pattern of our regular attack, it is the very heart of it!

Assuming that each team has its own arsenal of skills and strengths and has planned a carefully selected portion of their regular attack to meet the "Mayday" requirements, it is only necessary to know about using the clock as efficiently as possible.

Our two-minute offense concerns itself with two areas: (1) Saving time on the clock if tied or behind and (2) wasting time on the clock if ahead during the final minutes of the game.

Our ability to function smoothly and efficiently in these time periods can have a great effect on our season.

Knowledge of the rules as they apply to the game clock is the single most important factor in this phase of the game.

The wise use of our time-outs is the first factor to be considered. Each team is allowed three time-outs per half. It is imperative that we do not use any of our time-outs unnecessarily during the normal course of the game. If at all possible, we would like to have all three of our time-outs available for use in our two-minute offense.

Remember, during the last two minutes:

I. *The Game Clock Stops:*
   a. When time-out is called by official.
   b. Incomplete pass.
   c. Ball carrier goes out of bounds.
   d. During administration of a penalty.
   e. While chain gang measures for a first down.
   f. When either team makes the first down.
   g. When a fair catch is made or the ball is touched illegally.
   h. When a live ball goes out of bounds.

II. *The Game Clock Starts:*
   a. When ball is legally touched on a kickoff.
   b. With the snap of the ball:
      1. After a called time-out.
      2. Incomplete pass.
      3. After the ball carrier goes out of bounds.
      4. After the 2-minute notification (if applicable).
      5. After kickoff out of end zone (not legally touched).
      6. On exchange of possession.

7. For media time-out (televised games).
c. With the referee's whistle indicating ball is ready for play:
    1. After measurement for firstdown.
    2. After administration of a penalty.
    3. After an excess time-out.
    4. After a lateral out of bounds.
    5. After chains are advanced and set for first down.

Procedure for Two-Minute Offense

I. *Saving Time When Tied or Behind*
  a. General Team Principles
    1. Offensive team will have a play or plays ready when they **run** onto the field. They will come to the coach as a unit for a plan of attack.
    2. If the clock is not stopped, you will **immediately** line up and run either the second play called on the sidelines or you will take the automatic from the quarterback.
    3. If the clock is stopped, you will use the huddle and again receive a play or *plays* from the quarterback.
    4. When the clock is stopped for a measurement or penalty, use a huddle, but be on the ball and ready to play when the referee signals the ball ready for play.
    5. Ball carriers and receivers get as much yardage as possible, then get out of bounds.
    6. Hustle at top speed to your prearranged alignment any time the clock does not stop on a play.
    7. **Do not call time-out.** Time-outs will be called only by the quarterback—or other designated player.
  b. Quarterback Guide for Two-Minute Offense
    1. You must be absolutely positive about the number of time-outs remaining.
    2. Our basic rule will be to not use any of our time-outs until the final minute.
    3. You must be certain that the team is aware of the fact that you are in a two-minute offense.
    4. It is your responsibility to know all the rules regarding the stopping and starting of the game clock. You must be the absolute master of the situation.
    5. The ball carriers must be aware of whether you are thinking touchdown or field goal. They will be fighting harder to break for the long gainer when a touchdown is necessary. They will be more willing to get

out of bounds safely to stop the clock if we are working for a field goal.
    6. Always use a quick count during two-minute offense.
    7. Follow the game plan in calling plays that will allow the runner or receiver to get out of bounds if possible.
    8. Recognize the situation in which you must intentionally throw the incomplete pass to stop the clock.
    9. Follow the play closely, and be prepared to line up and call a play at the line of scrimmage if we do not get the clock stopped. (Keep one eye on the bench for a visual signal from the coach.)
    10. Request a measurement any time the ball is close.
    11. Remember when it is necessary to have a play called and have your team on the line of scrimmage ready to go as the referee signals the ball ready to play and starts the clock.
    12. You must understand the philosophy of when a called time-out is necessary, and you must hustle to be close to the correct official to get this time-out called quickly. You will call all time-outs unless the other designated player can expedite the time-out.
    13. Stay "cool" and remember that you are in charge!
II. *Wasting Time on the Clock When Ahead*
  a. Use the full twenty five-seconds on each play whenever possible.
  b. Keep the ball away from the sidelines.
  c. Warn runners to stay in bounds.
  d. Ball carriers should hold onto ball and get up slowly.
  e. If you must kick, do not kick out of bounds or over the goal line, and do not down the ball.
  f. Eliminate the penalty.
  g. **Never** call time-out.
  h. If less than twenty-five seconds are left, let the clock run without centering the ball.

Moving the Ball Upfield Quickly

As we stated previously, the offensive philosophy at Boise State is based on the two-minute offense in accordance with the "quick strike" objectives. Therefore, the personnel is already ideally positioned for playing the catch-up game, as all possess the skill requirements. The two-minute situation then becomes a selection problem: deciding which of our basic building blocks gives us the most efficient means of moving the football upfield quickly. At Boise State, this thinking is divided into three categories: formations, passing game, and running game.

Formations

These are some of the formations that we use during the regular course of the game and in our two-minute offense. All of them force the defense into full field coverage. If there is no huddle, we determine before the game the formation we want used and place the strength into the wide side of the field or the short side. This varies with the team we are playing. If there is a huddle, the quarterback can call any formation he wants.

If there is no huddle, we will line up in one of two basic formations. (See Diagrams 1 and 2.)

Diagram 1

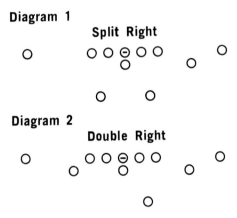

Split Right

Diagram 2

Double Right

If there is time for a huddle, we may have determined before the game to use another formation especially suited to attack the kind of prevent defense anticipated (See Diagrams 3 and 4). The quarterback can use it instead of the other two formations. Remember, no matter what the formation is, we have determined that we will be able to run our two-minute offense from it.

Diagram 3

Flood right

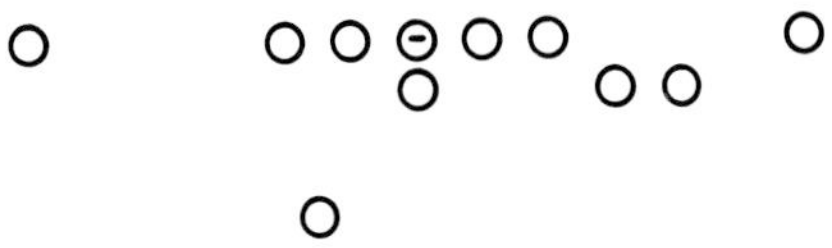

Diagram 4

Wing flood right

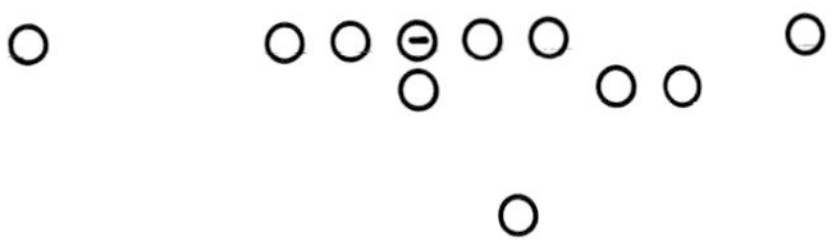

Passing Game

Pass patterns in our two-minute offense are plays we have chosen from our basic offense to be most productive in a two-minute situation. With these plays, we are able to strike deep, medium, or short, depending on what the defense will give us and what we have to do to conserve the clock. We divide our patterns into six types (See Diagrams 5–12).

Diagram 5

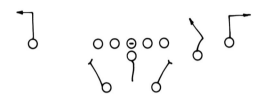

Quick passes. One- or three-step drop by the quarterback. (Usually a 5-yard pattern by receivers.)

Diagram 6

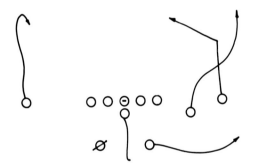

Strong side floods. Seven-step drop by the quarterback. (Usually 15-yard breaks by receivers.)

Diagram 7

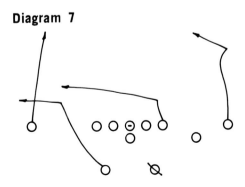

Weak side floods. Seven-step drop by the quarterback. (15-yard break by receivers.)

Diagram 8

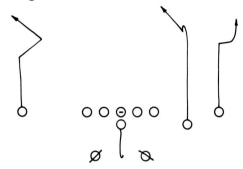

Deep floods. Seven-step drop by the quarterback. Receivers normally fake a pattern and then "go" deep.

Diagram 9

FB screen

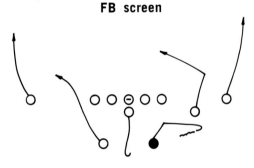

Diagram 10

HB -delay

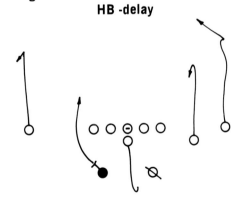

Delays and screens. These are run with a normal drop-back fake.

Diagram 11

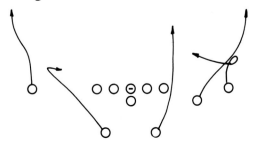

Diagram 12

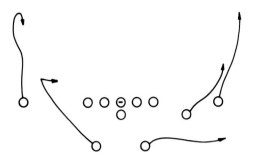

Combination. Seven-step drop by the quarterback. In these patterns, we try to use all of our receivers to strike deep, medium, and short simultaneously.

Running Plays

The philosophy underlying our running game in the course of executing the two-minute offense concerns itself with two important factors.

First, our running plays are designed and executed with time conservation being of foremost importance. Therefore, we expect our running attack to gain the maximum yards possible while making good use of the sidelines to stop the clock.

Second, our running attack is geared to take advantage of what the defense gives us in the two-minute situation. For example, against a tough pass rush, we would use the "quick" running attack utilizing the quick trap and the quick toss, or fake pass-run plays.

Diagrams 13–16 are examples of plays we would use, keeping these factors in mind.

Diagram 13

A. Quick trap

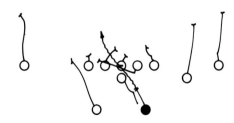

Diagram 14

B. Quick toss

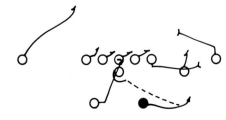

Diagram 15

C. Statue

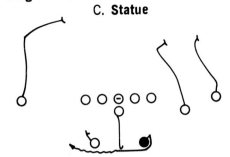

Diagram 16

D. Draw

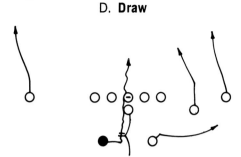

In conclusion, and in review, we feel that our basic offensive elements of formations, passing, and quick-striking running plays provide the best way to move the ball quickly. We realize that more offense is needed to go through the regular part of each game, and we have some power and some option plays that fit into the basic framework.

The place we begin it all, however, is chosen for its effectiveness in catching up if or when we get behind and time is of the essence. In the past seven years, the Broncos have found themselves behind thirty-four times in the fourth quarter and have managed to win seventeen of those games. The fans like that.

9
Halftime Organization

(From 1976 Summer Manual of the AFCA)

BOB STULL Assistant Coach, University of Washington

At the University of Washington we feel the key to a well-organized halftime is the proper utilization of facilities and an efficient time plan. During the twenty-minute intermission there are numerous things that must take place:

1. Players must be allowed to rest.
2. All injury and equipment problems must be taken care of.
3. The staff must analyze the first half and make plans for the second half.
4. The second half plans and adjustments must be transmitted to the players.

Organizing Space to Save Time

Before any coach or player leaves the locker room for the first half, each must know exactly where to report as he reenters at halftime. We feel this is extremely important because we cannot afford the time to look for players or coaches when so much has to be done in such a short period. It is not important exactly how you arrange your squad, just as long as your offense and defense are separated.

When we play at home, we assign the offense to the varsity locker room, the defense to the freshman locker room, and our staff to a room between. We also designate areas within the locker rooms for the various positions to congregate.

If we are playing an away game where we do not have the same facilities available, we simply divide the locker room into halves for the offense and defense, and our staff meets in any unoccupied space, which may even be the shower room area.

Budgeting Time

We have divided our halftime into four time periods.

1. First period (six minutes)
   a. Staff meets.
   b. Team rests.
2. Second period (five minutes)
   a. Position coaches meet with the players.
3. Third period (four minutes)
   a. Offensive coordinator meets with the entire offensive squad.
   b. Defensive coordinator meets with the entire defensive squad.
4. Fourth period (one to three minutes)
   a. Head coach meets with both the offense and defense.

In order to keep on this schedule, we feel that we have to begin our staff meeting as soon as we step into the locker room. To do this, all the information tabulated during the first half by our coaches in the press box must already be on the blackboard in our meeting area. So, actually our halftime schedule begins two minutes before the end of the first half since this is when one offensive coach and one defensive coach from the press box leave for the locker room with this information.

Period One

The first period is a critical one for the staff. At this time we are involved in an analysis of what has taken place during the first half and deciding what our plan of attack will be in the second half. The information we check before making these plans includes:

1. Offensively
   a. Fronts by down and distance.
   b. Secondary by down and distance.
   c. Short yardage and goal line defenses.
   d. Our calls by down and distance to check our tendencies and also to see what plays have been successful and what plays haven't.
2. Defensively
   a. Hits by formation.
   b. Hits by down and distance.
   c. Pass routes.
   d. Blocking variations.
   e. Our defensive calls by down and distance.
3. Kicking Game
   a. Have we had any assignment breakdowns in the punting game, kickoff returns, extra points, or field goals?
   b. Is the fake punt or field goal possible?
   c. How is our kickoff coverage?
   d. Should there be a change in philosophy as to whether we should punt blocks or returns?
4. General
   a. Personnel adjustments because of injuries or other reasons.
   b. How are playing conditions, such as rain, wind, and so on, affecting play?
   c. Any substitution changes?
   d. Analysis of Polaroid snapshots. (We have a photographer take various pictures of defensive fronts, offensive formations, and kick rushes from the press box.)

From all points listed above, our staff will arrive at a second-half philosophy. This philosophy will be based on how our opponent is attacking us both offensively and defensively and how we feel they will adjust to our attack during the second half. All blocking adjustments, route changes, and theory of attack is decided offensively. Also, any front alignments, coverage, or force adjustments are made to stop the opponent defensively. Of course, the score will also weigh heavily on our course of action for the second half.

While our staff is actively involved in the second-half strategy, our players are getting ready physically for the second half. All incidental injuries and equipment problems are taken care of in their designated assigned areas of the locker room. Liquids, towels, and other needs are brought to the players. This allows them to rest and prevents a lot of moving around. Any major injury is taken care of in the training room. We try and keep this initial period to approximately six minutes.

Period Two

The second period of our halftime is for each coach to meet with the players at his position. During this period, we hope to do two things. First, we quiz our players as to what is happening to them on the field. Our staff feels it is extremely important to have open communication with our players. Many times we will find that one of our players will come up with information that turns out to be very helpful the second half. Also, the coach needs to know, for instance, if a receiver can beat a corner on an out route or a streak, or if an offensive lineman can hook a defender on a sweep.

Second, our coaches transmit our second-half strategy to the players as it relates to their position. Alignments, techniques, and any adjustments are given at this time. This period lasts approximately five minutes.

Period Three

As soon as each position coach has met with his players, both the offense and defense meet with our coordinators to tie our scheme together. For instance, if we are having pass-protection problems because of confusion between our tackle and our halfback, it is the job of our coordinator to straighten this out. Also, many times our staff will decide on individual offensive and defensive goals in order to win the second half.

We may decide that in order to win the game, our defense must hold the opponent scoreless during the second half, and our offense must get one touchdown in the third quarter and a field goal or better the fourth. We have even broken this down further and have talked to our defensive players in terms of holding our opponents to a certain amount of rushing and passing yardage, and our offense gaining a determined amount of first downs, yardage rushing, yardage passing, and so on.

We have assigned graduate assistants the task of tabulating such information and reporting the progress to our players as they come off the field after each drive. In any case, we give our coordinators four minutes to relay any of this information to the squads.

Period Four

With five minutes remaining of the halftime, the officials will give us the five-minute warning. At this time our coaches with press box responsibilities and our team captains will leave the locker room for the field. The head coach will take control at this point and the offense and defense join together for final instructions. It is the job of our head coach to finalize all strategy and goals and to motivate our squad for the second half. This time period lasts usually not more than two or three minutes. Our team then departs for the second half of play.

Summary

Basically, our staff enters a game with a plan of attack for the offense, the defense, and our kicking game. How our opponent has adjusted to our attack during the first half and how we anticipate further adjustments in the second half determine our game plan after intermission. Our ability to decipher the information from our press box statistics and our players to make accurate halftime decisions and to present them to our squad has been most easily accomplished through our four-period time breakdown and the organization of our squad by positions.

10
The Sudden Change Is Ours

(From *1976 Summer Manual* of the AFCA)

LARRY SMITH Head Coach, Tulane University

How many times have you been involved in or watched a game where the sudden change situation has determined the outcome?

Sudden change is the situation during a game where your defensive unit has just stopped the opponent on a drive. The offensive unit takes over on, say, your own 32-yard line. On the succeeding play your offensive unit turns the ball over on a fumble or interception to the opponent. The defense has to go right back into the game. This is one of the toughest situations possible for a defense to experience. They are tired, confused, and not mentally ready to go back into the football game, let alone stop your opponent. Usually the offensive team scores in this situation.

During the past three seasons at Arizona our defense was successful in stopping the opponents in this situation 80 to 85 percent of the time. The keys to our success were mental preparation and practice time in actual situations.

Since coming to Tulane, we have tried to develop the sudden change strategy to fit offensive, defensive, and kicking situations. It is our belief that a football game is made up of a number of these situations. Whoever is successful in the majority of these situations is most likely to win the game. The following are lists of all the different types of situations that arise in a football game. (Those situations marked with an asterisk are discussed in this chapter.)

Offensive Situations

*1. Coming out (first down inside our 5-yard line).
2. Third down (long and short yardage).
3. Goal line (first down inside opponent's 10-yard line).
4. Two-minute offense (no huddle).
5. Hurry-hurry (no time-outs).
6. Slow-slow (keep clock running).
7. Two-point play.
*8. Sudden change (takeover after opponent turnover in four-down territory).

Defensive Situations

1. Goal line (first down inside our 10-yard line).
2. Third down (long and short yardage).
*3. Sudden change (opponent's offense takes over in four-down territory following turnover by your team).
*4. Hurry-hurry (no huddle offense or offense has no time-outs).
*5. Alert-alert (no cheap touchdowns right before halftime).
6. Prevent (definite pass-score situation).
7. Two-point defense.

Kicking Situations

*1. Two-point play and situation.
2. Punt or field goal from opponent's 40-yard line.
3. Receiving punt inside own 10-yard line.
4. Punt from inside own 5-yard line

It is quite obvious that these lists are nothing new to most coaches. We all spend time and preparation in our practice schedule on goal line offense and defense, long and short yardage situations, two-minute offense and defense, hurry-hurry offense and defense, and the various kicking situations. But there are a few situations that we may tend to overlook or take for granted.

Your team's efficiency in all of these situations can be improved with a minimum of practice time and a proper mental attitude. Here are six situations and how we treat them at Tulane.

Coming Out

This has to be one of the toughest positions an offense can be in. It can also be one of the most crucial series of downs for your whole team and the outcome of the game. The first thing we do is to educate our players as to what a coming out series actually is. We do this in an offensive team meeting and give them an actual situation. For example, our opponents just downed a punt inside our 3-yard line. We are in the game with a first and 10 to go on our own 2-yard line. Next we explain that we will run our best plays. There must be no mistakes and our execution here should be flawless. A turnover here is almost a sure score for our opponents.

The key to success here is the few minutes of a period in practice known as coming out. Here we give our offense the type of defenses we will see in this type of field position. We scrimmage this situation the same as we do goal line or long yardage in the spring or early fall practice. When a coming out situation occurs in a game, our players know what it is, are mentally ready for it, and have practiced it.

Offensive Sudden Change

In this situation our defense has just got the ball for us in our opponent's four-down territory. It is usually a turnover or some sudden exchange of the football. Our offense must have that "killer instinct" when this situation occurs. It is a great break for us since our opponent's defense is probably confused, tired, and not mentally ready to cope with the situation.

Offensively, we must score. There are two schools of thought here. First, I can play conservative, sound football, not make any mistakes, and take advantage of being in four-down territory. Second, we can try for the quick score, such as a play-action bomb. Actually, a combination of these two strategies is most effective. Once again the key to success is to have already presented this situation to your squad in meetings, practice, and scrimmages. They are ready mentally and have been in this situation before both on and off the practice field.

Defensive Sudden Change

How many times has your defense had to go back into the game immediately after stopping your opponent on a series of downs? They have done a good job on defense, they are resting and regenerating for the next series. On the first play your offense makes a mistake and the defense has to go right back into the game. The defense trundles back onto the field, unorganized and disgruntled.

Chances are your opponent will score in this situation because they have the mental edge.

Since working with Jim Young at Arizona we took the sudden change concept and sold it to our defense as a positive situation. It was one of the greatest challenges a defense could accept and win. Once again they had to be exposed to this situation in meetings and practices. Whenever anyone yelled, "Sudden change!" in practice or a game, it was like a battle cry. We found the most important thing for the defense to do when they heard this was to huddle up as a unit before they went onto the field. This gave them an organized team feeling. They went on the field as a defense with a positive feeling in a tough situation.

We practiced this every Thursday night for five minutes. Each week a different coach would make out a sudden change series of downs with field position and put it in the schedule. It was good for the coach calling defenses because he also had to react to this situation.

Hurry-Hurry

All defenses must be ready for the hurry-hurry series by an offense. It can be a no-huddle offense or a situation before the half or the end of the game when your opponent has no time-outs left. In all cases it is important to have your defense ready to call an automatic at the line of scrimmage. A defense has to be poised and set for each play. Confusion in your defense here means your opponent will move the ball and possibly score.

The key to success is preparation. We talk about hurry-hurry to our defense so they know what it is. Our linebackers and safety yell, "Hurry-hurry!" when the situation occurs. This alerts everyone on the field to our automatics. We practice five minutes every Thursday night on hurry-hurry. Our coaches make up actual situations that have occurred from our opponents' films. We are able to adjust our defenses on the field without confusion. Also, we are not stuck in just one defense because of a time limit in getting our defenses called. Our linebackers and safety know what to expect and what defenses to call. Again, the main ingredient for success is poise.

Alert-Alert

This situation occurs when there is only about two minutes left in the half. Your opponent has just taken possession of the ball deep in his own territory. Many times your defense goes into the game too relaxed or complacent in this situation. The end result is that your opponent moves the ball down the field and scores. The reason for this is that your defense is not mentally ready for this situation. Cheap touchdowns and long plays frequently occur with less than two minutes left in the half.

We call the last series in the half the alert-alert series. The key here is to play good, sound, heads-up defense. We strive not to gamble but to play an aggressive, forcing defense. Play preventive defense but not permissive defense. Time spent in meetings and on the field gets our players geared to this situation. Again the proper mental frame of mind is so important. Familiarity and knowing what to do ensure success.

The Two-Point Decision

The two-point decision is one that is evident most of the time, but, as coaches, we are not aware of certain times when it should be used. Also, time, field conditions, personnel, and momentum play a strong factor in this decision. If all factors are equal and it boils down to whether you try for it or not, we employ a computer card. We keep this on the sideline and in the press box to refer to for such a decision. (See Diagram 1.)

I know that we all win football games on how well our team performs and that we cannot spend the whole practice on situations. But I know that the more aware we can make our football team of special situations, the greater the chance we will have of winning.

Diagram 1

TULANE EXTRA POINT SYSTEM

TEAM AHEAD Recommendation				TEAM BEHIND Recommendation				
Points	Go For 1	Go For 2	Remarks	Points Behind	Go For 1	Go For 2	Remarks	Key to Remarks
0	x			0	x			
+1		x		−1	x			
+2	x			−2		x		
+3	x			−3	x			
+4		x		−4	x			
+5		x		−5		x		
+6	x			−6	x			
+7	x			−7	x			
+8	x			−8	x			
+9	x			−9	x			
+10	x			−10		x		
+11		x		−11	x			
+12		x		−12	x			
+13	x			−13	x			
+14	x			−14	x			
+15	x			−15	x			
+16	x			−16		x		
+17	x			−17		x		
+18	x			−18		x		
+19		x		−19	x			
+20	x			−20	x			
+21	x			−21		x		
+22		x		−22	x			
+23	x			−23	x			
+24	x			−24	x			
+25		x		−25		x		
+26	x			−26		x		
+27	x			−27	x			
+28	x			−28		x		

Part Three
Offense

11

The Houston Offense

(From 1968 Proceedings of the AFCA)

BILL YEOMAN Head Coach, University of Houston

The first thing we at Houston feel we must do is establish a basic offense in the minds of our players. I know this sounds rather elementary, but it took me a long time to understand it. Until a coach accepts this, he runs plays instead of an offense. We would prefer it be simple, but more important than simplicity is effectiveness, and, of course, we come immedi tely to execution. I know five or ten years ago I listened to people who said this and would say to myself, "Enough of the garbage, let's get to the meat of things."

In reality, execution is the meat of everything. We try to take what is a good defensive reaction and use it against the defense. While we try to establish the run, we feel we must be able to throw effectively. Because we do lean to the run, throwing out of the running game has been more productive than our drop back.

I won't get into our numbering system because I'm sure you have your own that is completely satisfactory. Our cadence is down—then a number—then "go," "go," and so on. We do call plays at the line of scrimmage by merely saying in the huddle, "Call it at the line." At the line the quarterback says, "down," then calls the play we want to run. We do not like to check or call plays at the line if we can possibly avoid it.

I won't go into personnel requirements as I believe it will be obvious as we get into the offense. Our entire basic offense running and throwing is built around the play we call the Houston option. We feel it puts a tremendous strain on an opponent's defense, and over the past three years has proved to be very effective. Our confidence in the play has been more responsible than any other item for our running an offense instead of plays.

Our basic formation is a pro set, split backfield,

wide end, and flanker back. The width of the split end, tight end, and flanker back is determined by their assignments and respective ability of the defensive personnel. Our line takes a 3-foot split. (See Diagram 1.)

Diagram No. 1

Our two running backs line up at 4½ yards, foot and foot with the offensive guards. (See Diagram 2.)

Diagram No. 2

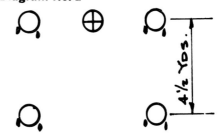

Let's get into the Houston option, and I believe you can see the reason for the alignment. There is nothing new about an option, and nothing new about releasing the end on an option, but threatening three holes at once while turning the two outside men on the line of scrimmage loose has forced some adjustment in the defensive thinking of our opponents. (See Diagrams 3–5.)

Our flanker back is responsible for the deep one-third. If the defense is in a zone, this becomes immediately obvious as he leaves the line of scrimmage. If the defense is in man-to-man coverage he blocks the outside man. The tight end releases outside the in man

Diagram No. 3

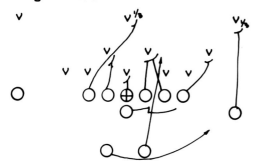

Diagram No. 4

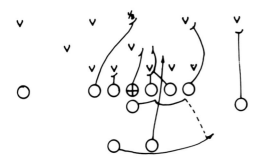

Diagram No. 5

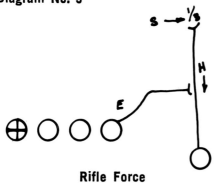

Rifle Force

on the line of scrimmage and blocks the man responsible for the flat. He blocks the inside man on man-to-man coverage. (See Diagrams 6–8.)

Diagram No. 6

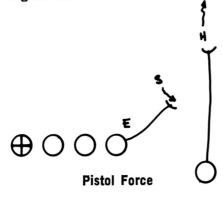

Pistol Force

Diagram No. 7

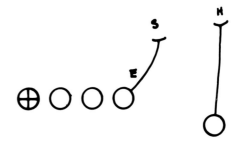

Man-To-Man

Diagram No. 8

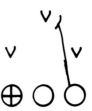

The strong tackle blocks the linebacker on his side. If there isn't one, then he helps the guard with his block and picks up the middle linebacker.

The strong guard blocks base. For those of you who use numbering, he blocks No. 1. For those who don't use numbering, he blocks the man over him.

Diagram No. 9

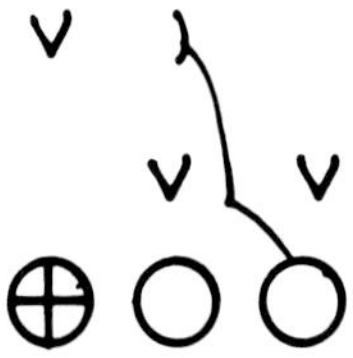

Diagram No. 10

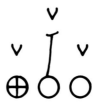

Diagram No. 11

Diagram No. 12

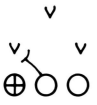

Diagram No. 16

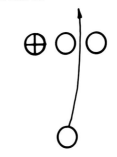

Diagram No. 13

Should the need arise, the guard, versus the odd, can be called off his block to help the center pick up the nose man.

The center blocks 0 or playside gap.

Diagram No. 14

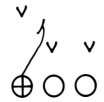

Diagram No 17

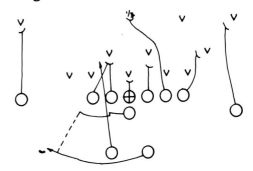

Diagram No. 15

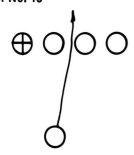

The quick guard blocks base (man over him).

The quick tackle forces an inside release and picks up the middle third.

The split end clears the quick third and picks up the movement of the linebacker and defensive end to his inside.

The fullback slashes at the seam between the guard and tackle, puts a "soft squeeze" on the ball when he feels it in his stomach, and runs with all the fury he can muster. He never knows whether or not he will get the ball.

The halfback takes off and maintains a pitch position. To us that means a position where the man forcing the quarterback cannot react and tackle the

man taking the pitchout. Obviously, the position will vary with defensive and offensive personnel.

The quarterback takes the snap, pushes off his left foot straight down the line of scrimmage, meshes with the fullback, and picks up in his vision the first man outside our offensive tackle. If he sees color across the line of scrimmage, he hands the ball to the fullback. If he sees color sitting on the line of scrimmage, he hands off to the fullback. If he sees color move inside, he withdraws the ball and runs a normal split T option on the end. This may sound somewhat difficult, but after a youngster has run it five or ten minutes for two or three years, it becomes instinct. As I have mentioned previously, this play is the focal point of our offense. From now on I may refer to the option as "the play" and I'm sure you will know what I mean.

When we run the play to the quick side, it is the same except the halfback is the dive man and the split end clears the quick third.

Diagram No. 18

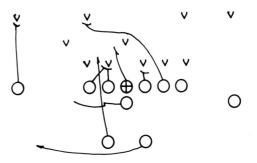

Diagram No. 19

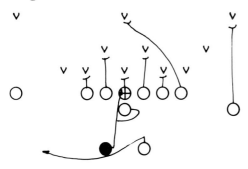

The basic ingredient of threatening three holes on one play is still there. One point that becomes obvious is that in some defenses we force the man responsible for containing to tackle our dive-back—this presents a problem.

As I have mentioned, the rest of our offense is used to keep the defense off the option. Teams have had some success in stopping the play, but in so doing have left themselves extremely vulnerable in other areas. We go into every game with the thought of running the option; what we must find out is the defensive adjustments the opponents are using to shut it down. I'll try to give you an example of our thinking when we determine what is stopping the option. For instance, if we are getting extremely quick flow from the interior linemen and linebackers, we run the counter.

Diagram No. 20

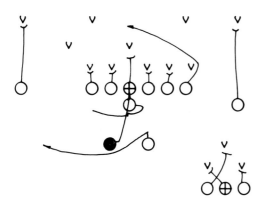

Diagram No. 21

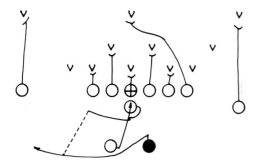

Our line uses a base block versus the odd and even. We do have one adjustment for the center and guard versus the even. They can use what we call a come around block.

Our quarterback takes a short jab step with his right foot, a short jab step with his left foot, reversing back toward the center, working parallel to the line of scrimmage and handing the ball off to the halfback. After the handoff, he continues on toward the defensive end, as if running an option.

The fullback takes a short jab step with his right foot toward the line of scrimmage, staying low, then pushes off his right foot and maintains a pitch position on the quarterback.

The halfback takes a slide step with his right foot, keeping his shoulders parallel to the line of scrimmage and slashes at the left leg of the center, breaking off the center's block (the guards block versus the even).

The counter, of course, goes both ways.

Say for example, the counter worked pretty well except the back side end or linebacker was falling into the middle and picking up the halfback. We then use the counter option.

Diagram No. 22

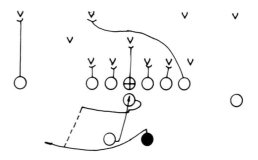

Diagram No. 23

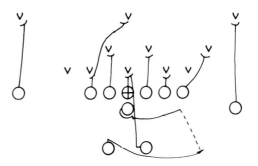

The line blocks base with the split end clearing the quick third, the tight end, the middle third, and the flanker back the strong third. The techniques of the back are the same, the only difference being the quarterback now withdraws the ball and runs an option on the end. The option, of course, goes both ways.

Diagram No. 24

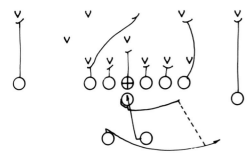

Diagram No. 25

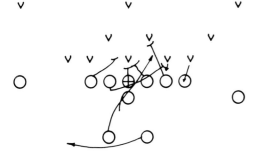

Another common defensive technique is quick pressure by the two men you turn loose on the line of scrimmage. If they become a problem and we need to soften the corners, we usually turn to the trap versus the odd or drop back versus even.

Diagram No. 26

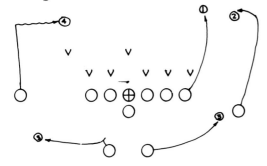

If we are getting severe pressure from the outside in the even alignment, we force the defense to stop our basic drop-back pass.

The quarterback keys the tight end as he is coming out from under the center. If the tight end is open, he dumps the ball. Obviously if the linebacker or end is coming, he will be open. If the tight end is covered the quarterback goes back and sets up at seven or eight yards and works down the order of receivers as indicated.

The flanker runs a curl. The fullback runs a flare. And the split end runs a drag. The halfback keys the defensive end or linebacker. If he is coming, he stays in the blocks. If the end or linebacker is falling off in pass coverage, the halfback flares. These are our basic cuts on our basic drop-back pass. We have all the individual cuts for the backs and wide people (delays, outs, flags, posts, drives, and so on), but we feel that if we can execute intelligently our basic drop back, then our quarterback will vary the routes with a good deal more understanding. He also should be better prepared to pick up the alternate receivers.

We do have a fullback set and run the same things that everyone runs. That is the fullback trap both ways, the halfback trap, and the power to the quick side.

You may have noticed that our line basically must be able to execute the short trap and the base block. We feel that if we can limit the number of plays, it should give our linemen more time to become proficient at executing these two blocks. We can of course run a left formation by bringing the tight end over to the left side. This doubles your offense. After being involved with this offense, I believe the players understand completely what has to be done, and adjustments that are required during the game can be accomplished quickly and with understanding.

I feel that the theory behind both the Houston option and the understanding of our players of what we are trying to do has permitted us to move the football with a good deal of consistency the last two years.

12

The Texas Offense

(From 1970 *Proceedings* of the AFCA)

DARRELL ROYAL Head Coach, University of Texas

Let me say, first of all, how we came about the wishbone T formation. It was not an original idea with the University of Texas, and we don't claim that the original concept is new to us. Homer Rice had fooled around with this thing years back, so there is nothing new in our thinking about this triple option thing.

It was probably made more popular and really brought to the attention of coaches when the University of Houston started having such fantastic success with the triple option. So we borrowed some ideas on the triple option from Homer and the University of Houston, and then we added a little different alignment.

During spring practice a year before our 1968 season, we worked with the wing T or the I. We had two of our boys, Steve Worster and Ted Coy, at the fullback position. It doesn't take an Einstein to figure out that that is too much talent to have in one position and that we needed to split those guys and put them somewhere in the backfield.

We were working with the wingback. None of our players was actually a wingback-type, but all of them had too much talent to sit on the bench. So, we wanted to get them back in the lineup. This meant that we were going to be in full backfield of some sort. The University of Houston was having great success with the triple option, as were West Texas State and several others in our section of the country, and we wanted to go with the triple option in some form.

Texas A & M was the conference champion that year, winning in the Cotton Bowl against the University of Alabama, and they were running a form of triple option with a tight fullback. We took a little bit from Texas A & M, and a little bit here, and a little bit there. We had taken different ideas and different

thoughts and put them together with a different look than had come out before.

I know we opened up with it against the University of Houston. We had decided to do this during the summer, and we started out the first day of September with no previous work at all on the triple option and certainly not in this particular alignment.

Some writers have asked us what we called it and we said, "Well, actually we don't have a name for it. We don't call it anything." They said, "Well, don't you think you ought to call it something?" "Well, I guess it is a good idea to call it something but I don't know what to call it." They said, "Why don't you call it a Y. Your backfield is like that."

I said, "Well, that's true. Call it a Y." And someone else said, "Well, it is more—people put a different connotation on the Y. There has been a Y." He said, "Why don't you call it wishbone. It is the shape of a wishbone." And I said, "That's good enough."

So that is the way the wishbone T got its name.

Reasons for Formation

There are three reasons why we use this formation. First, we wanted to maintain at least one split receiver at all times. We wanted a player who was to be selected strictly for his ability to run pass routes and catch the football. Thus, our line of scrimmage was to be a balanced line with one end split and the other end in tight alignment.

The next thing we had to decide was how to develop a sound running game toward the split end side. The play that was decided on was the triple option.

The third thing we needed to decide was the alignment of the backs. Our personnel was such that we wanted to utilize the running abilities of the backs that we had, and none of which were wingback types. We also wanted to establish a basic offense that was mirrored (which posed a constant threat to both sides) and balanced so that the abilities of all our backs could complement one another. Since the option was to be our basic play, we aligned the backs in the positions we thought would be the most conducive to consistent execution of the triple option. Thus, we came up with the formation that is commonly referred to as the wishbone T.

Formation

Diagram 1

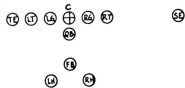

Guards: 2′ constant split (4-point stance).

Tackles: 2′–4′ variable split (4-point stance).

Tight end: 2′–4′ variable split (4-point stance) (will flip-flop).

Split end: 8–14 yards variable split (3-point stance) (will flip-flop).

Fullback: directly behind center, heels 13′ from ball (4-point stance).

Halfbacks: 18″ right and left of fullback and 15″ deep (3-point balanced stance).

Formation Variations

Basic Formations

Diagram 2 Right Formation

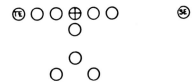

Diagram 3 Left Formation

Supplement Formations

To supplement our basic formations we decided on what we call "counter" formation. We knew there would be times when we would definitely want more than one deployed receiver. As stated previously, our backs were selected as runners and blockers and not as receivers. Therefore, we decided that the one position of alignment that we could put them in to force defenses to honor them as receivers, and without having to teach them to run a lot of routes and be dependent on them as No. 1 receivers, was this formation. This was also further substantiation of the fact that the triple option was to be the basis of our attack because we could still maintain the triple option to both sides even with one back deployed.

In summary: Make receivers out of our backs by alignment rather than by skills.

Broken Formations

Diagram 4 Counter Right Formation

Diagram 5 Counter Left Formation

We also decided on a third formation (pro formation) because against certain defenses we could get our split end on a three-deep halfback one-on-one and still maintain our basic running attack as a constant threat.

Diagram 6 Right Pro Formation

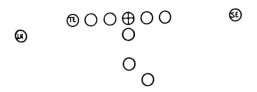

Diagram 7 Left Pro Formation

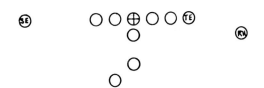

Basic Blocking and Mechanics of the Triple Option as We Run It

Ends—"Force." Always responsible for No. 1 (the man responsible for the deep third).

Tackles: "Inside."

Guards: "No. 1 LOS inside tackle."

Center: "Base."

Lead halfback: "Arc at 8 or 9." No. 2 from outside (which is the man who must take the pitch). Break straight lateral for the first three steps and start arc for the outside leg of No. 2. Take as aggressive an angle as possible.

Trailing halfback: Break straight parallel at maximum speed and ride the outside hip of your lead halfback and cut off his block.

Fullback: Break at maximum speed on direct path for guard-tackle gap. As ball is placed in your stomach take a soft hold on the ball and continue on veer course. If quarterback leaves ball, run with it—if he takes ball out of pocket, continue on course and become a blocker on inside pursuit. Your path must always be outside the block of the offensive tackle.

Quarterback: Mechanics—Open step with near foot on 45-degree angle. Pick up fullback with split vision, and place ball in fullback's pocket at earliest point. Stay down and work with extended arm. The ride with the fullback is from right to left (decision area). It is during this ride that your first option takes place. You will key the first man inside the defensive end and react as follows: (1) Key does not take the fullback—leave ball with the fullback; (2) Key takes the fullback—pull ball out and go to outside option. The outside option key is the defensive end and react as follows: freeze, force, and pitch the ball and take the obvious keep.

Diagram 8

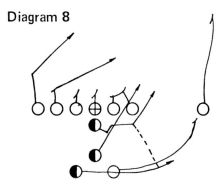

Line Blocking for the Triple Option

Stance: Our linemen get into a four-point stance because it is easier to get the lineman in his stance. Disadvantages of the four-point stance are that it is difficult to pull or trap from this stance and that it is more difficult to drop back and protect for a backup passer.

Our count is nonrhythmic and very simple—"hut" is one, "hut hut" is two, and "hut hut hut" is three. We vary our count; if we don't we will find defensive linemen charging better and quicker than our linemen. We spend a lot of time on getting off on the count. After our agility period, we will take our entire offensive team and go through our fire out drill. (See Diagram 9.) The linemen fire out straight ahead on dummies, and backs will execute the backfield action of play called. Here we check alignment of linemen, emphasize getting off as quickly as possible and getting proper splits.

Diagram 9 Fire Out Drill

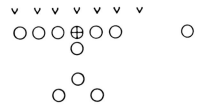

We always work on quickness and getting off on count in all of our drills. We never let our linemen fire out at half speed. Even when we are working on team polish, our linemen get off as quickly as possible into their assignment, hitting a man who carries a shield. We do this to learn assignments, get off on count, and pick up stunts.

In order for a linemen to be a good blocker he must understand the backfield action. Our linemen understand what we try to accomplish with our backfield maneuvers. We believe that he can be a much better blocker if he knows what is happening in the backfield.

Blocking Assignment for the Triple Option

End: Sprints off line of scrimmage, blocks man responsible for him in deep third.

Onside tackle: Blocks first man to inside on or off line of scrimmage.

Onside guard: First man inside of offensive tackle on line of scrimmage.

Center: Man over, no one there, check onside linebacker then block offside linebacker.

Offside guard: Block first man outside center to the offside.

Offside tackle: Release inside first man outside of guard, to point of attack and block first off-colored jersey.

Offside end: Block man in middle third.

Above are our rules for the triple option play. Different defenses will force us to block different ways. We will make calls on the line of scrimmage. In some games we emphasize blocking one individual and let someone else be free.

In order for the play to be successful, our linemen must create a lane between guard and tackle.

Diagram 10

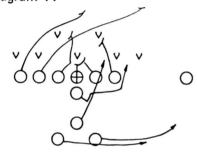

Blocking the Oklahoma 5–4 Defense

Diagram 11

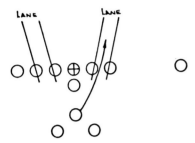

Onside tackle: Steps with outside foot into inside foot of man over him and goes for linebacker. Do not try to miss tackle.

Onside guard: Drive block man over center.

Center: Post block man over.

Offside guard: Steps toward center check for nose guard to slant. If he doesn't slant, block linebacker. We call this "zone" block.

Diagram 12 Slant Defense

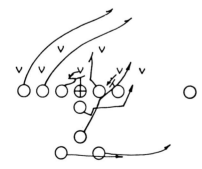

Onside tackle: Block in on slant tackle.

Guard: Goes in on nose guard, picks up shuffle linebacker.

Center: Ends up on nose guard with offside guard.

Offside guard: Picks up nose guard.

Diagram 13 Eagle

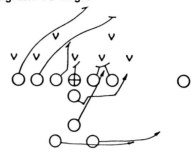

Onside tackle and guard: Double team the man between guard and tackle (our George block).

Center: Man over him.

Offside guard: Zone blocks.

Diagram 14 Underneath Technique

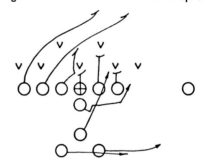

Onside tackle: Blocks man lined up underneath him.

Onside guard: Blocks linebacker (base block).

Center: Man over.

Offside guard: Zone.

Diagram 15 Blocking the Split 6

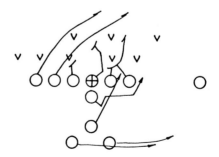

Onside tackle: Drives into tackle; if he feels that guard has him in a stalemate, he will slide off and block linebacker. We call this our co-op block. Tackle knows that we must have the lane between guard and tackle; therefore, we will end up in a George block.

Onside guard: Puts head in middle of tackle.

Center: Check onside linebacker; if he doesn't come, block offside linebacker.

Offside guard: First man outside center to offside.

Offside tackle: Clear.

Diagram 16 Split 6 with Inside Stunt

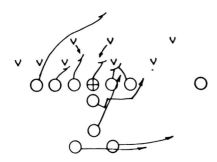

Diagram 17 Blocking 6-0 Defense

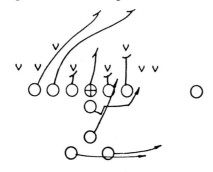

Onside tackle: Blocks linebacker.

Onside guard: Blocks first man on line of scrimmage inside of offensive tackle.

Center: Offside linebacker.

Offside guard: First man outside center to offside.

Diagram 18 Blocking the 6-1

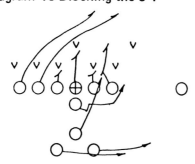

Onside tackle: Drive inside on man over guard—co-op block.

Onside guard: Head in middle of man over him.

Center: Block linebacker.

Offside guard: First man outside center to offside.

Diagram 19 Blocking the Inside Stunt from 6-1

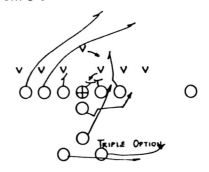

If we are having trouble reading keys for the option, we call the fullback handoff play with blocking. Or, if we want to go the outside option, we call it and go to the outside, faking first to fullback and go to the outside man and option him with the keep or pitch. The fullback knows that he will not get the ball; he becomes a key blocker on linebacker and he passes the line of scrimmage.

In order to run the triple option, we think that splits of our linemen are very important.

Diagram 20

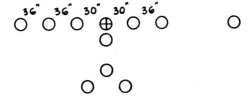

13
The Modern Wing T

(From 1975 Proceedings of the AFCA)

HAROLD RAYMOND Head Coach, University of Delaware

I think all football coaches recognize how fashion conscious they are. I think it is true nationally as well as sectionally. The teams we have played from the Midwest reflect Michigan and Ohio State influence. Many football teams show USC fraits, while still others have been influenced by the Houston veer and Alabama's or Texas's wishbone. Not only are there pockets of influence, but cycles with ideas returning to popularity after they have been discarded years before.

In 1974 Ara Parseghian said that in going to the wing T he backed into a cycle of interest popular ten years ago and became somewhat unique. In a sense we have remained with a philosophy and found ourselves on a sparsely trod path, creating a unique system for ourselves. Ara was kind enough to say that he had used some of our ideas, and I would be remiss if I didn't say that we learned a great deal from him. The Delaware wing T has been enhanced by his ideas, and its popularity has increased because of his interest in it.

What Is Wing T?

We often are carried away with public and newspaper interest in labeling everything. I think it difficult to label an offense, for most offenses make use of ideas from many disciplines. Just what is the wing T? It is more than a formation. It is an offensive system of moving the ball, and it is constantly undergoing change as we adjust to defensive trends, but the Delaware wing T does follow certain principles.

1. Its basis is a four-back, running-oriented offense with a balance of passing achieved through play-action passes. Ends are used as spread receivers.

2. It makes use of shoulder blocking as opposed to head or butt blocking.
3. It is a series or sequence football, threatening several points of attack with flow or misdirection.
4. It is designed to create defensive conflicts, that is, when a defensive player reacts to stop a particular play, he places himself in jeopardy for a related play.

We will use many formations and do a lot of shifting. The formations fall into two general categories: Those with a wing to the tight end and those with a slot (See Diagram 1).

Diagram 1

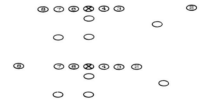

They may have a balanced line or become unbalanced with either a tackle or an end over (See Diagram 2).

Diagram 2

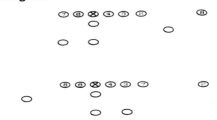

57

We will use extended motion to form certain formations. Our ends are regarded as interchangeable with respect to spread and tight—they will both block!

The use of varied formations with shifting has limited the number of adjustments we see and has been effective in creating blocking angles at the flanks. Without going into our entire offense, I can give you our theory of attack against an Oklahoma defense.

Diagram 3

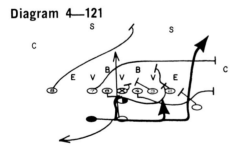

Diagram 3 is a basic wing T formation. The wing is 3½ yards outside the tackle and 2 yards from the ball. The line splits are 2'-3'-3' but our linemen will widen 1' with a man on them. The tackle versus an Oklahoma is split 3' and tight end 2 . We find that very few teams like to rotate, and no one has rotated to a wing into the sideline. We will often show a wing and a tight end to the wide side, then shift showing the wing and tight end into the sideline. This has been particularly effective against teams with a monster concept, because it's impossible for the monster to run from one side to another, and it is difficult for a defense to flip-flop personnel. The more concern they show for our shifting the more we will shift. Consequently we have a lot of teams making no adjustment at all to our wing.

Diagram 4—121

I would like to begin with the basic sweep from the simplest of our formations not only because it is an excellent football play, but because it is a good example of what we mean by misdirection and it creates several defensive assignment conflicts.

Let's begin by assuming the corner is dropped off and the end is outflanked by our wingback. Here is our buck sweep. The wingback blocks the first free man to his inside and steps first to prevent penetration by the end. If the end loops outside, the wing will let him go and continue inside to wall off.

The tight end steps to the gap and reads down. If the defensive tackle is coming hard or looping out, the tight end will block him, but if not, the tight end will wall off. The tackle also blocks the gap, read down. His first concern is the defensive tackle stunting inside, then the backer plugging, and finally the nose man chasing the guard.

The right guard pulls and reads the right half's block. If the wing has started to establish the flank, he will get 2½ yards of depth and block out at the flank. This depth brings him closer to the ball carrier and delays the cornerman's reaction. If the wing is unable to block the end, the guard will adjust his path and kick the end out. The center reaches, then blocks on.

The fullback fills the offside seam with a good dive fake. The quarterback hands off to the left half and fakes the bootleg. The left half takes the ball and reads the wing's block first. If it's good he will threaten to outrun the flank then turn upfield as the right guard blocks out. If the opening occurs inside, he will turn up quickly off tackle. Actually this play is either an off-tackle play or a sweep, depending on how it's played defensively. The play may be run from double wing.

Pressure Put on Defense

Let's take a minute to analyze the pressure on the defense. Both the defensive end and tackle are outflanked by a blocker and are playing on offensive men who are blocking down. If they don't react down, we will eventually trap them, but if they do react inside, they become vulnerable to our flanking position. The secondary has a problem, too. The quarterback is faking to the weak side and there are two potential receivers there: the fullback and the spread end.

Diagram 5—RT 921

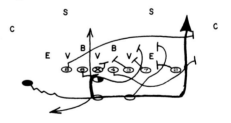

If we get a defensive end who is too tough for our wing, we will run the sweep from unbalanced with the wing to the weak side. This formation presents a conflict of adjustment. You can either move the line over or you can rotate to strength, but very few coaches like to rotate away from a wing.

The spread end now establishes the flank from a 3- to 5-yard split. The right half dives to prevent penetration. If there is none, he will turn inside and wall off. Everyone else blocks exactly as the original sweep to the wing. The onside guard still goes behind the right half and reads his block.

Diagram 6—121 WAG

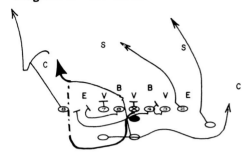

Our waggle pass is a good example of misdirection, and has become one of our most efficient plays. We find that it affects the support of the strong flank because its action affects the free safety. Let's assume our sweep action with the quarterback keeping the ball after faking to the fullback up the middle and the left half sweeping. The spread end releases and runs any one of several patterns: fly, out, curl, or angle flag. The attack side tackle blocks gap-on-area. The first guard pulls and blocks in on the first man he can block. The fullback checks the guards area, then slips into the flat. The center blocks a man on or to his right. The right guard pulls flat, allows the fullback to go in front of him, gets depth, reads the left guard's block, and blocks out on the next man. The offside tackle pulls to block the second man from the center. If the backer is coming, he will block him, and if not, he will block the man on. The left half blocks chase off the back side. The tight end fakes a "down" block, then runs a crossing pattern as he reads coverage. If the backers plug, he will run very flat and quick, but if not, he will work his way across to an open spot. The wing runs a post after faking his flank block. The quarterback reads the free safety. If he flows to the middle, the quarterback will execute a run-pass option at the flank. If the free safety stays, he will look for the crossing end. The waggle is particularly good to a tight end because the defensive end must seal an inside release. The halfback from this formation runs a crossing pattern.

Diagram 7—121 WAG SOL

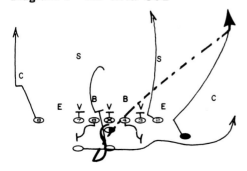

If the free safety will not flow to the middle and the strong corner supports quickly because of the flanking angle, we will run the waggle solid and the quarterback will not threaten the flank. This action is used if the strong corner and safety are supporting the flank quickly with run action. The left tackle blocks waggle as the left guard pulls and pivots the defensive end out. The fullback fills for the guard, then releases. The right guard blocks the backer if he comes, and, if not, will pivot the defensive end out. The right tackle blocks the man on him or to his outside. The left half reads the backer's action over the right guard. If this backer plugs, the left half will block the defensive end, but if not, the halfback will flare. The wing and tight end fake their sweep blocks and then release deep, tight end post and wing flag. This action gives our quarterback good protection with five potential receivers, and for some the quarterback may roll behind his fake to the left half.

First Option Is Called

The option plays a part in the wing T and becomes especially effective when the secondary becomes "man" conscious with the safety and the corner supporting fast when the wing and tight end block down. We are in a sense running the triple option principle, but will call it the first option.

Diagram 8—181 PIT

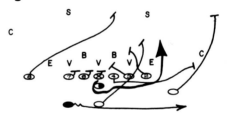

The wingback releases through the fifth defensive man, the man who must cover the flag. The tight end walls the backer off as the tackle blocks exactly as he did on the buck sweep. We do not like to release the end outside the defensive end because it relieves him of the pressure inside. The right guard pulls and blocks out on support. The center, left guard, and left tackle all reach, then block on. The left half takes two steps of motion, then runs flat for the pitch. The fullback slashes for the outside leg of his tackle and turns upfield with his fake. The quarterback reverse pivots, rides the ball to the fullback, and then executes the option, pitch or keep.

We can run the same option without a pulling guard and release the tight end to block out, but prefer to block the play with the end releasing inside because this is related to our sweep. We also have a keep pass series from this belly action. I would also like to point out that all of these plays under certain conditions may be used to any flank, to or away from a wing.

If we see linebackers chasing our guards, we will run the power sweep with the line firing straight out and the fullback blocking out. We have also run this sweep with the guards opposite as illustrated in Diagram 9.

Diagram 9—RT. Z131 G.O.

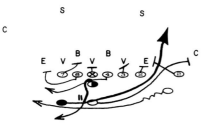

We have blocked down on the defensive end, forced him to contain the waggle and to control the option. Now we will trap him. A good example is our quick guard trap to the fullback, which looks like our option.

Diagram 10—182 DOWN

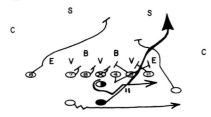

The end reads down, that is, he will block the tackle unless he stunts inside, and if so, the tight end will block the backer. The tackle also blocks down and will block the linebacker if possible. I should point out here that if the defensive tackle allows our tackle to block on the linebacker, we will trap or finesse him with another football play. The right guard pulls and traps the defensive end. The back side of the line reaches. The fullback starts for the outside of his tackle and takes the ball. He will read the block on the tackle.

Diagram 11—189 OPT

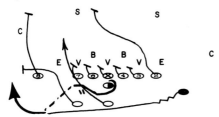

If we get rotation to our wing, we will also run the option away from the wing with motion. The flexed

end runs through the fifth defensive man. The left guard and tackle fire aggressively for outside position while the center and back side reach for position on men on or over them. The left half runs for flanking position on the end and then blocks out at the flank. The fullback slashes for the tackle's outside leg. The quarterback reverse pivots, rides the ball to the fullback, and then executes the option of keep or pitch.

Diagram 12—NO MO 189 PIT

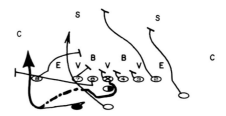

When the secondary rotates to the wing but flows with our motion, we will use a no-motion belly option. The left tackle will block down and the spread end will block the backer. The left guard pulls and blocks support to the flank. The wing runs to the cutoff. The quarterback reverse pivots, and rides the ball to the fullback. The left half fakes with a counter shoulder roll, then sprints for pitch position.

Diagram 13—RT 924 GUT

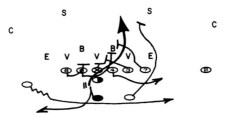

Now, let's take a look inside of the tackle. We have encouraged him to ignore our tackle blocking down in front of him. We still have our tackle trap counter, which we will use if our tackle can get to the backer, but the fullback up the middle has become equally effective to our old counter tackle trap.

We will block the fullback play with three types of blocking, depending on the defense and reaction, but we will probably begin with a finesse of the tackle. The quarterback precedes his cadence by calling "Odd set," "Even set," or "Gap set," describing the defense for the line and confirming their assignments. With a straight Oklahoma, when running the fullback play up the middle, the quarterback will confirm the spacing by calling "Odd set." The tight end will fake his "down" block and go to the backer. The right tackle will lead, doubling on the nose man with the center controlling him. The right guard will pull, faking the sweep. The left guard pulls and "folds" on the offside backer. The left tackle pulls for position if the backer stunts. The backfield shows back sweep action. The quarterback reverse pivots across the midline, giving the fullback a clean shot at the opening, and then fakes the waggle. If their line moves over, this play shortens and we finesse the man over the right guard as in Diagram 13.

Diagram 14

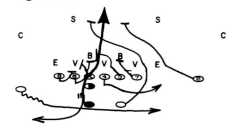

If we get an unusual spacing, the quarterback will call, "On set," and we will run the play with straight ahead blocking.

Diagram 15—134 CT. GUT

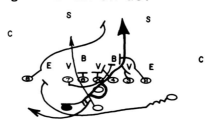

We have adjusted our tackle trap blocking when we can't get to the backer. Our attack side tackle will fight to control the tackle through the hole. The right guard will double with the center. The left guard blocks solid while the left tackle pulls and blocks through the hole.

14
Multi-Flex System at Harvard

(From 1975 Summer Manual of the AFCA)

JOE RESTIC Head Coach, Harvard University

A multi-flex system is one capable of many variations. The term "multi-flex" denotes multiplicity and flexibility in the truest sense. In order for a system to be totally multiple, it must have the built-in capacity to use a number of sets in a manner that places maximum pressure on the defense regardless of field position. Being totally multiple is not enough; the other capability that the system must have is complete flexibility. This dimension will allow you to put to work the most advantageous part of your offense.

If multiplicity and flexibility are the goals, then the system is the key to arriving at these goals. The system must be simple. This is the area that puts your knowledge and experience to the test as a football coach. How can I arrive at a totally multiple and completely flexible system that is simple? This may sound dichotomous, but it is in the realm of possibility and therein lies the challenge.

Where does one begin? The initial step and logical place is with the offensive sets. One must be able to incorporate a combination of zero-one-two and three back sets into the basic system.

A departure from basic thinking must take place in order to properly defense the zero back sets.

These sets present a five "off the line" receiver problem that must be effectively handled by the defense. In the trips set, four receivers out the same side forces a change in linebacker and deep back drop as well as positioning adjustment. This set can be most effective versus five-under coverage. The spread set, a combination of two out one side and three out the other, pressures the defense to play relatively balanced because of receiver deployment.

If man-blitz thinking is being used, a linebacker-receiver mismatch could result, or lack of proper coverage on one of the receivers could be the other possibility because of failure to identify the set.

This capability in your offensive system has value because of the time commitment and adjustment problems that it presents to the defense in a radically different way. In some cases, it forces the defense to come up with an automatic call when the zero back sets show. This in turn has to be advantageous to the offense if it has the built-in flexibility to capitalize on these defensive moves.

One Back Sets

Diagram 2A

Double Wing

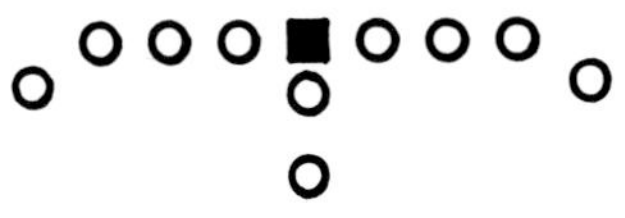

Diagram 2B

Deuces

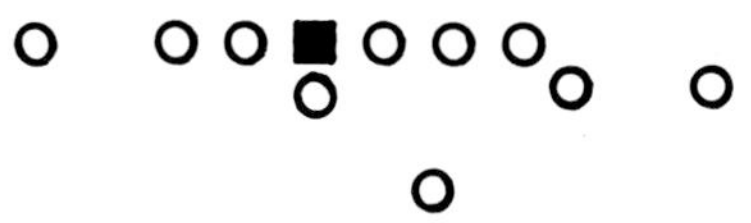

Zero Back Sets

Diagram 1A

Trips

Diagram 1B

Spread

Single back sets permit you to have a running back in one of three backfield positions. The fullback position can be stressed or your top running back can be put to maximum use as a primary ball carrier.

These looks also force opponents out of eight-man front—blitz—man-to-man thinking.

In the passing game, they present a four "off the line" receiver problem for the defense. These sets are convertible to the zero back sets by simply controlling the remaining back in a flare sense.

The deuces formation also gives the defense the wingback problem combined with the wide-out pass threat to either side.

Two Back Sets

Diagram 3A

Balanced

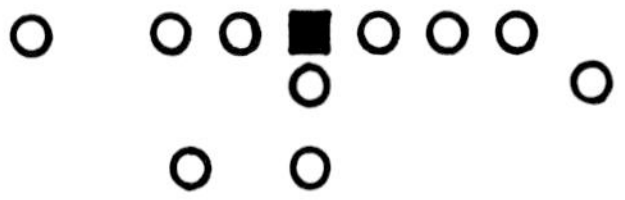

Diagram 3B

Split

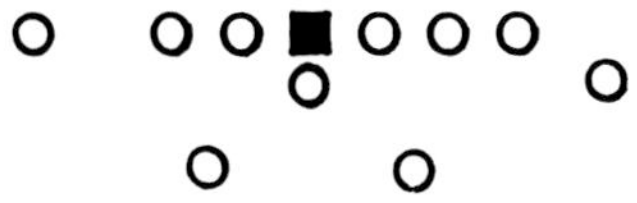

Diagram 3C

Strong

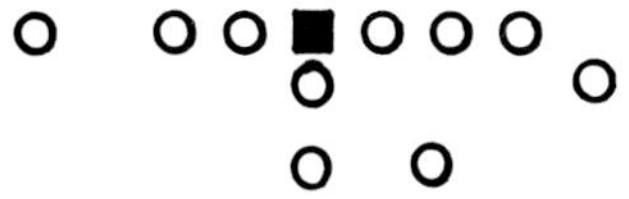

Diagram 3D

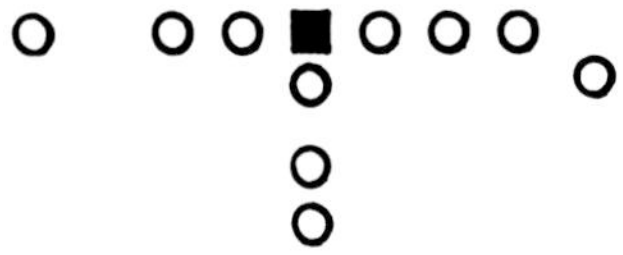

What are the advantages of the two-back sets? The immediate plus is a two-back run offense with the threat of the wideouts in the passing game. These sets give you the flexibility of placing the wingback in a position to pressure the contain portion of the defense and, at the same time, allow you to use him as a third running back.

A system of flare and check flare action must be incorporated to control the underneath coverage if you expect to fully capitalize on the pass. The remaining backs can also provide maximum protection when not being used in the above manner.

Three Back Sets

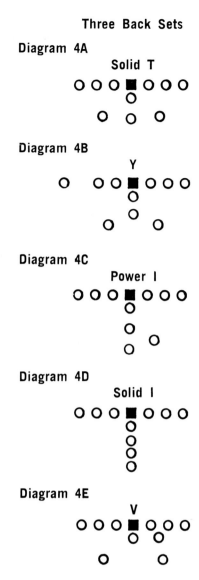

Diagram 4A

Solid T

Diagram 4B

Y

Diagram 4C

Power I

Diagram 4D

Solid I

Diagram 4E

V

How do the three-back sets add to your offensive package? These sets enable you to attack either side of the ball quickly with all of your backs. They also force the defense to play a balanced front with linebackers committed to the running game. The linebackers must be strong enough to handle two lead blockers versus the isolation game.

A most effective play pass and counter type action can be developed to take advantage of the defensive commitment to these run-oriented formations.

All the backs are in a position to fake, fill, block, or carry in a variety of offensive maneuvers.

The total set possibilities have just been presented. The key lies in the selection process. As a starting point, a minimum of one formation from each of the foregoing examples must be incorporated into your system based on the capabilities of the personnel at your command.

How to Use Motion

The second step in the development of the multi-flex system involves the use of motion.

How much and what type of motion do you need? These questions can be answered only after an assessment is made of the value of motion in an offensive system.

What are the values to be derived from the use of motion?

1. Motion can be used to change the nature and look of the offensive sets.

2. Motion can be used to get from one formation to another, thereby forcing a quick decision and adjustment on the part of the defense.

3. Motion can be used to confuse and to negate the ability of good football players by lessening the read and reaction time.

4. Motion can be used to put offensive people in a better position to get the job done that they are assigned to do.

5. Motion should be used to improve execution in the ball carrying, blocking, and receiving areas of the game. It should not be used as a frill.

The following examples project some of the possible ways to use motion.

Diagram 5

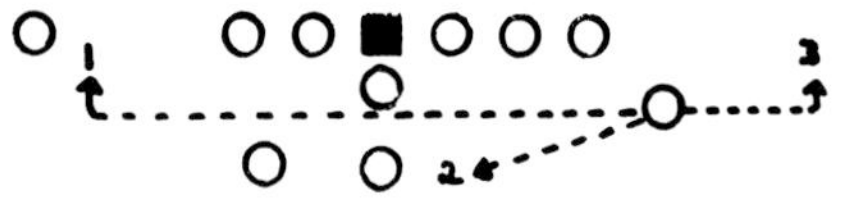

The above set initially presents a wing and wide-out problem to the defense.

1. Motion across the formation creates a wide twin set with a back in a position to establish a flood threat to that side.

2. Fly motion through the backfield places the back in a position to become a ball carrier, faking back or lead blocker to the other side of the formation.

3. Motion out from the formation presents the wide-out problem to either side of the formation.

In Diagram 4 the defense had to prepare for the wing, pro, solid T, and wide twin sets, which were created by the use of single-back motion.

The next example projects another look at single-back motion from the same basic wing T set.

Diagram 6

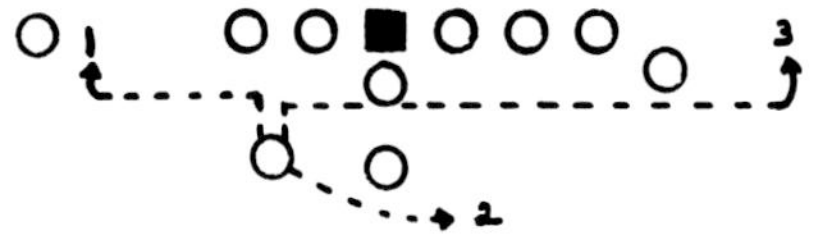

1. A double-wing set is created with the wide twin problems to the motion side.

2. Fly motion aids the back in execution of his assignment.

3. Deuce formation is the result of motion through the formation.

This formation presents the defense with a wing and wide-out problem to the same side. The pass defense must also handle three receivers off the line of scrimmage to that side.

In Diagram 5, the defense had to get ready for the wing T, double wing, and deuce formations.

The next example pictures a double wing-slot formation.

Diagram 7

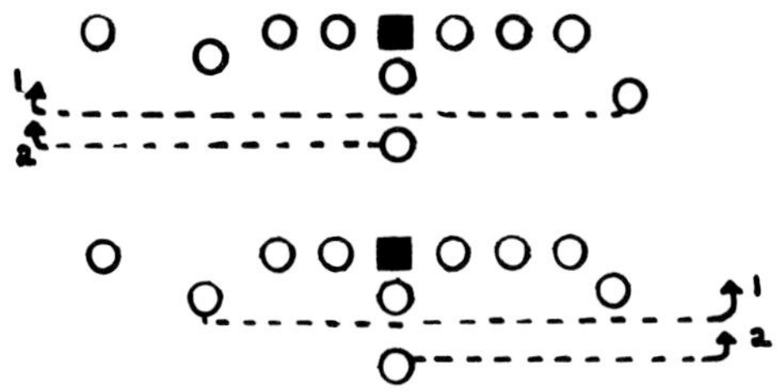

1. The deuce formations are created by set-back motion either direction.

2. In the single-back sets, remaining back motion results in the spread type looks.

The zero-one-two and three-back sets must be combined with single-back motion to give you the variations that are necessary to develop a totally multiple and completely flexible system. This system will put maximum pressure on the defense by allowing you to jump an offensive cycle every week during the season.

15
The Clemson Perimeter Attack

(From 1979 Summer Manual of the AFCA)

JIMMYE LAYCOCK Assistant Coach, Clemson University

At Clemson University our philosophy of offense is built on simplicity and execution. We believe that it is not necessary to have many different plays to attack a specific area of the defense. Instead, we limit our offense to a few basic plays and attempt to execute those flawlessly.

The importance of repetition to gain the desired execution cannot be overemphasized. In 1978, Clemson averaged 436.7 yards per game and ranked third nationally for turning the ball over only twenty times. These statistics reflect a combination of good players, super play selection, and continuous repetition during practice sessions.

An integral part of our offensive scheme is our perimeter attack. Basically, we use three plays for this purpose—two runs and a pass. The runs are the toss sweep and outside veer. Very seldom will we use both plays to a large degree in a single game. Which play to use is dictated by how tight the defensive ends align. If they are head up, we will feature the sweep, while the outside veer is used against an end who is aligned wider.

Diagram 1

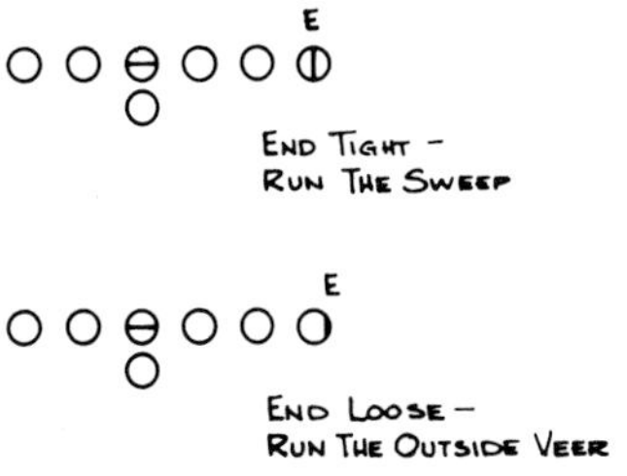

○ ○ Ө ○ ○ Ⓕ
　　○
　　E
END TIGHT –
RUN THE SWEEP

○ ○ Ө ○ ○ ○
　　○
　　　E
END LOOSE –
RUN THE OUTSIDE VEER

Both plays could hit anywhere from off tackle to the sideline. However, we feel with the threat of these two runs, the sprint pass takes on the added dimension for the defensive ends. Even though it is a designed pass, our quarterback will run about one-third of the time. When we vary our release of our tight end on our sprint pass, it can look very much like one of our runs.

The Toss Sweep

As we stated earlier, we prefer the sweep when our tight end can hook the defensive end. We also like it against soft run support. If it takes motion to get the secondary loose, we will use it. Internal stunts do not hurt the sweep; in fact, many times they help the play.

There are some basic reasons why we favor this particular play. There is minimal amount of ball handling; therefore, there are fewer chances for turnovers. In running the sweep, we put the burden for success on our linemen and backs, not on our quarterback. His execution is very simple on this play, so he is able to spend more practice time on something else. Our top quarterbacks will very seldom work on this play during practice other than during team work. Finally, the sweep takes advantage of a fine tailback. It allows him to use his ability to run to daylight.

Our blocking is very basic with the exception of the fullback and onside tackle. They must work together when we face a 52 defense. Our tackle will re-

Diagram 2

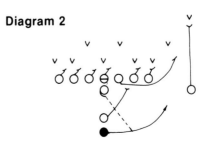

The Toss Sweep

lease outside the defensive tackle. If the defensive man goes inside, our tackle will continue on to the linebacker, and our fullback will block the defensive tackle.

Diagram 3

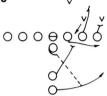

The fullback's landmark is the inside leg of our tackle. If the defensive tackle fights the release of the offensive tackle, then our man will stay with him, and the fullback must continue on to the linebacker.

Diagram 4

Against an eagle alignment, the fullback is responsible for the man over our guard.

Diagram 5

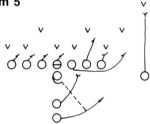

Our guard does not have many coaching points on his block. He must recognize where the run support is coming from. The worst mistakes he can make are to throw too soon and to duck his head. Our tailback has only a few coaching points. We first want him to receive the ball under control. He should then key the block of the pulling guard. When he sees 4 yards north, we want him to take it.

The Outside Veer

The outside veer is effective when the defensive ends are loose, thus enabling the tight end to block down and create a separation. The more room between the double team and the defensive end, the better the play. It also helps if the linebackers are tight. Rather than predetermine any element of this play, we put the burden on our quarterback and read it every time. To execute the play effectively, we feel the quar-

terback must be a good runner with better-than-average quickness. As opposed to the sweep, our top quarterbacks will spend a great deal of practice time on this play. However, it is worth it to us because of the versatility of the outside veer. By running it from the I formation, we not only can get the give off tackle and the quarterback keep, but the tailback is in an excellent position for the pitch.

Diagram 6

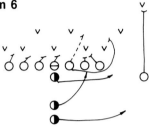

The Outside Veer

The blocking scheme is very basic. Our tight end will double with the tackle, unless the defensive tackle completely disappears inside. Movement on the double team is essential to the play's effectiveness. Our guard is responsible for the linebacker. He has the option whether to pull or not. When he pulls and mirrors the linebacker, he can turn upfield, either inside or outside the defensive end. The only time he should go inside the defensive end is on a definite give read. Against an eagle defense, our guard will still pull for linebacker.

Our tight end will block gap to backside linebacker. The offensive tackle blocks down to allow the guard to pull. It does not change anything for the quarterback's read with the exception that he may anticipate the give.

Diagram 7

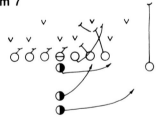

The fullback's aiming point is the outside hip of the offensive tackle. His course begins with a slightly open step as he works to get his head and shoulders square to the line of scrimmage. Hitting square is important because it makes the defensive end commit to the fullback. If the fullback does not receive the handoff, he should eliminate the defensive end, either by being tackled or blocking the end. With enough repetition, the fullback should know when he is to get the ball and when he is not.

We do not make a big issue out of the steps for the quarterback. He must get to the mesh point and feel comfortable. His eyes should focus outside the tight end's block. If he sees daylight, we want the handoff. Reading daylight has proved more effective to us than keying the defensive end. On a no-give look, the quarterback must accelerate off the fullback's hip and option the outside shoulder of number four (the strong safety or corner). The quarterback keeps the ball unless the defensive back takes a head-up position on him, at which point the quarterback comes under control and pitches the ball. It is our tailback's responsibility to maintain pitch relationship.

Sprint Pass

The third element to our perimeter attack is the sprint pass. There are very few instances when we would not feel comfortable with the sprint pass. We would rather have the defensive ends tight, but because of the arc of our quarterback, this is not a great concern. If we are getting internal stunts, the sprint serves basically the same purpose as the sweep. We tell our quarterbacks to pass first and run second on the sprint. Basically, we are throwing high percentage routes. If the receivers are not open, then the quarterback is in position to keep running on the corner. By sprinting, we are decreasing the distance of the throw, thus reducing the chance for an interception. Finally, we are creating a containment problem for the defense by incorporating the sprint with the sweep and outside veer.

Diagram 8

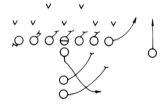

Sprint Pass

We zone block our sprint pass. Our onside guard and tackle are responsible for numbers one and two on defense. They must work together to pick up slants and stunts. The center and offside guard have zero and number one backside. The backside tackle will pick weak. We do want our linemen to block aggressively on the sprint. Against an eagle alignment, our blocking remains basically the same.

Our protection depends heavily on the backs. The fullback's aiming point is one yard outside and one yard behind the offensive tackle. He is responsible for blocking number three (the defensive end). The tailback's first rule is to block number four. If there is no

Diagram 9

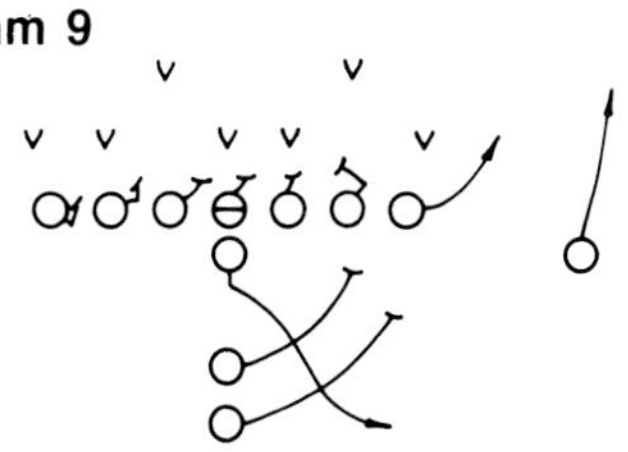

number four, he will clean up on the end with the fullback. He will lead around the corner and look inside if the end is down.

Our quarterback runs a deep arc because we are looking for the best possible throwing lane. We also want to make sure his shoulders are square to his target. His first step is straight back as is his second step. The third step is for depth and width. Our quarterback should be 6 yards deep behind the inside leg of our tackle. His eyes are on the receivers, but he must get a feel as to whether his throwing lane is outside or inside the defensive end.

Diagram 10

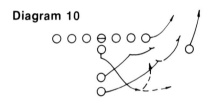

The base route for the wide receiver is a 10-yard out. He must make his break at 10 yards and then work back to 8 yards. The inside receiver runs a seam route at the outside shoulder of the strong safety and continues upfield running away from the linebacker.

Diagram 11

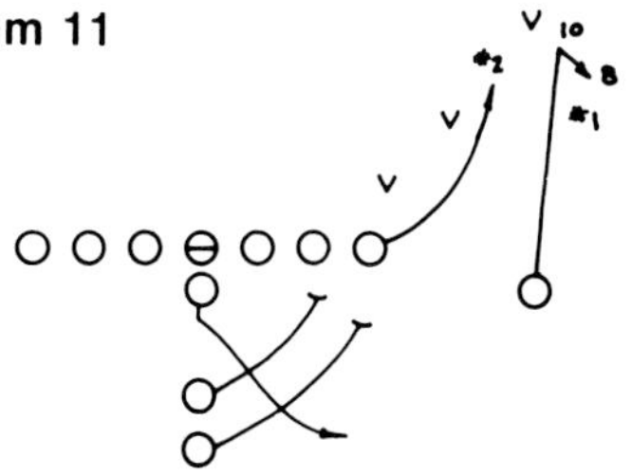

The quarterback reads by progression from the out to the seam. However, we emphasize throwing the out unless the strong safety sprints to the throwing lane. In the event neither receiver is open, the quarterback should continue running on the corner.

There are complements and counterattacks for each of these plays. However, these three plays are the base for our perimeter attack. If we have to choose between using a number of plays or desired execution, we believe execution is more important. It takes confidence to execute correctly and repetition builds confidence.

16
Perimeter Blocking in the Houston Veer

(From 1979 Summer Manual of the AFCA)

LARRY ZIERLEIN Assistant Coach, University of Houston

There has been much discussion and many articles written over the past few years concerning the veer offense. Offensive line play, backfield techniques, or the coordination of the two have been thoroughly covered. However, an area that seems to be often neglected is the all-important area of perimeter blocking. Breakdowns in this area appear to be quite common on all levels of football.

A tactic used by many teams in defensing the option is to take away the first two phases of the option and rely on their containing unit to defeat the blocks of the wide receivers and tight end. This is often successful because of either the lack of ability to block or the receiver's lack of training in this area. Usually it is the latter. In order for the offense to operate at maximum efficiency, the wideouts and tight end must be able to block on the corner and give us room to run when we pitch the football.

We are fortunate at Houston to have receivers who are good blockers. Their efforts contributed to our average of 6.4 yards per carry on all our option plays during the 1978 season. Our primary option plays are the zone option (see Diagram 1); counter option (see Diagram 2); and the trap option (see Diagram 3).

Diagram 1

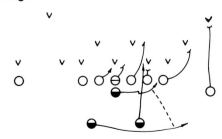

Diagram 2

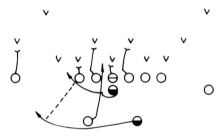

Diagram 3

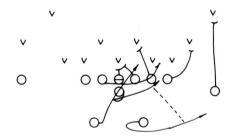

The receiver's assignments and techniques are the same on all three option plays. Although the technique of each receiver varies, there are two things each block has in common:

1. Patience. Don't overcommit. Be under control!
2. Invite the defender to commit to a certain side when he goes for the ball carrier.

In this article, the following areas of perimeter blocking will be covered:

1. Assignments
2. Techniques
3. Defensive tactics that cause problems and how we try to combat them.

68

Perimeter Blocking to the Tight End/Flanker Side

To the two-receiver side, the tight end will block the man responsible for the pitch and the flanker will block the defender responsible for the deep outside. (See Diagram 4.)

Diagram 4

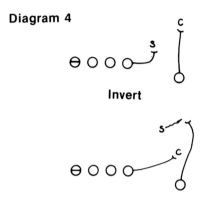

Invert

Tight End Technique versus Invert

1. Release flat across the face of the defensive end by pushing off the inside foot and lead stepping laterally with the outside foot. The second step is a crossover, and the third step reestablishes the initial position of the tight end. By the third step, the tight end will have read the secondary coverage and know if he is blocking the strong safety (invert) or the cornerback (roll).

2. It is very important that the tight end keep his shoulders square with the line of scrimmage throughout his approach to the strong safety. This can be accomplished by stressing to the tight end that he pull back with his inside arm as he releases and continue pulling back as he approaches the strong safety. This serves two purposes: (1) It insures the necessary squared-up position when the tight end reaches the strong safety; and (2) it facilitates the tight end's being able to come back on a strong safety who comes hard to the inside in an attempt to make a big play.

3. Continue gaining width flat down the line of scrimmage until reaching a position in which the tight end's body is aligned with the outside number of the strong safety. This is the relative position to be maintained throughout the block. Do not start gaining ground upfield until this relative position has been reached. (See Diagram 5.)

Diagram 5

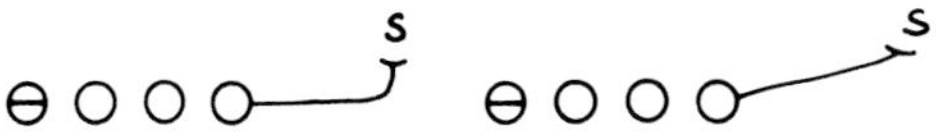

This   Not This

Gaining ground upfield too quickly is a common error and will result in a failure to maintain outside leverage on the strong safety when he goes for the pitch man.

4. After the proper width has been established, the tight end can then begin gaining depth on an arc, which allows for his maintaining outside leverage. He gains as much depth as possible before engaging the strong safety in order to give our pitch back more room to operate at the corner.

5. The arc block itself is not intended to knock the defender off his feet but to occupy him long enough for the back to go by. By gaining outside leverage, he will accomplish one of two things:
   a. Hook the defender so the back can run outside. (See Diagram 6.)

Diagram 6

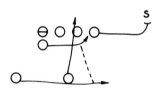

   b. In an effort to prevent being hooked, the strong safety will fight to the outside and open up an inside running lane. (See Diagram 7.)

Diagram 7

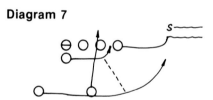

After engaging the strong safety, the tight end will continue to block on the outside number of the strong safety and then recoil until the defender has either been hooked or has been stretched to the sideline. To do this, he must operate from a good base with the tail down and head up. Overextension is one of the most common errors. The tight end hits up through the defender and not out at him. Overextension results in a loss of balance and the advantage then goes to the defender because he can get rid of the tight end and still have plenty of time to come up and make the tackle on or behind the line of scrimmage. (The relationship between the back and the tight end dictates that the block be maintained longer than when the blocker comes from the backfield, as in the wishbone.) The pressure is on the defender to get to the ball carrier, so let him be the one to make the first commitment. He has to come through the tight end to get to the ball carrier. The tight end does not have to go after the strong safety.

In summarizing the arc block versus the invert safety, the important points are:

1. Release flat across the face of the defensive end.
2. Recognize the secondary coverage by the third step.
3. Gain width to the outside number of the strong safety before gaining depth downfield.
4. Stay under control with the shoulders square to the line of scrimmage.
5. Do not overextend. Let the defender come to you. Keep a good base and hit up through the defender and not out at him.
6. Maintain outside leverage and either hook the strong safety or stretch him to the sideline.

The above is the tight end's technique in an ideal situation. Following are some defensive maneuvers that can cause problems for the tight end and how we try to cope with them:

1. After the tight end has established outside leverage, the defender tries to power through the blocker. (See Diagram 8.)

Diagram 8

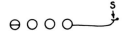

The tight end forgets about hitting and recoiling and meets force with force by exploding into the defender's outside number and locking on. Again, keep the shoulders square and either get him hooked or stretch him to the sidelines. Hitting and recoiling versus this defensive maneuver will result in the tight end's being driven back into the path of the ball carrier.

2. On the snap of the ball the strong safety charges hard upfield. (See Diagram 9.)

Diagram 9

A big defensive play can result if the tight end doesn't make this block. As soon as he recognizes the hard charge, he turns his shoulders parallel to the sideline and throws his body across the path of the defender. In this instance, we hope to get the strong safety on the ground. Attempting to block him high will again result in the tight end's being driven into the path of the ball carrier.

3. Strong safety comes hard to the inside trying to get behind the tight end. (See Diagram 10.)

Diagram 10

This is a defensive gamble but an effective one if the tight end is not prepared. If the tight end is under control with his shoulders square, and he gets no wider than the defender's outside number, he will be able to seal the strong safety to the inside and allow the running back an outside lane. (See Diagram 11.)

Diagram 11

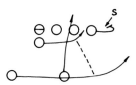

4. Immediately after the tight end begins his arc release, the strong safety fakes inside, then comes to the outside. (See Diagram 12.)

Diagram 12

The natural reaction to the fake will usually result in the tight end's losing outside leverage and then being forced to turn his shoulders parallel to the sideline in order to block the defender. The strong safety is not wide enough to allow the back to run inside of him, and the result is that the tight end blocks him into the path of the ball carrier. This can be a very effective defensive maneuver and the tight end must be drilled on it every day. The tight end should remember this: Any time the defender tries to go inside the block, he runs the risk of being sealed to the inside and providing us with a big outside running lane with the defensive pursuit having a long way to go to get the ball if it is pitched. If the strong safety is coming inside, the tight end has plenty of time to react and seal him on the inside without having to react immediately to the inside fake. By delaying reaction to the fake, he is in position to block the strong safety after he fakes and then attempts to come outside.

As stated previously, this must be drilled daily. It is a natural reaction to honor any fake. The tight end must see this often so that he becomes accustomed to not reacting too quickly to the inside move.

5. The strong safety goes hard to the outside, then comes back inside into the path of the ball carrier. (See Diagram 13.)

Diagram 13

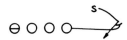

This can be good against the tight end who is very conscious of getting outside leverage. The hard outside move by the strong safety forces the tight end to turn his shoulders and run "out of control" if he is to get to the defender's outside number. This is exactly what the strong safety wants because he can come inside the blocker into the path of the ball carrier and probably not be touched by the tight end because of his poor position.

In handling this situation, the tight end should be aware of this fact. The strong safety is getting too wide and opening up an inside running lane any time he makes a move that forces the tight end to turn his shoulders and get out of control in order to get to the defender's outside number. Never get into a footrace with the strong safety. Stay under control with the shoulders square, and when the strong safety tries to come back inside, the tight end will be in position to apply an effective block. (See Diagram 14.)

Diagram 14

If the strong safety gains ground upfield until he is even with the tight end, then and only then would the tight end turn his shoulders to the sideline and block the defender out, thereby giving us an inside running lane. (See Diagram 15.)

Diagram 15

Again, don't get into a footrace with the strong safety. Any time the tight end has to get "out of control" to block the outside number, the strong safety is getting too wide.

Of course the best play against a constant dose of this defensive technique is the dump pass to the tight end (see Diagram 16), but if an option play has been called, we have to be able to block the strong safety.

Diagram 16

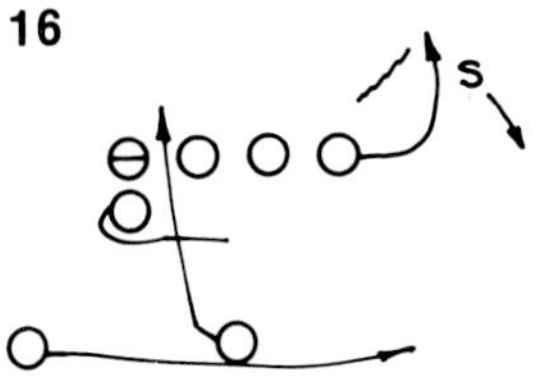

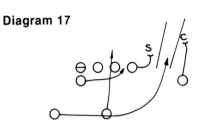

Flanker Technique versus the Invert

The flanker will block the defender responsible for the deep outside. Coaching points are:

1. Drive off hard to make the defender think you are running a deep route. Run at this outside shoulder in an attempt to widen him.

2. When the defender recognizes the run and breaks down to come back to the ball, the flanker will also break down and align his nose with the defender's inside number. (Some people get outside leverage, but we have found that our ball carriers have a tendency to head straight upfield after turning the corner rather than trying to get outside the flanker's block so that we get inside position and try to create a lane between the flanker's block and the block of the tight end.) (See Diagram 17.)

Diagram 17

3. From a break down position with the head up, tail down, and the nose aligned with the defender's inside number, the flanker mirrors the movement of the defensive back but does not initiate contact. Making contact too early gives the defender time to defeat the block, then come up and make the tackle for a short gain.

4. When the defender commits and contact can no longer be avoided, lock on and take him in the direction of his commitment (hopefully our inside alignment will have invited him to the outside). During contact, use the forearms to keep a good blocking surface and really work the feet to stay on the defender. We continually preach against lazy feet in this phase of the block.

We began by teaching the hit and recoil technique (much like offensive line pass blocking) to both wide receivers but found it required too much time and was a difficult technique to master, so we have gone to the simpler method of locking on, accelerating the feet, and staying glued to the defender.

In summarizing the flanker's block versus the deep outside defender, the important points are:

1. Widen the defender by driving at his outside shoulder.

2. When the defender recognizes the run, break down, assume inside number leverage, and mirror his movement. Delay contact as long as possible.

3. Do not commit too soon and do not overextend.

4. Invite him to get to the ball carrier by going to the outside. When he does commit, lock on with a good blocking surface, accelerate the feet, and hang on until the ball carrier has passed.

Tight End Technique versus Corner Rolled Up

1. Release flat across the face of the defensive end. By the third step the tight end will have read the coverage and know that he has to block the rolled up corner.

2. After recognizing coverage, the tight end turns his shoulders toward the sideline and approaches the cornerback from an inside-out relationship. He must accelerate and get as much width as possible before engaging the cornerback in order to create a wider running lane (the running lane is inside the block of the tight end versus the rolled up corner).

3. On reaching the cornerback, break down and align the nose with the inside number, inviting the defender to try to get to the ball carrier by escaping the block to the upfield side. (See Diagram 18.)

Diagram 18

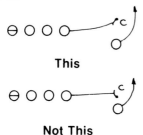

This

Not This

4. Mirror the movements of the cornerback, maintaining inside leverage. When he commits to the ball carrier, lock on, and take him in the direction he wants to go, hopefully upfield. If he escapes to the downfield side, he has a chance to make the play on the ball carrier, but if he tries to go around the upfield side and the tight end locks on, he will be taken out of the play. (See Diagram 19.)

Diagram 19

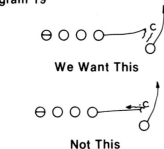

We Want This

Not This

Again, as with all perimeter blocks, the tight end must not commit too soon but should let the defender make the first move. Also, do not react too quickly to an upfield move since that might draw the tight end out of position and allow the cornerback to come inside into the path of the ball carrier. (See Diagram 20.)

Diagram 20

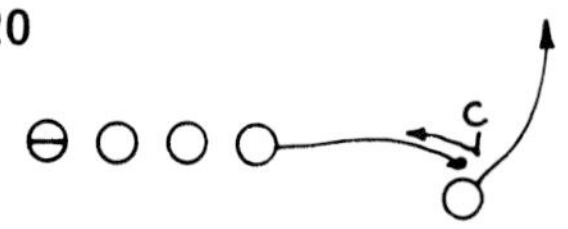

Be sure the cornerback is actually trying to come around to the upfield side before committing to the block.

Flanker Technique versus Corner Roll

The flanker recognizes the rolled up corner either by alignment or after the ball is snapped. Regardless, his first priority is to release outside the cornerback on his way to blocking the deep outside defender. The outside release accomplishes two things:

1. It widens the cornerback who is usually coached not to allow the outside release. This helps set up the block of the tight end and helps to widen the running lane. (See Diagram 21.)

Diagram 21

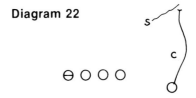

2. It will probably also widen the deep outside defender and help the flanker establish inside position on his block. (See Diagram 22.)

Diagram 22

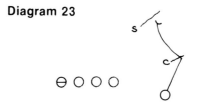

Attaining inside position is made more difficult by the outside release.

At times, the cornerback will simply not allow the outside release. If this happens, take the inside release but only after first widening the cornerback with the attempt of an outside release. (See Diagram 23.)

Diagram 23

If inside position cannot be attained on the deep outside defender, then get outside number leverage and use the same techniques as described before in blocking the deep defender.

Tight End—Flanker versus Overshift

Another coverage that we see occasionally is the overshifted secondary. (See Diagram 24.)

Diagram 24

As shown in the diagram, the tight end blocks the strong safety using the technique employed against the invert safety, and the flanker will block the cornerback using the techniques used by the split end versus the rolled up corner. These techniques will be described in the following section on split end play. The free safety is left unblocked.

Perimeter Blocking to the Split End Side

Despite the variety of coverages available to the defense, the split end will see basically two looks to his side. Either the cornerback will be rolled up to play the pitch, or he will be playing the deep outside and the pitch will either be taken from the line of scrimmage or by a secondary player, usually the free safety.

If the cornerback is playing the deep outside, the split end will use the same technique the flanker uses to block the deep outside defender to the tight end side. Although we will on occasion crack back on the safety if he is taking the pitch, we prefer to counter him on the play-action passes. We have found that reading the coverage to determine whether the corner or safety has pitch can be confusing and sometimes results in the split end's blocking neither the cornerback nor the safety.

Split End Technique versus Rolled Up Corner

The rolled up cornerback with no deep pass responsibility presents a difficult block for the split end. Correct technique is extremely important because of the length of time the blocker must occupy the defender before the ball carrier gets by. The running lane is inside the split end's block. (See Diagram 25.)

Diagram 25

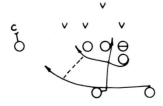

Coaching points:

1. Come off quickly but under control and establish a position that puts the split end about two yards from the cornerback and directly between the defender and the area where the ball carrier will receive the ball if it is pitched. (See Diagram 26.)

Diagram 26

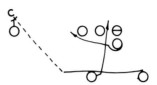

The first priority is to prevent the big hit; that is, the cornerback making the tackle at the same time the back receives the pitch. If that happens, the result is usually a fumble.

2. From a break down position and the nose aligned with the inside number of the cornerback, mirror the defender's movement. Do not initiate contact. Invite the defender to take an upfield route to get to the ball carrier. Delay contact as long as possible but maintain inside leverage.

3. When the defender commits to the ball or initiates contact, the split end then locks on with a good blocking surface. Keeping a good base, he maintains contact until the ball carrier has passed. Foot acceleration is important in order to stay glued to the defender.

The following are two problems presented to the split end by the rolled up corner.

1. The defender comes hard inside when the ball is snapped. (See Diagram 27.)

Diagram 27

In a situation where the split end doesn't have time to station himself between the cornerback and the ball carrier, the best he can hope for is to get his upper body across the front of the defender and drive him down the line of scrimmage to the inside. The ball carrier will now most likely run outside the split end's block.

If we face a cornerback who does this very often, we will make the play-action pass in the "hole" an integral part of our game plan. (See Diagram 28.)

2. The defender fakes upfield, then comes inside into the path of the ball carrier. (See Diagram 29.)

Diagram 28

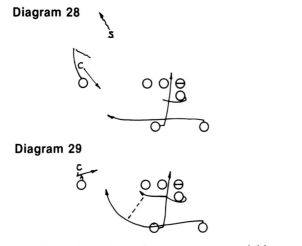

Diagram 29

The split end should not react too quickly to an upfield fake. He has time to react and block the de-

fender if the cornerback commits to the upfield move. (See Diagram 30.) However, he will not be in position to stop the inside move if he reacts too quickly to the upfield fake.

Diagram 30

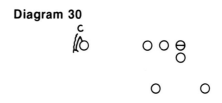

As defenses evolve, new techniques of perimeter blocking will need to be developed and different problems will present themselves, but the wide receivers and tight end must adjust to handle them. The perimeter blocking must be effective if the offense is to operate at maximum efficiency.

17

Gaining an Offensive Advantage Before the Snap

(From 1978 Summer Manual of the AFCA)

HAYDEN FRY Head Coach, and BILL SNYDER Assistant Coach, North Texas State University

We have always been impressed with the diversification of an offense like that of the Dallas Cowboys, primarily in their ability to create so many offensive looks through the utilization of motion and shifting while still maintaining a relatively basic attack.

Having to prepare defensively for such an attack has certainly given us a great deal of respect for its advantages. Perhaps one of the more convincing examples occurred several years back, in the summer All-Star Game between a group of pro-bound collegians coached by John McKay and a very sound representative of the NFL. On one play at the goal line, with the College All-Stars in possession, Coach McKay lined up his offense in a slot formation and sent the slot back in motion across the backfield to create a pro alignment (a very basic maneuver by today's standards). To adjust to that simple motion, that professional football team moved seven defensive people. From that point on we have been convinced that any time you can disrupt the continuity of a defense with offensive movement (motion or shifting) that much before the snap, you can create a distinct advantage.

After weighing the advantages against the disadvantages, we have committed ourselves to an offensive philosophy that stresses the use of multiple sets, extensive shifting, and motion. This type of offensive approach has met perfectly the needs of our personnel and our program. Among the most notable disadvantages are:

1. It can disrupt offensive timing and poor execution will result.
2. It may cause defensive adjustments that you are not prepared to block or throw into.
3. The threat of delay-of-game penalties always

exist because of the time required for shifting and motion.

There are certainly other problems that can occur, but these three are the ones we have to deal with most frequently. We might add that very basic to our attack is the concept that there must be a very definite purpose for each motion and each shifting pattern. We won't create movement without a purpose: one that should create an offensive advantage. We have found the following to be definite offensive advantages for us in the extensive use of presetting (shifting and motion), if our preparation is sound both on and off the field.

Advantages of Presetting (Motion and Shifting) and Multiple Sets

1. It neutralizes the defense to base alignments and secondary calls, limiting stunts and forcing a more controlled and balanced defense. The trend in defensing multiple sets, shifting, and motion has normally been to eliminate as many adjustments as possible and be as sound and simple as you can. Too much is involved in having a different adjustment from every defensive alignment, depending on weak motion, strong motion, trips, sets, and so on.

Most people also prefer to make all adjustments with only their secondary and not disrupt the continuity of the front seven. This further dictates the need to be simple and minimize the number of adjustments, as we all know the cost of one mental mistake in a defensive secondary. We, therefore, can virtually eliminate the overload secondaries that have become so popular in the past few years through the use of simple motion as indicated in Diagram 1, on the next page.

Diagram 1

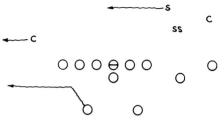

Motion to a balanced spread set forces the defense to disband overload coverage.

We have also found that with a variety of offensive sets and presetting that we often eliminate defensive pressure from linebackers (stunts) because they may be involved in making an adjustment. We often align in or shift to a "no back" offensive alignment (Diagram 2), which forces alignment adjustments by both the secondary and linebackers.

Diagram 2

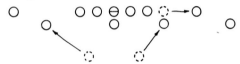

Shifting to a "no back" alignment.

And perhaps as important is the ability to preset in that same "no back" set and shift back into a basic pro or slot set with I or split backs. (See Diagram 3.)

Diagram 3

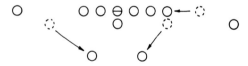

Presetting in a "no back" set and shifting back to basic alignment.

The value in this comes from the desire of the defense to keep their adjustments simple and basic, thereby taking their adjustment alignment first and then shifting back to their base alignment minus stunts when the offense shifts to a basic set.

2. It creates a personnel mismatch by changing the strength of the offensive formation and should eliminate flip-flopping of defensive personnel. The obvious situation is the slot motion, which forces the secondary to roll the free safety up as a strong safety (see Diagram 4) or run the strong safety across the backfield (Diagram 50), slowing and changing the angle of his support.

Against defenses that utilize strong and weak ends and/or linebackers (and in some cases tackles) the presetting of the tight end should force them into misalignments (strong end and linebacker on weak side

and weak end and linebacker on tight end side). This can easily be created by shifting the tight end from the true I alignment (Diagram 6), a move the Kansas City Chiefs made popular several years back, or aligning him on one side and shifting to the other. (See Diagram 7.)

Diagram 4

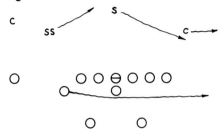

Slot motion causing free safety to roll up and play as strong safety.

Diagram 5

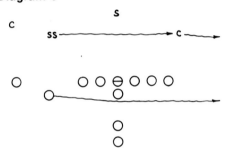

Slot motion causing the strong safety to change sides and alter his support angle.

Diagram 6

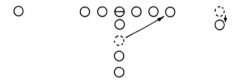

Shifting tight end from true I.

Diagram 7

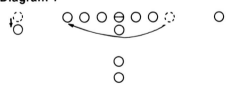

Shifting tight end from one side to the other.

In order to prevent the defense from determining the strength of the offense by placement of your flanker on a pro set, he and the split end can always align on the line of scrimmage (one always on the right, the other always on the left), and whichever one will become the flanker can back off when the tight end shifts (Diagrams 6 and 7). It should also be noted that when shifting from one side to the other (Diagram 7), the tight end should not touch a hand to the ground until after he has shifted to his final position. This would create an illegal procedure penalty if your wide receiver is on the line of scrimmage.

3. It disrupts defensive concentration and protects against the defensive recognition of offensive set tendencies. If offensive alignment is important to all eleven defensive players, then the change of that alignment must create a change in the defenders' alignment and/or responsibility and technique.

Against a nonpresetting offense where there is no motion or shifting, or at best predictable movement, the defender has considerable time to concentrate on alignment, responsibility, technique, and set tendencies. On the other hand, consider the uncertainty of a defender who has thought all of this through, has the play diagnosed, is ready to execute his assignment perfectly, and a sudden offensive shift takes place that changes his responsibility, technique, alignment, and even the tendency of what the offense might run. Being a "well-drilled player," he quickly fixes the new set of data in his mind and an offensive player now starts in motion. He must again assemble all the necessary information required for him to execute properly. We believe that establishes grounds for defensive confusion and little time to recognize offensive set tendencies.

4. It allows the offense the opportunity to control the defensive secondary coverage. With most defensive adjustments to motion and shifting coming from the secondary as mentioned above, it is necessary that that unit limit its coverages to a very minimum and not vary in the type of adjustments it makes to motion and shifting into spread and trip sets.

We have all seen or even been a part of a secondary that has a different coverage or responsibility for every single type of motion. The opportunities for confusion are obvious, which is why most defensive people now prefer to get back into the safest and most protective coverage they have against multiple set and presetting offenses. By presenting that threat, we feel we can force the coverage back to the base call. This allows us to devote more of our practice time working against base defensive alignments and less time preparing for all the variations that we feel we will not have to line up against.

5. It forces the defense to spend more preparation time on alignments and adjustments and less time on execution and repetition. Basic to any sound defense is to be certain that you do not get beat on alignment. To hold true to that philosophy takes a great deal of preparation and practice time, just making and coaching alignment adjustments in preparing for a multiple set team that utilizes extensive shifting and motion. This

certainly takes away practice time from the execution of the defense against each offensive play or series. The defense must prepare for your entire attack from all sets and possible types of motion, yet you may prepare only those "short list" plays that are best suited for that defense.

Diagram 8

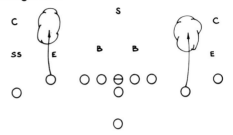

Double coverage against a spread often creates void seams for the inside receivers.

6. It can eliminate the ability of the defense to double cover or bump and run with your wide people. It has been our experience that motion and shifting have both prevented double coverage by a walked-off defensive end or linebacker or by a rolled-up corner or safety. For example, a balanced spread set (see Diagram 8) should seldom draw any type of double coverage because of the threat of the inside receivers.

If that holds true, you may eliminate double coverage by either executing your offense from a spread or presetting in a spread set, and motion or shift to the alignments you prefer. We find the same to be true with "no back" sets. They normally force the defense out of any double coverage.

Slot motion normally eliminates double coverage on your flanker back (see Diagram 9), although it may create timing difficulties for your quarterback.

Diagram 9

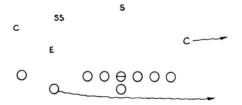

Slot motion to eliminate double coverage on flanker.

Shifting your tight end as shown in Diagrams 6 and 7 also allows you to eliminate or at least control the double coverage on the split end because the defense cannot distinguish which side is weak and which is strong until it is too late. If, for instance, the weak side defensive end chooses to double the split end and declares which side he is going to (as the offense comes out of the huddle) by following the split end, a shift by the tight end may leave him doubling the flanker and force him to check back to a normal alignment

Diagram 10a

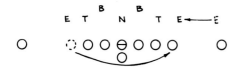

Shifting the tight end from one side to the other to eliminate double coverage by the weak side end or linebacker.

Diagram 10b

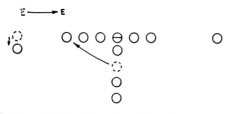

Shifting tight end from true I to eliminate double coverage by weak side end or linebacker.

(see Diagrams 10A and 10B), or allow the ball to be snapped without a strong side defensive end.

7. It creates a constant communication problem by the defensive signal callers.

8. It affords an exciting style of play for both the fans and the players. We may not do anything different than anyone else after the ball is snapped, but all the movement prior to that has created what our fans consider an exciting style of play. This becomes extremely important in a metroplex area such as Dallas–Fort Worth, where three other major schools and a professional team all compete for the same entertainment dollar.

The players are also motivated by this style of play and find it exciting, challenging, and fun. When executed properly, this style of offense adds points on the scoreboard in a hurry.

These few examples are only a few of the things we do in attempting to execute our philosophy of extensive motion, shifting, and multiple sets. We have adopted the philosophy in competing for the entertainment dollar, "Win or lose, look good doing it"! As each situation is different, this style of offense may or may not be best for every program, but it has certainly benefited ours at North Texas State University.

18
The "Gold Line" Running Game

(From 1977 Summer Manual of the AFCA)

ELLIOTT UZELAC Head Coach, Western Michigan University

At Western Michigan University, we spend a great deal of time on the "gold line," as we call it, inside our opponent's 10-yard line. We feel it is in this area that we make our offensive team physical and develop the punch that all great offensive teams have within their attack.

We have developed a separate theory and principles for the goal line offense that best uses the talents of our personnel and best attacks the defensive front that we see in our league. We feel it is very important that we first consider these two areas before we ever run a play. We must know the strengths and weaknesses of our own people and our opponents and then build our attack around these findings.

When our athletes arrive on campus in August for fall camp, the first thing that we do is establish our goals and objectives. In this all-important first meeting, we discuss at great length our goal line offense. For the fall of 1977, our team established one goal line goal—NEVER be stopped without a score with a first down on or inside the 10-yard line.

This was a very tough assignment and not only had to be thought about but also worked on very hard. Therefore, within our two weeks of fall camp, we set up two goal line scrimmages that would put great pressure on our offense and defense. We worked from the right, middle, and left hash. The ball was placed on the 10-, 9-, and 8-yard lines in each of these hash situations. It was first and goal in each of these situations and the offense had to score. Naturally, we also worked on our goal line offense when we scrimmaged on Saturdays.

This organization and pressure situations made us a much better offensive team in all areas as we could see we were becoming more physical and controlling the line of scrimmage with much more consistency. During the fall of 1977, Western Michigan University was never stopped without a score with a first down on or inside our opponent's 10-yard line. This was a great accomplishment for our young men and, more importantly, they achieved their goal for 1977.

Western Michigan's "goal line" offense has a number of theories and principles. They are:
1. Present a well-balanced offensive attack inside the 10-yard line.
2. Force the defense to balance up to our offensive formation.
3. Make use of motion to change the defense's run support rules or personnel.
4. Run option football inside the 10-yard line.
5. Make minimum line splits. Gap defenses force us to reduce splits.
6. Eliminate mistakes. (Fumbles, penalties, and missed assignments mean stops.)
7. Control the line of scrimmage; no penetration.
8. Sustain and block lower, front man; do not swing tail and get legs out of hole.
9. Backs run lower and harder, driving for the extra yard.
10. Throw the play-action pass, crossing patterns versus man and flood passes.

To develop these theories and principles, we felt the following formations would be best in order for us to attain success.

The series that we felt would best fit the abilities of our athletes were:

Our basic and most-used series would be our belly series. The important coaching points used are: 1) minimum splits; 2) movement at the point of attack;

3) seal the backside; 4) discrimination blocking and running; 5) no penetration; 6) backside end responsible for any fumble.

Diagram 1

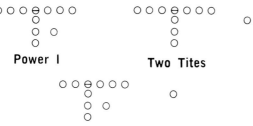

Power I   Two Tites

Unbalanced Power I

We use calls on the line of scrimmage to ensure that we are blocking the defensive look in the best possible way. An example would be a "run it" call made by our tackle versus a 6–5. On this call our tackle and end block rule and the wingback blocks opposite the defensive tackle to the strong safety.

Diagram 2

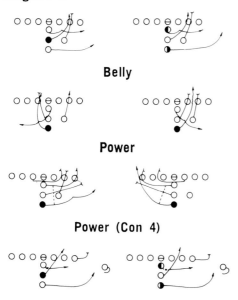

Belly

Power

Power (Con 4)

Veer Option Series

Diagram 3

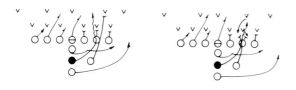

The fullback runs opposite the defensive tackle, and if there is a stalemate, he must take it inside the defensive tackle.

If we have an eight-man front, our tackle would make a "gap" call. On this call our tackle and end block inside gap and our wingback blocks the end-outside linebacker.

Diagram 4

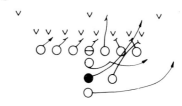

If we get a 70 look (Oklahoma), we can make either a "run it" or a "drive it" call, depending on the alignment of the strong safety.

Diagram 5

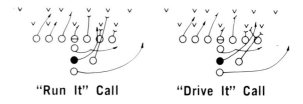

"Run It" Call   "Drive It" Call

On all belly series our frontside linemen use only our head-on block, which is the block used at the point of attack, when you have the option of taking the defender in either direction. We only use this block because we want no penetration and do not want our tails to swing and close up a running seam.

Diagram 6

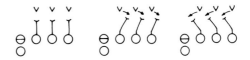

Examples of Head On Blocks

We want the belly option to look exactly like the fullback belly. Therefore, we dive our wingback in the tackle-end gap to the strong safety like we do on the fullback belly. However, the wingback reads the end's block to the strong safety on this play. The quarterback must get around the block on No. 3 and option No. 4. We can never pitch on No. 3.

Diagram 7

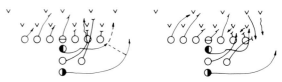

If an end has a wide alignment, the end will block down on the strong safety, and the wingback will block the end-outside linebacker the same as he would on a "gap" call versus an eight-man front.

Diagram 8

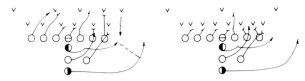

We also feel it is very good to run the fullback belly or the belly option from the unbalanced formation. We have now forced a change in alignment that we can take advantage of by going to strength or running the isolation or sweep away from formation strength.

Diagram 9

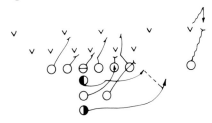

We then added the power series to the belly series, which gives us the complete package from the power I. The first play in the power series is the isolation. We use this to and away from formation strength. We definitely want to run the isolation play away from formation strength when people kick their defense down to our strength.

Diagram 10

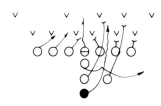

Our wingback blocks opposite the defensive tackle to the strong safety, and the fullback blocks opposite the defensive tackle to the middle linebacker. Our tailback will run opposite the defensive tackle to daylight.

When we run away from formation strength, our fullback will block opposite the defensive tackle to the free safety (or linebacker substitute).

Our tailback again runs opposite the defensive tackle to daylight. We dive our wingback away from playside to hold and/or block the middle linebacker to strong safety.

Diagram 11

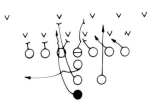

The power sweep has given us the ability to run strong or weak according to the defensive alignment. On the sweep to formation strength, we dive the wingback opposite the end to the strong safety. The fullback sprints, gaining one yard to a point behind where our tight end lines up. He reads the play of defensive end and supporting defensive back and blocks the defensive back using an overthrow technique. Our tailback uses a slight hesitation step to get separation from our fullback. He sprints laterally and expresses a wide sweep. He then reads and cuts off the block of the tight end on the end of line. Our quarterback reverses out, pitches to the tailback, stays 2 yards off the line of scrimmage, and goes opposite the tight end's block to seal the levels.

Diagram 12

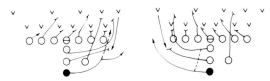

We also incorporated the "arc" technique used by the playside tight end. Now the fullback course was 1½ yards behind the tight end and worked for an overthrow block on defensive end. The tailback hesitates to get separation from the fullback. He then must read the fullback's block on the defensive end for his course.

Diagram 13

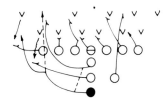

The veer option series completed our package. Again, as in other series, we would use line calls for the best blocking situations. This series was also developed because of its strength from motion off the power I. Against the 6–5, our tackle would make a "run it" call for the fullback dive. Against the 70 (Oklahoma) defense, our tackle would make a "lead it" call for the fullback dive. Our quarterback open pivots deep at a 45-degree angle. He brings up his back foot parallel to the fullback's course and extends the ball back to the fullback. He looks ball in and explodes the end-outside linebacker faking option. Our fullback takes a drive step directly toward the guard-tackle gap. Against the even defense, he reads the down man on the guard versus the odd defense, he must run the option cut on the "lead it" call.

Diagram 14

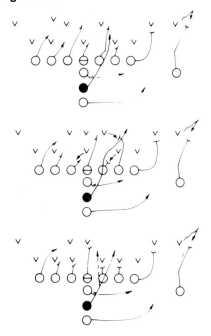

The calls are the same for our true option, in which we only option No. 3 unless a "stick" block is used. Then we clear No. 3 and option No. 4. On our outside play, our fullback is now used to flock block the levels (linebacker to free safety).

Diagram 15

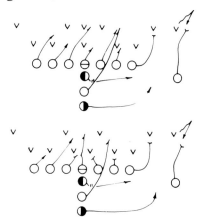

Our tailback must get in option phase, be ready to look the ball in, and run off the arc block. If a stick is called, the quarterback will option No. 4 and the tailback's course is a little wider before he hits into the crease.

Diagram 16

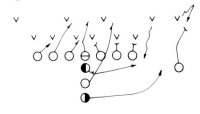

"Stick" Call

With the belly series, the power series, and the veer option series in, we then incorporated motion. This allowed us to attack on a broad front away from defense strength. We could attack with the sweep, the veer option and the buck pass to or away from motion.

Diagram 17

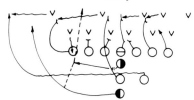

Arc Sweep

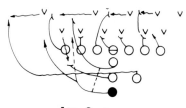

Veer Option

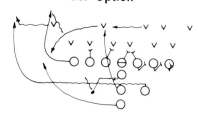

Buck Pass

We would run the buck pass when we received a very hard action by the supporting defensive halfback.

Part Four
Passing

19

Controlling the Ball with the Passing Game

(From 1979 Proceedings of the AFCA)

BILL WALSH Head Coach, Stanford University

Throughout most of my career I have been involved with the forward pass. At Stanford University I suppose we emphasized the forward pass, and this emphasis goes back, I believe, to the time I was an assistant coach with the Cincinnati Bengals. We had Virgil Carter as our quarterback. Virgil was a great Brigham Young quarterback, 6 feet in height without the deep-throwing arm. He was a good runner. We were contending with the Pittsburgh Steelers, Cleveland Browns, and other teams. Our best chance to win football games was to somehow control the ball. We were an expansion team, and it was important to make first downs.

So we developed what you might call a ball-control passing game. Virgil was not effective 20 yards or so beyond the line of scrimmage. We weren't that strong an offensive line to run the ball consistently, so we developed a ball-control passing game. Our hope was that if we could make twenty-five first downs in a given game and had good special team play, we would be in a ball game, and could be in the divisional championship. We played the Baltimore Colts in the playoffs and lost a close game.

Basic Fundamentals

Since that time my philosophy has been more toward controlling the ball with the forward pass. I can give you some basic fundamentals that we would follow.

First, with the pass you have to have versatility. You can't depend time after time on the same mechanical pattern you see a lot in college football. You can't practice it over and over in a fifteen-minute drill each day and then think that when it's third and 3, "Will

I go to this particular kind of pass?" We have to have versatility—versatility in the action of the quarterback. We certainly throw the dropback pass and we will emphasize, to some degree, a three-step drop pattern, but more often we will use a five-step drop pattern of timed patterns down the field. From there we go to a seven-step drop. Now I'm talking about the quarterback. When our quarterback takes a seven-step drop, he's allowing the receivers time to maneuver down the field. Therefore, we will use a three-step drop pattern when we are throwing a quickout or hitch or slant and, by and large, on those kinds of passes the defense is allowing you to complete by their alignment or by their coverage. If their coverage allows you to have a clean receiver on either side without a rollup, we can throw a quickout or a hitch, depending on the type of receiver we have.

If you can control their linebackers with certain play-action, you can throw the slant pattern behind people. But those three-step drop patterns are strictly patterns that break a defense that the defense is allowing you to complete a ball on. Any time we throw a three-step pattern, we have to have a completion. We don't want to waste time with an incomplete three-step pattern because, by and large, on a quickout, you are going to make 7 yards, on the hitch, 7 to 9, and on the slant, 8 to 12 yards.

As I recall, in professional football we might have thrown four or five of those a year other than the slant near the goal line. But we do throw the five-step pattern. The five-step drop pattern for the quarterback calls for a disciplined pattern by the receiver. He runs that pattern the same way every time. He doesn't maneuver to beat the defensive back. He doesn't concern himself with coverage other than a couple of fundamental things. He runs a disciplined pattern that's the same every time. The quarterback takes a disciplined drop of five steps and either throws with or without what we call a hitch step, and the ball is completed because of the coverage itself.

Then we go to a seven-step drop. While a five-step drop controls the ball, the seven-step pattern is where you try to score a touchdown. When our quarterback takes a seven-step drop, our receivers are now asked to maneuver, to read linebackers or defensive backs, to maneuver into openings and to maneuver on given individual patterns.

I recommend that with a drop-back scheme, you isolate it in those mechanics. So often in college football the quarterback is either standing there waiting for the receiver, or the receiver has broken before the quarterback can throw the ball. These are the biggest flaws you will see in the forward pass. Now when the receiver breaks before the ball can be thrown, the defensive back is adjusting to the receiver. Any time the quarterback holds the ball waiting for the receiver to break, the defensive back sees it and he breaks on the receiver. So the time pattern is vital.

Now you can't just drop back pass. You have to be able to do other things in order to keep the defense from zeroing in on your approach. So the play pass is vital. By and large, the play pass will score the touchdown. The drop back pass will control the ball.

For play-action passing we have certain blocking fundamentals that we use. We will show different backfield actions with basically the same offensive line blocking. We will go to the play pass as often as we can, especially as we get to the opponent's 25-yard line.

The third category of pass that most people use is what we call the action pass, where your quarterback moves outside. There are a couple of reasons for moving outside. One certainly is to avoid the inside pass rush. For a drop back passing team we will sprint, or waggle as we call it, outside to avoid blitzers who approach straight up the field on us. The other advantage is to bring yourself closer to the potential receiver.

We will get outside to throw the ball and get ourselves closer to the man we want to throw to. When you can get outside, the trajectory of the ball can be flatter because normally there isn't a man between you and the receiver. So we will come outside with Virgil Carter, we will play pass with Virgil Carter, and we will basically run a five-step drop, ball control-type passing. With a Ken Anderson you will go more to seven steps.

The versatility also includes changing your formations. We continuously change receiver width and spacing. We seldom will line up our receiver with about the same spacing on two or three given plays in a row. If we want to throw the ball to the outside, we will reduce the split of the receiver. We need running room to the outside. We don't want the ball in the air very long. So, we will reduce the split of our receivers. If we want to throw inside, we will extend the split of our receivers, so that there is more maneuvering room to the inside, and spread the defense. Our backs, as many teams know, will cheat to get where they have to be. We know that if we throw to backs, the first thing on their mind is how to release out of the backfield. We are quite willing to move the man to get the release and sometimes telegraph what we are doing. We are quite willing to do that with the idea that when we want to break a given tendency, we simply line them up there and run something else.

We will vary the split of the receivers according to the pattern and the coverage and, of course, to add versatility. The biggest problem you will have in the forward pass is when you have to throw the ball a number of times and, with a very limited inventory, you begin to throw the same pattern over and over. You get into trouble.

Pass on First Down

Don't isolate throwing the forward pass to a given down and distance. If you are going to throw the ball, you must be willing to throw on first down and not throw just a token pass hoping for the best, but a pass that is designed to get you a certain amount of yardage.

In our ball control passing, we will use the five-step drop pattern on first down, because we know through the drilling of our quarterback that we could get four or five dropping the ball off to a back, who is an outlet, or to a tight end. So we are quite willing to throw a ball control pass on first down. Come back with a running play on second down, and then go to our seven-step drop maneuvering pattern on third down.

You can see that these things fit together for us. Also, with ball control passing, it's like the running game. In our 1978 season, our quarterback threw two interceptions in his last 240 passes, so his percentages were good. You look at that and compare the interceptions with the fumbles of a team that runs 90 percent of the time and often you will see the team fumbling and giving up the ball more than the team that is passing.

Often the interception is down the field and the tackle is made and you gain a certain amount of field position with that interception. But most fumbles are near the line of scrimmage, so there is a dramatic loss there.

I think the argument that you will throw the interception has to be qualified with how much you know about the forward passing game versus the running game. In our last game our opponent fumbled five times and we threw no interceptions. That might have been the difference in the game.

You also have to develop consistent pass receiving, and a big part of it is continuous drilling of the pass pattern that each man is supposed to run. We don't stand there and play catch, thinking we are working on pass receiving. We run the specific pattern for a specific pass over and over and over. The quarterback has a way of throwing what we call an M pattern and a way of throwing a square out. He throws them over and over, much as a pitcher practices a change-up.

We have never used a net in practice. The point is that when we tell the quarterback a Z-in pattern, he is thinking about a type of throw, and our receiver is thinking about how he catches that pattern. When we talk to our fullback about an M pattern, he's thinking of a route and the ball being dropped over somebody's head a foot in front of his numbers.

We practice again and again, just as a running team will practice the option against different variations. We haven't used that many receiving drills. We do know that one of the key aspects of pass receiving is that as the man catches the ball, somebody gets in his way. One thing I developed, therefore, was to take an air dummy—one not filled with air, but stuffed and light—and stand in front of the receiver. As he caught an individual pattern, I would bust him just as he caught the ball. This helped to condition our players for receiving contact on the instant of the catch or on the instant afterward. I think that may be one of the most important things.

Don't Tamper Too Much

Another thing we allow for is the fact that each individual has a way of receiving a pass. You can take a receiver and keep saying, "catch it in your hands," and the man will graduate or leave school before he ever catches one in his hands. It might be more important to say, "Watch him catch it." Make sure he secures the ball the way he catches it, then slowly but surely work toward maybe a more efficient way.

Otis Taylor, one of the great pass receivers of all time, always caught the ball with his body. Fred Bilitenkoff always caught the ball out in front of his hands. We will let a man catch it with his body. We'll let him cradle the ball. We will let catch it any way in which he will begin to become consistent and efficient. Then, slowly but surely over a period of time, on a given pattern we'll say, "Try to open your hands a little more now that you can catch it." We try not to jump on people. Don't worry so much about the fundamentals of that particular pass pattern.

In the football I have coached, the coaches are involved. They hold the blocking bag. When I was with the Oakland Raiders, I held the blocking bag for Huart Dixon, and he busted it every day. It kept his enthusiasm up and I got a feel of how his pads hit that blocking dummy. The contact on the receiver just after the catch is vital. Throw the same pattern over and over until it registers what a wide player means and how the ball is thrown. I know our fullback this past season caught well over fifty passes and did not play the entire season.

Talk About Patterns

As far as the quarterback is concerned, we just don't talk to a quarterback about how strong his arm is or how far he can throw the football. We talk in terms of given patterns. When we throw a 20-yard out, we don't throw to a receiver, we throw to a spot. Put the ball up and let the receiver come to it. Anytime you are throwing the ball farther than 15 yards down the field, if your quarterback has to look at that receiver, and put that ball exactly to the receiver, he's going to be aiming the ball, and most often there will be an error. Mostly in that kind of pattern, if the pattern is clean, we throw to a spot. So the 20-yard out is thrown to a spot. The man should be near the sideline running back to the ball and catch the ball 17 yards deep.

For a square out, which is 12 yards, we take five steps and throw it on time. And as we step to throw the ball, if it's taken away, we hold it. It's a different pattern, you see. So for us, every pattern is a different throw for the quarterback. Now we don't have ninety-seven different throws. A pattern is developed where the quarterback thinks of a type of throw when he throws the pattern.

Now let's talk about play selection. One of the factors involved with our success a few years ago with the Cincinnati Bengals was that we would begin to set a game plan for the opening of the game. We continued that with the Chargers and at Stanford. My point is that at Stanford we got to a point where in a given game, say, for instance, against Southern California, we ran the first twelve plays we had decided on in order. Of course we ran out of lists because the first twelve worked and none worked after that. But the point is we went twelve plays in order, right down the line. We went eight straight games scoring the first time we had the ball. By the time we have completed eight to ten plays, we've forced him to adjust to a number of things. We've kept him off balance with the type of thing we were doing and we pretty much established in given series what we would come to next.

That is a good approach to offensive football. It forces you to go into that game with a certain calmness. You know where you are going, rather than having to say "What in the hell do we do now?" Occasionally planned plays don't work, but we just keep going. Against California this year, the first three didn't work. From that point on, however, they began to work. But we didn't change, we didn't worry about it. We were trying to create an effect on our opponent. The effect was he had to adjust. He saw different things. He had the ball run right at him. He had the ball thrown over his head. A lot of things happened. Meanwhile when we know what the play is going to be, we see what their adjustments are. We try to get a line on their first down defenses, but we take it from there.

Going for End Zone

We have a different form of pass offense from about our opponent's 25-yard line to his 5. From that area we are going for the end zone. I have seen so many teams march the ball beautifully, but right around the 15-yard line, they are already warming up their placekicker, because right at that point defenses change, the field you can operate in changes, and suddenly their basic offense goes all to pieces on them.

My contention is that if we are on their 25, we're going for the end zone, then we will kick a field goal. I don't want to try to take the ball from their 25 to the goal line in an evenly matched game by trying to smash it through people, because three out of four times, you won't make it. Unless you are superior. Of course if you are vastly superior it makes very little difference how you do it. But if it is head-to-head, a Southern Cal or an Oklahoma game for Stanford, when we're really scratching and battling, then we are going for the end zone from the 25-yard line.

Why? First, every defensive coach in the country is going to his blitzes right about there. He's starting to get a tight neck and he's going to start blitzing you. So we know the pass coverage, because by and large they are going to man-to-man coverage. We know that if they don't blitz one down, they're going to blitz the next down. Automatically. They'll seldom blitz twice in a row, but they'll blitz every other down. If we go a series where there haven't been blitzes on the first two downs, here comes the safety blitz on third down. So we are looking at that point to get into the end zone.

By the style of our football we'll have somebody to get the ball to a little bit late—just as an outlet to get 4 or 5 yards, try to keep it. But from the 25 to the 10, we're going for the end zone. I believe it is effective. Two years ago, with James Lofton as our flanker, James caught fourteen touchdown passes, ten of them right in that area.

We will go with patterns there designed to beat blitzes and go to man-to-man coverage. That part of our football is important.

The next part is the operating field offense. We know that on our first down basis our ball control passing is vital. You'll see us drop-back pass on first and 10, and we will be ready to drop the ball off to the backs. By and large, on first and 10 you'll get a two-deep zone—zone-type defense. We build into that the idea that we will drop the ball off. We have worked on it enough that we can drop the ball off to a back late and still make 4 to 5 yards. The 4 or 5 yards are as important to us as some other team making the same on an option play. We are looking for ball control on first and 10. You often will see us run with the ball on second and 10, because we want 5 yards. Often on second and 10, if you run a basic running play, you can get your 5. At third and 5, we are right back with a ball-control pass, dumping to a back, and we're making it. We said two years ago that if we can make thirty first downs a game, we'll win. We were right on that. Nationally, I think we were the No. 1 team on first downs because of that approach. Usually it would be drop-back pass on first down, run on second down, ball-control pass on third down. Get near the goal line, you're going for the end zone.

Strategy When Backed Up

Another consideration is what to do when you're backed up. At some point, to win a ball game, you're going to have to throw the ball inside your own 10-yard line. I've been in ball games where that has won it. And, I suppose, occasionally lost it.

What passes do you throw when you're backed up? You may have to do it. You have to decide for yourself what style of passing you are going to use there, and your players have to know it. We'll put ourselves in positions all over the field, throwing from our own 1-yard line and from their 20 when we have to, and most of your passes will hold constant for those situations.

There is situation passing, and it's not always the same basic pattern that you believe you're safe with and that you'll use up and down the field. Often you'll complete that hooking pattern for a couple of first downs and then go back to it just at the wrong time, when you don't have anything else to go to. Our pass offense is related to versatility, formations, different actions, the play calling itself, a sequence of things, or the field itself.

So much of your forward pass is related to your

opponent's goal line defense. You have standard passes to throw against a goal line. Often you are looking for the extra substitution to come into the game, but there are passes right for that goal line. Too often people go in there and butt heads with good linebackers on the goal line. Too often they don't make it.

We figure that if we get inside that 5-yard line, half the time we are going to throw the ball. Our percentages are as good or better than most teams of equal ability. If you're marching through somebody, you can just close your eyes and hand the ball off. When it's very competitive, that goal line pass is vital. So we have a series of those. We would never call them anywhere else on the field.

Another aspect of passing is short yardage. When we talk about short yardage passing, we're after two different things. One, we want to try to win the game right there. So anytime we are around their 35-yard line, if we don't see somebody standing deep down the middle, we are going to go for the 6 points, figuring that at that point we'll either kick a field goal or punt the ball. We want to get into the end zone with somebody chasing our guy. We don't want to have to shove them back into their own end zone to win the ball game.

Another category is to make it on third and 1 with the forward pass. That comes with the discipline of often throwing to a back out of the backfield. These are all combinations. Another thing that we will do is to include in our game plan a third and 3 category. That's the toughest one to make. What do you do on third and 3? If you outgun the other team, you don't have many of those. But when it's tough, what do you do?

We have a certain list of runs and a certain list of passes. When we have third and 3, we don't grope. We go to it.

I'll show you a ball-control pass that Sid Gillman may have developed some time ago. It's still the most effective forward pass that we used at Stanford. They call it "Go out for a long one."

Diagram 1

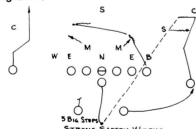

5 Big Steps

STRONG SAFETY WIDENS

We call this 22-Z in. This is a five-step drop pattern. The quarterback takes five big steps and a hitch step and throws on time. Not five short steps. The re-

ceiver splits 12 to 14 yards. He releases inside for 5 to 6 yards and then bursts hard to the outside foot of the cornerback. What he wants to do is to get that cornerback on his heels. He plants his outside foot and starts in. He'll only go in about three steps. Maybe four at the most, because we have to control linebackers. So he will go in, plant hard, and start in.

Meanwhile the quarterback has taken five steps, what we call a crossover hitch step, and throws the ball on time to that man and he should catch it 12 yards deep. That particular thing is done over and over.

The fullback runs what we call a scat pattern. He doesn't have any pickup, and he releases to the outside. He's shooting up going through the original position of the flanker. He never catches the ball more than 2 yards past the line of scrimmage, most often right at the line of scrimmage. If the backer blitzes, he looks for the ball early. In some instances in college ball we double read our guard and had very little trouble with this.

Our tight end picks off the near end backer. He'll put his head past that man's shoulder, slow down, and make contact. We bounce off it and go to the far guard position, and we turn and face the quarterback and watch his eyes because he's the last outlet.

The quarterback throws the ball related to that sky safety. If the safety gives ground, he'll throw to the fullback. If the safety flattens out, we'll throw in behind him, in this case to the flanker. If it's man-to-man, the flanker runs a man-to-man pattern trying to beat that corner. If it's man-to-man, the safety often will chase the tight end and there will be a good throwing lane with the backer coming out on the fullback. So we try to include all phases of it in that one pattern.

What happens when the fullback catches it? We tell the quarterback that the fullback should get the ball a foot in front of his number. That doesn't mean that as he is dropping back he's thinking, "I want to throw the ball a foot in front of his number." He's done it so many times that that is where it comes down. We found over a period of years that if he reaches, he takes his eye off the ball. If he slows down or breaks his stride, he doesn't get anything out of it.

Diagram 2

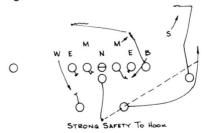

STRONG SAFETY TO HOOK

Diagram 3

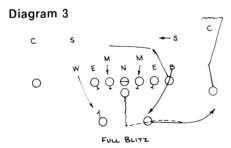

Full Blitz

Diagram 4

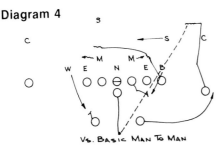

Vs. Basic Man To Man

to the sideline. He doesn't turn up the field. He gets width on that side.

What happens if they roll up in a two-deep? We simply change our priority to the outside man. Whether it be a safety or a cornerback, our receiver comes off the line thinking of that individual pattern, unless he reads the safety deep. If he reads the safety deep, he knows right away he has to defeat that cornerback. He sees that cornerback, and he works to get outside of him. Seldom will he ever make it. The cornerback moves laterally and cuts him off, but what he has done is widen that cornerback, then he jumps back up inside and hooks right to the inside. Everything else remains the same. If the cornerback gives ground with him, the fullback gets the ball. If the cornerback levels off, we'll throw the ball inside. If the inside is covered, we go right back to the tight end who maneuvers with the quarterback's eyes. That is the combination.

We can't do that on every play, so we have variations. Another thing we do is to put the fullback in motion. We get to their zone defense before they can get there themselves. So often when you coach defense you coach zone defense to spots on the field. We say go to the spot, and often we'll have more guys there than you have. We're going to run motion to get there.

We put the fullback in motion according to the quarterback's heel. How far he will go depends on what we're trying to accomplish. But he'll be almost there, then he'll turn it up. Now, we've stretched that zone long before they are ready for it. There's no way they are going to keep people inside and run out there to stop it. If they do, we can run other types of plays.

The next thing to do with that is to vary the width of the receiver, and attack a different portion of the defense. The flanker then would be only 6 yards. Now we can put the fullback in motion, and he can be outside the flanker when the ball is centered. This is really stretching the zone defense. When we move the fullback outside, the cornerback has no choice. He leaves the flanker. The flanker split will vary according to the opponent. One week 3 yards, then 6, then 14; one week with motion, next week tightened with no motion. With one pattern there are so many variations that you are going to have trouble practicing against it.

If people played for the inside break, we'd run what we call a circle out when we're trying to split the two-deep zone. Again, we're going to our right. We like to throw hooking patterns to our right, outbreaking patterns to our left. We need to see the hooking pattern develop, throwing to our right because we have to throw it off moving defenders. When we throw the out, we want to throw it without telegraphing. Therefore, you'll see us throwing 70 percent of our patterns to our left. The quarterback's shoulders are

When he catches it, he goes up the sideline. We tell our backs who catch the ball, "You want the sideline." The reason you want the sideline is that only one man can tackle you at a time and often he underestimates you along that sideline. What we are after there is a 7- to 9-yard gain to the fullback, or a 12-yard gain to the flanker. The fullback gets it about two out of three times.

As the quarterback goes through those mechanics, he comes back and looks at the tight end. As soon as the tight end sees his eyes, then the tight end slides laterally. We know the tight end stays stationary at that point, because as soon as the quarterback's eyes go back they engulf the tight end.

Diagram 5

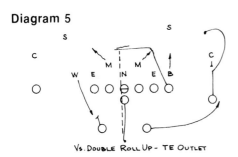

Vs. Double Roll Up - TE Outlet

At Cincinnati one year we were 20 of 22 going to our right on that pattern. We were averaging 8 to 9 yards a play. Often that would be our third and 3 pattern. Our quarterback knows that on third and 3, it's fullback, then flanker, then tight end. We would give them a different priority. We don't do any special keying. That is the 22-Z in as we know it. Now if we're looking for a blitz, this can be an audible.

If they are blitzing outside, covering men, the end backer has the fullback and we pick him off with our tight end, throw the ball to the fullback, and he runs facing right, so they can't get a jump on the throw to the left.

The next thing we would do with that particular action, the same pass protection, is to put our fullback in motion, start our receiver inside, and break him up to the safety and to the outside. Now we are splitting that zone deep, and we're isolating this man on the outside.

When we take that safety man on, we have to look him in the eye. When you coach pass receivers, you want to tell the pass receiver to look the defensive back in the eye. Don't take your eye off him. So much of defensive backfield play is instinct. It's nonverbal football.

It's the action of one competitive athlete against another. Any time we break inside we find that safety, look at him, and break away. At that point we are looking at the corner. If he is giving ground, the fullback gets the ball. If he's stationary or coming forward, we throw it over his head. But never attempt to throw it over a rotating corner's head when he's giving ground. You'll always underestimate how much ground he can give and his jumping height. He has to be coming forward or planting.

We are willing to throw to the fullback and get only 2 yards. So often a coach will put the forward pass as something you don't try unless you can make 20 yards with it.

The next step off 22-Z in is to go to our tight end and extend the split of the flanker. The tight end catches the hooking type pattern. He wants to get his body inside the defensive man and between defensive people. Whether we use motion or not, we run the wide flare. This man will clear straight up the field. We want him to release outside that corner if he has to fight until the whistle blows. Our tight end will release to the outside, but we know part way up the field he'll probably be going straight down the field. The problem with out breaks to tight ends is that once they're shown, they continue to move laterally before they finally break. What you get is a man staggering along sideways, and a defensive man can just walk along with him. At some point with his release he's got to work straight up the field 5 full yards.

As he goes up the field, he is aware of what's going on outside of him. If the corner rolls up in a zone, naturally he starts out and sets down between his position and the original position of the flanker. Now he doesn't mark that off with his feet. He simply senses where to set down. So if we overplay this, there's a hole in the defense right there.

Naturally, if it is man-to-man type of defense, or if it's a man-under type of thing with the backer covering him, he's going to run his out pattern full speed, and we throw the ball to the outside.

With 22 action, we have a Z-in bearing the split of the flanker, a Z-in with fullback motion. We've got a circle out with our flanker, and we've got a Y-out with the tight end. The key to the pass, as far as Stanford is concerned, is the fullback. You've got to be able to throw to the fullback effectively. He should average 7 to 8 yards a catch. We are not looking for giant gains out of him. We're looking for ball control throwing the ball to our fullback.

Now for the out pattern. This again is a five-step drop. We'll vary the formation on this. We can be in a slot, an open slot, or things of that nature. We are throwing a five-step timed pattern to, most often, our split end. He will split 8 yards. We seldom will change that, because on a timed pattern, a quarterback does not take a hitch step. When I say he doesn't take a hitch step, when he finally crosses over with his left foot, his right foot hits, he pivots, and throws the ball.

When I say he takes a hitch step, he crosses over, pushes back, hitch steps forward, and throws. Those differences in mechanics mean that a receiver can cover 5 yards, and the defensive man can cover 5 yards, whether you hitch step or not. It is very important that your quarterback's feet are right.

The receiver goes straight up the field as close to full speed as he can. At 10 yards he crosses over and breaks out. He catches the ball at 12. He doesn't fade down the field, which brings him closer to the defensive back. He crosses over and breaks to the sidelines. He doesn't care about the coverage, other than if they roll up; he runs a seam. He doesn't care where that defensive back is located, and he doesn't change his angle of release. He just runs the pattern.

The quarterback decides prior to the snap and just after the snap whether he's going to throw him the ball or not. It's up to the quarterback to decide if he wants him to have the ball. Not up to the receiver. The quarterback takes five quick steps. Notice I said five big steps in the Z-in. Now that we're throwing out, we take five quick steps. The right foot hits the ground, he pivots open, and throws the ball on time to that receiver. I know I can't lead him because any time you lead a receiver who is running parallel to the ball, he'll never catch up to the ball.

Diagram 6

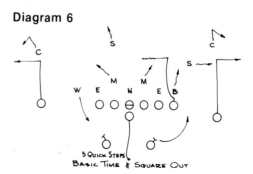

5 Quick Steps
Basic Time & Square Out

If I throw the ball to a receiver going parallel to it, both of them just keep running right into the tunnel. You throw the five-step drop right at the man's hip. We don't lead him on out. We don't lead him on the square-out. If you throw into his body, the defensive back doesn't have any way to get to it. What we are trying to get here is the defensive back giving ground this way and then losing lateral ground this way. That's on single coverage. We practice it over and over and over. We don't throw it over anybody's head to get it there.

On this particular pattern both receivers do the same thing, but I would say most often the flanker gets it. The tight end takes an inside release, goes straight up the field, and runs a full speed crossing pattern, but never crosses the ball. The tight end on his basic crossing pattern is the one you go to on man-under defense. If a team is running man-under, that kind of an out is suicide. So if our quarterback sees inside-out coverage on the wide receivers, reasonably close, his drop now goes right to the tight end; he's looking for the tight end to beat a man-under linebacker.

The backs are really the key to it. We check our backers on a blitz, although on certain times we can double read a guard and get him out. He runs what we call an M pattern. The fullback will run M pattern.

In the M pattern, the back sits for an instant reading for the blitz. Then he loses ground. He should get 1½ to 2 yards deeper than in his original position. I would say he is 6 yards deep, turns up the field, and he should be 3 yards outside the offensive tackle. This man is a little bit wider outside the tight end. Now they're looking for the M pattern. If we get a backer out from underneath it and another backer going to the zone, we aren't going to throw over his head. So we'll hold the ball, slide forward, and pop it right over their heads to that man. That is where all hell breaks loose if you're in a pure zone defense. We time a square out, they take it away, we hold the ball, slide forward in certain mechanics, and pop the ball over people to that back.

You never make a back reach for the football. No matter how good he is, the player is not going to go in there for that ball. We put it in front of the numbers. We don't want him to catch it any farther than 2 yards down the field. As soon as he catches the ball, he looks for the linebackers and splits them full speed. This is where the fine pass-receiving fullback is very important. We don't ever stop and dodge anybody in our football. We run between people at full speed. The only time we stop and dodge somebody is if there's nobody within 10 yards of us. Then we'll do it. As soon as I catch the ball, I'm looking for the two of them converging, and I split them. I want to run between

people. When I fall, I want my body to go down the field past their bodies. If they tackle me, my body gets closer to the goal line than theirs. That makes a little bit of difference in throwing to your backs because those extra 6 feet can give you second and 4. Now you can operate.

On the M pattern, the weak linebacker—some call him a defensive end—takes away the square out, we hold the ball, and pop it right off to the halfback.

Diagram 7

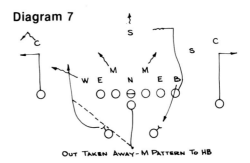

OUT TAKEN AWAY - M PATTERN TO HB

The double square out pattern is man-under and hold the ball—both of those backs are going to track backwards of their own—to the outside. They'll probably blitz one man, which isolates this man with a backer. Most of the time, with the way we teach our tight end, he has a good chance of beating the backer.

Diagram 8

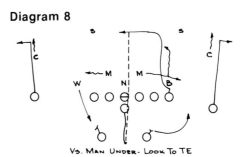

VS. MAN UNDER - LOOK TO TE

With a roll up zone, we hit the X on a square out. Practice, practice, practice. With a zone where the backer drops off, we hold the ball and hit the back on an in. We line up on their man-under defense, see it, and look at the tight end immediately. This is a ball control pass.

There's another ball-control pass that we will run often on first down. It has been an audible on the blitz.

The next thing we do is to try to get the halfback isolated against the zone. Our back is the primary receiver. We're going to double read our guard on a backer so that we can get that back out. If both of them come, we have to hit him with the ball. The whole idea here is for our back to release outside this man's rush, and break to the outside. If anything crosses his face along the way, he sets down between people.

That is what we call a halfback flat. If no one

crosses his face, whether it be a backer or a rollup corner, he runs a flat. We take five quick steps and hit him on time, then he gets up that sideline and makes one person at a time tackle him. We don't try to get him up the field too far on this type of play. If it's zone, take five quick steps and hold it. He sets down, and we throw it right in the middle of him.

If it were man-under and they locked on him, the tight end again is running that crossing pattern so that if we sense man-under by the location of the defensive backs, we then go to the man-under pattern for the tight end. Often our tight end is practicing mostly against man-under coverage against the backer. If he can beat man-under coverage against the backer, they're in trouble. If they put the safety on him, that opens up the outside receiver. If they don't put man-under on him, of course they're in a zone defense and everybody else starts getting the ball. The tight end is the man who goes against the man-under people.

There are four or five other things like that that we do for ball-control passing.

I will go from that to the seven-step drop pattern, but I'll show you just one play that is sort of worn out.

This is a seven-step drop, and we've already said that our receivers maneuver on a seven-step drop pattern. We're going to run a blue left for us, a right, which is motion, and we're going to run a 79, which is weak flow pass protection. We're going to say X-hook. Now X is going to run a pattern on the weak side, and the simplest thing they could do would be to drop people off. We'll put a man in motion, like that fullback in motion, turn up this alley, and set down right there.

Diagram 9

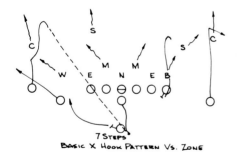

BASIC X HOOK PATTERN VS. ZONE

This could be a double-wing formation where he drags and sets down. You vary the width of the receiver. He may be 1 yard split or he may be 12 yards split, depending on which linebacker we are trying to beat. But he works up the field, gets past the man who has short coverage, and turns in. We tell him to get past the W and beat the M. As he gets past the W, he's aware of where he is. I suppose if he moved laterally, we'd go all the way by him, but we want to get between those two people.

The fullback checks and runs that M pattern. Now this is weak side passing. At one point three or four years ago, it was the best passing in football, as I judge it. Since then a lot of people use it, and people have found ways to take it away from you.

On this pattern we tell our receiver that on hooking patterns you must go at least 12 yards and never more than 18 yards on the hook. Not because you can't get open, but because the quarterback can't wait that long to throw. A lot of it is predicated on pass rush. We say never less than 12, because we can't have a hook develop at 12 when our quarterback takes seven steps. If the receiver hooks, the quarterback can't throw him the ball yet. If the receiver is standing there waiting, sooner or later a defensive man will notice him over there and go over and stand next to him.

We don't come back to the ball unless it is halfway to us. Then we start coming back. Often when you tell the receiver to come back to the ball, it comes to him so hard it comes off his chest. We will go from him stationary to him as the outlet. That is damn tough to handle against a basic zone defense.

Diagram 10

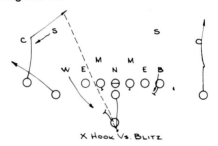

X HOOK VS. BLITZ

What happens on a blitz? The whole idea is to look for the blitz. One of the ways to take on a blitzing team is to use backfield motion. When you put the back in motion somebody has to cover him. If it's a linebacker, you're okay. They're not going to blitz you unless it's some kind of a special safety blitz. If it's the safety, you've got trouble. So we're sitting here and they are going to bring in people. Here they come. We go into motion—out of the middle he comes—we've got him. Our split end is sitting there looking at it. As soon as he sees that safety move, forward or laterally, he goes to the post.

The fullback picks up, of course, and we should have everybody picked up unless they fail to cover this man. So on a 79 X hook, our receivers hooking, he's beating a specific defensive man, but if everything's crowded down in there, he finds himself all alone standing out there. The motion starts, here comes the safety—we've got him beat.

20
The Air Option Offense

(From 1979 Proceedings of the AFCA)

HOMER RICE Head Coach, Rice University

Our offensive football philosophy is to develop the best of both worlds: a running game that attacks the defense and can control the ball when needed; and a passing game that exploits a wide-open attack that can also be utilized in catch-up tactics if needed. The blend comes out with the triple option as our running game and the pocket pass as our passing game.

Since we keep the ball in the air via the option pitch and/or the passing game with a variety of option keys, someone called our offense the "air option."

If a coach can perfect this combination, then he will dissect defenses to his advantage, becoming highly successful as an offensive unit. Naturally, talent is needed to execute any offense. In the air option, the quarterback must be an average runner with above-average ability as a passer.

In teaching football we strive to make the assignments as simple as possible in order to work primarily on technique. Thus, the simplicity of the offense enables this to be accomplished. We want security, but we are flexible in order to prepare adequately for any situation. The basic elements must be adhered to before we can add any flair, but our total thinking is simplicity with sound basic techniques.

Basic Formation

Our basic formation is the twin set with a split receiver.

Diagram 1

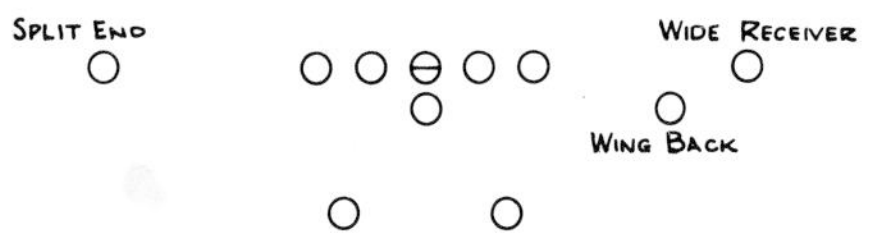

The spacing is highly important. Between the offensive linemen we split 1 yard or wider. Be certain you understand what a yard is—measure it. Most people do not adhere to this principle. We want our offensive linemen off the ball as much as the rule allows. This ties into our timing for both the running and passing game. It also aids in picking up stunts and allows the offensive linemen to block an inside gap charge without difficulty. The two running backs align directly behind the guards 4 yards deep.

Our wide receivers set one-third of the field from the ball, but are restricted by a boundary rule—never align any closer than 8 yards from the sideline. This is important in our passing game. The inside receiver or wingback sets 5 yards inside the wide receiver in the twin alignment.

Our team reports to the line of scrimmage in a prestance (the receivers are down ready to sprint off the line) because we snap the ball on a quick sound for our pocket passing game on many occasions.

After the quick sound we use a numbering system (26–26). If the numbers are live, that represents our audible calls. Going down, we then snap the ball on the first, second, third, or fourth sound. I believe the cadence should be an important phase of your operation. By varying the sounds and rhythm, you can keep the defensive charge from ever overpowering you. We number all our plays into double digits to simplify our audible and play calling. The formation, spacing, numbering, and cadence initiate the beginning of an exciting offense. Also, it is entertaining, which will create interest in selling tickets and which is very important in today's economy. We must be able to finance our programs.

We never execute the triple until we get it exactly

as we want it. Therefore, it is necessary to use our "check-with-me" audible system. We must first determine direction. This is determined by the alignment of the free safety. If he is in spot No. 1, we direct our attack toward the formation side.

Diagram 2

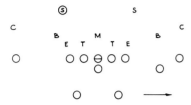

The nature of our wide-spaced formation permits our quarterback to easily identify the alignment of the free safety. Should the safety set in spot No. 3, then we will direct our plan away from formation toward the split end.

Diagram 3

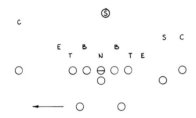

Some defenses play our two wide receivers tight man-for-man with the free safety backing them up deep.

When the free safety sets in the middle—spot No. 2—we can go either way. If the ball is on the hash mark, we favor going to the formation. When the ball moves toward the middle of the field, we favor the split end side.

Diagram 4

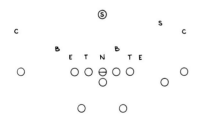

Once we determine direction we then ask our quarterback to decide upon either calling the triple or a designated pass to complement our intentions. Should the direction indicate formation side, we must count the defenders in the area. When the defense aligns three people in the twin area, we will call the triple.

Diagram 5

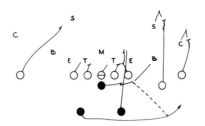

When only two defenders deploy into the twin area, we then call and execute a complementary pass.

Diagram 6

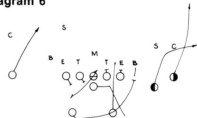

The "check-with-me" is a simple operation. The quarterback calls only the formation in the huddle and takes the team to the line. They do not have a play until he calls it on the line of scrimmage. This keeps everyone concentrating on the defensive alignment. Defensive recognition concentration plus superb technique will produce amazing results. Should the direction take us to the split end side, the quarterback will call the triple when two defenders play our split end. If only one defender covers our end, we will immediately call and execute a pass.

Our blocking scheme for the triple allows us to block areas rather than people. Versus an even front, we approach the handoff area with our center pivoting into the strong gap. Our strong guard blocks through the defender's outside leg and the strong tackle comes down on the linebacker. The quarterback handles the next defender with his "read."

Diagram 7

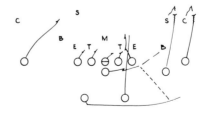

Should the "read" take the handoff, then the quarterback steps around the collision and sprints to the inside shoulder of the outside rush for the pitch or keep. The soft corner presents the quarterback with a true option picture. In the beginning we always instruct the option pitch. The keep and handoff then become reactions rather than concentration points.

The blocking scheme versus an odd front is similar to the even except that our tackle does not block down. The center and quick guard lead on the nose guard. The strong guard pivots toward the defensive tackle, with our strong tackle driving through the outside leg of the defensive tackle. If the defensive tackle steps out, our tackle will block him; our strong guard then picks up the linebacker. The ball will be handed off to the running back.

Diagram 8

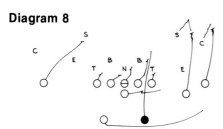

Should the tackle close, the strong guard picks him up with our tackle on the linebacker. The quarterback read will take the ball outside for the option on the soft corner.

Diagram 9

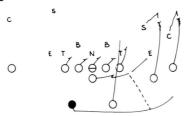

Establishing the triple necessitates our spending 75 percent of our practice time allotted to the running game and all the intricacies involved. We divide our practice time 50-50: 50 percent in passing and 50 percent in running. So you can readily realize we do not add many supplementary running plays to our offense. This keeps us less complicated. When you become diversified, you are spreading the offense too thin.

Technique and execution are more important to us. We have utilized a quick trap, the quick toss, an isolation, the counter option, and a quarterback sneak. As a change of pace we have employed the I set, particularly to expose a top running back from time to time.

The passing plan unfolds from the dropback or pocket concept. Again we work for simplicity. By injecting only a few pass routes, we can teach technique and execution. By reading coverages correctly and adding flexibility on the many ways to get the ball to the receivers, we create an awesome passing game.

The entire passing game success depends on tim-

ing. It starts with the quarterback. He must learn to set up just short of 10 yards deep in 1.7. He accomplishes this by sprinting back in seven steps. By dropping his right foot back on the snap, he is able to sprint back the required seven steps on time. This portion takes a lot of dedicated work by your quarterback.

The receivers learn three basic routes, although we become more sophisticated with several combinations later on. It is imperative that they learn the step counts to perform the basic technique.

The three basic routes stem from the release (four steps), the controlled area (three steps), and the stick (three steps). The quarterback starts his release on the seventh step, throwing to the receiver actually before he turns his head. This enables the receiver to catch the ball, put it under his arm, and turn and run before the defender can hit.

Diagram 10

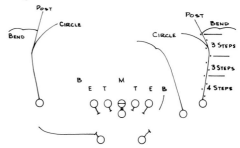

The two wide receivers run the same route called in the huddle, either the post, bend, or circle.

The key to the passing game is timing, protection, and reading the coverage. We again utilize the alignment of the free safety, as indicated in Diagrams 2, 3, and 4, to determine direction. Should our direction be the split end side, then it's a simple matter to drop back and hit our split receiver. This will change only in the event that the outside linebacker drops deep enough into the throwing lane. Should this occur, the quarterback dumps the ball out to the halfback. The halfback can release since the linebacker is his blocking assignment if he rushes.

Diagram 11

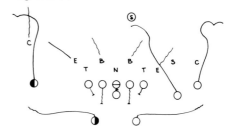

Should the free safety align in spot No. 1, then we direct our pass to the formation side. Now the quarterback must read the strong safety on the way back in the pocket to set because we have two receivers on the formation side and we cannot always determine the coverage. Should the strong safety stay with our inside receiver (wingback), we will go to the wide receiver because this indicates man (one-on-one) coverage. We then have the same situation as we had on the split end side, throwing to the wide receiver unless the outside linebacker drops deep into the throwing lane, whereby we can dump the ball to the halfback on that side.

Diagram 12

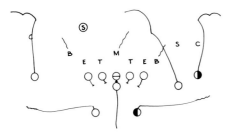

When the strong safety performs any other action—roll, invert, drop—we stay with the inside receiver (wingback) because this registers zone coverages. We are better off if we allow the wingback to work on the inside linebacker into open areas.

Once you are able to establish the basic plan with its techniques, you can lock in on one side or the other

with a variety of combinations. We work on the vulnerable areas, versus two-deep coverages with five or six defenders underneath.

Diagram 13

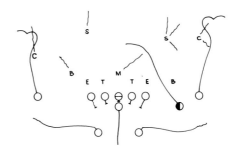

Diagram 14

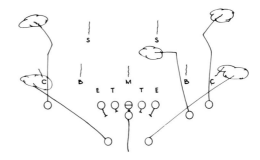

The combination of the triple-pocket combination is a stimulating experience. Your players will be exciting and it's a lot of fun to coach.

21
Practicing the Passing Game

(From 1979 Summer Manual of the AFCA)

DAVE CURREY Head Coach, California State University, Long Beach

One of the most important elements in a successful offense is to be known for something. California State University, Long Beach, has been ranked in the top ten and has been the number one passing team in the PCAA in 1978–1979. We believe in and are committed to throwing the football successfully. The number of passes thrown during a game is not so important as how effective you are in throwing them. You can win the big games by having the ability to throw the football.

To be an effective passing team, you must commit valuable time practicing it. This requires approximately 50 percent of your practice time. The ability to pass must coincide with keeping the opponent off balance. To some degree, therefore, we pass on running downs and run on passing downs.

There are a number of important characteristics that are brought about because of the forward pass. Enthusiasm, motivation, discipline, concentration, purpose, commitment, fundamentals, poise, and so on, all play a part toward the ultimate common goal of winning. We utilize these characteristics in practicing our passing game. Each practice session and each particular drill is implemented with the preceding characteristics and all aid in helping us improve as a total team.

Early Group

A typical practice day starts with a daily 10-minute warmup. This includes all of our receiving corps (quarterbacks, receivers, backs, and tight ends). At

---

PRACTICE PLAN

Period	Time	
Early Group	2:30	
Prepractice	2:45	On line drill
Period 1	3:00	Hookup drill
Period 2	3:15	Teaching, seven-on-seven (linemen working on blitzes)
Period 3	3:30	Competitive seven-on-seven versus varsity secondary (linemen working on pass protection)
Period 4	3:45	Team passing versus defensive scouts
Period 5	4:00	Team run versus defensive scouts (open field)
Period 6	4:15	Team run versus defensive scouts (short yardage and goal line)
Period 7	4:30	Kicking phase
Period 8	4:45	Team conditioning—extra emphasis

NOTE: As seen above, a minimum of 50 percent of the time is spent on some facet of the forward pass. This is essential in order to be able to have a successful passing attack. Ultimately, this should enhance the success of your total offense.

this time, we emphasize hand selection, concentration, hand-and-eye coordination, throwing to a target, follow-through, etc. This is an important coaching time. Coaches should make sure everything done in this period is a game-like drill. The attitude and acceptance of this warmup time has a lot to do with how your remaining day's practice is going to be.

Diagram 1

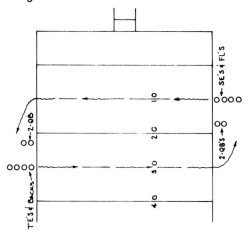

Prepractice

Prepractice begins with all the receiving corps going through the on-the-line drill. (See Diagram 1.) Two quarterbacks stand on one sideline with split ends and flankers. Two other quarterbacks stand across the field, on the other sideline, with the tight ends and backs. The quarterback calls the cadence, takes three steps, and sets. He allows a receiver to cover at least 5 yards before he releases the ball over his head. The receiver should run directly on the line. (This is a good time to observe receiver running form.) The ball should drop down over the receiver's inside shoulder.

Coaching points here are to stress drifting to the ball, never turning the hips, and always keeping the ball to the receiver's inside shoulder. Once the ball arrives, drift to it, catch it, look it into the hands, tuck it away, and continue running to the other side of the field. Keep a constant stride and try to make a smooth reception. The quarterbacks can progress with the drill, allowing receivers to run 20 and 30 yards before releasing the ball. This is an excellent time to observe a quarterback's release and follow-through. Also, receiver's running form, hand selection, and concentration should be stressed. The purpose of this drill is to teach good throwing form, running form, and skill of drifting to and catching the football.

Hookup Drill

The hookup period stresses fundamentals. (See Diagram 2.) We usually spend fifteen minutes a day

Diagram 2

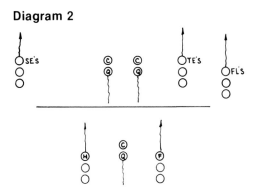

on hookup versus air. Emphasis is on correct footwork of routes, depth of patterns, hand selection, and execution. No ball should ever be dropped during this period. It must be done every day with strong coaching emphasis on having success in throwing and catching the ball. This is also a good time to teach new patterns and discipline route running. We never get enough hookup work. Quarterbacks can switch from day-to-day, throwing to backs and receivers. Sometimes the tight ends can go with the backs for hookup. The best and simplest way to teach a person how to gain confidence in catching the football is to throw it to him time after time. For every pass caught in a game, our receivers must catch one hundred during practice that week. The purpose of the hookup drill is to build confidence.

Teaching Seven-on-Seven

This is a key time to introduce opponents' coverages and concepts. This is a very important explanation time. Receivers and quarterbacks must understand what the defense is trying to do. The "why" is as important as "what." A well-organized scout secondary is necessary for proper teaching. It is important that the scout secondary know the opponents' coverages before this drill starts. During the drill, we introduce game plans and explain new patterns. Full-speed tempo of this drill is not important. Teaching and understanding what is necessary is. This drill should be highly organized in order to eliminate a lot of standing around. The purpose of this drill is to teach concepts and opponents' coverages.

Diagram 3

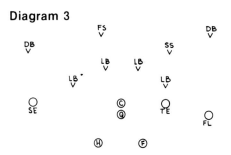

Competitive Seven-on-Seven

Fifteen minutes is minimum for competitive seven-on-seven. Sometimes we take 5 minutes off our teaching seven-on-seven and make this a 20-minute drill. It is important for your best athletes to practice against each other. We put one against one here and make it highly competitive. The defense may not exactly see what the opponent runs; however, full-speed reaction toward any pass play helps one improve. You only improve when you work full speed against good people.

During this drill, we run our base patterns. This drill will help both your offensive and defensive groups improve. At certain times you may want to use your good receivers to run some of your opponents' patterns. This will allow you to service your defense. Seven-on-seven must be a competitive time. We expect both sides to be going full speed at the ball. This is probably the best drill for a successful pass offense. Repetition is most important.

A changeup to make it even more competitive is to move the ball up and down the field. Another changeup idea is to bring the linemen down and make it an eleven-on-eleven pass scrimmage with no tackling. Do not touch the quarterback in this drill. The purpose of the seven-on-seven drill is to improve pass offense, as well as defensive secondary coverage. The key is to make the drill highly competitive.

Team Pass versus Defensive Scouts

After a seven-on-seven, usually there is a dropoff in practice tempo. For this reason, we move into a team pass versus defensive scouts drill. The scout team is the key here. Getting your scouts cranked up about giving a good pass rush is important. This is the time to incorporate screens and draws. Screens and draws require so much timing that you must get a full speed and no tackling defensive picture.

This period is also a good time to work on game-like situations. Play selection versus different defenses is important, and working against your opponents' defensive picture is essential. This is a time you can develop your passing game around the entire offensive team. This drill can be designed to teach offensive consistency with good tempo. Timing and execution are key areas of concentration. The purpose of this drill is to take a part of your offensive game plan and practice it against your opponents' defense.

Remainder of Practice Plan

The remainder of the practice includes working on the running game and kicking phases. At all times,

consistency and a balanced run and pass offense are our goals. In order for us to be able to run the ball effectively, we must be able to pass. This is why so much time is needed to prepare for the passing game.

The success of the passing game is evaluated in the percentage of completions, the amount of yardage per pass play called, amount of yardage per pass play completed, yards gained after the ball is caught, ability to control the game with the passing game, protection, interceptions, and bad plays resulting from the passing game. It is important you practice all phases so that proper execution can come from learned habits.

Other areas of concentration for passing efficiency are goal line routes and long yardage passes. These must be incorporated into your practice plan throughout the week. Also, one-on-one drills with defensive backs allow receivers to learn to get open with man-to-man coverage. This is especially important in building confidence with your receiving corps.

So many of us like to throw, but so few are committed to spending the time necessary to perfect it. If you want to have a successful pass offense, you must allow the necessary time to practice it.

Defense still wins the majority of ball games. The stronger you are on defense, the more chances you may take on offense. The forward pass is considered a high risk. You eliminate the percentage of the risk by practicing. Six factors must be considered in utilizing the time to practice throwing the football.

1. The forward pass is a great equalizer and it will allow you at some time to defeat a superior team—it allows you a weapon to win the big game.

2. Players enjoy throwing and catching the football. It is fun and entertaining. It is a tremendous recruiting tool. Athletes love to throw and catch. They look for programs that excel at it. You can recruit skilled people if you can convince them that you throw and catch effectively. Linemen are also attracted because they will learn how to pass protect. If a lineman can pass protect, then his chances of professional football are enhanced.

3. The forward pass allows you total utilization of the field. A drop-back passing game gives you more holes to throw into. It is fun to coach and enjoyable to the players. It gives you full rein for attacking from anywhere on the field and having the possibility of scoring at any time.

4. It is not the number of times you throw, but the fact that sooner or later you will have to throw. It is not how many times your opponent is concerned about your throwing. Throwing enough times to win and being able to throw successfully will enhance your ability to win.

5. At some time you will need a two-minute catch-up offense. The ability to drop back and throw

the football gives you a built-in catch-up offense. You are practicing it all the time, and sooner or later, you will need it. A catch-up two-minute offense is ideal with a successful passing game.

6. Because of the reputation of throwing the football, your opponents will try to incorporate a strong pass rush. The emphasis on pass rush will enhance your running game. Pass rush lanes are important. This usually creates standardized fronts, thus giving the running game an advantage. The greater the threat of a pass, the greater the opportunity for successful running plays.

Most successful teams are well balanced. The balance is evident on both sides of the football. Defense, kicking, and offense are all important to winning programs.

The passing game is by no means the sole answer to success. Knowing when to pass and recognizing what is happening is more important than the pass itself. The forward pass has its appropriate place with philosophy and personnel. Most important is that whatever you do, practice it.

22

Pass Protection, Screens, and Draws

(From *1977 Summer Manual* of the AFCA)

HOMER SMITH Head Football Coach, U.S. Military Academy

Pass Protection

Our offensive staff, led by Bruce Tarbox, believes that protection assignments for all of our pass plays can and should begin with one system for identifying defenders and, further, that assignments for screen passes and draw runs can begin with the same system.

An onside and an offside are established by the number-name of the play. The center is considered a part of the offside unit and a defender over him is an offside target. The offside targets are not counted but are grouped as a picture of four potential rushers. The onside targets are counted one, two, three, four with the guard and tackle assigned to No. 1 and No. 2. Diagram 1 shows four defenses with offside targets blackened and onside numbered.

What is different from conventional pass protection systems? The application of one identification system to all passes and the concept of grouping offside defenders into a picture are different. We keep the two-receiver side as the onside on all drop-back passes, believing that it is difficult to rush four defenders over the onside, but not over the offside, and wanting solid protection where the biggest rush problem exists. This is different, as is our system for varying assignments, to get either more or fewer blockers or to change targets by using code words than can be communicated by the quarterback.

Basically, the onside is the side of the play. With our drop-back passes, however, the onside is always the two-receiver side. It is a simple matter to get a primary receiver identified. By having the two-receiver side as the onside, we keep four potential blockers on the side where there is the greatest chance of facing four rushers. If a fourth man rushes on the two-receiver side, it is much easier to make him pay a price because the tight end can catch a short pass behind the rush.

Diagram 1

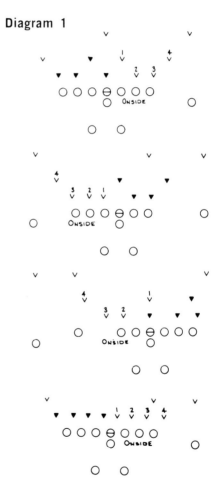

Diagram 2 shows four-man rushes to each side, with the offside rush being blocked and the onside beaten by the pass pattern. The backs find it helpful to know that on the one-receiver side, when they are needed as a complementary receiver, they are always assigned to the outside defender in the grouping. This

Diagram 2

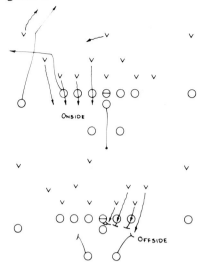

defender is least likely to rush, so we can have our cake and eat it too.

Blocking techniques vary with the type of pass being thrown, of course. Diagram 3 shows three plays when the right guard is on the onside and is assigned to No. 1, but where three different blocking techniques could be employed.

Diagram 3

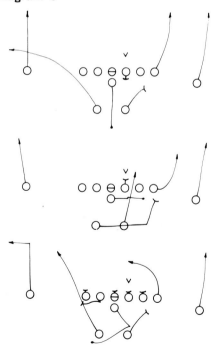

The drop-back problem is simple. Referring to the second play in Diagram 3, with the back faking outside of the guard, somewhat more aggressiveness can be applied. Referring to the third play, the guard is asked to protect an onside and then allow for bootleg

movement toward the offside. Sorting out No. 1 as the target is just a start for a guard, as the diagram shows.

Varying Assignments

With the one system for identifying onside and offside defenders established, it is not confusing to learn a short list of variations. Each variation has a code-word name and is defined simply and positively in terms of exactly what a blocker or a group of blockers does.

1. *Uncovered.* When we want to handle the four-man rushing threats on the offside with just three blockers, we call for either uncovered or hinge blocking. With uncovered blocking specified, the center, offside guard, and offside tackle watch the four defenders and block the three who rush. The man with the linebacker over him checks the linebacker and, if he does not rush, steps out to take the defensive end. (See Diagram 4.)

Diagram 4

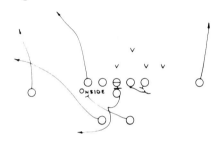

2. *Hinge.* The center, offside guard, and offside tackle watch the four defenders and swing or hinge out to take the three who rush. Both men must watch the linebacker, because, if he rushes, they cannot hinge. (See Diagram 5.)

Diagram 5

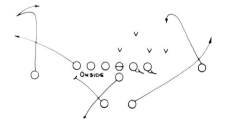

3. *Mike.* The offside tight end blocks the outside man in the four-man rushing threat. Mike is implied in many plays. (See Diagram 6.)

4. *Sierra.* The offside back does what the offside end does in Mike—he blocks the outside man in the four-man rushing threat. This is usually called in the huddle, but it can be implied in a play. (See Diagram 7.)

Diagram 6

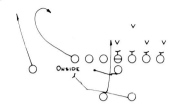

Diagram 7

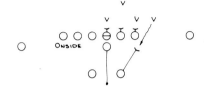

5. *Big-on-Big.* When assigning a back to the end man on the line, Sierra protection would have him blocking a big lineman while one of his own big linemen checks a linebacker. The solution is to call for big man to block big man. (See Diagram 8.)

Diagram 8

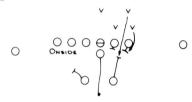

6. *Alpha.* When a back can be used to block a linebacker over the center or over an onside lineman, the blockers to the offside of that linebacker can block away. This obviously enables us to get four blockers on the offside four-man rushing threat while releasing the offside tight end. (See Diagram 9.)

Diagram 9

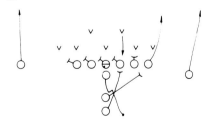

Calls 1 to 6 involve the offside. Following are those that involve the onside:

7. *Romeo.* All blockers think of reaching toward the onside to stop a fourth defender who rushes over the onside three blockers. (This is a skimpy explanation of an assignment that requires combo blocking technique to deny penetration.) This cannot be used with uncovered or hinge protection. (See Diagram 10.)

Diagram 10

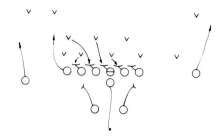

8. *Down.* The tight end on the onside blocks to his inside because a fourth defender threatens to rush to the inside. This is used when Romeo protection cannot be used because only three blockers are available on the offside. (See Diagram 11.)

Diagram 11

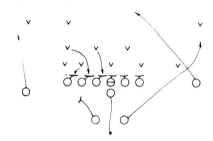

9. *Shoulders.* This can be a call or an assumption. Throughout pass protection, linemen close their shoulders while they wait to see which defender comes to the inside and which to the outside. The shoulders technique gets its toughest tests in the defensive maneuvers shown. (See Diagram 12.)

Diagram 12

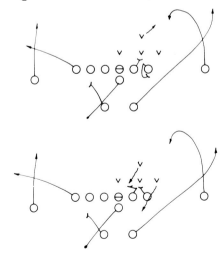

10. *Check.* An onside lineman with a linebacker on him checks to make sure the linebacker is not rushing and then helps another lineman. (See Diagram 13.)

11. *Area.* There are two defenders outside of an offender. He takes the one who threatens the play. The word means exactly what it does in running offense. (See Diagram 14.)

Diagram 13

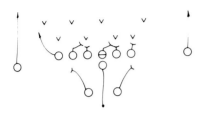

Diagram 14

12. *Rush.* A fourth defender is rushing from the outside on the onside. It implies that the pass pattern must beat the extra man. (See Diagram 15.)

Diagram 15

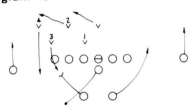

13. *Blitz.* A defensive back is an extra man in the inside rush. Blitz means to stop the blitzer by blocking toward the inside and to make any unblocked man come from the outside. (See Diagram 16.)

Diagram 16

This is a lot of words. If we did not standardize words for use in this way, however, we would have to use sentences and paragraphs to explain what inevitably must be done in pass protection. The descriptive words listed can be used in huddle calls, in line of scrimmage communications, or in simply discussing plays and defenses.

Visioning

The key to pass protection is vision. A blocker must find the man to whom he is assigned, look for cross charge or linebacker run-through possibilities, communicate with other blockers if necessary, and use his eyes. Most pass protection failures are a result of poor visioning.

When defenders attempt to surprise blockers, they must hold relative positions in the blocking front. Assignments are area assignments for purposes of picking up cross charges and linebacker run-throughs. Blockers close shoulder pads to deny penetration and then block the defenders who rush on their respective sides. Four examples are shown in Diagram 17.

Diagram 17

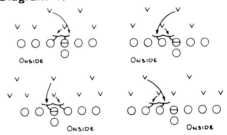

Special Problems

The overshifted seven-man fronts present special problems. We do not want to recount the outside defenders because inside defenders jump one way or another. Our solution is to block standard and overshifted defenses the same, helping ourselves with Romeo and gap calls where possible. Diagram 18 shows two problems and our blocking solutions.

The eight-man front that threatens four rushers over three onside blockers requires the Romeo call or, on passes that require hinge or uncovered blocking on the offside, a gap call. The diagram shows both calls with plays that require them.

Diagram 18

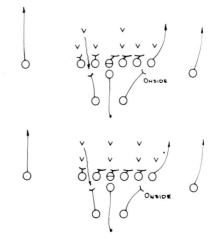

A No. 3 lined up over the tackle calls for big-on-big blocking. The man assigned to 3 watches both linebackers and takes the most dangerous. A Romeo or gap call is a possibility.

Launch Points

There are essentially six spots from which the ball will be launched. We have more than six pass actions, but for purposes of blocking, just the six points need to be defined. Passes that fake option plays are thrown close to the line of scrimmage, approximately behind a tackle. Halfback passes and sprint outs are thrown well outside of the blockers. When we fake run action and then move to a side, the movement of the quarterback is delayed. This needs to be distinguished from the action where the quarterback moves away from the center, showing pass. Bootleg passes move the quarterback to a side but with extreme delay. Drop backs and certain play actions leave the quarterback directly behind the center. Diagram 19 shows the six launch points.

Diagram 19

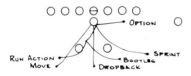

Screens

Screens, like draws, require more than the learning of assignments. The following material is essentially what we require players to understand. As with most aspects of football, an understanding is like a good computer program that is ready to fit and relate any information it receives.

A screen is first a pass. A pass play is called, an action is protected, and a pattern is run. Everything that is done in pass protection blocking against a defense is done in a screen play, because it is first an actual pass play. At a point, the screen blocking unit—both guards and the center—breaks off to the outside, and the pattern runners wheel around to block for a play that is trying to get to the outside. Blockers start after 2 seconds, after two quick but good pass protection blows, then break off together with the first man pulling the other two. (I have used the names Huey, Dewey, and Louie as an example of men in good formation for screen blocking.) Moving, waiting for a "go" call from the receiver, starting downfield with proper timing, obeying rules that say that you cannot block downfield until the ball is in the air—these things are not difficult to do. For the receiver, sneaking out without giving the play away is difficult, but

it can be learned. The problem is to stop a rusher completely with one blow and then to fake losing him.

What is really difficult about a screen is calling it properly while having an accurate prediction of defensive vulnerability. It needs a space between rushers and defenders. How many defenders rush and drop off is not primarily important. It is how they rush and drop and how much space is created. We search for the space in scouting and during game action. The diagrams show one defensive end going with a receiver and another holding a shallow position waiting counter action. Is there a space to set up a screen? Everyone can help determine whether or not there is.

Diagram 20

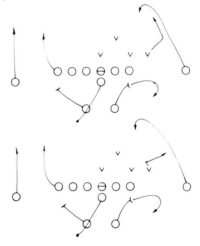

What is next most difficult is getting the ball exchanged. The quarterback's enacting of the pass play must pull rushers; the blocking by those who break off must leave no hint of a screen. The blockers in moving down the line must look—in order of their places in line—to the outside, straight ahead and to the inside. They are protecting a reception point not unlike how pass blockers protect a passer's launch point. Nothing can come between them, the receiver is behind them—unless there are more than four defenders collapsing on the reception point, the ball exchange should be made. Diagram 21 shows the most common blocking problems.

After experiencing dozens of screen plays, scouting an opponent, practicing, and visioning the defense before the snap, a screen blocking unit will be as confident as a pass protection unit.

Blocks by the downfield receivers should be aimed high because they cannot be certain where the ball carrier will go, and they should be executed with speed. Get to a defender by the shortest route and in the fastest way! The three-man unit, on hearing "go," sprints out, looking to the outside, straight ahead, and to the inside. Blocks are high. Everyone, including the ball carrier, tries to get the ball to the outside.

Diagram 21

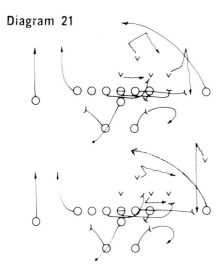

Diagram 22

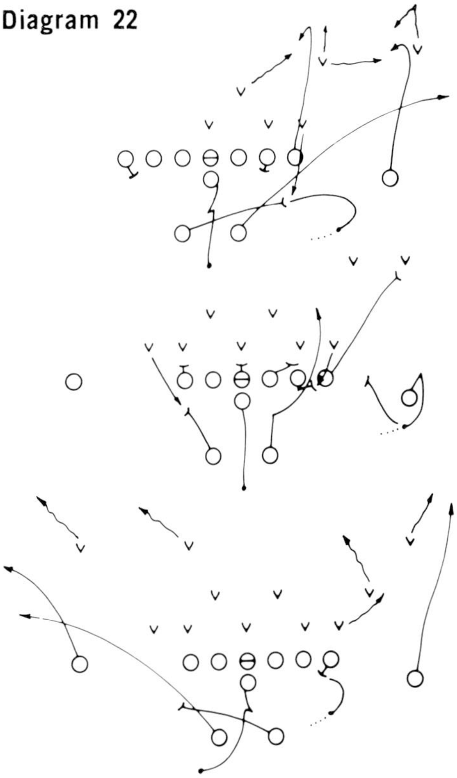

With these points ringing in their ears, players should be able to coach themselves on screen plays. As on the draws, they are asked to coach themselves as a way of demonstrating the potential in mastery and self-correcting. The only situation in which they do not have a chance to execute the screen is the one where a defender gets between the passer and the receiver, smells screen, and backs off into the play. When this happens, the discipline is not going downfield before the "go" call is practiced as is the quarterback's discipline in preventing lost yardage. The quarterback is making decisions from the time he says "hut"—he can make a regular pass play out of it, he can execute the screen, he can throw the ball away or run a quarterback draw, he can use the back not involved in the screen as a target, he can do something before he gets thrown for a loss. Examples of three more screens are shown in Diagram 22.

Draws

Like screens, draws lend themselves to understanding more than to the memorizing of assignments. The idea is to fake as much pass as possible to get the rushers rushing and the pass droppers dropping! In assignments, the blocking is exactly the same as it is in pass plays—onside/offside. In execution, the blocking is different in that we never want two linemen teamed on one defender. We will always have a blocker for each of seven targets—four on the offside and three on the onside. Understanding this paragraph will take care of many of the questions that players ordinarily have about our draw plays.

Next, points of attack, blocking timing, and blocking technique. The blocker at the point of attack takes a man over him either way or takes a man in the gap to the inside. Other blockers keep their men away from the point of attack, if they can, but, if they can-

not, they keep them covered. Turn a defender away from the point or keep him covered. Whether he is a lineman or a linebacker, turn him away from the point or keep him covered. Points of attack are shown in Diagram 23.

Diagram 23

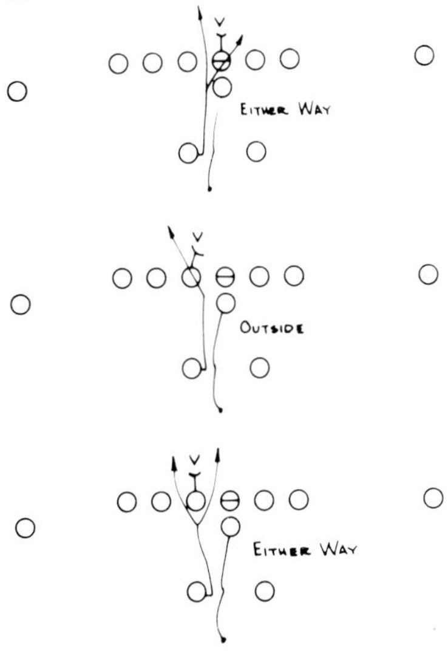

Against the split linebacker look, a call must be made to get either the guard or the tackle stepping around. (See Diagram 24.)

Step-around blocking should be used freely because it results in better protection of the point of at-

Diagram 24

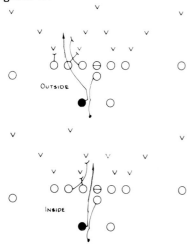

tack against pinching and in better timing of blocks on linebackers. Technique is dictated by knowledge of where the ball is going and the feeling of when it will arrive at the points where blocks are being executed. Our square block tells the blocker and the runner that the ball can go either way. Because the play is slow hitting, a square block should never spill a defender to a side. Other blocks used are the standard gap and wall, the shoulder with timing on either a lineman or a linebacker, and area, where there is a cross charge possibility from the perimeter.

The play can be run from split backs or I backs. With split backs, in order to have seven blockers, the tight receiver must block on the onside; with I backs, the fullback will block the third man. On the offside, with split backs, there is a back to serve as the fourth blocker; with the I, there must be a tight receiver. The diagrams make these points. The key is to remember that we want seven blockers—three onside, four offside.

Diagram 25

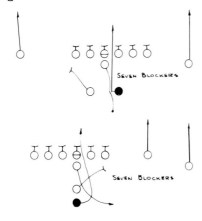

Next, assignments for the two receivers not involved in the seven-man blocking unit. A spread man

does not attempt to block. He is run outside of the man on him and deep, taking advantage of a chance to threaten the defender deep. An offside tight receiver (from a split formation) influences the inside linebacker and blocks the safety.

Diagram 26

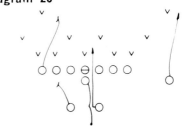

An onside tight receiver (from an I formation) influences the inside linebacker and then helps all that he can. Diagram 27 shows him blocking No. 4 against normal rotation and the inside safety against outside rotation.

When it is not clear who is to block whom, the players are to think pass protection. Problems are solved in the same way. The subsection Special Problems under Pass Protection on page 105 applies to the

Diagram 27

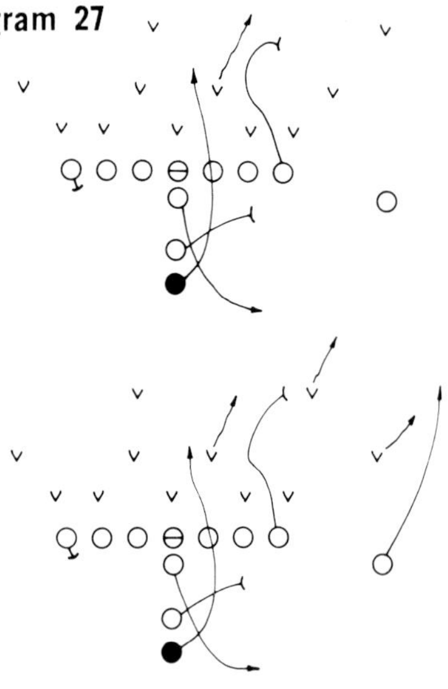

draw plays. The draw is blocked like a pass; the same seven defenders must be stopped; if eight defenders rush, the same man is left unblocked.

Summary

The simplification of having just the one system for identifying defenders in no way restricts us. Pass protection, screens, and draws work because players understand what is going on around them. Having the one system is a steadying factor, a solid foundation upon which to learn.

23
Attacking Zone Coverages

(From 1975 Proceedings of the AFCA)

ROGER THEDER Assistant Coach, University of California

There are a variety of ways to prepare your quarterback on the field through the various drills many of us use. We have selected a few basic drills to get a quarterback ready and have a progression we use. Our system is to:

1. Teach the two-, five-, and seven-step drop.
2. Time the two-, five-, and seven-step drop and throw.
3. Teach the hot receiver principle with an executed blitz and throw.
4. Throw individual patterns.
5. Teach flare control with one underneath linebacker.
6. Work a strongside drill.
7. Execute our seven-on-seven drill.
8. Pass scrimmage.

We have now become such strong believers in teaching this zone principle of flare-flood control that once the fundamentals are taught we immediately go to this three-on-two attack.

The quarterback and receivers must understand that we are placing three quick receivers in two zones to outnumber the defense and allow us to be successful. The pattern number is immaterial, but the flood idea is now executed.

Diagram 1

Drop Drill

In attacking the five-under defense we have found that the outside flat zone is the area most changeable. Because of this our quarterback begins the attack in the hook zone, where the pass can more easily be thrown. The lead shortside underneath pattern is the in. The shortside hook area will now be exploited with the split end and fullback and the flat zone controlled with the running back.

Diagram 2

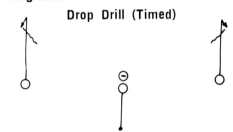

Drop Drill (Timed)

Diagram 3

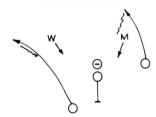

Hot Receiver

Diagram 4

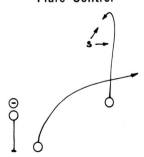

Flare Control

Diagram 5

Strong and Short Side

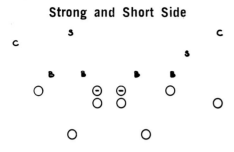

Diagram 6

7 on 7

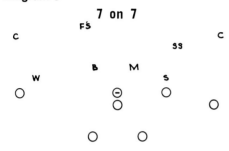

Diagram 7

Pass Scrimmage

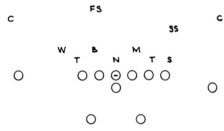

Diagram 8

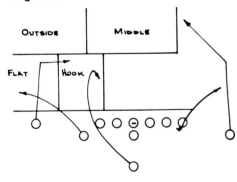

A receiver is now placed in the deep alley and a back in the short alley on the isolated linebacker. This package forces the linebacker to make his decision, and he is also affected as the near back comes out. We hope to create movement to open the lane or cause the linebacker to stop his drop, thus opening the split end as the primary receiver.

This package handles the blitz or the zone concept as the fullback must be alert should his blocking assignment be blitzing.

We have the mirrored play to the strong side through the use of our tight end, flanker, and fullback. The weak side flood has been the most effective because of the drop of the strong linebackers who have a tendency to favor the tight end side.

The hook area may also be exploited through the flood attack where the outside linebacker is isolated in this zone. In this package, the quarterback should throw the out should it be uncovered because of coverage and alignment.

Diagram 9

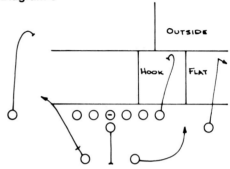

If in the five short zone coverage the ball will be thrown to the tight end or fullback based on linebacker drop and angle. We do not feel you will ever put two defenders in this hook area.

As in the in package, we have the mirror of this pattern to the short side. Before showing how to attack the flat underneath zone, let me get into our principle of attacking the three-deep zones. When confronted with the three-deep coverage, this deep area will not be our primary area of attack. Most teams tend to show a high percentage of the two-deep coverage, and now the lead pass is our double streak or double Z.

Diagram 10

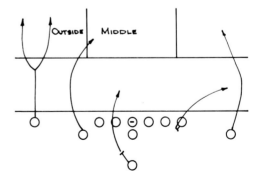

The deep flood idea is to place two receivers in these two deep zones covered by one defender. The primary attack is the drop back, but the sprint-out is an excellent way to beat this coverage. Often a formation variation or motion will dictate a coverage and help the quarterback's initial read. Pressure is now on the safety to make a decision and favor the wide receiver or running back. Should the underneath coverage get deep enough to be a factor, the fullback delay is built in and the fullback will catch the ball in the short alley moving upfield.

When confronted with the three-deep zones covered, the tight end is coached to hook up, and now the flare-flood package once again is effected in the hook area. As mentioned, the toughest area to predict is the flat zone, yet teams become very consistent with their corner play as a game progresses. Immediate pressure must be placed on the flat coverage man through the bench pattern or sprint corner pattern. In the bench pattern the talents of our wide receiver and fullback are used. This pattern is most effective when attacking the 5 under 2 deep defense.

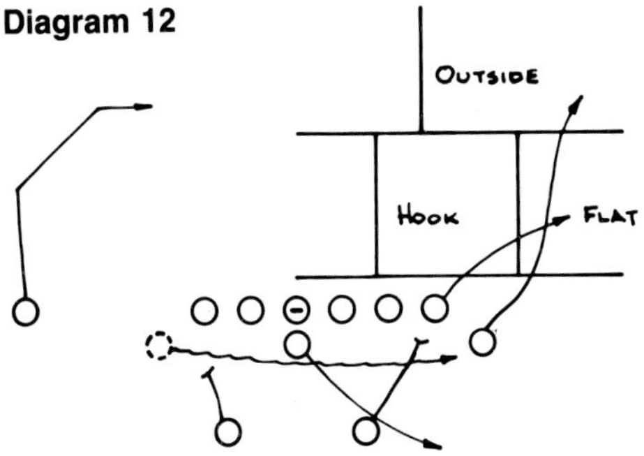

In each of these patterns the flat coverage defender must make an immediate decision, and the quarterback can determine the primary receiver and throw the completion.

The final package is the very effective sprint-out series. In this package the quarterback is given all the weapons to make correct decisions based on coverage and the application of the flare-flood attack.

Diagram 13

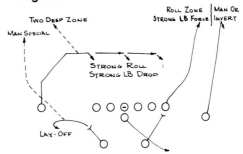

The strong feeling here is that in this package the defense will dictate the primary immediately or the quarterback decision will be made after the snap. Here the entire field is attacked and the backside becomes our flare-flood combination. The number one choice is the strong side out to our flanker. Secondly, the tight end is our primary if coverage doubles on the flanker out pattern and only a hook coverage defender can take this pattern away.

Should the quarterback be forced to come to the backside, it would only happen because the defense overmoved the underneath zone and placed more than one defender in the middle, hook, or strong flat zones. The split end in pattern and running back hook becomes the primary. This one package was probably our most successful and consistent gainer in 1974. There are a variety of combinations of this strong sprint-out attack to keep the defense off balance.

Diagram 11

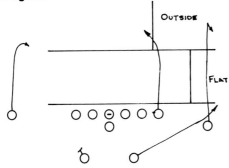

Diagram 12

24
Maryland Quarterbacks Sprint-Out

(From 1979 Summer Manual of the AFCA)

JERRY EISAMAN Assistant Coach, University of Maryland

The sprint-out pass is an integral part of the Maryland multiple I offense. We try to average 5 yards every time we call the sprint-out pass.

Blessed with some fine quarterbacks over the years, for example, Bob Avellini (Chicago Bears), Mark Manges (St. Louis Cardinals), Larry Dick (Saskatchewan Roughriders), and others of lesser ability, we have consistently maintained 5 yards per call with our sprint-out pass. The point being made is that the sprint-out pass has been successful despite the fact that our quarterbacks have possessed different types of ability; some had running ability and others did not. So, fundamentally, because of its proven success and consistency, the Maryland sprint-out has become a vital play in our offense.

In teaching the sprint-out pass we begin with our quarterbacks and centers on a straight line 5 yards apart. We use the following steps of progression: First, on the snap from center, the quarterback instantly turns his head and eyes in the direction of the sprint-out. His weight is on the ball of the left foot before the snap when sprinting right; when sprinting left, the weight is on the ball of the right foot. This weight distribution is the fastest way to get the quarterback away from the line of scrimmage. Next, the quarterback's first step is straight backward, away from the line of scrimmage. Third, the quarterback must sprint to a depth of 5 to 7 yards; he must quickly get width and depth.

Diagram 1

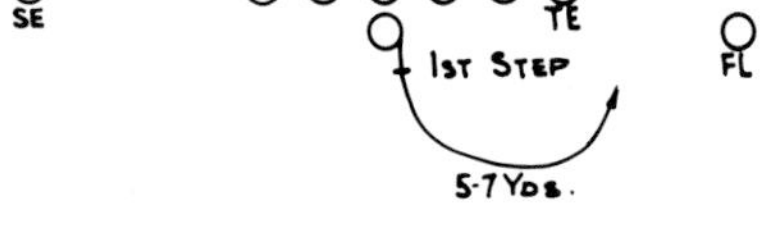

We have our tight end release outside at a 45-degree angle. The quarterback and tight end read the strong safety.

Diagram 2

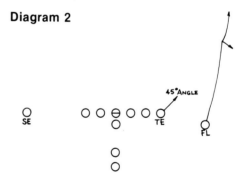

Our flankerback's alignment is a good stretch (distance) from the tight end, in order to stretch the distance between the tight end and the flankerback. Of course, this varies according to whether the ball is placed on, or near, the hash marks. The flankerback never gets closer than 5 yards from the sideline.

The flankerback releases downfield at full speed trying to make a defender in the secondary cover the deep outside one-third. If the flankerback sees he cannot get open in the deep outside one-third, he immediately executes a sideline cut at approximately 12 yards deep, working back to the sideline.

Each receiver has certain reads, which tell him what pass pattern to run. If the quarterback can run, we tell him to put pressure on the line of scrimmage and exploit the threat of the run. If the quarterback does not have the run threat, we tell him to read his keys, to pull up when he gets his width and depth, and then to throw the ball to the open receiver. When the quarterback does not have running ability, oftentimes he is pulled up on the sprint-out. Because of this, we have our offside or back receiver (split end) away from the direction we are sprinting. He releases downfield to a depth of 14 to 16 yards and then drifts across, trying to get in an open passing lane or hole where the quarterback can find him. If the split end is covered, the quarterback should tuck the ball under his arm, run back to a split in the backside defense, and gain as much yardage as possible. (See Diagram 3.)

Diagram 3

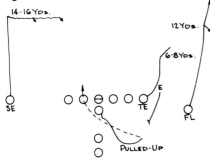

When the quarterbacks and receivers know their pass patterns, we try to put the sprint-out pass together and break down the defensive coverage. On the snap from center, all receivers release from the line of scrimmage. As the quarterback comes from center, he reads the strong safety. If the strong safety is blitzing, the quarterback will dump the ball on his third step, to the tight end, who is releasing outside at a 45-degree angle and who also is reading the strong safety. The tight end, upon releasing and reading the strong safety's blitz, will turn out immediately and look for the ball. (See Diagram 4.)

This is how we handle the blitz from the outside, which is the first type of defensive coverage that might be encountered.

If no blitz occurs from the strong safety, the tight end will not turn out but will continue at a 45-degree angle in the seam, continually reading the strong safety. If the strong safety goes to the flat or to the deep outside (rolling up the defense), the tight end will look over his outside shoulder at a depth of approximately 6 to 8 yards from the line of scrimmage, where he will receive the ball. The quarterback should have his

Diagram 4

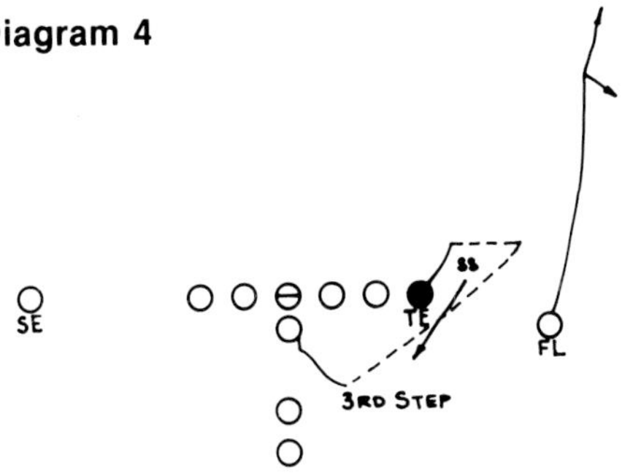

width and depth and should have sprinted into the approximate area where the tight end originally lined up on the line of scrimmage.

We tell our quarterback that this is the area we want him to be in when he passes the ball to the tight end. (See Diagram 5.)

Diagram 5

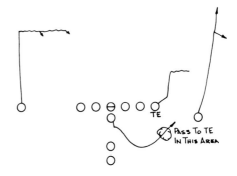

If the quarterback cannot get the ball to the tight end, we tell him to forget the tight end and to put pressure on the line of scrimmage with the run threat. As he approaches the line of scrimmage, the quarterback looks for the flankerback and decides whether he can get the ball to the flankerback on the deep pattern. If not, he tries to hit the flankerback on the sideline cut before he (the quarterback) crosses the line of scrimmage. If there is any doubt, the quarterback puts the ball under his arm and gets as much yardage as he can run for.

Another type of defensive coverage we often encounter is the "pure man across," which covers each receiver as tight as possible. As we read this coverage, the tight end will continue straight down the field taking the strong safety with him. Also, our flankerback will continue straight downfield, deep, taking the outside corner with him. When the quarterback and receivers read this type of coverage, they immediately know that the quarterback will run with the ball. As soon as the quarterback reads "pure man," he will yell "block," and all deep receivers will try to get into position to block the deep secondary people. All linemen will release their blocks on the line of scrimmage and will sprint downfield in the direction of the sprint-out to get a block, or they will be alert for a cutback from the quarterback. The linemen do this immediately when they hear the quarterback yell "block."

We really like to sprint out toward our formation. That's where the tight end and the flankerback line up. This causes the defense to overshift to that side. These overshifted defenses usually are rotated from the secondary to cover the formation side. Frequently, also, linebackers will slide over to our formation side. When this occurs, we will sprint out away from our formation side, that is, away from our tight end and flankerback. Now, we will be sprinting out to our split end.

The split end will usually be covered one-on-one. The quarterback will sprint out in the same manner as we described earlier. Now, however, he will concentrate on the split end beating the cornerback. The split end has an option route to beat the cornerback deep. If he has a "cushion" and cannot beat the cornerback deep, he will do a "sideline" at approximately 12 yards deep. He will then work back to the sideline. The quarterback will read him low to the outside and the split end should catch the ball for approximately a 10-yard gain.

When we sprint out away from our formation side, we sometimes encounter double coverage on our split end. (See Diagram 6.) This is usually a defensive

Diagram 6

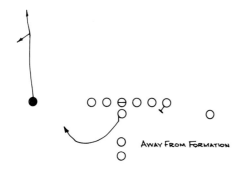

Away From Formation

end dropped off from the line of scrimmage, or a linebacker. As the quarterback sprints out toward the split end, he must read the defensive end or the linebacker and must make the decision to run or throw, depending on the depth of the end or linebacker. If the end or linebacker takes the sideline away, and the cornerback takes the deep outside away, then the quarterback should elect to run. This should result in a 5-yard gain, or more.

When a quarterback has the running ability of a Mark Manges, the sprint-out pass can be called from anywhere on the field and in practically any down-and-distance situation. One further suggestion offered from our experience with the sprint-out pass concerns the speed of the quarterback. If a quarterback does not have the speed or running ability to capture the line of scrimmage when he gets a "run" read, the "throw-back pass" must be utilized as one of the counterplays to complement the sprint-out offense.

Keep in mind that an effective sprint-out pass offense requires repetition of practice. A large portion of the weekly practice schedule should be devoted to repetition of practice against the defensive coverages that quarterbacks and receivers will encounter in each succeeding game.

Part Five
Positions and Techniques

25
The Army Receiver Sequence

(From 1974 Summer Manual of the AFCA)

MIKE MIKOLAYUNAS Assistant Coach, U.S. Military Academy

At West Point we have tried to identify the "art of catching the ball" in a way that builds pride and confidence for those who learn it. We have outlined for our receiver athletes a way to practice and learn what we feel are the important techniques needed to catch and advance the ball. We call the list the army receiver sequence.

Every receiver is required to learn the sequence point by point and teach it to coaches. During organized practice sessions we work on all points of the sequence every practice day and in sequence where and when we can. Because catching skills are developed for the most part away from organized football practice, we make sure that our athletes know how to improve with our receiver sequence on their own. We have an organized way to practice all that is needed to be successful.

Ball Tricks

We warm up our ball handling reactions by doing ball tricks. The following is a list of some things to do with a football to develop hand-eye coordination and concentration on the football. We recommend that players work twice as often with their weaker hands.

1. *Air Dribble.* Drop a ball and catch it with fast repetition, giving the effect of dribbling it in the air. Do it alternately with both hands.

2. *Finger Roll.* Hold the ball at one end with the palm down. Roll it over on its back so that it is resting on the back of your hand with your palm still down. Return it to its original position.

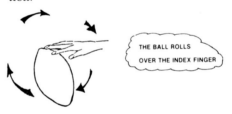

3. *Finger Flip.* Holding the ball as you do for the finger roll, give it a full back flip, then hit it just enough to give it a full forward flip, and catch it in its original position. Do it with two balls and both hands at the same time.

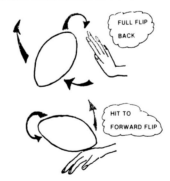

4. *Hand Roll.* Hold the ball at one end but with the palm down and the ball line perpendicular to the arm/hand line. Roll it over the back of the hand and grab it by the other end. Return it to the original position. Do it with two balls and both hands. See page 118.

ROLL IT OVER
THE BACK ON
THE HAND

5. *Hand Circle.* Hold the ball as you do for the air dribble. Drop it as you lift it slightly, circle your hand around it, and grab it in the original position. Do it with two balls and both hands.

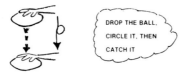

DROP THE BALL,
CIRCLE IT, THEN
CATCH IT

6. *Globetrotter.* Pass the ball from one hand to the other around the waist and between the legs, changing directions, Harlem Globetrotter style.

7. *Juggle, two balls.* Juggle two spinning balls with one hand.

8. *Juggle, three balls.* Juggle three balls with both hands.

Ball Security

We practice these things every day. Taking the ball out of the air and getting it to our pocket involves all of these coaching points.

1. *Strengthen Your Grip.* Hold the ball in front of you in both hands, try to pop it with your fingers and hands. If you have a partner, grip wrestle with him.

GRIP WRESTLE

2. *The Ball Tucked Away.* Holding the ball under your arm in proper ball-carrying position, try to pop the air out of it by squeezing it hard.

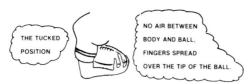

THE TUCKED
POSITION

NO AIR BETWEEN
BODY AND BALL.
FINGERS SPREAD
OVER THE TIP OF THE BALL.

Hold the ball under your arm and have a buddy try to wrestle it away from you. Simulate approaching a crowd and practice covering the ball with the second hand. Holding the ball under your arm, run and cut to eliminate the action of the arm that makes the ball break away from the body.

3. *Snap It In.* Now test your hand and arm position over the ball. Flip the ball into the air or bounce it off a wall and, as fast as possible, grab it and snap it to a tucked position. Do it to both pockets.

Stationary Catching

Practice these with a partner. The passer and receiver do not need to move. The passer must be able to throw the ball hard and with some accuracy to drill you properly. Again, twice as much attention and work should be given to your weaker hand.

1. *Check Hand Position First.* To warm up, throw and catch going "around the clock." Concentrate on catching the ball with relaxed, well-spread fingers, positioned properly.

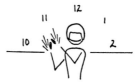

Thumbs in. With shoulders open to the direction of the pass and the ball at or above shoulder level.

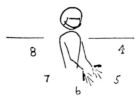

Thumbs out. With the shoulders open to the pass and the ball lower than shoulder level.

See the ball into your hands. At nine and three o'clock you are tested.

2. *Check the "Pinchers" and "Arm Give."* Have the ball thrown at your face. Catching the ball with your pinchers spread and arms relaxed to give with the force of the ball, snap it to your ball-carrying pocket.

RECEIVER

3. *Low Passes.* The scoop technique must be practiced for low balls. Work to keep the elbows together and the fingers spread while you bend for the ball. Lunge to scoop the ball off the grass tips ready to roll to either side when you hit the ground. See page 119.

4. *Pocket Catching.* In the pocket is the surest way to catch the ball. Throw wobbly balls, spirals, and wet ones at times. The weakest pocket needs the extra work. Have the ball thrown at your sternum. You must adjust for a pocket catch.

THE HANDS, ARMS, AND BODY FORM A FUNNEL SHAPED POCKET

5. *Check Concentration on the Ball.* Catch knuckle balls. Because a knuckle ball floats and changes flight erratically, the demand is for you to watch the ball all the way into your hands. Snap the ball to your pocket. Go "around the clock."

UNDERHAND THROW—DO NOT TUMBLE IT.

To throw a knuckle ball.

6. *Snap the Head.* The receiver's reaction to snap his head to the passer and focus instantly on the thrown ball can be greatly developed. The passer holds the ball at waist level initially, then cocks and throws as fast as possible. The receiver focuses on the ball at the waist, then snaps the head and shoulders around for a complete turn as the passer moves to cock.

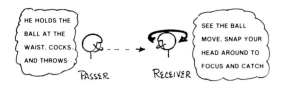

HE HOLDS THE BALL AT THE WAIST, COCKS, AND THROWS
SEE THE BALL MOVE, SNAP YOUR HEAD AROUND TO FOCUS AND CATCH
PASSER   RECEIVER

7. *Bother Drill.* To test your concentration on the ball, the bother drill is great. Have two, three, or four defenders distract you while you catch. They can bump you, jolt you slightly, wave their hands in your field of vision, and even tip the pass.

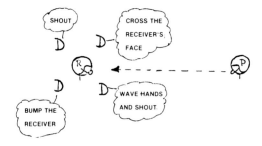

SHOUT | CROSS THE RECEIVER'S FACE
BUMP THE RECEIVER | WAVE HANDS AND SHOUT.

Catching on the Move

Again with a partner who can throw, move on all angles from him practicing catching techniques with all the different sighting angles.

1. *Come Back for the Ball.* With the shoulders square to the passer move back to him as he releases the ball. Catch balls thrown "around the clock."

BEND TO LOOK DOWN THE FLIGHT OF THE BALL

Try to catch all you can bending to look down the flight of the ball as you move back into it. Looking down the flight reduces the speed of the ball and allows you the chance to see it into your hands or pocket.

2. *Across the Passer's Face.* Move on a line in front of the passer to the right and then the left. You should adjust your speed for balls thrown out in front of you or to your rear. You should bend whenever possible to look down the flight of the ball.

OUR KNIFING TECHNIQUE
A LEVERAGE STEP TO GET DIRECTLY UPFIELD, DIP THE INSIDE SHOULDER.

Practice knifing after catching these balls. Knifing is a technique we define as moving directly to the goal line at the point of a reception. It involves stabbing a leverage step to direct oneself upfield and a dip of the inside shoulder as the ball is tucked away. This is a reaction that must come immediately at the point of reception. It needs constant practice.

3. *Moving to the Sideline.* Moving to a line boundary you need to keep your feet close to

the ground, with shorter, quicker strides. Develop your peripheral feel for the boundary. Throw balls that will keep you in bounds. On these the knifing technique is again practiced.

Throw balls that will force you to drag one foot in bounds.

4. *Deep Ball Catching.* On all deep balls you must be able to hold your speed as you look back for the ball. This means you must try to concentrate on your body lean. Turn your head to look back keeping your chin close to your shoulder. Practice one-hand catches first. With your hips turned downfield from the passer, let him lead you with a pass over your shoulder. You should adjust your speed on the ball and practice extending with one hand to stop the ball, then catch it with two.

Next, work on looking down the flight of a deep ball. Run deep under a high long ball. Adjust on it and without trying to catch it see how close to your nose the ball can drop. Doing this you will experience looking down the flight of the ball. You will reduce the speed of the ball. Then run under the same pass and extend your hands back for the ball to see the ball into your hands. This is the most consistent way to catch deep balls. This is the position under deep balls we want you to get whenever you can.

Third, practice fading on deep balls. Have the ball thrown deep and well to your outside. You must strain to keep your sight on it as you look over your inside shoulder and widen your course to get under it.

Then, practice closing on the ball. Fight the tendency of the hips to run straight downfield and close in your course to get to the ball.

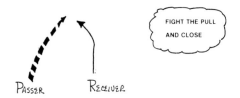

The fifth deep ball technique that we practice is the slow and go technique. Here you judge the ball as underthrown initially. You slow, then readjust to a full sprint to catch the ball running away with it, running away from a defensive back whom you would ideally have pinned to your inside.

Endline catches must be practiced for deep balls. You must know the boundary of the end zone. Dragging the foot in is the technique.

The last point we coach is our reaction for deep balls that are well underthrown. The techniques are to adjust back for the ball and catch it at our highest jump point, or to practice stripping a defender who has position on the ball so to prevent an interception.

This then is our checklist of techniques that our receivers learn and practice. By outlining these coaching points and techniques, we feel we have accomplished three major objectives with our players.

First, we think that we have shown them that there is a limit to the knowledge that is needed to be successful. By fencing in the set of things to be mastered, learning is enhanced.

Second, we feel that in having our players learn these points in a logical progression, learning again is facilitated. The memory is aided and the stress is on the player being able to develop on his own.

And finally, in having players learn, teach, and practice these skills they know that they have done all they can to develop their skill. And they can be proud and confident of what their skills are.

26
Training the
Wishbone Quarterback

(From 1974 *Proceedings* of the AFCA)

PEPPER RODGERS Head Coach, Georgia Tech University

There is one absolute requirement: the quarterback must be an aggressive runner. Without an athlete who is looking for spaces between pursuing defenders and who is eager to keep the ball himself, the offense will not work. Speed and size help at the quarterback position just as they do at any position, but the aggressiveness is the key and the only absolute requirement.

A wishbone quarterback—with the reading of defensive linemen on the triple-option play, in addition to the passing, ball handling and optioning—has a bigger job than other T quarterbacks do, and the offense needs an athlete who will work hard to prepare himself, think positively, and concentrate totally on game action. However, aggressiveness is the element without which the offense will not work.

Execution of the Read

The first problem is to find which defender to read. Option theory holds that a single defender cannot take both the quarterback and the pitch man or both the pitch man and the receiver who releases downfield. It takes three defenders to stop the outside dimensions of the play. If a fourth can be moved to the outside defense, there is no way to handle him. Assuming that one of the eleven defenders is over the center or at middle safety, there are just five defenders on each side and two of them must play the inside dimension. Diagram 1 shows the three most familiar defensive placements of players. In each defense there are just three men to play the quarterback, the pitch man, and the receiver.

In simplest terms, then, and counting from the outside in, the fourth man in must either be blocked or eliminated by the read. That suggests the rule for triple optioning—the fourth man in must be blocked

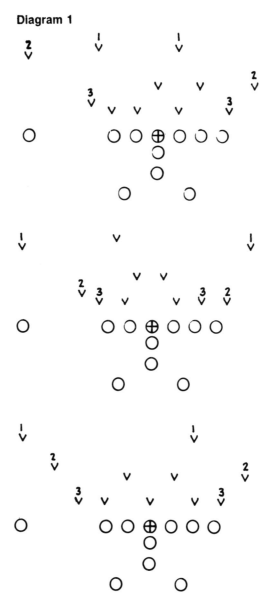

Diagram 1

or read. A later section deals exhaustively with counting problems. Basically, if the fourth man is a linebacker, he will be blocked. If the fourth man is a lineman inside of the tackle, he will be blocked by the tackle. But, if he is a lineman on or outside of the tackle, he will be read.

The problem of dealing with the latter will be discussed first. It is on this type of man that the fundamentals must be learned. The all-important thought process will be explained first, followed by the geometry of fitting the athletes together for smooth ball handling.

The execution of the basic play begins in the mind of the quarterback. Which man does he read? What are that man's responsibilities? Is he No. 4 or is he No. 3? Is there a cross stunt possibility? Where is the man who will take the quarterback if the ball is taken to the outside? And so on. The most difficult part of the execution takes place in the thought process, before the ball is snapped. And it can be impossibly difficult unless the athlete understands something about mind/eye/muscle coordination time.

An analogy will make the point. A baseball hitter, in his mind, does not think of hitting the ball if it comes across the plate and not hitting it if it does not. He makes a move to hit every ball. His only reaction is to check up and not swing. In other words, he does not give his mind/eye/muscle coordination two reactions to make; just one.

This principle applies in the making of the quarterback's decision to give the ball or disconnect it. For the easiest reads he might not need to think this way, but for the toughest, for the fast ball, he will. He steps away from the center with the intention of giving the ball to the fullback and leaves himself only the reaction of disconnecting on certain reads. Or he steps with the intention of disconnecting and gives only if he gets a certain signal. An athlete will not grasp this approach the first time, or the first five or fifty times, he tries to read, but he will in time, and it will help him.

Again, the most difficult part of the execution takes place in the mind of the quarterback before the ball is ever snapped. If the defense and the tackle movements shown in Diagram 2 were the only ones to read, there would be no problem, but they get difficult

Diagram 2

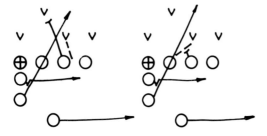

to the point where the give and disconnect signals are equally strong.

Having an approach clearly in mind before stepping away from the center can be every bit as important as it is for a baseball hitter to move to hit the fast ball before it ever comes off the pitcher's hand.

Working with Fullback

Along with the clear and positive thought process, a quarterback needs a smooth and sure hookup with his fullback. The exchange from the center has something to do with this, as does the position of the fullback's bottom hand, extension of the quarterback's arms, and a number of other details. First, the exact positioning and movements of the center, quarterback, and fullback will be explained; next, the actual mechanics of handling the ball will be explained.

The quarterback's first movement with the ball is sharply away from the center, and the ball exchange technique must fit accordingly. On no other T formation play is the movement of the ball more sharply away from the center, because the quarterback tries to get the ball hooked up with the fullback as fast as possible. The center should grip the ball just as he would if he were going to pass it. The quarterback fits his hands together, the anchor points being the fingernail of the middle finger of the right hand, which is pressed against the middle seam of the center's pants, and the inside of the right thumb, which touches the center's butt. If an imaginary line bisecting the angle formed by the quarterback's hands points at the rear tip of the ball as it lies flat, the position is good.

The quarterback's arms are slightly bent at the elbows, and the fingers are taut as though they are reaching for the ball. The ball is moved on a line so that it will wedge into the quarterback's hands. This means that the center must use only one hand to move the ball and that his elbow must bend during the motion. The middle finger of the quarterback's left hand is pointed out at 45 degrees and the hand of the center rotated somewhat less than 90 degrees. This takes pressure off the hands of both athletes.

The purpose of the technique is to ensure the exchange for the extreme movement of the ball that happens on 90 percent of the plays in the wishbone offense. Having the center actually push the ball through the V formed by the quarterback's hands and having the ball wedge into rather than slap onto the hands gives the assurance. When a quarterback operates along the line of scrimmage, or when he is not pressured to move the ball quickly, a less precise technique will suffice.

The quarterback's feet should have a sensation of gripping the ground through the cleats. The first step places a foot on a line 45 degrees from the other foot. The arm opposite the direction of the step is extended until it is completely straight. The ball is not pulled into the belly and then extended; neither is it swung around with straight arms. It is merely moved as efficiently as possible to the fullback's pocket.

If the fullback's heels are lined up 13 feet from the forward tip of the ball, and if a short lead step puts him on a course that will run the middle of his body over the outside foot of a guard who has split twenty-four inches, then the quarterback's extension of the ball should put it in the fullback's pocket. The quarterback's step actually cannot control how far his arms reach. The angle of the body along with the length of the step controls this. It is enough to tell the quarterback to form the 45-degree line between his feet and to ride the fullback with straight arms.

There are two more important fundamental moves on this technique of getting everything hooked up so that a read can take place and a give or a disconnect can be made. The ride movement of the arms must be started as soon as the one arm is extended on the 45-degree angle. For the quarterback to ride by feel as he might in a belly series attack would put too much ball pressure on the fullback.

Ideally the ball would be fitted into the pocket with the fullback feeling it with his arms but with only the back of a wrist touching his belly 6 inches from the center of the pocket. While the ride takes place, the fullback folds his arms and hands softly over the ball, but he should not be aware of pressure on his stomach until the decision is made by the quarterback to give. This ideal position will be approached if the ride action is started as soon as the arm is extended.

The other important fundamental has to do with the positioning of the head. A defender is watched but the head should allow for the peripheral vision to see as much of the ride as possible. The eyes go to the defender, but the head turns slightly farther away.

With thought processes in order and hookup geometry accurate, the giving and disconnecting mechanics are not difficult. To give, the back hand is pulled away, the front hand presses the ball, and the arm follows the fullback slightly farther than it does on the disconnect. The hands are then brought together for the fake. To disconnect, the ball is snapped away with the back of a wrist keeping the fullback from feeling any ball pressure. The grip on the ball must be secure because it is often pulled through the hands of the fullback.

The quarterback's movement off the fullback's tail is an acceleration, whether he has the ball or not. In faking, acceleration is the single most important thing; in optioning at the perimeter, acceleration means inches gained on the defense. In order to accelerate, the quarterback's second step is not forward with the ride. Instead, it hangs in the air waiting to start the sprint. The ride is actually made on one foot, although it does not seem to help the quarterback kinesthetically to think of actually being on the one foot as the arm ride is made.

Confidence Is Key

It is a mistake to try to read until there is confidence about everything that leads up to it. Confidence, not perfection, is the key, and with it the quarterback can proceed to make the simplest of all reads. A defensive lineman can be put outside of the offensive tackle and told to move straight ahead or down the line. The defensive movement shows even before the hookup, and deciding to give or disconnect is a simple matter. It was to deal with almost this clear a movement that the triple-option play was developed, but today it is seldom that simple. The next step is to have the defender not move at all part of the time to get a dividing line between give and disconnect reads.

At first the quarterback will tend to stare at the defender, but after some days of work he will begin picking up more and more in his peripheral vision. And the encouraging thing about starting a quarterback in this technique is that he can be assured that he will not have to execute anything he is not confident about. Remember, always, that the option play from the wishbone formation with no read at all is a very good football play.

27
The Name of the Game—Punting!

(From 1974 Summer Manual of the AFCA)

JIM HOGGATT Assistant Coach, University of Southern Mississippi

The ability to punt the football is a number one factor in the success of any football team. I have had the opportunity to work for two head coaches, Billy (Spook) Murphy at Memphis State University and P. W. (Bear) Underwood at the University of Southern Mississippi. Both of these men believe strongly in the kicking game and both put it in the important category of furnishing the "winning edge." The axiom, "More games are won or lost in the kicking game" is still true, and this makes a winning team's punting efficiency of prime importance.

I personally feel like I have actually punted more footballs than any boy I ever coached. I did not say better, I just had more opportunities. I grew up on the playgrounds of Jacksonville, Florida, and was the punter on my high school, junior college, and the Memphis State University teams. Punting a rubber football barefooted until the top of your foot is blistered will teach you to place the ball correctly. However, I had an excellent coach in high school and junior college in Rankin Hudson. He had the ability to teach and demonstrate at the same time. He probably can still outkick me. My senior college playing days were spent under Ralph Hatley, and, with his Tennessee background, I fell further under the need of stressing the kicking game.

The University of Southern Mississippi has been blessed with many outstanding punters, but the current spotlight falls on All-America Ray Guy, now of the Oakland Raiders, and on Jerrell Wilson of the Kansas City Chiefs. They are considered the top two professional punters in football as their record in the 1973 season proved. The fact that Oakland drafted Ray Guy in the first round of the 1973 draft would also tend to prove the importance the professional teams put on the punting game.

The schedule provides me thirty minutes a day to work on improving the skills of our punters. This time is labeled prepractice and comes before the entire squad comes on the field. In addition, some phase of the kicking game is covered in every practice, and all phases are reviewed two days prior to each game. Even with this schedule most punters do not get the necessary kicking opportunities they need to really improve their ability to punt a football.

I try to encourage a year-round kicking schedule, but this is not possible in most cases. So, I will stay after practice and allow more opportunities to kick as the need arises.

Fundamentals

The actual fundamentals, step by step, of the punter are as follows.

Stance

The punter stands in a comfortable position with his knees slightly bent, the arms from the elbows to the hands parallel to the ground and the hands slightly above the right knee. The punter should have open palms with his thumbs out and should give an inviting target to the center in a direct path that the center snap should follow. This is the same as a baseball catcher giving a target for the pitcher to hit. The punter can never expect a perfect snap and must be in a position to move quickly to the ball in any direction.

The feet should be in a comfortable position about 6 inches apart. The feet should be parallel to each other. Both feet should be flat on the ground, and any weight shift should be on the left foot. The right foot is forward of the left foot so that the toe of the left foot

124

reaches the instep of the right foot. Now we are ready to receive the football.

The punter must wait on the center snap to reach him and not "walk" into his kick. Regardless of where we catch the snap, we would like to return to the correct fundamental position as we adjust the football. For example, if the snap is high and makes the punter stand straight up, we want him to catch the football and return quickly to his fundamental position.

When the ball hits the hands, he must spin the ball so that the laces are on the top. As the ball is rotated, the right hand is placed under the ball with the fingers apart to form a resting place for the ball. The middle finger should be the main support of the ball. The left hand is in slight contact with the ball on the left side of the ball only to help the alignment that the right hand directs. The left hand should not try to control the ball. The right arm and hand should be in complete control of the football. The right arm from the elbow to the shoulder is comfortable against the side. The left hand is slightly forward so that it is a relaxed pocket that is formed for the football. The football must be treated with "tender loving care" during this process. This again guards against a fumble, and this is the last fundamental before actually dropping and kicking the ball.

Steps

There are some punters who need three steps to punt, but we teach and use the two-step method. Once the ball is in place in the righthand pocket, a short step is taken with the right foot, then a normal step with the left foot, and then the ball is kicked.

The first short step with the right foot gets the body momentum moving forward, and the step with the left foot gives the body thrust to aid the right leg in providing force to the ball. The ball is kicked with the left foot on the ground, and the balance that is needed will come from this step. Once contact has been made, then the motion of the follow-through will pull the heel from the ground. The two steps must be smooth and not hurried or strained.

The steps should be taken in a straight line. Usually the left foot will give direction to the flight of the ball. The steps should not be splayed, and after many opportunities these steps should be performed the same way every time and should not have to be consciously thought out.

Drop

The ball is placed on the instep with the right hand. The ball should be motionless when placed on the instep, with the nose slightly elevated. The distance that the ball remains in the air after release by the right hand should only be a few inches. The greater this distance is, the more chance of error in the placing of the ball. The arm extension will vary with each punter. In general, the arm should be extended with a slight bend at the elbow and the arm directly over the kicking foot. The rhythm of the drop and kick should be the same each time you kick.

Follow-through

Follow-through is actually the continuation of the momentum that is generated by the act of punting. The method of punting previously described is designed to keep the punter in balance and under control at all times, so the follow-through is a reflection of the skill of the punter.

At the moment of contact with the ball, the punter has his left foot firmly set so as to give stable, firm leverage for the punt. After the kick, the forward momentum of the body of the punter is forward, straight ahead. The follow-through step by the right foot should be in the same line as was the path of the steps prior to the kick.

The right leg should be directly forward during the follow-through. The same applies to the left leg. Since the ball is kicked from a position in front, and slightly above the right knee, the punter will be under control once the right foot has touched the ground. The forward trajectory of the ball will be at a 45-degree angle so that the follow-through is only a consequence of the speed of the leg during the kick. Follow-through is perhaps most important because it reveals errors in the punter's form.

Spread Formation

It is important that the punter's fundamentals time is directly with the team effort and plan in the punting game. We use the spread punt formation shown in Diagram 1.

Diagram 1

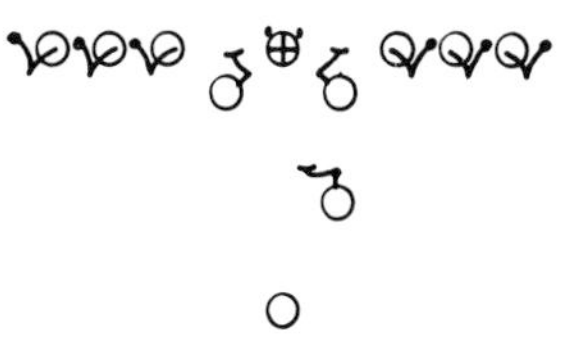

There is a 3-foot split between each lineman. We want them in a balanced but wide-based two-point stance with their elbows on their knees and their heads up. The fundamental step they learn and execute each time is a step with their outside foot and hitting a blow with their head and elbow extended to the next man.

They never move the inside foot until the ball is kicked.

The two up-backs line themselves in a two-point stance in a legal position from the line of scrimmage. They take a short jab step inside and then block out across the hole on each side of the center. The center is very important to the team success in the punting game. He must snap the ball 14 yards deep in .7 or .8 of a second and then snap up and protect his area before covering the football.

We use the following method to call the spread punt. The punter calls the signal in the huddle and says, "Spread punt, when the center is READY!" We do this to emphasize the importance of the snap! The deep back lines up 6 yards deep and takes a step up as the ball is snapped, and then slides over after the ball passes. We want him to block the most dangerous man, inside out, on every snap. This is the only man who blocks a man; all others block an area! With this arrangement we ask the punter to get the punt off in 1.2 seconds from the time it hits his hands. We work on this 2.0 second goal at every opportunity. We use a stopwatch to time each segment: the snap, the punter's time, and the flight time of the football. We also time the entire operation for the team's benefit. The punter lines up 14 yards from the football, and we work toward his steps not covering over 5 yards in length. The good snap, the fundamental steps, and the right rhythm by the punter will ensure your getting the football airborne.

Lanes of Coverage

After the punt is in the air, the importance of the coverage becomes the number one fundamental of the punting team. Of course, the actual time that the punt-

er keeps the ball in the air is very important also. We have had much success in teaching the lanes of coverage in Diagram 2.

Diagram 2

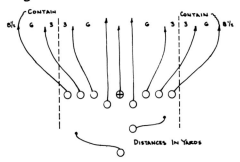

The center covers the middle of the field. The only time he may deviate from this lane is when he is the first man down the field; then he is free to go to the ball.

The tackles cover lanes 3 yards inside hash marks. A tackle may deviate from his lane only when he is the first man downfield; then he may go to ball.

The guards cover lanes 3 yards outside hash mark. A guard should never deviate from his lane until he is sure where the ball is going. If the ball goes away, a guard stays 5 yards short of the ball until he has a chance to make the tackle. He must be very alert for a "kick in" block because the favorite return lane is between the first and second man from the sideline.

The ends cover lanes 8 yards from the sideline. Don't let the ball carrier get around you, but be very alert for the "kick out" block. Stay in your lane until you are sure where the ball is going.

The up backs go directly to the football. On the fair catch signal, the up backs break down behind the receiver.

28
Technique of the Long Snap

(From *1974 Summer Manual* of the AFCA)

JIM SOCHOR Head Coach, and BILL BRYANT Head Freshman Coach, University of California, Davis

The kicking game has been considered for many years as one of the three essential phases of the game of football. An important phase of the kicking game itself is the long snap. The center snap for the field goal, the point after touchdown, and the punt is generally referred to as the long snap.

The significance of the long snap is felt most when it goes awry. How many games have been lost due to a poor snap from center? How many punts have been blocked or kicked badly due to a poorly delivered pass from center? When a field goal or point after touchdown is blocked, one can usually relate it to an ineffective snap from center.

In reviewing our 32–31 loss to Boise State in the last game of 1973, we found the crucial turning point to have been their blocking of our field goal attempt inside their 30-yard line in the third quarter. Why? A poor snap from center. Our center had lost speed on his snap due to a sprained ankle that had weakened as the game progressed.

Over the past four seasons, I can recall eight to ten of our games that were won with the kicking game. For the most part, the kicking game begins with the long snap. If the snap is good, the desired result has a real chance of occurring, like the good drive in golf setting up the par for the hole. If the snap is slow or off target, it puts added strain on your kicker, and poor kicks are usually a result of pressure, either real or imagined (self-imposed).

Characteristics of the Snapper

The center who assumes the duties of the long snap should have certain physical and emotional qualities. While it is not so important that he be overwhelming in size, it is vital that he have strong hands and wrists and the leg power to send the ball spiraling back firmly and accurately.

The desired emotional qualities would be the ability to handle pressure and a "nothing ever bothers me" attitude. The snapper must have a "cool" personality with the ability to be "right" regardless of the conditions prevalent that day (cold, wet, windy). You would want him to possess a positive attitude and to exude confidence. He may have to be tougher mentally and physically than others along the offensive line as he is ripped many times just as he releases the ball.

The player who hikes the ball for the long snap need not be your regular center. It is so important a task that the player with the most ability in this particular phase should be sought out early and assigned to gear himself to it for the season. The most important requisite is that the player must want to be in that position and have the desire to work at its perfection. The duties of blocking and covering downfield, while important, still remain secondary to the ability to get the ball back with consistency and zip.

Stance and Positioning of the Ball

The stance for the snapper should be a little wider than the T formation center stance, to ensure a good, solid base of support. A toe-to-instep staggered stance is generally favored with most of the weight on the balls of the feet.

The snapper should grasp the ball much the same way as the quarterback does in throwing a forward pass. For the righthanded player, the right hand grasps the ball toward the forward end with the fingers well spread, covering the laces. The left hand can be placed toward the rear portion of the ball or on top of the ball depending on comfort and convenience.

While the two hands must work in unison, the right hand is the power hand and the left hand serves more as a guide.

The ball should be delivered with the arms and hands moving in one continuous motion. A common fault here is picking the ball up before delivery, losing brief, but precious, time. It is the speed and accuracy of delivery, however, that are crucial.

The arms at address should be slightly bent to gain the most propitious angle for maximum power. The weight of the snapper should be evenly balanced with just enough weight on the ball as you might fall forward slowly if it was taken away. Even pressure must be kept on the ball so as to not key the time of delivery. The snapper must keep the defense off balance (beware of dropping the butt just before the snap). As the delivery is made, the hands and arms should follow through directly at the target. The first and most important responsibility of the snapper is to get the ball back with speed and accuracy. Wrist snap must be developed to gain maximum power. The snapper must not watch the ball all the way to the punter or holder. He must get into a blocking position quickly.

Action Analysis

Dr. William Harrison, an optometrist in Davis, California, who has a special interest in analyzing sports skills, suggests a four-step approach when performing any sports skill.

1. Analyze the skill to be performed. What does it entail? Note all of the prevailing conditions such as wind, rain, and wetness. Check difficult angles and the position of the ball on the field. Determine exactly how you are going to perform the skill.

2. Visualize in your mind actually doing the skill. This takes only a few seconds. The many repetitions on the practice field allow for easy visualizing in the game itself. There are times on the golf course when you step to the tee and you know you will hit the ball well; you can visualize yourself doing it even before you hit. You gain a kinesthetic feel for the shot by "seeing" it happen in your mind beforehand. It is vital that the performer come up with the correct visual image of the skill. This will aid in ensuring that the right neurological patterns develop. It is suggested that thinking about the proper techniques to be performed on your way to the game or even the night before can be beneficial to performance.

3. Centering means focusing in on your target. If you soft center on your target, you will see a broad picture. If you fine center you will be zooming in and only seeing a specific thing, for example, a number, the hands, and so on. It is important that the snapper

utilize a soft center when aligning himself to gain a broad field of vision; he then zooms in to fine center on his target. By fine centering on his specific target unnecessary objects will be excluded from his vision and extraneous noises will be eliminated.

4. Execution. The actual execution of the skill will be facilitated by the three previous steps. The long snap for the punt should be executed by firing the ball back low, fast, and accurately in a good spiral. The time factor from snapper to punter should be executed in .9 of a second or better. In executing the snap for the field goal and point after touchdown, accuracy is the key factor. The ball must be delivered as firmly as the holder's ability to handle it, and it must always be on target (hit the hands of the holder). The center may have to adjust his speed in early practice until the holder gains in his ability to handle the faster snap. Additional practice time must be provided for the holder and snapper until they are harmonious from snap to placement. The timing for the long snap for a field goal and a point after touchdown should be .7 of a second or better. As the snap is made, the snapper is fine centering on the holder's hands. He then comes up quickly with head and shoulders in a blocking position. The snapper should always take plenty of time before snapping to ensure that all players are set at the line and the punter (or holder) has time to adjust himself and is ready.

Progression Training

While there are several important steps in the training of the centering specialist for the kicking game, the overall psychological approach is of paramount importance. The duties of the long snapper can be tedious and demanding and will usually go unnoticed by the fans and the media. For these reasons, the center must receive praise and encouragement from coaches and other players, particularly the kickers and holders. Both the center and the coach must develop and maintain a positive attitude in practice and during the pressure of games. To facilitate the attainment of this positive attitude, achievable objectives and goals should be set for the long snapper at all stages of training.

Learning to consistently make the long snap under pressure requires patience and practice. Except in an emergency, no athlete should be expected to perfect the necessary skills in early season practice. The training process must begin in the off-season or during spring practice, so that the new long snapper can report for fall practice with some skill development and confidence in his abilities to make the snap.

The actual training progression can be summarized as follows:

Passing Action

The first step in the development of the kicking game center is to learn the proper passing action. He should begin by passing from a standing or kneeling position, depending on his ability. Many of the basic passing drills that are used in the training of the quarterback can be utilized in teaching the center to pass. One drill that should be included is the two-hand overhead pass. This is an excellent warmup drill for experienced long snappers, as well as an effective drill for learning to make the proper wrist snap.

Passing from a Center Stance

When coach and center are satisfied with his ability to pass the ball smoothly and comfortably, he can begin to pass from a center's stance. At first this pass will be limited to a distance of 8 to 10 yards. This distance can be gradually increased to 13 yards when the new center feels comfortable and confident in making the short snap. The emphasis, at this point, should be on developing correct form and on executing a sharp, crisp pass.

The Long Snap

Only when the center feels confident in his ability to make the long snap consistently should he begin to drill for accuracy. If he begins to concentrate on accuracy too soon, he may become frustrated or sacrifice speed to achieve accuracy. While he should strive for perfection, a good initial objective might be to make eight out of ten accurate snaps—to the punter's hands at about waist level. When he can consistently achieve the desired accuracy, his snaps should be timed. Although he must achieve some degree of speed in his delivery, one of the most common mistakes a coach can make is to overemphasize the speed of the pass. Many bad snaps are attributable to the center trying to get it back "a little faster."

Passing for the Field Goal and Point After Touchdown

In working on centering skills for the field goal point after touchdown, the snapper must constantly work with a holder to develop the crisp and accurate pass necessary for success. The center should try to get the ball back as fast as possible, as long as the holder is still able to handle it with relative ease and confidence. When the center and holder have developed a smooth working relationship, they should begin to work with the kicker on the timing of the whole unit. The primary drill for developing this pass is constant practice between center and holder. A good rapport between center and holder will facilitate communication, thereby speeding up progress and creating a greater desire to practice and improve their skills.

Versus a Defender

When the long snapper has developed confidence in his abilities and consistency in his snaps, he should begin to face a defender. At first the defender need only make his presence felt by a light slap to the head or shoulders; he may later make more vigorous contact. Once the center has learned to handle contact from a single defensive man he is probably ready to face the pressure of "live in the line" kicking drills.

Practice Pressure

All snaps could be charted and timed. This will not only catch any consistent faults but will also put added pressure on the center. As many pressure situations as possible should be created in practice to prepare the center for actual game pressure.

Other Practice Needs

There are certain other factors that must be considered in preparing the long snapper for a game or season. He should learn to snap wet and muddy balls with accuracy and consistency, and also learn to adjust his target in excessive winds. In order to prevent the center from giving away a fake kick, he must practice snapping to the up backs. At all times the center should practice taking an extra second before snapping so that this will become an ingrained habit.

Off-Season

In the off-season, the dedicated long snapper must work hard to perfect the skills of his specialty. Even in the off-season, however, practice should be as specific as possible. To this end, the center should practice making both snaps, using the same kind of ball he will use during a game. All snaps should be made wearing shoulder pads and helmet, if at all possible.

Because we desire this specificity in practice we do not recommend the use of a weighted ball. The snapper can, however, work on making a longer snap of 15 to 17 yards to psychologically "shorten" the 13-yard snap. He can also work on developing stronger wrists and quicker hands through weight training, the Exergenie, playing handball, and doing fingertip push-ups. The emphasis of his practice should be on making repeated 13-yard snaps to a punter and 7-yard snaps to a holder.

The real key to the success of your kicking game is how much time and enthusiasm you are willing to commit to it. If the belief is there that the kicking game is a significant factor in winning or losing, the commitment will be there, and, for the most part, the kicking game begins with the long snap.

29
Center Play at Nebraska

(From 1976 Summer Manual of the AFCA)

MILT TENOPIR Assistant Coach, University of Nebraska

At the University of Nebraska the offensive center must possess several characteristics in order to do the job required of him.

He must be an individual who has leadership, because as the hub of our offensive line, he is responsible for initiating every offensive play. He must influence our entire offensive line, if we are to get the job done up front. We expect the center to show a great deal of hustle and dedication because of the fact that he is our most important cog in the entire line. The center is normally our best athlete in the offensive line.

We have, in the past, required our center to do a lot of one-on-one blocking because of all the 50 fronts we face in the Big Eight Conference. He is also required to be a good post blocker since we use the center and offensive guard on many double team blocks.

We need pretty good agility in our centers as we require him to reach a full man on some plays. (See Diagram 1.)

Diagram 1

In making the difficult reach block shown in Diagram 2, we require the center to get a good lead step nearly parallel to the line of scrimmage.

Diagram 2

We also require our center to be agile enough to execute what we refer to as a do-dad on a linebacker (see Diagram 3), because of the slanting defenses we face.

Diagram 3

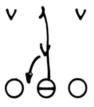

In addition to the responsibilities of run blocking, the center must be able to pass protect. We do a great deal of pocket passing at Nebraska and require the center to handle a nose guard many times without help. He must get back off the ball quickly in order to keep the nose guard away from the quarterback. (See Diagram 4.)

Diagram 4

On occasion we require the center to pull out of the line and pick up a defensive lineman on the backside. (See Diagram 5.)

Size is an important factor for our center at Nebraska. We don't always find the ideal center with respect to size, but when recruiting for a center we look for an individual about 6 feet, 2 to 3 inches tall who

Diagram 5

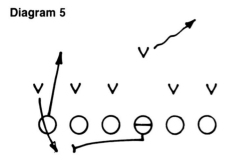

possesses the strength needed to handle our run requirements versus a nose guard and also to handle our pass protection needs.

The taller and larger center offers the quarterback immediate protection, allows for our quarterback to be more erect when receiving the snap, and enables the quarterback to survey the defensive situation with more ease.

The center really performs two basic tasks. The first task is snapping the ball. He must do so properly each time in order to initiate the play successfully. A poor snap means a poor play. The second task is that of blocking. After each successful snap, the center must do the best possible job of blocking his opponent.

Before snapping the ball and executing a block, we must first get our center into a comfortable stance. We are quite liberal in demanding a particular stance at Nebraska; however, we find that in most cases the candidates for center use a toe-instep relationship. We don't really want more of a stagger than this as we feel he can move equally well in all directions from this stance. (See Diagram 6.)

We like to have the feet a little wider than shoulder's width, knees flexed, back straight, head up, but not in a tensed position. Because of our demands on the center to pass protect, reach block, and pull out to cover the back side, we do not like to have our centers put any weight on the ball. In aligning a center into

Diagram 6

his stance, make certain that his feet are pointed straight ahead, and his shoulders are parallel to the line of scrimmage.

We insist that the center have a good grip on the ball to ensure a proper exchange. We prefer the center to grip the ball with his primary hand with the laces straight up and the thumb of his lifting arm over the laces. When the center snaps the ball we want him to bring it up to the crotch area by breaking his wrist and elbow and allowing one-quarter natural rotation. This natural rotation should allow the quarterback to receive the ball with the laces upward, and assures the quarterback of getting the proper grip on the ball for passing or handing off.

The most important aspect of the exchange is that it be consistent at each snap and that the snap is very firm and not mushy. The ball should pop the quarterback's hands.

At Nebraska, we work on the exchange between centers and quarterbacks daily during our specialty period. We rotate the centers and quarterbacks daily, so that in case of a substitution during a game, we do not put either in an unfamiliar situation.

During our specialty period we work with our centers on making the long snap for punts and points after touchdown. For the long snap, we prefer a toe-to-instep staggered stance, with the feet a little wider than the normal center-to-quarterback exchange.

We put very little weight on the football. We want much of the center's weight on the balls of his feet. His back should be relatively straight. (See Diagram 7.)

Diagram 7

The eyes of the center should be on the target. For the snap to the punter, the center's eyes should be focused just below the numbers of the punter.

The center should grip the ball just as a passer would grip the ball to pass, with the fingertips on the laces. The other hand is used merely as a guide and should be placed accordingly for the type of snap desired.

Diagram 8

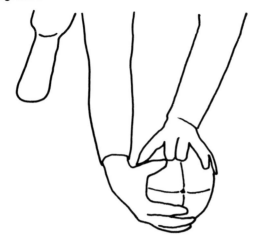

Before snapping the ball, the center should cock the power wrist to the point of exaggeration. (See Diagram 8.) The power arm should remain straight at all times during the snap, with pressure put downward throughout the snap.

The top hand can be placed forward for the punt snap (Diagram 9) and toward the back of the ball for the lower point after touchdown snap (Diagram 10).

In making the snap, both arms should snap

Diagram 9

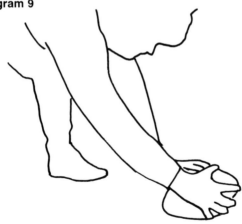

Diagram 10

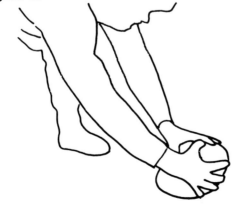

Diagram 11

through the legs at the target. The tail should not be raised. (Diagram 11.)

The wrist snap will take care of itself naturally. It is very important to get the ball to the punter or holder as quickly as possible. At Nebraska, we want our centers to get the ball to the punter in about .7 second. The punter is approximately 13½ yards deep.

We make an effort to time our centers and punters each day in practice. Immediately upon completing the snap for a punt, the center should snap his head upward, both eyes open, looking for an opponent coming into his area.

If the center is not covered, however, he will normally release immediately to help cover the punt.

In the point after touchdown and field goal formations, the center should hold his ground and allow the defender to come to him rather than seek him out. He must maintain a good football position and have good balance. He cannot be driven backward into the kicking area.

We do not use a cadence on the long snaps. The punter or holder will shout his ready command, alerting the center that he is ready for the snap any time the center is ready to deliver. Because of the importance of the long snap, we want our center to be able to snap when he is ready, not when the holder or punter says go!

We try to snap at least twenty-five long snaps daily.

In developing a center, we use repetition in our daily drills. Basically, we use three drills to teach the reach block, double team, do-dad, and pass protection. To become proficient with the reach block we use a drill we refer to as pin-trap. (See Diagram 12.)

In the pin-trap drill we stress the lead step constantly. We want the center to gain something with his lead step.

For teaching the do-dad and double team we work a three-on-three drill. (See Diagram 13.)

This is a very simple drill, but we stress it in all of our daily workouts. The blocking scheme dictates which of the above blocks may develop. When the center knows he has a possible do-dad, he is going through the playside hip of the nose guard. If that hip disappears away from the play, the center automatically thinks of the do-dad.

If a double team is in order according to the blocking scheme, the center fires at the numbers of the nose guard, knowing that he will get help from the guard.

In working on pass protection, we will normally work our entire five interior linemen versus five defensive ball players and concentrate our coaching efforts on getting the people off the ball as quickly as possible in order to get a read on the defensive man.

Each team has its own philosophy on the play of the center. We have presented many of the things that we do that have proved successful for us.

Diagram 12

Diagram 13

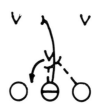

30
Defensive End Play

(From 1972 Summer Manual of the AFCA)

ESCO SARKKINEN Assistant Coach, Ohio State University

Gertrude Stein's oft-quoted line, "A rose is a rose is a rose," is paraphrased by Woody Hayes's identity of defensive end play—"An end is an end is an end." The ultimate purpose of a defensive end is to play as an end—not as a linebacker, not as a tackle, not as a combination linebacker-tackle-end—only as an end, period. That is why he is out there.

The initial approach that we use in our coaching is to work from the "whole" to the "parts." The player gets the broad concept first as to his part and as to his play in a defense. The importance of the "parts," such as stance, alignment, keys, and techniques, is undeniable, but we want to make sure that the player understands the general notion of his defensive play. He must get the basic idea first. The format of this article will be based on the same principle—overall concepts first and details second.

We flip-flop all our defenders except for the interior linemen. The reasons for doing this are to simplify the learning assignments, to enable easier teaching, to work players in units, and to get our best personnel to the side of the big play.

The first broad concept of our defensive thinking is that football is a game of vertical position or depth—going up and down from goal line to goal line. Football is also a game of lateral position—going side to side from one boundary to another. Over 80 percent of the offensive plays will originate on or near the hash mark. To the offense, the open side of the field is "gold" country. There is where the great back and the great play like to operate. But the closed side of the field (boundary) is "nickel and dime" country. The plays into the boundary usually end up with half the yardage of plays to the wide side.

A few years ago our staff saw on film an astounding play by Jim Grabowski of Illinois. The projector clicked off as we looked at each other in disbelief. From the hash mark this young man ran an option pitch sweep into the boundary. He scored a 65-yard touchdown with every one of the eleven defensive players completely pinned to his inside! There was no overrun of pursuit by a defender and no cutback by the runner as he swept into that narrow patch of sideline to outskirt the complete defense. Except for goal line plays, a run of this caliber was a landmark.

"Sammy Sideline" is the defender's best friend and the game's deadliest tackler. Naturally, our boundary end gets the "axiom" to force the sweep wide into the sideline. Look at the odds in his favor. Only Grabowski has done it (scored) in twenty-five years of Big Ten football.

If the open end has more territory to defend, roughly two-thirds of the field, compared to the boundary end's one-third, it is reasonable to assume that the physical requirements of each will differ. Furthermore, the open end gets burned in his brain the positive axiom "Stay on your feet," or its negative counterpart, "Never go down." The end who comes closest to being a nimble, sure-footed mountain goat type gets the call to play this position. Meanwhile, the steady-heady, more physical end plays into the boundary. By flip-flopping the two types, we expect to have the odds in our favor. Until the rules put the hash marks exactly in midfield, we will continue to believe that each side of a defense has distinctive needs; hence, the need for differences in their play.

We are a multiple defensive football team. Like most staffs, a recurring tug of war exists on what to carry versus what to drop. The forces of reduction usually win out. Likewise, we try to clarify terminology and communication so there are no "busted" assignments. There are showdowns between the number of defensive "looks" versus defensive "stunts." Which is better? More looks with fewer stunts, or a few looks but more stunts? If we favor the latter, the techniques and responsibilities should be kept to a minimum. "Consistency as much as possible" is the key phrase in our odd, even, seven- or eight-man front defenses. For example, we do not want such complex or varied option rules that the assignments for the dive, the quarterback, and the pitch cannot be immediately determined by reaction rather than by rote.

Areas of Defensive End Play

We have four basic assignments in the four major areas of defensive end play. These assignments involve our regular 52 defense.

Pull Up the Quarterback

How many times is the sprint or rollout pass effective into the sideline with the ball favoring the hash mark? Not very often, since the receivers run into cramped areas, and the quarterback has restricted running room. The quarterback usually aborts his course to deliver the ball early. Consequently, our boundary end has more of a routine force to contain this pass. The open end does not enjoy this built-in luxury. The difficulty in pulling up a quarterback going to the two-thirds side is more pronounced.

The open end has a subtle but wider alignment. If his keys (tight end or near back) release, he makes a quick read of the quarterback's course. A "down the line" course will hold or "hang" the end on the line of scrimmage for the apparent option play. An "off the line" course will force the end to accelerate and get leverage up field. Quick read and quick acceleration will firm up his course so that the quarterback and his blockers are on his inside shoulder. Hand and arm strength are his basic weapons on the blocker. He uses less butts, but more hand tools in order to keep a cushion on the blocker. Tangled feet are caused by proximity to the blocker's body. Tattoo on his brain, "Stay on your feet" and "Never go down," but also teach him how and why. The answers to good or bad pass rush lie in these areas—his alignment, read, acceleration, course, and hit.

Squeeze the Off-Tackle Hole

In our basic 52 look, the boundary end has a heavier alignment—his nose is on the tight end's shoulder. His basic play is to level or hang on the line of scrimmage. Conversely, the open end has more

width—his inside foot on the tight end's outside foot. His action is to get depth, which makes his "seal" at the off-tackle hole more difficult. Both ends are the primary containment elements. We expect them to contain first and to constrict the off-tackle hole second.

When the blocker's head is on his inside, the end holds up on any upfield force. He tightens the angle to the ball. His block protection is a forearm flipper. The knees are flexed in a breakdown position so that he delivers hard joints—the inside shoulder, elbow, and knee—to this pressure. The big coaching axiom at this crossroads is to point the feet toward the goal line. The body falls in place, which ensures a braced football position. The shoulders will be parallel to the line of scrimmage while the outside leg and the outside arm remain free.

The "open end of the funnel" is a term we use to indicate separation between two defenders, in this case our end and tackle. To negate this split on an off-tackle play, we give the end a few "no-no's." Do not be a "chaser," do not turn out or up, do not go around the tail of the blocker. In a more positive vein, work through the blocker's head. If caught upfield, execute a spinout release to get back toward the ball.

Force the Sweep Wide

From 1968 to 1971, no team had had its defenses against the sweep receive a more severe test than Ohio State. Five outstanding pro-type backs tested our front. This test usually came after each back had made a fabulous performance in the week prior to our game. Statistics can be twisted to prove any point, but we feel the following is illustrative.

Prior to our 1968 game, Purdue's Leroy Keyes had many running totals of 200 yards a game. We held him in 1968 to 19 yards. Iowa's Ed Podolak had gained a total of 320 yards in his previous game. We held him to 45 yards. O. J. Simpson gained a few miles of territory prior to our Rose Bowl encounter, but we held him to twenty-seven carries and 91 yards. In 1971 Michigan State's Eric Allen gained 350 yards (NCAA record) prior to our game. We held him to 79 yards. In both games he had twenty-nine carries.

The factors that allowed these great backs most of the yardage for their record-setting performances were:

1. Run the pitch sweep or option.
2. Run it to the open side of the field.
3. Run against a defense that gives them the inverted line of scrimmage or the open end of the funnel.

There are additional factors that complement the above. If a sweep breaks upfield (north-south direction) in an area approximately 1 to 4 yards outside the offensive end, this play will average three times the yardage of a sweep that breaks upfield in an area approximately 5 to 8 yards or more outside the offensive end. Obviously, the first dictum from this study is to force the back to run in an east-west direction as long as possible.

Diagram 1

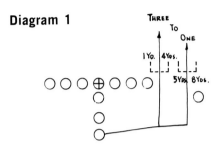

Relative speed of the ball carrier is the next important sweep factor. In O. J. Simpson's 80-yard Rose Bowl touchdown against us, he ran his first 10 yards laterally (east-west) in eight steps. This meant he was operating roughly at three-quarter speed or less. When he turned upfield (north-south) in that critical zone 4 yards from his end, he took 7- to 8-foot strides and covered 10 yards or 30 feet in four steps. Worse, he was approaching his 9.4 speed. Hence the maxim "force the sweep wide."

Another factor in this touchdown run was that O. J. broke inside of six defenders who overran their pursuit courses and then frantically tried to recover. Not only was O. J. opening his throttle to his 9.4 speed, but he was breaking reach-back arm tackles like toothpicks as he broke against the grain of the defense. In this same context, Ohio State's Paul Warfield once ran an 86-yard touchdown countersweep that broke inside of eight defenders! Once more, the reminder: Force the sweep wide.

To meet the dilemma of a Simpson or Warfield sweep, the end has three stepping stones of reaction in time lapse order. First, react to movement (key). Second, react to the blocker's head (block protection). Third, react to the ball (course). Let us put these reactions in order against the sweep.

1. The end moves with movement. First things first, jab step with the near foot if blocked by the tight end. There is no time for anything else. Jap step and shuffle if blocked by any other player.

2. React to the blocker's head. Meet his outside pressure with a hand shiver and a crossover step. Fight around his head, never into his body. Keep the outside leg and arm free with crossover steps.

3. Disengage or release from the block. Get nose-up on the ball carrier and stay there as long as his direction is east-west. Prevent the cutback (north-south). Do not offer the inverted line of scrimmage or

Diagram 2

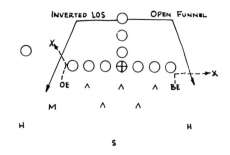

the open end of the funnel. The open end permits the former when he comes upfield too deep and wide. The boundary end permits the latter when he slides too quickly to his outside. In either case, the ball carrier finds this "daylight" readily and he quickly shifts to the deadlier north-south track. As we say, give him the "midnight" look instead. The end's perimeter support comes from his outside. He must stay in phase, eyeball to eyeball with the ball carrier, even if stymied by a blocker. When techniques are disciplined, the ball carrier is forced into a lateral course; his speed is reduced; and best of all, "Sammy Sideline" awaits yonder. Admittedly, it is the coordinated play of the perimeter that blunts the sweep, not the singular play of the end, but we do remember that the end is an end is an end.

Feather the Option Play

The standard approach to a three-way option is to assign two people to the dive, one person to the quarterback, and two people to the pitch, particularly when there is an overload or lead blocker. The double assignments usually call for one of the two to have the primary responsibility, while the one "searches" and helps as a second hitter. Our normal option assignment for the end is to "lock up" on the quarterback.

Just about every kind of option play—dive, triple, veer, counter, inside belly, outside belly, blast, and speed option—has a common denominator: the quarterback runs down the line. This action holds the end on the line, since the ball is now his ultimate key. The end should present a clean running lane to the quarterback. He takes an inside attitude on the quarterback; that is, he positions himself off the inside (near) hip of the quarterback in an approximate 1 yard off and a 1 yard out alignment. This alignment will vary according to the quarterback's running ability, the opponent's strategic tendencies on pitch or keep, and the game's tactical situations in both the vertical and lateral field positions. For example, the boundary end locks on the quarterback somewhat tighter. He reacts with a Pavlovian response, knowing that the pitch is relatively ineffective into the sideline despite Grabowski's run.

The end's next approach to the option is to play for time and let the quarterback run (east-west) as long as possible. This is very true for the open end. Understandably, this brings the inside pursuit into the picture as well as outside rotation to the potential pitch. In normal play we do not like to pop or jump the quarterback with the end. This action forces a quick pitch, but it takes the end out of his pursuit. It stretches the defense at the perimeter; and it enhances the possibilities of a breakout because the following pursuit to the pitch is delayed or diverted.

We prefer the technique called "cat 'n' mouse." Its main coaching points are:

1. Position fairly well off the quarterback's near hip.
2. Cushion just close enough to make the tackle if the quarterback turns up.
3. Give ground with a controlled shuffle step as the quarterback angles in.
4. Run the line on the pitch.

With proper execution the end has:

1. Closed that critical zone just outside the offensive end (the one to 4-yard north-south cowpath).
2. Kept the ball moving laterally (relatively little danger here).
3. Reduced the speed of the ball carrier.
4. Allowed the pursuit and rollup to form up including his own release when the pitch occurs.

Any time the pitch is made, then there is no alternative. A good back now has the ball. We do not like a one-on-one confrontation in those wide-open spaces where a missed tackle means trouble. It is almost impossible to stop an option pitch that has a lead blocker with just one defender, unless your defender is one who wears a jersey with the great big letter "S" on it. Not many option pitches are made perpendicular to the line of scrimmage. The quarterback will angle in on the end and make a long pitch toward the sideline. The rollup of a single defender cannot handle both the ball carrier and his blocker because the long lead pitch enables the ball carrier to turn upfield al

most immediately after his catch, and this puts him in that dangerous north-south axis.

To defend the pitch there should be relief—an outside and an inside attitude made by two people. In Diagram 3 the open end makes an inside approach after the pitch, while the open corner makes an outside approach. The assignments of outside and inside responsibility will vary with the structure of the defense, the change-ups, and the stunts.

Diagram 3

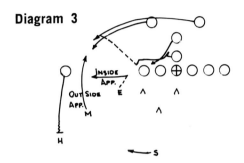

Diagram 4 shows a similar approach, with the option going into the boundary. Again, this principle will not always be played with the same people. A change-up defense will dictate the coverage.

Diagram 4

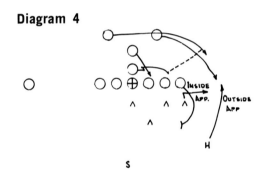

In the total picture we ask the defensive end to do many things. He handles his job almost entirely by his reactions. If we had to pick one physical characteristic of defensive end play that is more critical than any other, we would select "footwork." This has many meanings, such as speed, agility, quickness, pursuit, containment, and others, but football is a game of movement and this is what defense is especially about.

31
Fundamentals and Principles of Linebacker Play

(From 1978 *Proceedings* of the AFCA)

JERRY SANDUSKY Assistant Coach, Pennsylvania State University

All of us realize that football is a game of execution and that football games are won with sound fundamentals. It is very important that linebackers know what to do and are able to execute in the most efficient manner.

One of the most difficult jobs for any coach is the task of drawing the line between having the necessary discipline and making robots out of the players. It is felt that linebackers should be trained to perform within certain guidelines, but must perform with a degree of recklessness. We believe that regardless of the position you coach, there are a few very important points that must be emphasized before the athlete takes over.

In order to be consistent in our expectations and to avoid misunderstandings, we have developed the following principles of linebacker play. It must be understood that these principles are based on our multiple defensive scheme and the responsibilities that the linebackers have within this scheme.

Stance

The type of stance used should be dictated by the linebacker's initial movements. Most of the initial movements of linebackers are lateral; therefore, we use a parallel, two-point stance. Essentially, it is football's basic hitting position.

The feet are about shoulder width apart or wider in a parallel position and pointed straight ahead. The heels of both feet are on the ground, but the weight of the body is on the balls of the feet. The legs are alert and bent slightly at the knees. The amount of bend will vary with different body builds, but the end result should be a good balanced position. The linebacker should bend at the waist so that his hands dangle at approximately knee height. His upper body should be prepared but not tense. It is important that he appear confident; his head and eyes should be concentrating on the offensive key. The easiest way to get into this position is to start with a basic hitting position with hands on knees, then slide the hands a little forward and below the knees, and lower the buttocks slightly. It is very important that he not raise up or lower himself to move laterally.

Movement

Most of the movement of our linebackers is lateral. The linebacker should not raise or lower himself from his initial stance, and he must maintain his shoulders as close as possible to the line of scrimmage while in lateral movement. The manner in which a linebacker moves laterally is dictated by a key or the ball.

The first fundamental movement is the slide or the shuffle. This is the easiest movement from which to change direction, because the feet never cross. Sometimes it is only necessary to slide once. Analysis shows that the linebacker leans in the direction to which he wants to go, slides his back foot (the one opposite the direction that he wants to go) in the direction of the body lean, then slides the foot on the side of the direction he is going. It is very important that he not hop or cross his feet. It must be a quick move, keeping the feet as close to the ground as possible. The elbows should be kept close to the body with a minimum amount of upper-body motion. If necessary, he continues to slide in this same manner.

If sliding is not fast enough, then it is necessary to

run laterally. To run in this manner, the linebacker should keep his shoulders square and swing his arms naturally. Again, the linebacker leads with his back foot (the one opposite the direction that he wants to go), but this time he crosses over the other foot. Example: If going to the left, it is right over, left out, and so on.

The linebacker should remember to:

1. Turn his shoulders to run only as a last resort.
2. Not waste motion or become overextended.
3. Become quicker by doing the things that are necessary for his position with an all-out effort. Everything must be done with a maximum effort, whether it is one slide or a 40-yard sprint; any effort less than maximum can become a bad habit.

Shedding Blockers

The linebacker should not do anything that isn't necessary. The object is to make tackles, not to play off blocks. If it is necessary to play off a block, it is recommended that when a blocker approaches the linebacker at an angle (not straight ahead) or comes at him below the waist, he should use his hands to protect himself and get rid of the blocker. If playing off a low block the linebacker should:

1. Concentrate on the blocker, while seeing the ball carrier out of his periphery.
2. React to the blocker's head, slide in the direction of his head, and strive to maintain position.
3. Use his hands to stop the offensive man's charge. In order to do this, it is best to aim his hands in the area of the offensive player's shoulder pads.
4. Push with his hands on contact and give with his feet to clear the offensive man's charge.
5. Keep his shoulders square and make his second move before his opponent (that is, be the first to move after contact).
6. If necessary, give ground to keep his shoulders square. He should not go around behind the blocker in the "easy way" if the offensive man has good position. He must keep moving in the direction the offensive man is trying to go.

If the blocker comes at the linebacker above his waist and straight ahead with the ball carrier behind him, he should deliver a blow. In playing off these high blocks the linebacker should:

1. Stay square with the blocker and not take a side.
2. Take a short step with the foot on the same side of the forearm that is being used. Drive his shoulder and forearm underneath the hel-

met of the offensive blocker. Lower his tail at the same time so that his feet are underneath him.
3. Not wind up or waste motion but create maximum explosion with a minimum amount of wasted effort. Think of "stinging" the blocker.
4. Not get overextended but maintain a balanced position.
5. Accelerate his feet on contact in short, choppy steps, keeping his head up and back arched.
6. Strain upward and into the pressure of the block.
7. Make an all-out effort to get rid of the blocker. Use the hand that is not delivering the blow to push and throw off the offensive man. Do not stay blocked.
8. Prevent the blocker from getting position between himself and the ball carrier.
9. Never spin away from the blocker.
10. Strain into the pressure of the block, give ground, keep his shoulders square, and take a proper pursuit angle if a blocker has got position between himself and the ball.

When the linebacker is outflanked (a potential blocker is outside of him), it is important to stay alert for a crack-back block, that is, a blocker coming from the outside to block a defensive man who is positioned to the inside. If a blocker is approaching from the outside, it is recommended that the linebacker first try to beat the blocker (get upfield before the blocker makes contact). If he gets blocked or is on a poor pursuit angle to the ball by trying to beat the block, he should be ready to give ground, keep his shoulders square, and take a proper angle to meet the ball carrier. The most common mistake in this case is to stop and look for the blocker. The block should probably not be played in the same manner every time. Occasionally, he should unload on the blocker and come off the block as he would any other high block.

Tackling

Desire, proper body position, and balance are essential in tackling. It is recommended that when a linebacker is making a tackle he should:

1. Not raise or lower himself from a good hitting position but stay square when approaching the ball carrier.
2. Keep his elbows close to his sides and not wind up.
3. Bull his neck, keep his eyes open, and stay square to the ball carrier.
4. Accelerate his feet with short, choppy steps

and wrap his arms around the ball carrier on contact.

5. Keep his head up, back arched, and always try to look at the ball carrier.
6. Drive through the ball carrier while trying to take him back 5 yards and put him on his back.
7. Keep his eyes open when assisting on a tackle so that he doesn't knock off the other tackler.
8. Spring from his stance and attempt to meet a ball carrier in the air who is diving to score a touchdown or make a first down.
9. Attack ball carriers in the open field most of the time. Force the ball carrier into a decision.
10. Use the sideline to advantage when making a tackle by coming under control, taking away the runner's inside cut, and forcing him out of bounds.

Pursuit

It is important that defensive players approach ball carriers at the proper angles. Using good judgment and taking the proper lane of pursuit can help to overcome the advantage of speed enjoyed by most offensive backs. When pursuing a ball carrier, some important points for the linebacker to remember are:

1. Inside linebackers should try to keep everything on their outside shoulder when the action has come to their side. They should pursue in a lateral direction until the ball carrier has turned upfield and then attack from the inside position.
2. When a ball carrier goes away from a linebacker, he should maintain a position slightly to the inside so that he can protect against the cutback.
3. Attempt to make ball carriers continue to run in a lateral direction. Try not to create a seam so that a back can run upfield.
4. Take a steeper angle of pursuit (from the line of scrimmage) in order to save a touchdown when the ball carrier is farther away.
5. When playing the quarterback against the option, pursuit should be at least at a flat angle to intersect the ball carrier's path once the quarterback has pitched the ball. If the ball is pitched well out in front of the quarterback, it is necessary to take a steeper angle (from the line of scrimmage) to meet the ball carrier.
6. Outside linebackers (playing a flat zone) should attack flare and screen passes from an outside position, attempting to force the ball carrier into the middle.

Zone Pass Coverage

The recommended techniques for the linebackers in playing zone pass defense are:

1. As soon as a linebacker recognizes a pass play, he should call it out and start running to his area of responsibility as fast as possible. Initial depth gives him an opportunity to come under better body control when the ball is about to be thrown.
2. Most of the time he should turn and run laterally, looking over his inside shoulder at the quarterback.
3. As he is going to his zone, he should glance for receivers who might be coming into his area, but he should never turn completely away from the ball. He must know where receivers are, yet still be able to react if the quarterback throws quickly or in another area.
4. He should position himself between the ball and a potential receiver in his zone. Once he has got within about 3 yards of the receiver, he should settle down (stop in a basic hitting position) where he can see both the receiver and the quarterback (match up with the receiver). He should be turned at about a 45-degree angle toward the outside (receiver), aligned 3 yards in front of the receiver and 3 yards to his inside; concentrate on the ball but see the receiver out of his periphery, and be ready to go to any throws that would be made to the outside. If the receiver works wider or the ball is thrown to the outside, the linebacker should run at an angle to make the interception in front of the receiver. If the receiver breaks to the inside behind the linebacker, he should pivot back to face the ball and react to it.
5. If no receiver is in his zone (12 to 15 yards deep), he should square his shoulders to the line of scrimmage and begin to back pedal. While running backward, his weight should be on the balls of his feet, his arms should move as if running, and his elbows should be close to his sides. As he is retreating, he should glance for receivers.
6. He should react to all looks of the quarterback in his area. When the quarterback looks, he should turn his shoulders and sprint at an angle to make the interception in front of the receiver.
7. He should try to catch the ball at its highest point, look it into his hands, shout "fire," and spring toward his goal.

8. All of the linebackers should communicate with each other. They must tell the adjacent linebacker if a receiver is crossing into his area.

9. If a receiver crosses a linebacker's path, he should be knocked to the ground or at least off stride, but in the process the linebacker should not get overextended or go out of his way to hit the receiver. The linebacker should not lose his position in trying to knock down a receiver.

10. Once the ball is thrown, all linebackers must be running at full speed toward the ball until it falls to the ground.

Man-for-Man Pass Defense

Two types of man-to-man pass coverage techniques are used. The linebacker will play reckless man-for-man coverage when he has help in the deep secondary. Reckless techniques are used to take away the underneath passes (from the line of scrimmage to a depth of about 18 yards), while cautious man-for-man techniques are used when the linebacker does not have any help in the deep zones, and he must protect them. When playing cautious man-for-man pass defense the linebacker:

1. Aligns himself approximately 1 yard inside the offensive receiver at a depth of about 4 yards with his inside foot forward.

2. Concentrates on the receiver.

3. Begins to run backward, leading with his front foot, as the receiver comes forward.

4. Tries to maintain a distance of 2 to 3 yards between himself and the receiver and maintains a position of 1 yard to the receiver's inside. As the receiver gets closer to him, he begins to run laterally in order to maintain his position.

5. Breaks parallel to the receiver's changes of directions, and then gradually gets closer to the receiver as the ball is thrown.

6. Must protect against any deep pass.

7. Turns his back to the ball in pursuit if the receiver has got beyond him. Concentrates on the receiver, especially his hands; turns toward the receiver to look for the ball when the receiver's hands come up.

When playing reckless man-for-man with two defensive halfbacks helping in the deep outside, the linebacker:

1. Aligns in the same manner as if playing cautious man-for-man. Can align on a tight receiver (tight end or tight slot) and to his inside.

2. Concentrates on the receiver.

3. Does not immediately react to any moves by the receiver toward the inside.

4. Does not let the receiver go to his inside; jams him if he tries to get the inside position.

5. If the receiver releases to the outside, he waits (does not move) until the receiver reaches his outside shoulder and then turns and jams him with his hands. He also lets the receiver get slightly ahead so that he can cover the underneath passes.

6. Chases the receiver, staying to the inside and slightly behind him.

7. Plays all pass cuts of the receiver from underneath (the side closer to the ball), concentrates on the receiver's hands, and goes for the interception when the receiver reaches for the ball.

Blitzing

When blitzing, the linebacker should:

1. Not alert the offense by altering his stance or starting too soon.

2. Go immediately on the snap of the ball.

3. Attempt to penetrate across the line of scrimmage.

4. Notice the offensive linemen and the action of the ball and adjust as they are moving; inside linebackers should follow pulling guards, and so on.

5. Guard against losing himself.

6. React to the pressure of blocks as if he were playing normally.

7. Use his hands when rushing the passer.

8. Make quick moves but stay in his rushing lane.

9. Try to get the offensive man turned one way and then go in the opposite direction.

Additional Points to Remember

The linebacker should:

1. Not dive (leave his feet) to make a tackle except as a last resort.

2. Use his hands when playing lead blockers in the open field where the ball carrier has plenty of running room.

3. Try to make the blocker miss or give ground in order to save the touchdown.

4. Not become impatient or attempt to make every tackle without an offensive gain.

5. Give ground around piles of blockers and defenders in order to make plays for a 2- or 3-

yard gain instead of creating potential "big plays."

6. Recognize the blocking direction and react to the pressure of the block.
7. Take care of immediate problems first.
8. Learn to concentrate on blockers while seeing ball carriers out of his periphery.
9. Not waste motion and effort.
10. Have a sense of timing and know when to exert himself.
11. Not be a "robot" or afraid to take a chance in order to make things happen.

Part Six
Defense

32
Drills at Alabama for Defensive Players

(From 1976 Proceedings of the AFCA)

BILL OLIVER, KEN DONAHUE, and PAUL CRANE
University of Alabama

Introduction (Bill Oliver)

I've been to many football clinics where I only found one or two things I liked or could use, but they are still being used today. The following techniques and drills are some of those used at the University of Alabama. Each is illustrated and the objective of the drill and coaching points are also included.

We spend more time during the spring and two-a-days using drills than during the regular season. Certainly we do some in the regular season and, at the same time, we try to use drills that might apply to the type of coverage or coverages we are using. It is imperative that the player understands why he is doing a drill.

Break Drill

Diagram 1

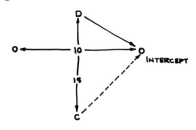

Objective: To teach the defender to get the jump on the ball and measure the distance he can break on the ball in the air.

Coaching Points: Always break into the direction the coach steps and break when he steps.

Hash Mark Tip

Objective: To teach the defensive back to react on the

Diagram 2

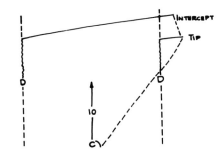

ball thrown to the opposite side of field and to make an interception on a tip ball.

Coaching Points: Sprint back maintaining a constant cushion and break on the ball when the passer steps.

Great Hash Mark

Diagram 3

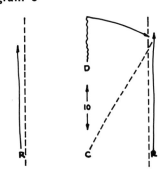

Objective: To teach defensive backs that they can cover two receivers in a deep zone by keeping good position and breaking on the ball.

Coaching Points: Keep equal distance between the two receivers as quarterback steps, break to the receiver, and intercept the ball.

Everybody Tip It

Diagram 4

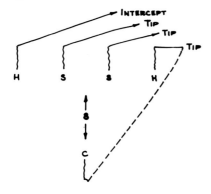

Objective: To teach all defensive people to react to the ball thrown to the opposite field.

Coaching Points: Everyone sprints to the ball, each player maintaining a position so that he can get his hands on the ball, assisting the next man.

Hash Mark Drill

Diagram 5

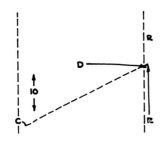

Objective: To build confidence in a defender in the amount of area he can cover while the ball is in the air.

Coaching Points: Break when the coach steps to throw.

Check Drill

Diagram 6

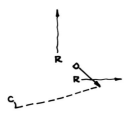

Objective: To teach the defensive man to read the quarterback and get the jump on the ball.

Coaching Points: Throw the ball quickly so the defensive man can intercept it. Make sure the two receivers start first.

Comeback Drill

Diagram 7

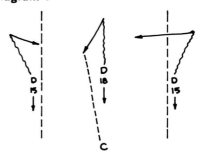

Objective: To teach a defender to come back on the ball a great distance.

Coaching Points: Keep in a coiled position reading the arm of the passer. Plant the outside foot and roll forward intercepting the football.

Finesse Drill

Diagram 8

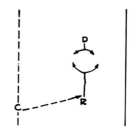

Objective: To build confidence in a player that he can make a sure tackle from a big cushion.

Coaching Points: Keep position on receiver and make the sure tackle.

Circle Tip

Diagram 9

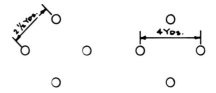

Objective: To develop quick eye-hand coordination.

Coaching Points: Keep the football moving as fast as possible without letting it hit the ground. Try to keep the ball moving between the knees and shoulders.

Wave Drill

Diagram 10

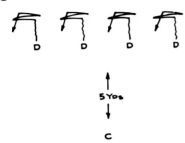

Objective: To teach body balance, quickness, and co-ordination while changing direction 180 degrees.
Coaching Points: Keep in good football position. When pivoting, always drop outside weight over the balls of your pivoting foot. Always gain ground when you step with lead foot.

Take Off Drill

Diagram 11

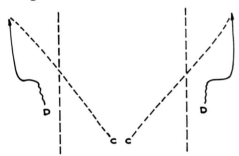

Objective: To develop the reaction of a defender intercepting or getting his hands on the football with a receiver going deep.
Coaching Points: Maintain good position on receiver. At the last second get higher than receiver after locating the ball.

Weave

Diagram 12

Objective: To develop a shoulder relationship with the receiver.
Coaching Points: Backpedal, then start weaving no wider than 4 yards and never crossing feet over. Keep shoulder perpendicular to line of scrimmage.

Basic Defensive Drills (Ken Donahue)

Before I get into defensive drills, I would like to give you a little insight into Alabama's philosophy and scheme of defense. We believe in a multiple scheme, but we try to keep it as simple as we can by using and teaching only a few defensive techniques. Over the period of a season, we may use as many as four or five basic fronts with variations. We want to make it complicated to the offense and simple to our defense.

We try to teach our defensive linemen a read technique, a gap technique, a loop technique, a short-yardage technique, and at least two pass-rush techniques. Of course we teach tackling and the other basic fundamentals.

Our drills are designed to develop skills in these defensive techniques and fundamentals.

We have a few basic principles that we follow in our drills that we think are important.

1. If feasible, start the drill on movement of the ball and end it with linemen in a football position.
2. Change drills frequently to keep them from getting monotonous.
3. Use extra motivation in drill.
4. Put emphasis on strengthening the weakness of an individual.
5. Place the emphasis in drills according to the strength of the opponent's offense.
6. Display enthusiasm for and compliment an outstanding performance.

The first basic drill I would like to cover is a basic tackling drill. We call it gauntlet tackling drill, and some form of this drill has been used down through the years. We usually have three different groups or setups in this drill at the same time, with our defensive linemen and ends in one setup, our linebacker in another setup, and our secondary in another. We try to get our bigger and stronger junior varsity backs to be the ball carriers versus the defensive linemen and ends. We want the ball carriers to run as if they were running inside and to either make one fake or no fake.

The coaching points we stress in this drill are:
1. Start from a coiled stance.
2. Focus just above the belt buckle of the ball carrier.
3. Go after the ball carrier at controlled speed.
4. Attack the ball carrier in the middle from a coiled position.

Diagram 13

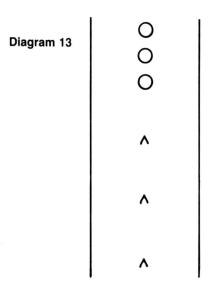

5. Tackle on the rise through ball carrier, lock arms, and gain yardage.

Normally we let a defensive man get three tackles and get out. If he makes an outstanding tackle on the first one, we will have him get out. If he is a poor tackler, we may let him get an extra one. After the season gets underway, we do not put the ball carrier on the ground.

We have a pass-rush drill in our practice plans on Monday and Tuesday and sometimes on Wednesday. Our favorite pass-rush drill is what we call the two-on-one pass-rush drill.

Diagram 14

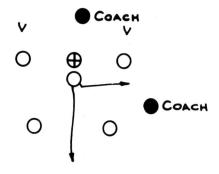

In this drill a manager acts as a quarterback, and our scout team offensive linemen are the blockers. Our scout team offensive line coach stands in front of offense and uses hand signals to give the snap count and play. Most of the time he will call a play-action or drop-back pass. Infrequently, he will call an inside handoff or an option. The two offensive linemen line up approximately 5 yards back and use drop-back protection if a pass is called. The quarterback carries out the called play. On a pass, he throws from a depth of about 12 yards to a man standing downfield. We have

the offensive linemen use the same blocking techniques as our opponent.

The coaching points we stress to defensive linemen on the pass-rush drill are:

1. Do not let blocker get body-to-body contact.
2. Use the hands and a good pass-rush technique.
3. Be in position to get in the rush lane.
4. Move quickly and lower the center of balance as you get to blocker.
5. Never come to a complete stop.
6. Jump as quarterback releases ball if he is facing.

The one basic running play drill that we use almost every day that players are wearing pads is what we call the read drill.

Diagram 15

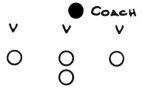

The scout team coach signals the offensive play and snap count. The defensive coach signals the defensive technique he wants used. The managers act as quarterback and simulate play. This is basically a drill where defensive linemen work on defensive techniques versus the running game, although a pass is called infrequently. In this drill we work on a hand shiver read, a shoulder read, and a gap technique.

Another drill that we use a great deal in spring practice and in early fall is the three-on-three drill.

Diagram 16

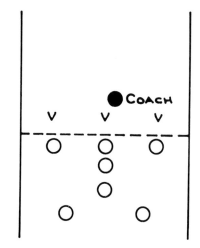

This is also an excellent offensive drill. In this drill we try to defend a 10-yard area with three defensive people. We normally have two setups of this drill with the first offensive line against our first defensive front in one setup and our second offensive line against our second defensive front in the other setup. Usually, we use the scout team and freshman backs in this drill, but at times we use our first and second team backs. To make this a successful drill, the defensive men cannot jump through the gaps and the backs cannot block. At times we make a game out of this drill, with the offense trying to make 10 yards in three downs. An offensive coach lined up in front of the offense calls the snap and play with hand signals. Players are usually rotated after six or seven plays. This drill usually lasts from twenty to twenty-five minutes and is very competitive, since the offense and defense try to outdo each other. A great deal of fun is had by both coaches and players in this drill.

Drills for Linebackers (Paul Crane)

I would like to cover three of the basic skills that a linebacker must physically be able to execute in order to play. At Alabama we feel our linebackers must be able to play blockers, tackle, and play pass defense. They must also have the movement and recognition to put them in a position to accomplish these basic fundamentals. We try to incorporate movement and recognition as a basic in all our drills. I would like to concentrate on several of the drills we use to teach the basic fundamentals of playing blockers, tackling, and pass defense.

Drills for Playing Blockers

One of our favorite drills is the three-man circle drill. This is a reaction drill used to teach the linebacker to react to and play a blocker. The drill is set up using four players and one coach.

Diagram 17

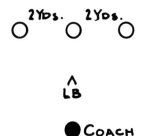

Three of the players become offensive linemen and line up approximately 2 yards apart facing the linebacker, who lines head-up on the middle man about 2 to 2½ yards away. The coach stands behind the linebacker, and on his signal (points), one of the offensive players fires into the linebacker to block him. The

blocker does not try to sustain the block, but delivers an initial block and returns to his original position ready to block again on the coach's signal.

The linebacker reacts to the blocker by stepping to him with his onside foot and exploding into him with his flipper and shoulder, whipping and shedding the blocker and then reacting back to his original position ready to react to the next blocker. We normally have the linebacker hit each blocker twice before he rotates to become an offensive blocker and another linebacker rotates over to the defensive position.

This drill provides an opportunity for the coach to check the linebacker's stance before and after he makes contact and reacts back to his original position.

Another drill we use during the spring and early fall is a one-on-one drill with a ball carrier. We use this drill to teach our linebackers to play and shed a blocker and make the tackle on the ball carrier. We place two dummies about 3 yards apart.

Diagram 18

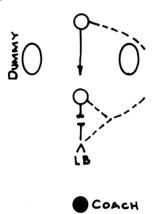

Have a blocker on the line and a ball carrier behind the blocker. The linebacker is about 2½ yards off the ball. The coach stands behind the linebacker and signals the offensive players either to block straight on the linebacker or to use a cutoff block and run wide. This is a good drill to teach the linebacker to see both the guard and back and to react to the different types of blocks and flow. He must be able to whip the straight-on block with his shoulder and forearm and make the tackle. He must also be able to beat the cutoff block with his hands and movement and make the tackle. The ball carrier must stay inside the dummies on the straight block and run outside the dummy on the cutoff block.

Drills for Tackling

We use several drills in teaching our players to tackle. One drill we use every day during our warmups is a simple form tackling drill. We divide the lineback-

Diagram 19

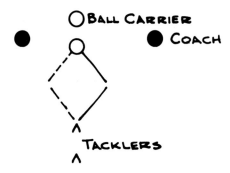

ers into two lines that face each other. One line becomes ball carriers, the other tacklers.

The ball carrier runs at about three-quarter speed to the tackler's left side. The tackler makes an angle tackle on the ball carrier, then rotates to the ball carrier line, and the ball carrier rotates to the tackling line. When all the tacklers have made a tackle to their left side, then the ball carriers run to the tackler's right side. After making an angle tackle to each side, they then make a head-on tackle. The coach should stand behind the ball carrier in order to watch the tackler's approach and to make sure he keeps his eyes open and head up. The tackler should put his head across the front of the ball carrier, wrapping his arms around him and hitting on the rise. This is a simple drill, but still an excellent teaching drill.

Another tackling drill we like for linebackers is an open field tackling drill. We use this drill to teach the linebackers to come under control and make the sure tackle. We place two dummies about 8 yards apart and put a ball carrier about 10 yards deep and the linebacker about 10 yards deep on the opposite side. The ball carrier must run within the dummies. On the coach's signal the ball carrier tries to run between the dummies, avoiding the linebacker. The linebacker tries to prevent the runner from passing between the dum-

Diagram 20

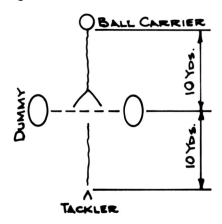

mies by closing the area between them as much as possible and then coming under control and making a sure tackle. The coach should be in a position to watch the linebacker's eyes and body control. This is a good drill to teach the linebacker how not to overcommit himself in the open field.

Drills for Pass Defense

We try to put a number of pass catching drills into our warmup and specialty periods. We do this to give the linebacker a chance to improve his ability and confidence in catching and handling the football and to make practice more interesting. We use several drills to help our linebackers with their pass drops. One of them is a combination of a pass drop with a tip man. We place a player about 15 to 20 yards deep to the side of the linebacker drop.

Diagram 21

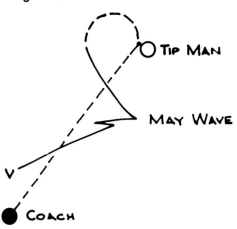

The coach has the linebacker make his regular pass drop and react on the ball as in a wave drill. The coach may throw the ball for the linebacker to intercept, over his head, or behind him to the tip man. The tip man tips the pass up in the air, and the linebacker must react to the overthrown ball and intercept the tip at its highest point. This drill is used to work on pass drops, maintaining a football position, and reacting to and finding the football.

Another drill we use for pass defense is called "man in the middle." We use this drill to show the linebacker how far he can move on reaction to the ball, to give him confidence in handling the ball and for fun. This drill is best done in front of a net. We place two players about 8 yards apart and then place a linebacker between them.

The coach stands about 12 yards in front of the linebacker. The linebacker should be in a good football position, with his weight on the balls of his feet, ready to move. The coach tries to throw the ball to one of the end men while the linebacker tries to move on the coach's motion and intercept the pass. This is a good reaction drill and a drill the players enjoy. We make it a contest drill between the players and coach. If the coach completes so many passes he wins, if the players intercept so many passes they win.

These are a few of the individual drills we use to help our linebackers play blockers, tackle, and play pass defense. We feel the best recognition drills for linebackers are team drills, such as secondary or front drills and scrimmages.

Diagram 22

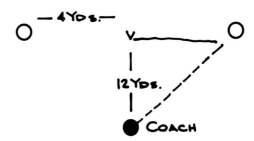

33
Development of Individual Defensive Techniques at Maryland

(From *1974 Summer Manual* of the AFCA)

JOHN DEVLIN, Defensive End and Linebacker Coach; GEORGE FOUSSEKIS, Defensive Guard Coach; and TERRY STROCK, Secondary, University of Maryland

Defensive Guards and Tackles
(George Foussekis)

At the University of Maryland, we use a multiple defense. We teach our defensive personnel by techniques, thus simplifying our system and saving valuable time for game preparation. Each technique carries a specific assignment; therefore, we can get our people where we want them without wasting time.

Playing a multiple front, our defensive linemen are called on to line up in several different positions. However, we ask them to execute and master only a few basic techniques. We have found that the players take a great deal of pride in learning only a few techniques that they are able to execute well. As a coaching point, our tackles must be able to execute the six and seven techniques; our guards must be able to master the two technique. When a coach talks to a player about these particular techniques, the player understands him immediately.

Stance

The stance is the first step we take in teaching our defensive linemen. We are not overly particular about the stance, but we feel that the most important thing is that it be comfortable. We want our players in a stance in which they can uncoil, make good contact, and move quickly.

Coaching points that we stress to our players include not taking a stance in which a player will get overextended (too much weight on hands or heels) and not getting into a stance with too wide a base. If you have a wide stance and take the proper step, you become locked in your stance or off balance. Watch the feet in studying films to see if a player's first step is a false one back under him. He may be doing this in order to correct his stance or regain balance.

Guard Play

Our guards line up in a four-point stance with their feet even and about shoulder width apart. The weight must be slightly forward and their tail slightly lower than their shoulders. The weight should be evenly distributed on the hands and feet. A good way of checking weight distribution is to check the tail to see if it is even with the heels of the feet.

The two technique is the technique our guards must master in order to play the wide tackle six defense successfully. The alignment in a two technique is head on a normal offensive guard. We tell them to keep their spacing on each other and not let the offensive guard oversplit them. We like them to line up arms length apart, although this will vary depending on the player's experience or ability. If they are getting oversplit, we tell them to move back off the ball or jump in the gap and shoot the gap.

Another way we control big splits is by our linebackers' checking to our inside stunting game. The distance they line up off the ball is about 2 feet; however, this is determined by ability, line splits, and game plan. We always start our young guards farther off the ball until they gain confidence and become salty in their skills. If we are playing a reading defense, the guards read a triangle consisting of the offensive guard, center, and the feet of the fullback. If we are stunting, they read the football.

Our guards' responsibility in the two technique is 60 percent inside and 40 percent outside, but he must never be trapped or beaten to the inside. If the play is a run to your side, pursue laterally. If it is a play pass, pursue deeper in the backfield and rush the passer. If the play is a backup pass, one guard must stay head up until the threat of the draw is gone, then rush. The other guard has a free rush. When playing a two technique, they always keep their inside arm free and never run around a block. Once our guards become experienced, they have the option of moving around on their own trying to disguise the front of the defense. Our guards spend the majority of their practice time on the two technique, because this is the one technique they must master in order to be successful.

Personnel for the Two Technique

In choosing our personnel for the two technique we look for someone who is strong enough to stop the inside running game and able to control the line of scrimmage. It also helps if he possesses good reaction and quickness because of our reading and inside stunting game. He does not necessarily have to have good speed, but he must have good lateral movement. You can get by with a lesser athlete at the two technique if he is tough and willing to work.

Tackle Play

The stance of our defensive tackles is basically the same as our guards, except that at certain times we tell them to stagger their outside foot about heel and toe. We stress to our tackles that their first step must be a short lateral step. In fact, we spend about five minutes a practice session taking the correct steps and not overstriding.

The basic alignment of our tackles is what we call a seven technique. The tackle will line up with his outside foot on the outside ear of a normally split offensive end. His distance off the ball is about 2 feet, but this will vary from game to game depending on the type of offense we face. The coaching points we stress to our tackles are to stay on the line of scrimmage and not to be in a hurry to do something. This is one of the biggest problems we have with our young tackles, as they have a tendency to get upfield or turn their shoulders before locating the ball. They must remember, due to their alignment, that it takes the ball longer to get to their area of responsibility.

Each tackle's responsibility in the seven technique is to take a short lateral step on the movement of the offensive end. Play him head on while looking to the inside to read the action of the tackle and near back. He must keep his inside arm free. If it is run his way, he has the off-tackle responsibility and then pursues laterally. If the flow is away, he is the trail man, but before he crosses the line of scrimmage, he checks for inside trap and reverses. Don't be in a hurry! If the flow passes his way, he rushes the passer, and with a backup pass, he has a contain rush.

Personnel for the Seven Technique

In choosing our personnel for the seven technique, we look for someone who is strong enough to plug the off-tackle hole. Yet he must possess the necessary agility and speed to contain the passer and wide running plays. As you can see, our defensive tackles have to be pretty good athletes who possess good reaction and speed.

Drills

The first drill we teach our defensive linemen is an explosion drill. (See Diagram 1.) They must be able to deliver a good lick and control the line of scrimmage. This is a must.

Diagram 1

SIX POINT STANCE

STRESS TUCK OF TAIL!

We have several big wooden single buckers on which we teach extension and explosion. We start off by lining up in front of the buckers in a six-point stance. From this stance we explode with our legs. At this point we are stressing to them to tuck their tails and try to find the sky with their eyes. He should end up after the blow on his stomach at the base of the bucker. His feet should not move. We feel this drill really teaches our people to tuck their tails in delivering a blow. We also will do this drill from a four-point stance, again stressing the tuck of the tail. This is one drill we work on every day.

The next step for our defensive linemen is learning how to whip a man one-on-one. (See Diagram 1a.) Here we mainly work on the drive block, concentrating on getting underneath the offensive man's pad and again tucking that tail. This is also a good toughness drill, and is a must drill for our defensive linemen.

Diagram 1a

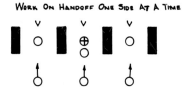

Next we try to teach the defensive man to read the blocker's head while looking back to the inside to read the flow. (See Diagram 2.)

Diagram 2

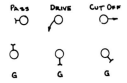

This is a great drill for teaching drive block, cutoff block, and pass recognition. The first step is one of the most important factors in defensive line play. A great majority of the time our people get themselves in trouble because of a poor or incorrect first step. This drill gives our people the opportunity to practice taking the correct steps, so we feel this is another must drill and one they must master. Our next progressive step is the two-on-one drill. We use an offensive guard and center plus a fullback for our guards. For our tackles, we use an offensive tackle and end, plus a ball carrier. (See Diagram 3.)

In this drill, we try to expose our people to as many blocking situations as possible. This is an excellent recognition and reaction drill.

The next drill is one we use mainly for our defensive guards, which they probably use more than any other drill. It is the five-on-two drill and a drill we must perfect. (See Diagram 4.)

This drill exposes our guards to every situation they will face in a ball game. This is a drill we use a great deal during the season.

Another drill we really like, which helps us strike a blow, take correct step, release the block, and make the tackle is called our "hustle" drill. (See Diagram 5.) This drill not only teaches the basics of football, but also becomes very competitive between the defense

Diagram 3

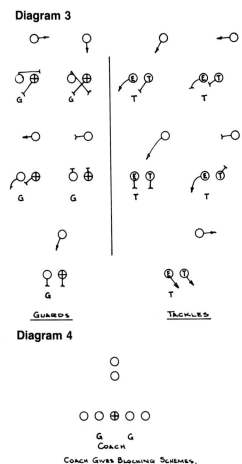

Diagram 4

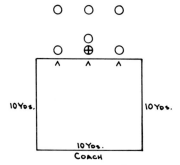

and offense players. Also, our coaches have been known to get carried away emotionally in this drill.

The offense is given three downs to make 10 yards. A coach standing behind the defense gives the snap count and direction of the ball.

Diagram 5

We spend a great deal of time in our "post area." In this particular area we have seven padded posts, forming an offensive line. (See Diagram 6.)

In this area we can work on striking a blow, our

Diagram 6

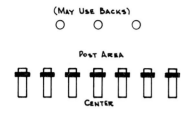

(May Use Backs)

Post Area

Center

stunting game, and reaction drills. Also, it's great for learning team defenses, taking proper steps, and getting assignments down.

In our stunting drills, we are basically concerned with two things: Getting off on the ball and redirecting on our second step. We tell our players to read on the run, when they are involved in a stunt. We spend a great deal of our practice time on our stunting game because of the number of times our linemen are involved in stunts. We feel our stunting game can be improved by repetition and work.

We are finding ourselves spending more time in our practice schedules on pass-rush techniques. In today's game a great deal more passes are being thrown. Therefore, we must spend more time on learning how to rush the passer. We have several different drills we use; some are for techniques, others are to improve effort.

In conclusion, I would just like to mention a few other points. We go over seven dummies every day, working on foot movement. Also, we do certain wave drills on the post, which help our foot work. We try to do most of our agility drills from a four-point stance. (Since they have to play from a four-point stance, we put them in that position as much as possible.) Also, during practice and scrimmages, we stress to our linemen the importance of always knowing the down and distance and field position (being aware of this will help them in pass-rush and stunt selection). We attempt to simulate our drills as close as possible to actual game situations. We do not believe in employing drills that are not functional. We want to drill and rehearse our players in practice the way we want them to perform in a game.

One final point, and probably the most important: We attempt to inspire our young men to the degree that they think and know they are capable of doing what it takes to win. Teaching them how to accomplish this is extremely gratifying and one of the rewards of coaching.

Defensive Ends and Linebackers (John Devlin)

In selecting personnel to operate at our end and linebacker positions, we must search our roster to find athletes who are capable of performing many different techniques. Our ends and linebackers are our "big play" people. We attempt to train them along these lines.

Our defensive ends, as a rule, are required to make many more basic adjustments and play more varied techniques than even our linebackers.

The following are the techniques our ends must master.

1. Defeat a drive, "G," hook, kick out, and roll block from a 50 end position. (See Diagram 7.)

Diagram 7

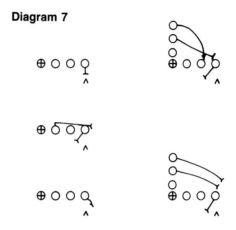

The end in a 50 position uses a balanced, feet-parallel stance, with his weight slightly on his outside foot. His key is the helmet of the third man from the center.

When the key fires straight out, the end steps into the key, rolling his hips and tucking his tail, striking a blow with his inside arm. He uses his free outside arm to shed the defeated blocker. He must keep his shoulders square and control the line of scrimmage.

When the key goes down to his inside, he steps down and into the key with his inside foot, taking a short shuffle step with his outside foot. He strikes a blow with his inside forearm or both his hands keeping the key from double-teaming the defensive tackle. He keeps his shoulders square in a good football position. If a pulling guard or a back is trying to kick him out, he crosses the blocker's face, squeezing as hard as he can, keeping his outside arm free. If the ball is moving deep and wide to his side and they are attempting to roll block him, he works his way upfield, through the outside shoulder of the blockers, containing the play.

2. Defeat a turn out, kick out, and roll block from the wide tackle position. (See Diagram 8.)

When the end is in the wide 6 position, the techniques are basically the same as the 50 position.

As a true end, he doesn't have to contend with a tight end and has more time to read and carry out his assignment. Our end uses a balanced, feet-parallel stance. His weight is slightly on his outside foot. One

Diagram 8

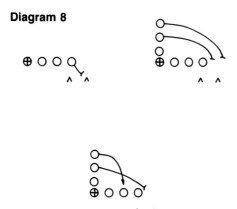

also is responsible for reverse or counterplays. If a run breaks down the opposite sideline, he should be the man to keep it from being a touchdown. Flow away—pass. He revolves deeper and is involved in the under coverage. He also is depended on to help on throwback or bootleg. Experience teaches the correct angle of the revolve.

   5. Play the option from all basic positions. (See Diagram 11.)

Diagram 11

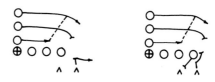

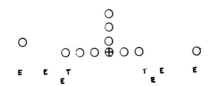

technique that he must master in this position, however, not in the 50 position, is the turn out by the tight end or wingback.

On the snap of the football, the defensive end takes a step with his inside foot. On seeing the turnout block, he explodes into the tight end—squeezing as hard as he can, keeping his outside arm free. He controls the tight end and is always ready to fall back inside to make the tackle.

   3. Defeat the slow block by the tight end, split end, and wingback. (See Diagram 9.)

Diagram 9

To be able to defeat a slow block in the three positions pictured in Diagram 9 is a must for a defensive end and very vital to the overall defenses.

In aligning himself to defeat the slow block, the end must assume a nose-on position. On the snap of the ball he must be careful not to charge the offensive man. He then must use his hands to control the blocker until the ball reaches him. Then, he attempts to shed the blocker opposite of the way the ball is breaking. In all positions he must never let the blocker release easy to his inside.

   4. Learn to revolve from the off and "on" positions. (See Diagram 10.)

Diagram 10

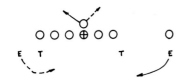

The end in an on position reads flow away. His assignment is revolve. Flow away, run—means his angle is shallower, depending on the type of run he sees. He

Learning to play the option is more important because most offenses now feature some type of option. As in Diagram 11, our end must sometimes take the quarterback and on other occasions take the pitch man. In the off position he sometimes must take on a back who is running the arc for the tailback. In taking the pitch from the on position, his key is the speed and width of the pitch man.

When tackling the quarterback, he tries never to attack with the shoulder facing the opposite sideline.

   6. Play pass defense (man and zone) from all positions. (See Diagram 12.)

Diagram 12

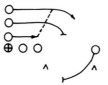

The first principle of zone defense is to hit all receivers. Never let a potential receiver release clean off the line of scrimmage. Then, you must pick up the quarterback and read the pattern as best you can. Depth is most important, and, finally, the break on the ball after it has been thrown is a technique that must be worked on time and time again.

In most cases, the end in man coverage has help deep—this allows him to be super aggressive and take chances. The techniques are very similar to man defense in basketball.

7. Learn to stunt.

Diagram 13

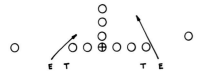

Our ends must learn two basic stunts. (See Diagram 13.) One is a controlled charge toward the remaining back. He now keeps contain responsibility, but he is able to get a jump on the ball and get a sharper angle into the backfield. He must always keep his outside arm free, and when taking on a blocker he must have his weight on his outside foot so that he can step into the offensive man.

His other stunt is the easiest because now he has no contain responsibility, and all he has to do is let no one turn him out.

Our linebackers are our defensive quarterbacks and must be able to perform many techniques. Most outstanding linebackers have a natural "nose" for the ball. It is our job to fill the gap between their natural asset and all the other techniques they must master.

The following are the basic techniques vital to linebackers' plays.

1. Defeat the drive block by the guard or tackle. (See Diagram 14.)

Diagram 14

When being blocked by a lineman, the linebacker must step up with his inside foot. He strikes a blow with his inside forearm—always free the outside arm. It is most important to hit on the rise with tail tucked.

2. Defeat the isolation block by the fullback or wingback. (See Diagram 15.)

The linebacker reads the "over" block, and at this point, the key is for him to step up over the line of scrimmage and take on the fullback with his inside forearm. It is important that he gets almost down the middle of the blocker and keeps his head up.

Diagram 15

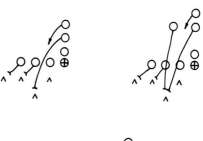

When taking on the double "ice" (wing and fullback), the linebacker must try to split them and cause a stalemate.

3. Defeat the down block by the tight end and tackle.

On flow wide to his side, a linebacker must be alert for the blocks seen in Diagram 16.

Diagram 16

He must drive his inside arm across the face of the blocker, working to free his outside arm, always keeping his shoulders square. It is most important for the linebacker to know who will have an opportunity to block down on him on wide flow.

4. Fight the roll block. (See Diagram 17.)

Diagram 17

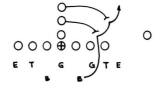

The technique is the same as the end in a peel-off technique.

5. Defeat the guard or center on flow away. (See Diagram 18.)

This technique is one of the most difficult to teach. When the linebacker reads flow away, he leads his steps to the flow and drives his backside arm and shoulder pad through the center and comes up running.

Diagram 18

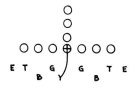

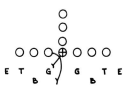

The blocking angle of the center or guard dictates the angle the linebacker takes in going to the football.

6. Pass defense. Man and zone.

When in zone coverage, linebackers must first read routes and work for depth. It is most important in our scheme that both linebackers are conscious of the area under the safety man in our three deep. Linebackers must always be alert for crossing receivers and delays by backs and the tight end.

Most man coverage by the linebackers will be on backs coming out of the backfield.

The angle of the back will tell the linebacker how he will play. If he fires right up over him, he will collide with him and then run with him. If the back flares, he will flare with him, keeping inside out leverage and maintaining his depth. (See Diagram 19.)

Diagram 19

7. Learn to stunt.
   (a) Never give your stunt away.
   (b) Keep your shoulders square.
   (c) Don't be trapped.
   (d) Read on the run.
   (e) Go flat to ball.

The following are basic drills for ends and linebackers.
1. Strike a blow.
   (a) Posts.
   (b) Hand bucker.
Ends and linebackers work their way down the sled, striking a blow with their hands. They should have their inside leg up, tucked tail, and hit on the rise. Form tackle a bag at the end of the sled. (See Diagram 20.)

Diagram 20

2. Peel off.

With weight on the outside foot, work your way through the outside shoulder of the blocker. (See Diagram 21.)

Diagram 21

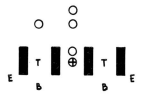

3. Eye closer.

You can work on all basic techniques for the ends and linebacker with this drill. (See Diagram 22.)

Diagram 22

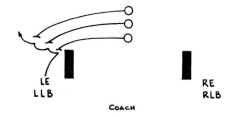

4. Basic drill.

This is small half-line drill. You will be able to teach basic techniques easier in this confined area. (See Diagram 23.)

Diagram 23

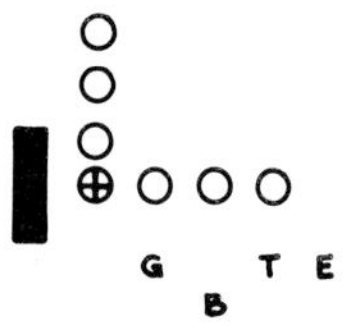

5. Go to spot.

Diagram 24

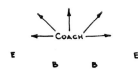

All basic moves for the ends and linebackers can be taught and checked with this drill. Coach gives flow. (See Diagram 24.)

    6. Tip drills (pass defense).
        (a) Intercept at highest point.
        (b) Tip.
        (c) Over shoulder catch.
        (d) Turn around on first sound.
        (e) Play eyes.
        (f) Play routes.
    7. Tackling drills. (See Diagram 25.)

Diagram 25

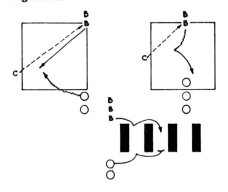

    (a) Five-yard squares.
    (b) Eye opener.

We spend a lot of time in team drill during the season because coordination between the ends and linebackers and the line and secondary is vital. Play recognition is vital and time must be allotted to perfect this area. This is really a team defense.

Developing the Three-Deep Secondary (Terry Strock)

We have always believed in the theory that most football games are won or lost in the defensive secondary. A team can be beaten more quickly by a mistake in the secondary than in any other phase of the game. Conversely, you can change the complexion of a game by a great play in the secondary, such as an interception, fumble, or punt return.

It is very important that our defensive backs realize they are the last line of defense to the goal line. Thus, we strive to eliminate five basic mistakes that can break down this barrier.

    1. Do not allow a long pass to be completed over our secondary.
    2. Do not miss a tackle.
    3. Do not get knocked down in the secondary.
    4. Do not run around a block.
    5. Do not bust an assignment.

If any one of these errors occurs, it could easily result in a score for the opponent.

While stressing the elimination of these errors, we also impress upon our players five objectives they must attain to have a successful pass defense. First, we must prevent the touchdown pass. This is an extremely difficult objective to accomplish due to the highly skilled passers and receivers we face each week. Second, we must prevent the long-gain passes. We consider a long pass one over 17 yards. Third, we must keep the gain per completion to a minimum. Our minimum is 12 yards per completion. Fourth, we must intercept. Our objective is to intercept one out of every eight passes attempted or three interceptions per game. Our fifth objective is to punish the receiver or ball carriers by gang tackling. In doing so, we will create fumbles or at least make the receiver pay for catching the ball in our secondary.

Any good defensive back must have confidence in himself and his ability to play pass defense. We want to create confidence in our backs so they can cover their area and have a tremendous desire to get to the ball when it is thrown. By instilling this confidence, the defensive back will want the opponent to throw it into his area so he will have an opportunity to intercept.

We are basically an eight-man front team with a three-deep secondary. Our two halfbacks and safety are responsible for pass first and run second. We consider every play a pass until a run shows. We key the football through the eligible pass receiver and know what the receiver on our side is doing.

Since the secondary is primarily responsible for the pass, we gear our practice time accordingly. Most of our individual and group drills are designed to improve our skills against the pass. We want our players to know their weaknesses and strive each day to improve in our drills.

There are many excellent drills for teaching pass defense. Regardless of the drills used, every drill should have a definite purpose and should closely correlate to a game type situation. The players should not be allowed to perform the drills carelessly. The manner in which a player practices is the way he will execute on game day.

The following are the drills we feel are best suited for developing the individual techniques needed to have an overall successful defense.

Ball Drills

We tell our players there is only one football in the game and every time it is put in the air it is meant for us. Therefore, we must catch as many passes each practice as the offensive receivers are catching.

Clock Drill

Purpose: To teach backs to catch the ball at var-

ious spots while developing good hands. (See Diagram 26.)
1. Line up defensive backs facing the coach.
2. Throw passes at various spots.
3. Stress relaxation of hands, fingers, and wrists.
4. Look ball into hands and tuck away.

Diagram 26

One-hand Catch

Purpose: To teach concentration on the ball and develop a touch.
1. Line up defensive backs facing coach.
2. Throw high passes having backs catching the ball with both right and left hands.

Half Turn and Catch

Purpose: To teach reaction to the ball when back is turned to the passer. (See Diagram 27.)
1. Line up backs facing away from coach.
2. Throw ball and give the command "ball"; the back must turn, locate, and make the catch.

You may vary the distance the ball is from the back when the command is given. Also vary the distance between the coach and players.

Diagram 27

Maze Drill

Purpose: To teach concentration on the ball while disregarding the receiver. (See Diagram 28.)
1. Line up a player directly in front of the back.

Diagram 28

2. Throw the ball and have the player in front frame the ball but not touch it.
3. The back must make the catch and tuck the ball away.
4. Stress concentration.

Start with 3 yards between receiver and defender, then shorten the distance.

Maze Drill with Half Turn

Purpose: To teach reaction to the ball and concentration.
1. Combine the half turn with the maze drill.

Agility Drills

These drills are designed to develop and improve footwork, body balance, and quickness.

Carioca

Purpose: To improve foot movements and loosen hip movement.

Have backs do drill with an upright stance and a flexed body in a low football position.

Crossover

Purpose: To improve hip movement. (See Diagram 29.)

Have backs do drill on a line, trying to get a yard on either side of the line. Do not have them gain much yardage up the line. Drill can be done in one spot.

Diagram 29

Balance Run

Purpose: To teach backs to be good ball carriers and keep balance when hit. (See Diagram 30.)
1. Drill should be run in a 5-yard area across the field.
2. Have back run at right sideline and hit on his

Diagram 30

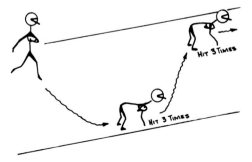

left hand three times, keep balance, change ball, and crossover to left sideline and hit on right hand three times.

3. Stress that players do not go out of bounds and that the back gains ground upfield.

Run the Line

Purpose: To teach foot movement and body co-ordination. (See Diagram 31.)

1. Drill should be run on a yard line across the field.
2. Have back rotate hips right and left while sprinting backward. Keep eyes on the ball. Feet should stay on the line.
3. On command, plant foot and sprint to the passer. The ball should be thrown requiring the back to catch it at the highest point.

Diagram 31

Defensive Cuts

Purpose: To teach foot movement and breaking on the ball.

1. Similar to run the line drill.
2. The back breaks on a 45-degree angle instead of remaining on the line. Concentrate on rotating the hips.
3. After a series of breaks, the ball is thrown at different spots.

Backward Run

Purpose: To teach proper footwork used in man coverage.

1. The back assumes his stance used in man coverage.
2. Use shuffle steps keeping weight over front knee. Do not pick feet up high. Sprint to ball when thrown.

Interception Drills

Intercepting a pass is a skill that consists of timing, hand and eye coordination, relaxation of hands, fingers, and wrists, and concentration.

Straight Line Interception

Purpose: To teach intercepting while sprinting toward passer.

1. Align backs about 20 yards from passer. Have them sprint toward passer and break on ball.
2. Stress intercepting at highest point and sprint past coach.

Tip Drill

Purpose: To teach backs to react to tipped pass.

1. Align backs about 20 yards from passer. Have two backs sprinting toward passer with about 5 yards between them.
2. The first back tips ball to second back, then gets in position to block.
3. Stress intercepting at highest point and both backs sprinting past coach.

Interception Through Receiver (Missed Pass)

Purpose: To teach concentration on ball while intercepting. (See Diagram 32.)

1. Set up a one-on-one situation with receiver and defensive back.
2. Have receiver run sideline or circle route. Let back know what route is being run.
3. The receiver frames the ball but does not touch the ball. The back must concentrate on the ball and make interception.

Diagram 32

Dog Fight

Purpose: To teach backs to play through the receiver and fight for ball.

1. The same drill as interception through receiver, except the receiver now attempts to catch the ball.
2. Stress fundamentals of playing through the receiver.

Three-Man Dog Fight

Purpose: To teach backs to fight for the ball. (See Diagram 33.)

1. Have three backs about 3 yards apart running toward the passer. The middle man is the re-

Diagram 33

ceiver and the two outside men are defensive backs.

2. Throw the ball between them having one back and the receiver fight for the ball while the other defensive back is looking for the tip.

Tackling Drills

We feel that tackling is 90 percent desire and 10 percent skill. We can teach the players if they are short on skill, but the defensive backs must have the courage and desire.

Sideline Tackling
Purpose: To teach backs to keep leverage on the ball carrier near the sidelines. (See Diagram 34.)
1. Place marker 8–10 yards from sideline.
2. The ball carrier sprints between the marker and the sideline. The back must make the tackle using the help of the sideline.

Diagram 34

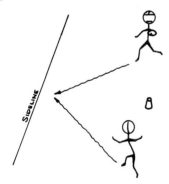

Open Field Tackling
Purpose: To teach the back to make open field tackles.
1. Same drill as sideline tackle except the marker is now placed 20 yards from the sideline.

Goal Line Tackling
Purpose: To teach the fundamentals of tackling on the goal line. (See Diagram 35.)
1. Set up the drill in a 5-yard square. The tackler

Diagram 35

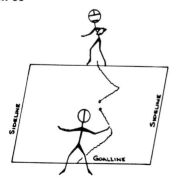

is 1 yard behind the goal line with the ball carrier 5 yards from the goal line.

2. On the command the tackler sprints to get in front of the goal line and make the tackle before the ball carrier can score.

3. Stress proper breakdown, use of sidelines, and tackling high and strong.

Clean-Up Tackling
Purpose: To teach tackler to keep leverage and try to force fumble by second man on tackle. (See Diagram 36.)
1. Set up the drill with markers 12 yards apart. One ball carrier and two tacklers are 10 yards apart between the markers.
2. On command, the ball carrier sprints to one of the markers, then may break anywhere.
3. The first back makes the tackle with the second man cleaning up and attempting to create a fumble.

Diagram 36

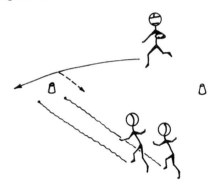

Unit Drills

Individual drills are very important, but the best way to teach pass defense is through unit drills. It is important that the defensive backs develop a togetherness and sense of pride in their responsibility. Nothing is more important than constant communication between secondary people.

Covering Thirds
Purpose: To teach the principle of covering the deep one-third areas. (See Diagram 37.)
1. Align receiver on the sideline and hash marks with the defensive backs assuming their proper position.
2. For the left halfback have the receiver on the defensive left sideline and left hash mark sprint downfield on a streak route. The halfback must cover deep one-third area and sprint to intercept when the ball is thrown.
3. The ball should be thrown at different spots (short or long on the sideline or on the hash mark).

4. Next go to the safety and use a receiver on each hash mark. The safety must cover his middle one third.

5. Then go to right halfback.

   Use different kinds of pass action (drop back, sprint toward, and sprint away).

Diagram 37

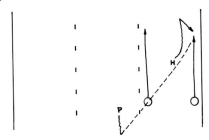

Covering One-third with Five Receivers
Purpose: to teach the three-deep to cover the field.

1. Same as the covering thirds drill in Diagram 37 except all three backs are used at the same time with five receivers, as shown in Diagram 38.

Diagram 38

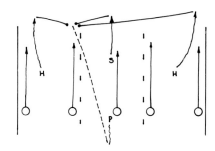

Call Coverage—Flow—Field Position—Go to Ball
Purpose: To teach backs their responsibility as to assignments, field position, and importance of sprinting to the ball.

1. Set up an offensive skeleton versus a set of defensive backs.

2. Have coverage called by the safety.

3. The receivers run their patterns but do not go for the ball.

4. Check the secondary for proper alignment, stance, reads, rotation, field position, and sprinting to the ball.

Diagram 39

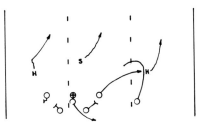

Be sure to move the ball from hash mark to hash mark. Use different types of passes (drop back, sprint out, play action, and bootlegs).

Basic Backfield Techniques

1. Call: All of our defensive alignments are called by the linebacker and our secondary coverage by our safety man. It is necessary that our backs hear both calls and know the defensive ends assignment.

2. Alignment: Our basic alignment for the halfback is 7 yards deep and 4 yards outside a normal tight end. His split rule is to line up outside a split receiver until he can cover him into the boundary by lining up on his inside. The safety lines up 11 yards deep over the football. Against a wide receiver his depth will depend upon the width of the receivers.

3. Stance: The halfback's feet are shoulder width apart with his outside foot back. His weight is evenly distributed on the inside balls of his feet. The ankles and knees are flexed so that the knees are over the toes. The back should be straight and head erect with eyes looking through the eligible receiver on his side to the football. The arms are hanging freely in front of the knees.

   The safety's stance is the same except his feet are parallel to the line of scrimmage. The safety should see the receiver on both sides using peripheral vision.

4. Skate: On the snap of the ball, the halfbacks take shuffle steps back and out, then react to the flow of the ball according to the defensive call.

5. Key: We key the football, which tells us what our assignment will be.

Basic Zone Coverages

Cover 3
Coverage:
1. Backup Pass
   a. Halfbacks—Deep outside one-thirds.
   b. Safety—Deep middle one-third.
2. Flow Pass Either Way
   a. Halfbacks—Deep outside one-thirds.
   b. Safety—Deep middle one-third.
      Keep relative position on ball.
Technique:
1. Deep Coverage—Slow—Fast—Faster—Faster—Faster. Halfbacks curl away from the boundary as you get depth.

Diagram 40

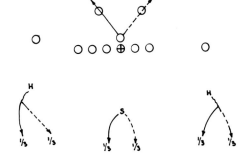

Coverage:

1. Backup pass
   a. Halfbacks—Deep outside one-thirds.
   b. Safety—Deep middle one-third.
2. Flow Pass Either Way
   a. Halfback toward flow—level off 7 to 9 yards.
   b. Safety—Deep outside one-third toward flow.
   c. Halfback away from flow—revolve, deep two-thirds away from flow.

Diagram 41

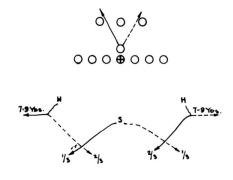

Coverage:

1. Backup pass
   a. Halfbacks—Deep outside one-thirds.

   b. Safety—Deep middle one-third.
2. Flow Pass away from Leveling Side
   a. Halfbacks—Deep outside one-thirds.
   b. Safety—Deep middle one-third.
3. Flow Pass Toward Leveling Side
   a. Halfback toward flow—level of 7 to 9 yards.
   b. Safety—Deep outside one-third toward flow.
   c. Halfback away from flow—revolve. Deep two-thirds away from flow.

Diagram 42

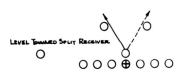

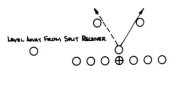

Diagram 43

We coordinate these basic zone coverages with our ends, linebackers, guards, and tackles to develop our overall defense. It takes eleven to play pass defense, so if there is a breakdown, we must see if all eleven men carried out their assignment.

34
Line Play and Adjustments from Wide-Tackle 6 Defense

(From 1979 *Proceedings* of the AFCA)

JERRY CLAIBORNE Head Coach, University of Maryland

I want to share some of the techniques we use in our defensive line play at the University of Maryland. The techniques and drills are ones we have used over the years. I believe the key to coaching is doing what you know best and what you can get across to your players. The head coach must be completely sold on what he is doing.

I personally am completely sold on the wide-tackle 6 philosophy of our defensive scheme. Next, you must be able to sell your philosophy to your staff, because it is the staff that is really going to get the techniques across to your players. After you have sold your staff, the people you really have to sell are your players. We feel our players are completely sold on our defensive scheme. They like to play it and they enjoy practicing it. We feel the philosophy we have of a multiple defensive front, moving around on defense and stunting, might be a little more fun practicing than just lining up in a straight defense.

Our basic defensive front is the wide-tackle 6. (See Diagram 1.)

Diagram 1

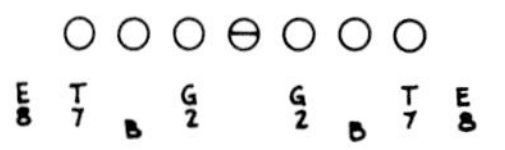

O O O ⊖ O O O

E T G   G T E
8 7 2   2 7 8

First, I want to discuss the play of our guards. We line up our guards on the offensive guards. (See Diagram 2.)

Diagram 2

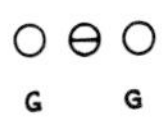

O ⊖ O

G   G

The distance between the guards is normally about two arms' length. We tell them to try to touch hands with each other. Of course, the splits of the offense will make us adjust, but I am going to discuss our normal alignment.

The distance off the ball will vary with down and distance, but it depends on the ability of our guards as much as anything. We like for them to get as close to the line of scrimmage as they can but still be able to read and react at the snap of the ball. The slower the individual reacts, the farther off the ball he is going to have to play. Since it will take him longer to read and his reaction time is slower, the slower the athlete the farther off the ball he will play. The better the athlete, the closer he will play since he can crowd the ball and still react to his reads.

The number-one assignment of our guards is to control the offensive guards. Our players must at least get a stalemate on the initial blow. The guards' responsibilities are 50 percent inside and 50 percent outside, but they are never to get beat inside. Read the triangle made by the offensive guard, center, quarterback and fullback. (See Diagram 3.)

Diagram 3

One of the first drills we teach our guards is to deliver a blow. We have an old wooden sled that our maintenance man made for us and we start with the six-point extension. (See Diagram 4.)

Diagram 4

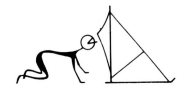

The hands, knees, and toes are on the ground and we get as close to the bucker as we can. We want our players to learn how to explode into that bucker, bringing their tail and all the weight of their tail with maximum force as they explode with their forearm, knees, and toes all extending as their head drives up and past the pad. We want them to fall on their stomachs. If they do not fall on their stomachs but end up on their hands and knees, they are not really getting the explosive motion and power we want.

We go from the six-point stance to the four-point stance but using the same drill. From the four-point stance we are able to deliver a stronger blow but still concentrate on exploding. We drive the head up and past the pad, bringing the forearm up and hitting with a good wide base, tucking the tail, and getting all of those leg muscles, the butt, and the weight of the butt into the blow. This is what we call the six-point and four-point explosion drill.

From the explosion drill on the single bucker we go to one-on-one. (See Diagram 5.) Even when we are working one-on-one, we like to have a quarterback in his position so we get used to looking inside and reading.

Diagram 5

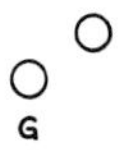

In the one-on-one drill our guard learns to deliver a blow on the offensive guard while looking back inside to read the quarterback's feet. In this drill, we work on the drive block, cutoff, and reading pass. (See Diagram 6.)

Diagram 6

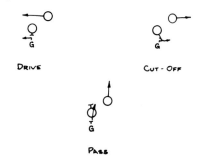

As he plays the guard's block he is always reading back inside to react also to the action of the quarterback. As he reads the action of the quarterback, the guard will give lateral pursuit as he defeats the different type blocks of the guard.

For the next step we add the center to the drill. (See Diagram 7.)

Diagram 7

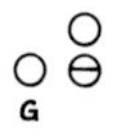

We now have the opportunity to read the inside short triangle and react to the different blocks of the guard and center. Now we are able to play the drive block, junction block, cut-off block, reach block, cross block, and pass. (See Diagram 8.)

Diagram 8

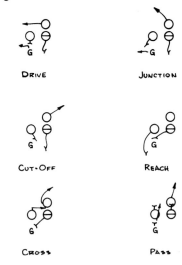

We really concentrate on lateral pursuit and read in the short triangle.

The next drill is the one our guards practice the most. We call it three-on-two. (See Diagram 9.)

Diagram 9

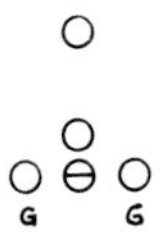

Eighty percent of the time the three offensive linemen in this drill are going to be the players who will be blocking our guards in a game situation. Our guards must be able to read and react to this offensive alignment. Almost every possible block they will see during the game can be assimilated in this drill. (See Diagram 10.) This drill is done over and over again.

Diagram 10

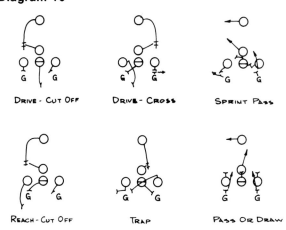

We also add some offensive tackles to this drill and call it five-on-two. (See Diagram 11.)

Diagram 11

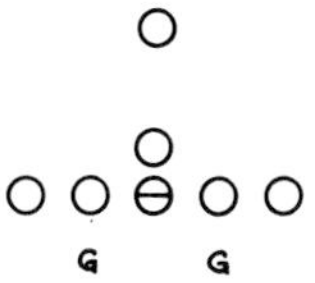

We use this drill when we feel our opponent will block down with their tackles and pull the guards on our linebackers or trap our tackles. We can also add split backs to the drills when we are playing a veer team to enable our guards to recognize the angle of the backs and quarterbacks.

Diagram 12

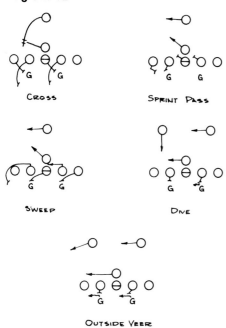

Some points to emphasize for our guards: strike a blow, read inside triangle, lateral pursuit, never run around a block.

The next technique I want to discuss is that used by our defensive tackles. We call it the seven technique. (Diagram 13). The alignment is for our tackle to line up 2 feet off the ball with his outside foot on the outside ear of the normal aligned offensive end.

Diagram 13

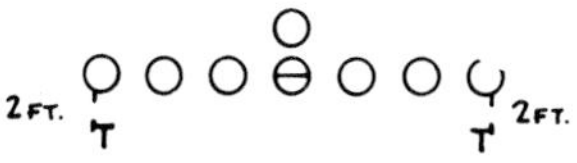

His assignment is to take a short lateral step on the movement of the offensive end playing him head on, while looking inside to read the movement of the offensive tackle and near back. He should free his in-

side forearm. If it is a run toward the tackle, he has the off-tackle responsibility and then pursues laterally. If a flow pass is to the side of the tackle, he will rush the passer. If the flow is away, the tackle is the trail man; but he should not cross the line of scrimmage until he checks inside for a trap. On a backup pass, our tackle has contain rush.

The teaching process is started exactly the same way as with our guards. The tackles must be able to deliver a blow on the line of scrimmage and stop the charge of the offensive end. We take the six-point stance explosion. From the six-point explosion, we move to the four-point stance. We definitely work hard to learn how to deliver a blow with both flippers.

Our first live drill is one-on-one. (See Diagram 14.)

Diagram 14

We like to have an offensive back in this drill, either at the veer position or the I position, to give us a flow. We do not use a ball in this drill since we want to learn to read the movement of the offensive end and react on his movement. In the one-on-one drill, we concentrate on delivering a blow to the end, stepping laterally and not moving upfield. We must feel the end as we read back to the inside. (See Diagram 15.)

Diagram 15

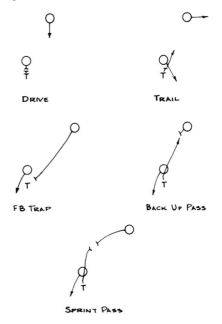

We next go the two-on-one by adding the offensive tackle to the drill. (See Diagram 16.)

Diagram 16

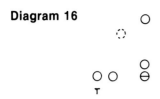

Most of the time our tackle will be blocked by the offensive end or tackle. Therefore, this is the drill our defensive tackles use the most and must learn in order to read and react. In this drill, our defensive tackle will take a short lateral step with his outside foot and feel the block of the tight end as he reads back through the offensive tackle. If their end is blocking our tackle and the tackle fires straight out, our tackle will keep pressure to that end, playing the ball. (See Diagram 17.) If the end slips our tackle and their offensive tackle fires out on our tackle, our man will move back to the inside playing through the tackle's block. Our tackle will stop the tackle's charge by stepping with his inside foot and striking a blow with his inside flipper. (See Diagram 18.)

Diagram 17

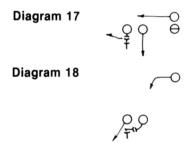

Diagram 18

If the end slips our tackle and the offensive tackle fires out straight ahead, our tackle will look for the fullback's block. (See Diagram 19.)

Diagram 19

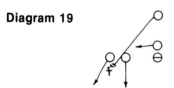

Other blocks we can work on by using this drill are illustrated in Diagram 20.

Diagram 20

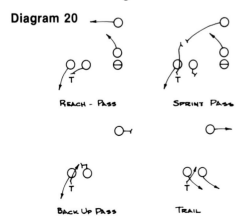

REACH - PASS   SPRINT PASS

BACK UP PASS   TRAIL

When a team uses a wing set, we back our tackle off the ball a little more and move him head on the end. This puts us in a better position to read the wingback and offensive tackle to see which way the block is coming. (See Diagram 21.)

Diagram 21

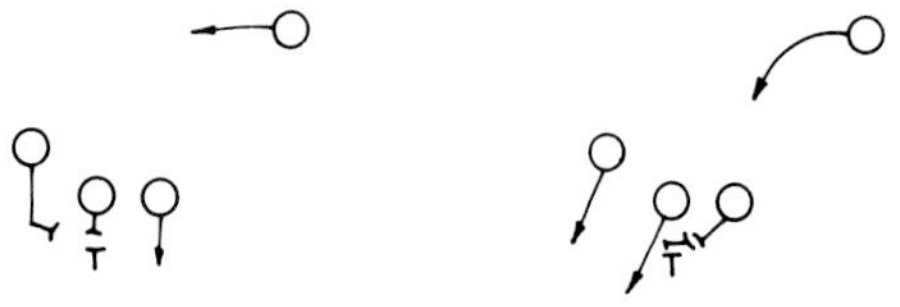

We also have to set up drills to the split end side since we will see this type of formation most of the time on one side of our defense. Most of the time we play this type of formation without any adjustment. We tell our tackle to play as if the end is still lined up in front of him. He uses the same movements but does not have to worry about being blocked by the end. (See Diagram 22.)

Diagram 22

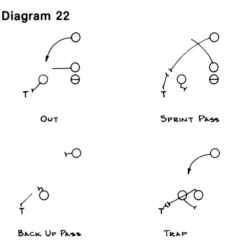

OUT   SPRINT PASS

BACK UP PASS   TRAP

Some points to emphasize for our tackles: Strike a blow; do not cross the line of scrimmage; feel the end and look back inside at the angle of the offensive tackle and back; flow away trail.

Our end in our wide-tackle 6 scheme is more like a cornerback or monster man, as some people refer to him. We teach our ends to align 2 yards outside of the defensive tackles, but we very seldom line up in this position.

Diagram 23

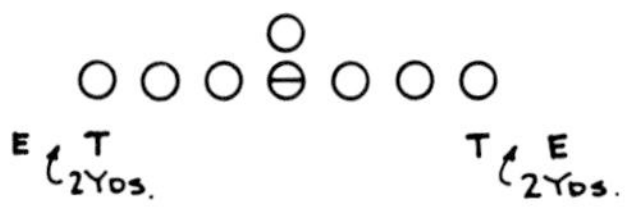

We want the ends to line up with their feet parallel and shoulders square. On the snap of the ball he looks through the offensive end reading the action of the offensive back nearest to him while seeing the ball.

The end must know where the ball is going. If the ball stays on the line of scrimmage, he stays on the line of scrimmage. If the ball goes in the backfield, he goes in the backfield, getting in the running lane. The running lane is a yard in front and a yard outside the ball. If the ball goes away from our end, he has a slow revolve looking for inside cutbacks and then a deep revolve. If a backup pass develops, our end will drop off to cover his flat area. On an option play, our end will be responsible for the pitch man. (See Diagram 24.)

Diagram 24

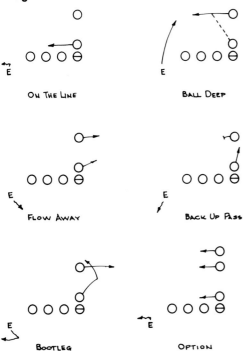

ON THE LINE

BALL DEEP

FLOW AWAY

BACK UP PASS

BOOTLEG

OPTION

Very seldom does our end line up on the line of scrimmage in his basic position. We want him to move around to try to confuse the quarterback with his alignment.

The two techniques he must perfect in order to play good defense against the running game is to overcome the climb block and the roll block. He must be strong enough to stop the climb block and agile enough to keep from getting knocked off his feet with a roll block.

We start out playing the climb block by teaching our end to put his weight on his back foot as he prepares to deliver a blow to the blocker. We feel the end puts himself at an extreme disadvantage if he has his weight on the forward foot as he prepares to deliver a blow on a moving blocker. We work on moving across

the line of scrimmage, stopping to put the weight on the back foot, keeping the shoulders square and protecting the forward knee with a lowered forearm. (See Diagram 25.)

Diagram 25

This drill is half speed, just trying to learn the proper position to whip the climb block. We also use this drill to learn to recognize the difference between the climb block and the roll block. This is just a matter of repetition and recognition.

If a roll block develops, we use our hands to stop the blocker charge and move our feet as quick as possible to avoid getting knocked down. If our end gets overpowered, we want him to retreat the way he came across the line. We do not want him to go to the sideline or run around a block. We must not create a big hole for our tackle to defend. (See Diagram 26.)

Diagram 26

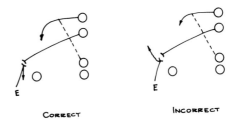

CORRECT

INCORRECT

In the drills we use for defensive ends, we have one back come out to the end using either the roll or climb block. We then add one or two more blockers and let one use a climb block, the second a roll block, and so on. We will add a pulling guard to the drill as some people do use this type of blocking scheme, and our end must be able to play the climb block of a pulling guard. When you are using several blockers in the drill, be sure to have them staggered with enough space between them so that no one is hurt.

Some points to emphasize for our defensive ends: Have the weight on your back foot when playing blocker; keep your shoulders parallel to the goal line; protect your forward knee with your forearm; stay low; retreat the way you went in; and never get knocked down.

35

Use of Multiple Defenses at the Air Force Academy

(From 1973 Proceedings of the AFCA)

BEN MARTIN, Head Coach, United States Air Force Academy

There has been a trend in defensive football toward the use of multiple defenses rather than using one basic defense that was altered only near the goal line. In the early 1970s most teams utilized a single alignment. The principle was to teach the individual players strong techniques as well as to show them how to make personal adjustments to combat specific problems. As usual, the offensive planners devised formations and play patterns to attack a single alignment effectively. There always seemed to be one play (pass or run) or one play series that would work against the basic defense. The problem, lacking truly superior personnel, was the inflexibility of the defense to adjust to a major problem. Thus, the multiple defensive approach came into football and has generally been accepted, even by squads of clearly superior manpower.

With the built-in versatility of a multiple defense package, coaches and players are able to do something positive to shut off a particularly troublesome offensive weapon. These adjustments can readily be made on the field without detailed discussion or time-consuming conferences; merely call the defense that was designed to counter the problem—make the big adjustment right now to discourage the offense from a bread-and-butter play or series. In a multiple defense system, such major changes in alignment can be made along the line of scrimmage to improve defense against the frontal attack, at the perimeter to assist versus options, sweeps, and roll outs, and in the secondary to defeat certain pass patterns, which otherwise would be gifts.

There can be little doubt that multiple defenses have made a big impact on the game, for now we all are aware of the staff designation of "defensive coordinator." That coach has an extremely important role

and is considered by many to be the head coach of the defensive unit. With such responsibility, the coordinator also has to be creative and imaginative in expanding the scope of multiple defenses so that the adjustments anticipated for each opponent are thoroughly researched and taught prior to the contests. The entire package gives the defensive coordinator an arsenal of alignments that almost matches in numbers the weapons that an offensive unit can mount. Thus defensive strategy has become increasingly important to the outcome of a game.

The defensive package can be derived from a basic seven-man front or a basic eight-man front. Or in some programs that are really flexible, there can be a mixture of seven- and eight-man fronts. The change to eight from seven normally entails a down lineman (middle guard, for example) dropping back to be a linebacker, while a defensive back (strong safety) eases up to be a line-of-scrimmage defender.

Choosing Basic Defense

The base alignment from which we flex the defenses is the standard 54. We believe that there are three factors that should be considered in deciding exactly which base you select—first, the type and numbers of football players available to the defense; second, the style of offense anticipated from the scheduled opponents; and, third, your staff's background knowledge and belief in any particular basic defense. All of these important factors formed the foundation of the Falcons 54 defense.

Like so many football squads we are not in the position to recruit definite physical types of athletes to fit into one specific base defense. But our experience over

Diagram 1

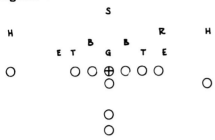

the years has indicated that those athletes that we naturally acquire can best be utilized in the base 54 defense. To start with, there is a dearth of big downlinemen, which precludes the four-man front so popular as a split-6 look, or the 43 pro defense. Both of these basic defenses require four big anchor men, while the 54 requires only two at the tackle spots. Another short supply of football types in our program is at linebacker, especially those with adequate size to withstand a frontal assault. The split 6 requires four linebacker types and the pro 43 requires three, but the 54 requires only two, one of which can easily be used on the weak side, away from the power plays. So the 54 basic defense is a natural for our program.

We normally get a good number of middle guard types. They are usually of medium size with quickness and are able to adapt easily to dropping back as a part-time linebacker. Another normally adequate supply of athletes in our program is at end. I mean "true" end, the player who can slash in to stop the off-tackle play, widen with the sweep, and put pressure and containment on the passer. He additionally is versatile enough to drop off into a pass defense zone and join the secondary. Here again the strongest end would be basically a lineman while the smaller end could very well be used as a weak side or space defender, applying the same principle as was used by the linebacker corps.

The same principle of best use of available athletes applies in the secondary as well. Any defense requires two halfbacks or cornerbacks who should be fast as well as tough against the run. Although we don't get an abundance of defensive halfbacks, we put our fastest men at the corners. Safety men are usually available as space-oriented conservative players who are content to stay back, read the big picture, and get involved in the contact when it becomes absolutely necessary. Perhaps the best football player in our defensive secondary is the strong safety or rover back. He actually prefers to be around the ball, and so in our flexible approach we move him tactically to be nearest the anticipated action. Thus, he could play up front as an end or linebacker as well as back as a strong safety or deep back. The safety blitz is his favorite move!

The second factor in picking a basic defense style

of play of the scheduled opponents is of vital importance to our particular approach because we play teams from all the main geographic sections of the country—and football is definitely played differently in each area. We also play against some very sophisticated, pro-style, passing attacks as well as option-style running games. Thus it follows that we need four men trained in the secondary to adequately defend the pass, but we need the rover's help against the perimeter attack of the option teams. He also figures in to bolster control of the primary line of scrimmage as we shift from a seven- to an eight-man front. There's no doubt that our nationwide schedule dictates a maximum amount of flexibility on defense.

The third factor, staff knowledge and beliefs, can best be stated as the way we have been doing things with confidence for a good number of seasons. What you believe in, and are familiar with, can be taught to the players who must use the format in the most confident and positive way. Belief not only helps the staff as teachers; but their good experience makes them effective salesmen to build up the squad's confidence.

Teaching the Defense

Once the basic defense has been determined, the next important step is to package the entire format for efficient teaching. We have found that the best staff organization for our program and for our staff is to delegate three areas of responsibility: (1) line, (2) linebackers, and (3) backs. For drill work the staff would assume teaching roles within the team as indicated in Diagrams 2 and 3.

In our approach to multiple defenses, a coordination is required whenever we shift to an eight-man front from the basic seven-man front of the 54. This usually takes the form of a 53 or perhaps the 44 as shown in Diagram 3. The key man is the rover back, and the next key man in such a move is the middle guard. Thus, the rover back falls into the area of responsibility of the linebacker coach, or on occasion, the line coach who also handles ends. When the defense dictates that the rover become a primary de-

Diagram 2

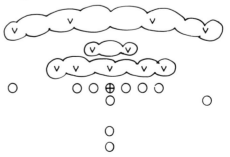

Diagram 3

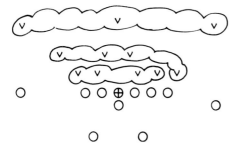

fender, the backfield coach then has only three men to teach: the two halfbacks and the true safety man.

In actual usage, concealing the final alignment until just prior to the snap is an important aspect of the multiple defenses program. Therefore, the rover back moves into position at the last second and the middle guard drops back quite late. Sometimes he will move on the snap and still be effective in the defense called.

The staff plans at length to ascertain the proper balance of coaching time on the practice field between the individual techniques required and the unit coordination necessary with each defense. With the exception of the middle guard and the rover back, the fundamental techniques are fairly simple and can be applied from all alignments of the multiple defenses. For instance, the tackles learn to play head up or on either shoulder. Then they learn to play a gap and to slant left and right. Then the defense called dictates which individual technique will be employed. Just as in all basic defenses, some reading of an opponent is taught, as well as directional keys for linebackers and backs. But in the multiple defensive approach the techniques are not stressed quite so much as are alignment, execution of a move, and clarification of each player's responsibility. Thus, a lot of the coaching involves mental grasp of the unit as well as physically teaching techniques within that unit.

The Falcon multiple defenses include the 54 package, the 53 package, and the 44 package. Each one of these is a complete format within itself with the added flexibility of having an odd or an even front, an overshifted primary defense plus a versatile set of stunts to perform from each base. Although the secondary adjustments are quite extensive, too, they will not be covered in detail in this presentation. Suffice it to say that the defensive package includes, among others, pure zone, man-for-man, combination, and rotation principles on key or opponent tendencies.

Making Use of Stunts

In the basic 54 or seven-man front each player is taught his responsibility against the run and the pass.

Then the various stunts are taught. The stunts change the responsibility for two or more individuals; but those players not involved in the stunt continue to execute their basic responsibility. We believe that stunts should be applied to confuse blocking assignments, to exert pressure at a point of attack, to break up the offense's timing and play patterns as well as to give a single player a precalled technique to use. Such a technique tends to relieve the player of reading and also adds a sense of recklessness to his reaction. It also gives him an opportunity to avoid his opponent's getting a hook on him as a sitting target.

Diagram 4

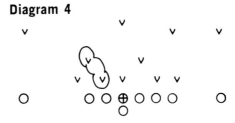

The simplest kind of stunt is what we call a change stunt. In this case, the tackle and linebacker merely change positions and responsibilities, either by prior alignment or by a movement reaction at the snap. The change stunt, as illustrated in Diagram 4, gives the tackle more power to his inside to counter a trap block or to close off with authority the inside hole while at the same time affording the linebacker relief from the frontal assault. The linebacker is also better positioned to execute his move when a pass shows. When any stunt is utilized, it should be fully understood what it will accomplish and what exposed weakness may be a by-product. To stunt merely to be cute is usually ineffectual and can be costly by giving up cheap yardage or a score.

Our so-called pinching stunts, as shown in Diagrams 5 and 6, involve either two or three men on one side of the center only. Here again a change in basic responsibilities is involved with quick pressure to the inside being paramount and containment to the outside being secondary. These moves force the play to

Diagram 5

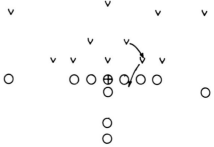

Diagram 6

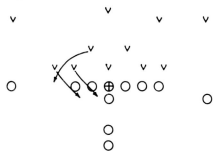

develop perhaps quicker than designed. The good things (defensively) that can happen are arrival by a pinching lineman at the ball exchange point or the hasty forcing of an errant pitchout on the option play. Most offensive coaches abhor quick penetration and/or clean breakthroughs. Many turnovers have been caused this way.

Diagram 7

Diagram 8

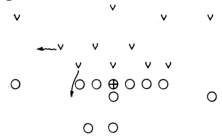

The variety that is built into our end play by called stunts in the 54 package is best shown in Diagrams 7 and 8. The end can smash in quickly for penetration and containment or excellent pass rush, for he knows that his outside duty is being assumed by a teammate. Then, too, especially on the open, or weak, side the end is in excellent position to play very soft in the cover spot. Thus he can protect a pass defense zone or be in position to defend the wide runs. He literally can be out there waiting for the action where previously he attacked deep and to the inside like a dart. The change of execution by called stunts can be quite dramatic, as well as effective.

Diagram 9

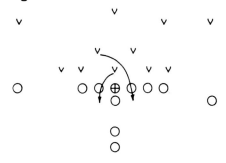

A simple and oft-used stunt utilized by quick middle guards is the loop move to right or left of the center. (See Diagram 9.) It is coordinated with a linebacker so that the guards' territory away from his move is guaranteed. It will contribute to clean misses on blocking assignments, aid in penetration across the line of scrimmage, as well as get a player started rapidly into the pursuit pattern on wide flowing plays. The linebacker may or may not penetrate on execution of the loop. Perhaps his key tells him to stay at home or to drop back for a pass.

Diagram 10

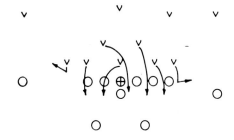

The blitz stunt involves more players than the others and very few individuals retain their basic roles. (See Diagram 10.) It's a full pressure stunt designed for quick penetration to the inside where four defenders normally have to be blocked by three offenders. Someone usually breaks clean whether a pass play develops or not. Some blitzes are designed for maximum pressure from off-tackle and outside. This can be accomplished by the addition of the safety blitz or, more conveniently, in our 53, eight-man front, package.

Diagram 11

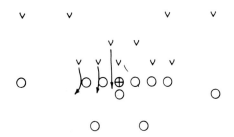

Our staff has found that the pressure stunt, shown in Diagram 11, which is primarily a weak side gap involving four players, is particularly effective in the pass rush and against teams that pull their weak side guard a lot. It can be executed in two ways—merely by a linebacker call, or tap, with the tackle. The end draws a block and then does not continue to pressure. Rather he assumes outside run responsibility as well as flat coverage should a pass develop.

Diagram 12

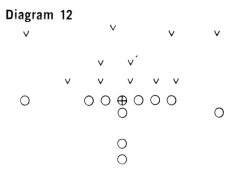

In an effort to bolster the defense against a frontal attack and to protect the linebackers from being blocked quickly, we will stack both linebackers behind two down linemen who are in the gaps. (See Diagram 12.) The linemen go for quick penetration through the cracks to reduce the effectiveness of a cross block or to draw a double team block, which would free up the linebacker as a tackler. We stack weak or strong according to the problem posed by the offense. The linebackers also may key to fill across the line of scrimmage as a back side leverage man when flow goes away.

Diagram 13

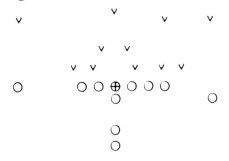

The split 6 look can readily be adopted from the 54 front when the offense splits out an end. This popular and effective alignment, depicted in Diagram 13, really confuses blocking assignments, strengthens the strong side versus power plays, and again protects the linebackers from immediate blocks. All of the linemen merely execute techniques within the split defense that they have learned; but to the offense, it's a whole new look.

Our basic four front is arrived at by dropping the middle guard to his linebacker role in the fashion

Diagram 14

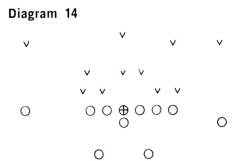

made popular by Tennessee. We designate it the 43, as in Diagram 14. The weak side linebacker normally "changes" position with the tackle and the strong side linebacker might also "change" versus a two–tight end opponent. The linebackers use quick keys, and a pinch call for the tackles can also be built into the 43 format.

Diagram 15

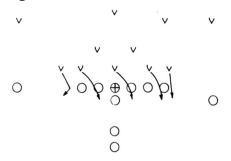

We employ a slant move with either two or three down linemen whenever we have a strong tendency developed by an opponent toward which we'd like to have a running start for pursuit. (See Diagram 15.) For example, we might slant to the wide side of the field, the strong side of the formation or toward a particular player. Whenever a slant is called, the linebackers are mentally prepared to cover away from the slant. They are in excellent shape to scrape through the line of scrimmage in a direction counter to the slant move. The slanting linemen are normally head up and about 2 or 3 feet off the ball. They aim for the far number of the opponent one man over toward the slant. Their technique is to stay low and to deliver a blow to avoid being cut off. Then they find the ball. Should it be going in the opposite direction, they are drilled to quickly come under control and follow the prescribed pursuit angle.

Using the 53 Defense

In the Falcon multiple defensive format the basic eight-man front is the 53. It is most easily taught because the front seven defenders have already learned the techniques that are to be utilized. The learning problem is mainly for the rover back, who is taken out of his secondary role and becomes a linebacker. But since he is usually the best athlete in the defensive backfield, our experience has told us that the rover fits in nicely with his teammates in the trenches. Of course, his practice time must be coordinated so that he is well prepared to be an eight-man front defender as in the regular 53 alignment shown in Diagram 16.

Diagram 16

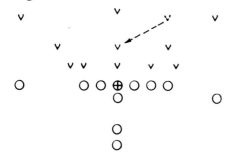

Many coaches believe that, in addition to the advantage of flexing from a seven- to an eight-man front, some problems that any option series causes can be countered best from an eight-man front. It very simply gets another player up in the ball game. There are many basic and effective stunts that can be employed within the 53 package.

The moves incorporated in Diagram 17 have proved to be quite effective versus the off-tackle and slant plays. We have also used it in short yardage situations. Here again concealment of the pending pressure by the outside linebacker is vitally important. It's best that he come full speed from out of nowhere and is not touched by a blocker.

Diagram 17

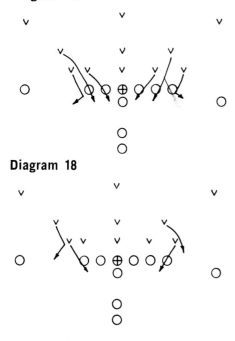

Diagram 18

As a change-up stunt from the same 53 lineup, the end can "smash" with strength from the outside to squeeze off the off-tackle hole or to get quick pressure on the passer. All the while, as in Diagram 18, he is protected to the outside by the linebacker. Many times the varied pressure applied at the off-tackle area is confusing to the blockers and worrisome to the ball handlers who have to hurry their play patterns. It also affords the defense additional weapons to handle the sweeps and options that are aimed their way.

Diagram 19

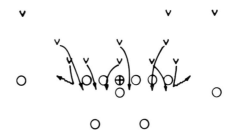

One of the favorites of all the linebackers is the full blitz from the 53 set. (See Diagram 19.) It sets an attitude of reckless abandon and provides them the chance to throw the offense for a loss. The blitz can be called left or right, weak or strong. The net result is a gap defense inside after cross charges set up the breakthroughs. The ends appear to be coming across hard with penetration to "draw a block"; but their responsibility is outside on the run and flat coverage versus the pass. It's a "go get 'em" stunt that should be applied for surprise and change-up. It, too, has some short yardage value.

Employing the 44 Defense

Finally, to round out the multiple-defense format, we add to the 54 and 53 packages the 44 (see Diagram 20).

Diagram 20

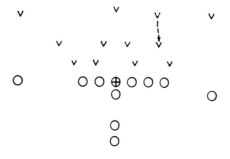

Once again the middle guard assumes the role of a linebacker. The rover is also involved as a primary defender. This eight-man front defense provides great flexibility in defending against the pass, has proved effective against option plays, and can be a fine pressure alignment by calling stunts from the 44 basic alignment. The inside linebackers can fire straight ahead, cross paths with each other, and scrape off to their side whenever the tackle pinches and fill on a quick key. The same flexibility in stunting is true outside with the ends and linebackers who can pressure or change responsibilities.

We believe that multiple defenses are extremely valuable, not at all difficult to teach, and are well received by the players. Both the squad and the staff like the feeling of having lots of tactical weapons to help themselves during the games. It's not necessary to utilize all the packages but it's comforting to realize that something else can be done to stem the tide and turn the game around.

36
Using Multiple Defenses

(From 1977 Summer Manual of the AFCA)

JIM McKINLEY Head Coach, North Carolina Agricultural and Technical University

In early staff meetings at Central State University (Wilberforce, Ohio), it was decided to use multiple defenses, rather than go with a base defense, as the backbone of our defensive philosophy. This came about because of our limited knowledge of personnel and our limited knowledge of what they had been exposed to. However, we did decide that the defensive personnel at Central State was weak and definitely in need of improvement.

We were looking for a system in which our weaknesses could be hidden and an ability to stunt to apply pressure. Our intent was to limit opposing offenses' ability to read our defense. By protecting our weaknesses and showing our opponent many different looks, it would force them to spend a greater amount of time preparing for us. By using multiple fronts, we could keep our weaker defenders from being constantly attacked.

I have always been of the philosophy of "bending but never breaking." We wanted to eliminate the easy score and make our opponents work for everything, even first downs. We also felt that we needed to work on the psychological aspect of defense. Instilling a defensive confidence and spirit began immediately. We knew if people had to work to score or move the ball, our defenders would begin to believe in themselves.

By "bending but never breaking" we felt that offenses would stop themselves 65 percent of the time with penalties, broken assignments, turnovers, or incomplete passes, thereby helping us to develop the desired psychological effect. This spirit, coupled with an ever-changing look on defense, could help to bring about the desired offensive mistakes. We also wanted to stunt and stem to give us more flexibility and to apply pressure and destroy timing.

Everybody on the defensive unit was continuously exposed to positive basic beliefs to help speed up our confidence and spirit-building process. Our defenders found the coaches stressing believing in themselves and their teammates, to be leaders, to make the "big play," to battle for every foot, to force our opponents to go the hard way, and to communicate with other defenders.

As our system began to take shape, we wanted to play both seven- and eight-man fronts, emphasizing sound techniques, pursuit, and zone pass coverage. We wanted to use multiple fronts and occasional stunts to confuse the offense while maintaining simplicity for ourselves. We decided on a four-lineman system using numbers to align our ends and tackles to give us variations and combinations and add a great deal of flexibility.

We wanted to play zone pass defense to prevent the most psychologically damaging effect to our defensive football team—the long run and long pass. Our system would also require the ability to contain any type of offensive system without forcing us to add new things or learn new techniques during the season. It also had to provide a very sound platform for defensive football.

Communications Needed

It was decided that our greatest problem in becoming a multiple-defensive football team was the need for a great communication system. The system we used was not only excellent for communication, but we also found it a great system for teaching techniques. We also found that our playbook page had to be broken down to help facilitate the individual learning process. (See Diagrams 1, 2, 3, 4.)

We added words for some alignments to further

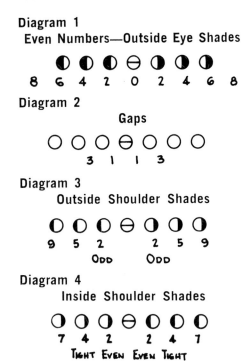

Diagram 1
Even Numbers—Outside Eye Shades

8   6   4   2   0   2   4   6   8

Diagram 2
Gaps

3   1   1   3

Diagram 3
Outside Shoulder Shades

9   5   2   2   5   9
ODD   ODD

Diagram 4
Inside Shoulder Shades

7   4   2   2   4   7
TIGHT   EVEN   EVEN   TIGHT

aid communication, not only for teaching, but also for on-the-field adjustments. After breaking the huddle a defensive call may be made to stem or move the tackles in a position to take advantage of an offensive alignment or to take away blocking angles from the offensive linemen.

Along with our numbering system we found that we had to give names to our individual linebacker positions. This procedure allowed us to give our four linebackers flexibility within our system. We also felt this would aid in the teaching process. Our system had a middle linebacker, weak outside, strong outside, and a rover.

The middle and strong linebackers would always play a truer linebacker technique. Our weak linebacker and rover would have to learn some defensive end assignments. Our rover would also have to learn to be a defensive back in a four-deep. By learning to play only one of the linebacker positions, it would cut the amount of information in half, plus they would only practice those techniques needed for their specific assignments.

Four separate linebacking positions also allowed us to place our personnel according to the strengths of their abilities. A smaller, quicker pass defender type would, for example, be a rover because of his total assignment with more stress on pass defense. Where a weak outside linebacker would have to be able to play a variety of defensive end techniques, he could be a larger individual to perform his physical tasks.

A careful organizational procedure for practice would have to be devised so that those individuals

would receive a maximum amount of time to develop given skills. The rover, for example, would quite naturally have to spend time with the defensive secondary.

To accommodate the flexibility of our four separate linebackers, we had to devise a system to get our linebackers into the variety of positions needed for our defenses. We came up with a preshift alignment for post-huddle procedure, which allowed us to flip-flop our linebackers. The preshift alignment gave us the time to make a strength call; this was important because we would at times make a double set of digits call in our defensive huddle, with each set referring to a strong and weak side. This was the preshift alignment that we settled on. (See Diagram 5.)

Diagram 5
Pre-Shift Alignment

E   T   T   E
        MLB
        SLB
H   ROVER WLB   H
        S

While we may use these numbers to describe anyone's alignment and technique for practice purposes, we use these numbers to call our different defense sets. The first number called is the tackles alignment, the second number is the ends alignment. In the case of two sets of numbers, the first two refer to the strong side, the second set refers to the weak side. Diagrams 6, 7, 8, and 9 are examples of the eight-man defensive fronts that could be called.

Further communication was needed within the numbers called. There had to be a way to call either

Diagram 6

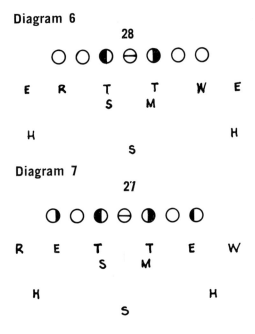

28

E   R   T   T   W   E
        S   M
H   H
            S

Diagram 7

27

R   E   T   T   E   W
        S   M
H   H
            S

Diagram 8

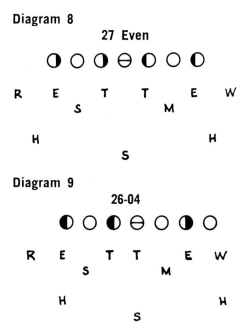

27 Even

Diagram 9

26-04

a three-deep or four-deep secondary alignment. To do this we added a digit before the call for only the four-deep; no number was added for the three deep. For example, the "27" call (split-6 alignment) would be a 3-deep. By adding a word after the numbers, you could give the desired pass coverage, "27-base" or "27-man." The four-deep would be conveyed "4-26-base," or "4-26-man safety free," giving a college 4–3 defense with either a zone or man coverage.

Also by placing the number "four" before the defensive call, the rover knows that we are going to call a seven-man front. His responsibilities will become more secondary oriented. This allows us to play more

Diagram 10

4-59-05

Diagram 11

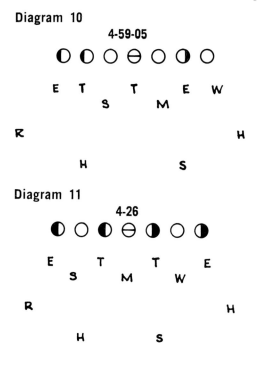

4-26

sophisticated pass defenses versus stronger throwing attacks. Diagrams 10 and 11 are our seven-man fronts, one odd and one even.

The basic alignment of the linebackers was handled by having the rule that with all seven-man fronts the defensive lineman will cover four offensive linemen and the linebackers will cover the remaining offensive linemen. If you have only six offensive linemen, the weak outside linebacker is given alignment rules to adjust to the weak split. He may align in a "hip" or a "walk away" position. The linebacking unit must however memorize their alignments for all the eight-man fronts you may desire to employ.

The problem of communicating stunts in the defensive call was handled by using words before the coverage. For example, in "27-go-man" (Diagram 12), the word "go" represented the stunt desired and meant that both outside linebackers and defensive ends would stunt.

Diagram 12

27-Go-Man

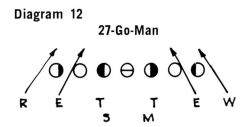

However, if we wanted to send only one outside linebacker and defensive end, we incorporated in all our stunts a system of what we referred to as SWRL, which stood for "strong, weak, right, or left." So, in the huddle, if we wanted to use 27-go to the strong side only, we would look like Diagram 13.

Diagram 13

27-Go-Strong

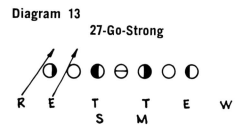

A team could also be employed in the same basic manner deciding whether you wanted all to go or just half the line. It was very easy to incorporate SWRL into the scheme. In a basic 50 look when we wanted to send both inside linebackers to the strongside guard gaps, we would call 4-59-05 fire strong (Diagram 14).

To aid us with stunts in pressuring the offense, we wanted to stem, changing the picture at the line of scrimmage. Now, not only would the opposing team be forced to expect many different looks, they would be forced to face a new problem at the line of scrimmage. If they had prepared to run any extensive check

Diagram 14
4-59-05 Fire Strong

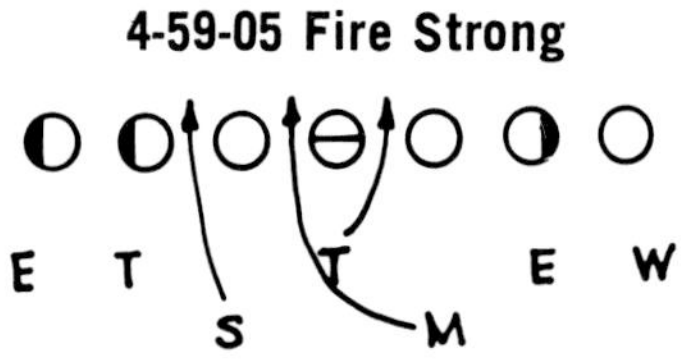

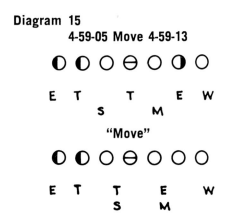

off system to pick the best play for the front they were facing, our front would change just prior to the snap.

After acquiring some degree of success defensively versus a checkoff system, we had begun to create confusion and doubt in our opponent's offensive team. This is a great factor in deciding the outcome of the contest because a confused football player cannot be an aggressive football player. Our defensive team would gain some vital ground versus the offense. It would also help us to destroy offensive timing and consistency, while allowing us to control tempo and momentum.

We handled this in the huddle by calling two defenses: the first set of numbers the defense we lined up, the second set of numbers the defense we used. For example, stemming from a 50 to a 50 gap stack, the huddle call would be 4-59-05 move 4-59-13 (Diagram 15).

Diagram 15
4-59-05 Move 4-59-13

"Move"

We had to consider various types of huddle procedures to handle the calls without any misinterpretation. We have found using a linebacker to call the fronts and the safety to call the coverage to be most effective. Excellent huddle procedure must be practiced and stressed at all times. Our system of calling defenses forces the players to be more alert at all times in the huddle, because every player must listen to the call to get his alignment, technique, and assignment, all of which may change on every down.

Central's defensive system may seem very compli-

cated when looking at it from the total picture. However, the defensive tackle is only burdened with learning an outside shade, inside shade, and gap techniques. If the tackle played in another system, he may have to memorize what to do for each individual defense, rather than working with the numbers not only to call defenses, but also to teach him his assignment and technique. We feel our system of breaking down the calls by position to be simpler and easier to learn and to execute while maintaining the desired effectiveness.

Flexibility Acquired

We originally planned to go to one basic front after we were able to acquire better personnel and become a better defensive football team. But we found that as our players improved with this system, we had acquired a great deal of flexibility that we were not ready to abandon. With each set of new defenders, we were able to grasp quickly what our strengths and weaknesses were to take advantage of this flexibility.

One other insight we found was that, with our schedule and with being an independent university, we faced a far greater variety of offenses. In a conference many schools have a tendency to follow the better teams' offensive and defensive trends. We did not have that type of trend from week to week. Central State was faced with option teams both veer and wishbone, wing T, pro running attacks, and the slot I on its schedule.

Interestingly enough, the variety did not stop there. As varied as our opponents' running attacks were, so were their passing games. We faced pro drop backs, sprint-outs, play-action, and a variety of different types of motion. We were forced to play accordingly with our secondary from week to week. However, our system was able to adjust to the run and the pass easily from week to week.

Certainly no one particular way is the right way. You have to do what you believe in and sell the players on your philosophy and make them believe in themselves. These factors will help to overcome shortcomings your squad may have. If you couple this with hard work, dedication, and sound preparation, you will have a pretty tough edge for your opponent to beat.

There are teams around that use a multiple defensive system but very few offer a complete defensive package as varied as calling the defense by the numbers.

37
Defensive Game-Week Preparation

(From 1976 Summer Manual of the AFCA)

FRANK MALONEY Head Coach, Syracuse University

We feel defense is the key and essence to winning football. We will make any sacrifice in our program to help our defense. Our substantial improvement in 1975 was due largely to a defense that statistically improved by cutting its 1974 totals almost in half. I would like to share our thoughts on how we prepare our defensive team during game week.

The first thing that we are concerned with is our opponent, and the scouting that we have on our opponent.

Scouting

There are twelve basic things that we try to scout on our opponent as we try to prepare a defensive game plan:

Personnel

We get most of this from films. That doesn't mean that we are going to go into a detailed study of each individual, but we certainly want to take a good long look at their personnel and try to categorize which personnel can hurt us the most. Which offensive lineman can hurt us the most? Which back can hurt us the most? Certain teams have certain tendencies to do certain things either with or to certain personnel.

Statistics

We like to take the statistics of the team into consideration. We think that statistics can tell you a lot that you may overlook just scouting or viewing films. It can give you vital information on frequencies in ball carriers, receivers, and so on.

Formations

We like to chart all the formations that they may possibly run. We don't try to prepare in full detail for every formation, but we want to be ready to be able to attack each formation. Naturally, we are going to limit ourselves to their base formations, and, of course, the plays that they run.

Running Profile

How we handle the running profile is something like this: We draw a diagram of a running formation and use our own numbering system and translate their plays into our system. We chart the frequency of how many times they run a play. We can take the sheet and tell in a quick flash exactly what we feel their top plays are going to be.

Diagram 1

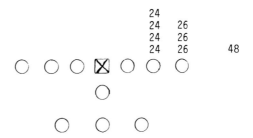

Blocking Patterns

We try, through the use of film and what not, to look at their blocking patterns. How many different ways do they block a particular play? Some teams, for example, would not have a great number of plays, but have a great number of blocking patterns. You want to chart the whole offensive line blocking patterns.

Passing Profile

We draw up the passing tree, and chart all the different areas on the field where they throw the football and what type of play action they like to throw.

Individual Patterns

We try to draw the individual patterns and the routes that they run with all the various complementary routes.

Hash Tendencies

Do they have strong hash tendencies? Some teams have great tendencies to run their plays to the field. Some run their plays to the sidelines. We feel that in planning and preparing our game plan, we are going to have to know the hash tendencies.

Down and Distance

We will try and chart every down and distance situation. If you are preparing for a team that will run the ball 98 percent of the time on first and 10, that will mean a great deal for your defensive strategy if that is going to be their percentage. Whereas, if you are preparing for a team that throws the ball 50 percent of the time on first down, your defensive strategy should change markedly.

10–20 Yard Line

We like to chart our own 10–20 yard line as they are coming in because that is where our defense drastically changes. We feel that we have really got to go after them. We can't sit back and play passively; we can't sit back and play zone type defenses. We have to go after them with blitzes and semi-blitzes and a lot of man coverage. We want to know what they are going to do in that area so we can be very careful that we are setting up the right defense. We now know that they have an extra down in there to do things.

Goal Line

What is their tendency on the goal line? We must know their run-pass ratio as well as all the possible formations they use.

Kicking Game

We must have all of their punt, kickoff return, and field goal formations and patterns charted.

This is the information that we want to know right off the bat as we get ready to prepare our game for the week. We naturally get most, if not all, of this information from films that we have exchanged with our opponents.

Game Plan

There are six things we feel we have to have when we go into every football game as a defensive team:

Basic Defenses

What are we going to try to beat them with? We have to have a basic defense or two to go out and beat this team.

Special Secondary Coverage

This doesn't necessarily mean that we are going to use these coverages, but we have to have special coverages ready to anticipate special pass patterns or things done to defeat basic zone coverages. We also need coverages for something that might come up unexpectedly from a formation that we know they have the capability of doing but haven't done as yet.

Pressure Run Defenses

The worst thing in football is to have a team run the football down your throat. It is a feeling of helplessness and one of the worst things psychologically that can happen to your football team. When they are overpowering you, it is demoralizing. So, we want to have some pressure run defenses ready. These may be a semiblitz or a little cross game here and there. If they are beating our basic defense, then we have some change-up to try to attack them with.

Pass Blitzes

We don't try to put in a lot of pass blitzes each week, but we feel that we have to have them whether we use them or not. We try to change our pass blitzes every week. They are completely out of our basic defense. We will line up in any front when we want to blitz. We don't care what we line up in—6, 8, 7, 5. But we like to change it each week so that an opponent can't categorize it.

Goal Line Defenses

Naturally this depends on our opponent's style of goal line offense. We must determine which three or four looks will be best for us on the goal line.

These are defenses that we don't normally use, but if all else fails, it is something we can fall back on.

Daily Schedule—Defensive Game Week

Sunday Night

We will try to review our opponent's film and make a great effort to get as much film as we possibly can. We are willing to give up our own films, trade with opponents, do anything, just so we can obtain the maximum number of films. I think this is a lot easier and simpler than doing it any other way.

The next thing that we do is prepare the scouting report to give to the players on Monday. I think there is a great misconception in football coaching about a scouting report. Some coaches feel it is going to become like a bible to players, but most don't read and study it enough for that. They really don't absorb a fixed scouting report. We feel very strongly that the scouting report is the coaches' bible. Throughout the week, we check back to the scouting report to see that we, as coaches, are getting prepared properly.

Monday

We want to have the scouting report finalized by noon. Our defensive report runs about thirty to thirty-five pages. You might think that is a lengthy report, but it is primarily for the coaches. Also, we want to finalize our game plan by noon. By Monday noon, we want to be sure that we know how to stop their best plays. We don't feel we can necessarily stop every play, but we certainly want to stop our opponent's base offense.

Monday Practice

First of all, we have prepractice. We try to get our players in on Monday, Tuesday, Wednesday, and Thursday for thirty to forty-five minutes before they go out to practice. We try to get them during their lunch hour, or some time during the day.

On our Monday prepractice, we will give them a position tip sheet. Now what is a position tip sheet? We will take that thirty-five page scouting report and break it down according to position. Each section, usually two typewritten pages, is applicable only to

one position and prepared by the individual position coach.

We try to show the players films of their opponents as much as possible.

Scouting report is presented at 4:00 in a fifteen-to-twenty-minute period. We then divide the players into offense and defense and show them more film.

At 4:50, we go out onto the practice field. Our Monday practices are, according to some of our players, practices of the week. What we do on Monday is run. And boy, do we run! One of the great problems in coaching today is that we do a great job in the summer of getting our players in condition, and by mid-season we have lost our condition. Monday is the day when we try to keep our conditioning throughout the whole season.

When we come out to practice to start our running, we are in sweatsuits. We warm up and separate into offense and defense. The first thing that we do is run sprints. We set up little formulas to try to make it interesting. For example, our defense runs ten 40-yard sprints plus one for every point you have given up over a touchdown. If our formulas don't work out, or we don't think that we are getting enough running, we think of some other formula.

After the wind sprints, we come together and walk through the defenses we anticipate using that week. We go through our kicking game. We especially walk through and discuss new defenses, special adjustments, and special problems.

We close practice with distance running. We run about 2½–3 miles. We run the alphabet letter of whomever we are going to play that week. If it is Maryland, we run the big M.

When we come off the field at 5:50, and we are really exhausted. Monday night, as a staff, we go over the game plan.

Tuesday

In the prepractice, our players meet for forty-five minutes with their respective coaches. We try to show them more film. The second thing that we do at this meeting is play a tape recorder for them. We try to take the tip sheet and put it on the tape recorder. We do this for two reasons. Number one, it is a change-up learning technique. The coach shuts up and the tape takes about three to four minutes, and the player listens to the coach on the tape explaining what is important for that player in the ball game. The second thing we tell the player is that he should listen to the tape recorder because there is going to be a test on it at the end of the week. That way, we feel our players will know our opponent pretty well.

Tuesday Practice

Our two-hour practices run like clockwork. First there is the warm up—five minutes. Second is punting—five minutes. One thing that is very important is to get our kicking in at the beginning of practice. So many coaches put their kicking at the end of practice. When they do, two things will happen: One, sometimes there is little time and they cut short their kicking game; and two, by the time the players get to the kicking game, they psychologically think that practice is over and they don't do the job with the kicking game that they should. Third is our tackling practice—five minutes, and fourth, agility—five minutes. The fifth part of our practice is for the individual—fifteen minutes. Each coach takes his players and goes over individual techniques. Sixth, we have key and perimeter drill—fifteen minutes. The key drill consists of the down linemen and the linebackers. They work against the opponents' plays. The defensive ends and backs run a perimeter drill and they work against the option and the wide plays of the opponent's offense. Seventh, we work the full line—fifteen minutes. We have our ends, tackles, middle guards, and linebackers work against our opponent's running game. We incorporate the off-tackle hole and some sweeps. Our backs will work mostly on passing plays. Eighth, we work with the full team—forty minutes. The full team usually incorporates four areas of football: pressure run defenses—five to seven minutes, pass blitz—five to seven minutes, goal line—five to seven minutes, Field defense—twenty minutes. After practice, we get some running in with wind sprints or team pursuit drills.

Wednesday

Identical to Tuesday. The only difference is in the prepractice period, where we have another mental technique. We prepare a list of "areas to improve." We evaluate the practice that we had on Tuesday and we make up a sheet on all of the mistakes that we made. Each player looks to see if his name is on it. It is not a critical sheet, but it has been my experience that the chances of making the same mistake is a lot less if it is clearly spelled out to the player.

Thursday

We really start working on mental attitude on Thursday. In prepractice, we start establishing individual and team goals for the game, and we start decreasing our meeting time. Our prepractice meeting is now about twenty minutes instead of forty. Each member indicates his personal goals, and he will be given a report card on how he did the day following the game. We think we get better performances by having team goals.

Thursday Practice

We shorten our practice to about one hour. We do all phases of kicking for about twenty to twenty-five minutes. We go over any fake or tricks that an opponent might do. We put in two or three fakes or tricks. We conclude practice with about thirty minutes of full team defense where we work basically on our bread-and-butter defenses and on our goal line defenses.

After practice, we have a short meeting. We give each player a sheet called the "What to Expect Sheet." The coaches sit down and try to guess what the other guys are going to try and do; what to expect in general, formations, runs, passes, and so on. This gets the players thinking more about the game.

We ask the players to visualize the big play, to just sit there, close your eyes for twenty to thirty seconds, and picture making the big play. If you can get mental images of success, your chances of success are going to be much greater.

We finalize team goals. Then, we show them a short film of about five to eight minutes.

Friday

We have the players come in any time in the day when they have ten to fifteen minutes and we give them a position test. It is amazing how high the kids will score.

Friday Practice

We go about thirty minutes in sweats. We review all our defenses. After the practice, we get together for about fifteen to twenty minutes and we do three things:

(1) We try to reemphasize our preseason goals. We are a great believer in goals. They have to be tough as hell, but they have to be realistic.
(2) We review our game goals. We try to preach confidence. Everything is a positive direction of what he is going to do.
(3) We close our meeting Friday visualizing team success. We work a lot for mental preparation.

Mental Preparation Checklist

1. Goals.
2. Areas for improvement sheet.
3. Visualization.
4. Tape recorder.

5. Decrease meeting time, plus getting our information out early.
6. Test.
7. Signs.
8. Charts; tackles, punt returns, kickoff, club, defensive team objectives.
9. Categories.

12 Championship Defensive Objectives

We also have some defensive objectives that we think are necessary to achieve championship defensive football. These are our objectives:

1. Hold opponent to:
   a) One touchdown or less.
   b) 125 yards or less rushing.
   c) 125 yards or less passing.
   d) 250 yards total.
   e) No run over 20 yards.
   f) No touchdown passes.
2. Score or set up one or more touchdowns.
3. Intercept or recover four balls.
4. Trap the passer one out of nine pass plays.
5. Average 20 yards or less on kickoff coverage.
6. Average 10 yards or more on punt returns.
7. Hold opponents to less than twelve successive plays.

If you achieve seven or eight of these objectives, you are playing pretty good defense.

This is approximately what our defensive staff and defensive team do in preparation for a Saturday game. Of course, we hope this preparation will culminate in an outstanding performance. I believe very strongly in our method of preparation as it has proved successful over several years.

38
Ohio State's Goal Line Defensive Package

(From 1974 Summer Manual of the AFCA)

GEORGE HILL Defensive Coordinator, Ohio State University

At Ohio State University we basically use an adjusting 6–5 goal line defensive package. Most of the time we will play our defense straight, but we will utilize certain stunts that we feel will take advantage of the offensive sets or the tendencies that an offensive team may present us at the goal line.

Before I get into the specific alignments and techniques that we teach our personnel, I would like to talk a little bit about our strategy and the utilization of our personnel in going to our basic 6–5 goal line. First of all, we substitute two tackles into our defense and take out our two safeties. We feel that we must get the most physical athlete that we can in on the goal line to keep the offensive line from punching us off the line of scrimmage down where each inch is very important. Therefore, as we line up our goal line defense, we will have two inside tackles, which we call guards, two tackles, which are normally our regular tackles, and two defensive ends. We then utilize our three linebackers to play the inside linebacking positions and our two defensive halfbacks to play the outside position or the wide position, depending on what offensive set we face. In reality, we essentially play with six linemen and five linebackers, although two of these people are halfbacks.

Our goal line defense is truly a goal line defense. We very rarely will use this defense in the middle of the field or out on the field. Late in a football game, if we were behind and we felt we must get the ball back, we have gone to goal line defense; or on a particular down-and-distance situation where it is a must that we stop a first down, we have gone to it. But basically, we do not use the goal line defense until we get to the 5-yard line. This is a rule of thumb; however, we have gone to goal line defense on the 4-, 7-, 8-, or 9-yard line.

Down and distance will also play a part. For example, a fourth down and 1 on the 8 generally will bring us to goal line defense. As the ball gets nearer to our goal line, but before the 5-yard line, we generally feel that some type of pressure defense or blitzing defense from our basic package is a little more sound than going to the goal line defense. When we go to a goal line and our backs are against the wall, our players have very specific thoughts in their minds—keep them out of the end zone.

As I have said earlier, we basically play our line defense straight, and we think it is sound against most offensive plays and offensive sets. However, I think one would be remiss in not utilizing certain stunts to take advantage of offensive sets, the particular offensive play that people run, and the offensive tendencies that a team might show. We also feel that our stunts will keep an opponent off balance, and they must prepare to block these stunts in order for their goal line attack to be sound. As we prepare each week to defend our goal line, the most important thing is to stop the play or plays that an opponent runs or has been successful running on the goal line. Sometimes this involves a specific play, but more times than not it involves a specific player. Most offensive people have a tendency to run their great back on the goal line, and we feel, to be successful, we must be able to stop the bread-and-butter back.

There are times on the goal line that it is important to just flat out gamble. You are going to take a chance because you anticipate what an opponent may do and you know if a particular stunt in your goal line package can take advantage of what they are doing, then you flat out gamble. If you get crossed up, you may end up giving us a score, but sometimes the gamble is worth it.

Basically, we play a zone pass defense from the goal line. However, we do feel it is important to play man-to-man against certain teams and against certain offensive sets, as we know that some people like to pass a little bit more on the goal line and we know that our man-to-man pass defense can play the receivers a little tighter than our zone. I think you must mix up your zone and man-to-man pass defense if you intend to be successful in defending the goal line against the pass. I do know, however, that if you play one or the other all the time, your offensive opponent will take advantage of what your tendencies may be in playing your pass defense on the goal line. For example, if you are basically a man-to-man pass defense team on the goal line, you can rest assured that you will see an awful lot of option plays and a great deal of pick plays on the passing game, where they will pick off your inside linebackers with outside receivers to free an inside receiver into the outside of the end zone. We also feel it is very difficult to play a good option football team on the goal line playing man-to-man, as your defensive backs or your linebackers are involved with man coverage and generally are a little bit slower getting up to support the option game.

Meet Strength with Strength

First of all, we feel that it is very important that we always meet strength with strength—that is to say that we will always be in a balanced goal line defense. Our goal line defense will always be balanced with the offensive set. We feel on the goal line that it is extremely important to defend the areas at both perimeters equally well. Therefore, if you overshift your offensive set, rest assured that we will adjust our defense to balance it with the offensive set that you give us. If you use motion or shift your offensive set, our goal line defense will adjust at the same time to put our defensive people in a position in which we feel we can take advantage of the offensive sets that you are giving us.

Second, we feel it is extremely important that we keep our people tight on the goal line. We have basic split rules and we will not allow our inside people to be split out of the ball game. We are going to line up in certain areas and we are going to play those areas. By keeping this tight alignment, we feel that we are going to stop the opponent from the easiest avenue to the goal line, that is, directly up the middle or just outside the tackle. We feel, if we can stop the inside areas, which are the quickest, easiest way to get in the end zone, we can force the opponent to do two things: either go outside with some type of an outside gain or pass to score. Then we feel that our goal line defense basically will start on a successful premise.

I think the offensive strategist, if he can bang the ball inside the tackles and be successful at it, will see very few offensive people going to the perimeter or throwing the football on the goal line. They would much prefer to bang it into the end zone the easy way, right up the middle, and I think your basic goal line defense must be able to make this the hard way to score.

Our guards (two techniques) have three basic alignments. They are "regular," which means the fullback is at home; "I," some type of "I" formation; or "C," which means there are split backs. (See Diagram 1.) Our middle linebacker will call as the offensive formation deploys these terms: "regular," "I," or "C." This will tell our defensive guards specifically what alignment and what technique they will use in our basic goal line defense.

Diagram 1

Guards

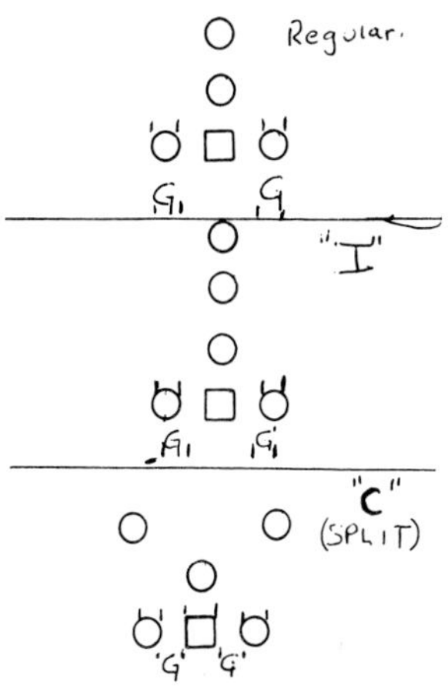

If we are playing our regular alignment, our guards line up with their shoes inside the shoes of the offensive guards, pretty much in a head-up technique. They are going to charge the line of scrimmage with a hard, low charge using their outside flipper. Their intent is to knock the guards back off the line of scrimmage as far as possible and keep them from blocking our Mike linebacker.

If we get an "I" alignment, we bring our guards in a little tighter, that is, we will split the stance of the offensive guard, putting our outside shoe in the middle of his stance. The defensive charge is exactly the same, striking with the outside flipper, keeping the inside flipper free, and attacking the line of scrimmage and establishing ourselves as deeply in the offensive set as we can.

If we get a "C" formation, then our guards tighten a little bit more. We try to keep about a yard in between the two guards when we get a "C" call. They are responsible to strip the quarterback and take the inside gap. We call this our reach through technique.

Our guards know that they must not be blown off the line of scrimmage, but more important, they must never be able to be reached on by the offensive center. If a play is going to their side, they must be part of the run the line defense if the center tries to reach on them. We do not use a real low charge, but our charge is through the knee of the offensive man. We aggressively keep our shoulder plane down and attack the line of scrimmage and try to get as much penetration as possible. In reality, we are like an offensive blocker coming off the ball hard and low, popping the hips into the offensive man as we come across the line of scrimmage.

I think the most important thing for the guards is that they cannot be overblocked by either the center or the backside guard on a play away. If this occurs, our guard must be able to beat this type of block, work the line of scrimmage shoulders square and take the place of a linebacker. Any time an offensive team uses the reach block or the overblock, they are trying to free a lineman to the play side to block one of our linebackers—most often, our Mike.

Our tackles play a very hard, tight 5 technique. (See Diagram 2.) We line up heavy 5 and play an aggressive 5 technique, attack the line of scrimmage with a low shoulder plane, destroying the block of the offensive tackles, and again we tell the tackles you cannot be overblocked by the offensive tackle. You are responsible to protect the 5 area, and you must defend that area before you leave to pursue the ball.

Diagram 2   **Tackles**

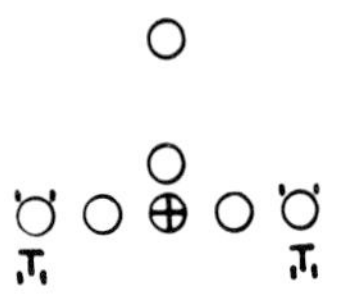

Our ends play a hard 9 technique. (See Diagram 3.) They play heavy on the tight end and he is basically responsible for stopping the off tackle holes first. He must play the quarterback very tight on all option plays and keep them from darting inside for the easy score. If the offensive end blocks down, we key the halfback or the nearback and close the off tackle hole. If the end punches at you or tries to turn you out, you must hold your ground and play the block. If the end and the halfback release, the end must get up field very rapidly and contain the quarterback. This is

Diagram 3   **Ends**

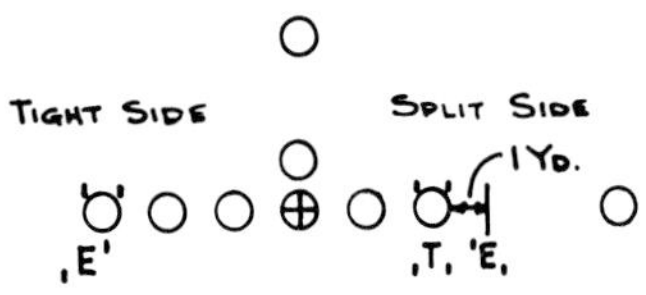

probably the most difficult technique that we ask anyone to deploy on our goal line defense.

The alignment of our linebackers, which include our halfbacks, probably is a little different from the way most people play their 6–5 goal line. These people make the adjustments to meet the strength of the offensive set.

We basically go by a very simple rule of thumb. Our halfbacks are responsible to line up outside the first eligible receiver, which means a tight end, a flanker, or a split end, depending on the offensive set that we see. Our inside linebackers are responsible to line up with an outside attitude on the second eligible receiver. This could be a tight end with a flanker outside, it could be a slot back with a split end outside, or it may be a halfback at home in the halfback's position in a normal T formation.

The one exception to this basic rule for the outside linebacker is the I formation. Because of the tandem, it is virtually impossible for him to line up with an outside attitude on the tandem backs. Therefore, the Mike linebacker and the outside linebacker away from the strength of the offensive set will line up in what we call the tandem, and this allows us to get quick run fill to the quick areas that the I formation can hit; mainly the quick handoff to the fullback or the isolation play.

Because we utilize the tandem with our linebackers, it ties in now with the deployment of our guards as they have tightened their alignment to take a little more of the middle seam away from the offense. Diagrams 4, 5, and 6 show some offensive sets that we see, and I think they will show you how we deploy our personnel using these rules of thumb that I have given you and also the terminology of "regular," "I," and "C."

As you can quickly see, no matter what the offensive set, we will automatically adjust our goal line defense by our basic alignment rules to meet strength

Diagram 4

Linebackers—HB

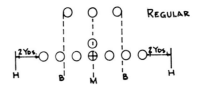

Diagram 5

Linebacker—HB

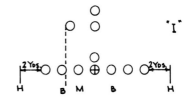

Diagram 6

Linebacker—HB

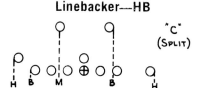

with strength and balance our defense to the strength of the offensive set. If an offensive team now wishes to send motion or to shift to one formation or another, it simply means that our linebackers now will follow their rule of thumb and continue to line up on the first eligible, the second eligible, and our Mike linebacker on the third eligible. (See Diagram 7.)

Diagram 7

Linebackers—HB

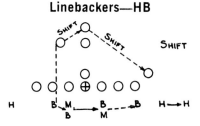

Basic Goal Line Plays

Now, let's put the defense together and go over a couple basic goal line plays, and we will illustrate the fills of the linebacker and the techniques of the defensive linemen to show how our basic linebacker fills take care of the blocking schemes that the offense may deploy.

Diagram 8

Double Isolation

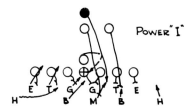

Let's look at the double isolation from the power "I." (See Diagram 8.) As we start across from the front side of the play, our end plays the heavy 9 technique and keeps from being punched off the line. Our tackle plays a heavy 5 technique and does his best to keep from getting punched off the line and turned out on by the offensive tackle. They are double teaming our guard in an "I" alignment. He must neutralize the double-team block and hold his ground. The backside guard, being reached by the backside guard, must beat the reach block and work the line of scrimmage to be able to take care of the cutback play.

The tackle must neutralize the offensive tackle and work back the line of scrimmage and our backside end has chase contained. The halfback on the front side will support outside the end for a play that bounces to the outside. Our inside linebacker will meet the block of the offensive isolation back. Our Mike linebacker has a hard 3 fill and will meet the block of the fullback as deep across the line of scrimmage as possible. Our backside inside linebacker has a 0 fill. He is going to fill the gap between the guard, being in position to take care of the cutback play, or to take the play as it bounces over the top. Our backside halfback has a 3 fill. Again, looking for a play cutting back to the backside deep, he must fill up each hole in our goal line defense.

Now let's look at an option play. (See Diagram 9.)

Diagram 9

Dive Option

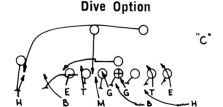

This is something I think each of us sees on the goal line. I'll draw it out of a splitback formation, or what we call our "C" alignment. Our defensive end will bump the tight end as much as possible and, as he sees the ball coming down the line, will be in position to take the quarterback quickly. Our tackle will force hard in the 5 technique. Our Mike will drive hard through the 3 technique taking the dive. Our guard, being reached on by the center, will beat the reach block, work down the line of scrimmage and seal off the cutback play. Our guard on the backside, also being reached on, will do likewise. Our tackle will force hard and work back the line of scrimmage and our backside end is the case contain. Our halfback will have to take on the flanker back on the stop block, being certain that it is not a halfback pass or a pass play and give us late support on the pitch man. Our linebacker lined up on the second eligible, the tight end, and must work up through this tight end in a position to take on the pitch man and force him wide and deep. Our Mike fills 3 and our backside linebacker will fill back through the 0. Our backside halfback has a 3 fill, again looking for a play that might cut back.

Defending Against Pass

To defend against the pass in zone coverage, we will play five deep zones versus the drop back pass. However, we do not see the drop back pass very often on the goal line. Mostly, we see the sprint type or play action, which means that our linebacker to the strength side or to the flow side will cover the flat and our other four linebackers will cover the deep quarters.

Diagram 10

Play Pass

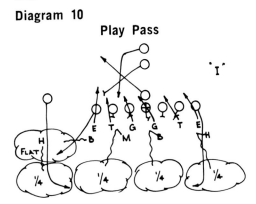

As you can see in Diagram 10, our linebacker can take away the quick, flat route of the right end, releasing into the flat, our halfback will take away the out-cut and ride the curl, and this will buy time for our inside linebackers to come off the play action and get back underneath the outside cuts working back to the inside.

Three Basic Stunts

We use three basic stunts on the goal line.

Diagram 11

GL Shoot

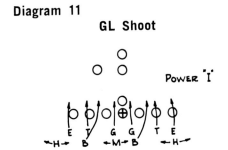

The first is goal line shoot. (See Diagram 11.) This simply means that our outside linebackers are going to shoot the 3 gap on both sides, giving us in effect a gap 8 defense. The other three linebackers find the ball and work to stuff anything coming over the top and do the best they can on pass defense. Obviously, we are short some people to play pass defense when we are in this type of a stunt.

The next stunt that we use is a pinch. (See Diagram 12.) That means that we are going to bring our interior people into the inside gaps, trying to squeeze off an inside play with our more physical football players. This frees all of our linebackers to take on the ball carrier at the point of attack. But obviously, our defense is weak at the perimeter.

Diagram 12

GL Pinch

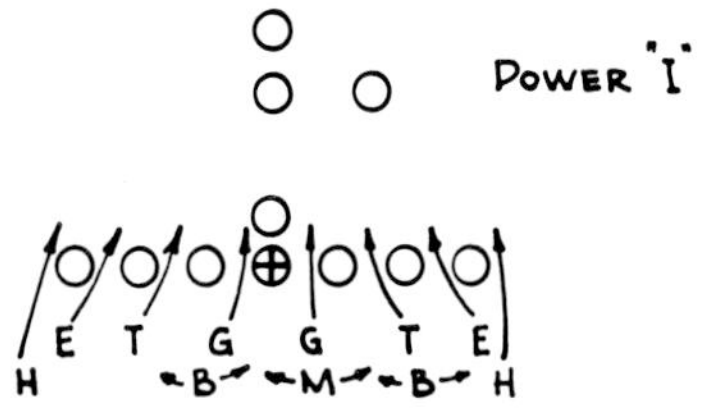

The third stunt that we use is what we call an "out." (See Diagram 13.) Against certain types of blocking schemes, we will execute our out move, getting our guard into the 3 gap, our tackle into the 5 gap and our end outside with our linebacker plugging hard on the inside one gap.

Diagram 13

GL Out

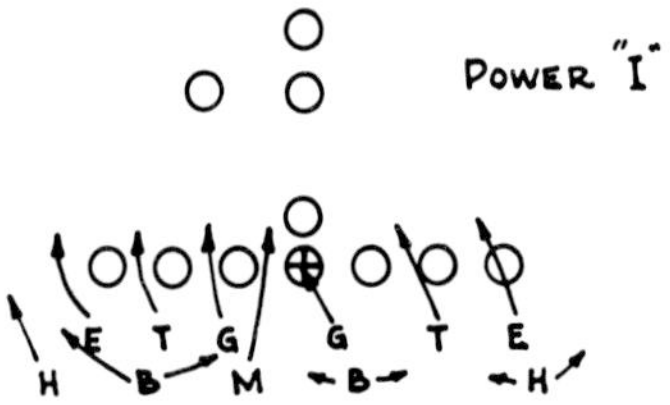

We feel by utilizing these three different stunts along with our basic goal line defense, our opponent must be able to block these three stunts if he expects to be able to run the offense that he chooses on the goal line. When we combine these with our basic goal line defense, we think this gives us a pretty full package to defend against most of the things that we will see during the season. But as you know, no goal line package is totally complete because you must make adjustments from week to week to take advantage of things that you know about your opponent, such as their offensive set, their tendencies, who their great back is, and the blocking schemes that they like to deploy in their goal line attack. If you will take the basic, utilize the stunts, and make the necessary adjustments week to week, I think you will have a complete goal line package.

The single factor that does not show up in the X's and O's is the physical personnel that you utilize and their mental attitude when they go to goal line defense. We have won several ball games in the past few years because of our ability to play great goal line defense. If you sell your players on this, and they believe that if the ball is on the 1-yard line and the opponent has a first down, we have a chance to win with our goal line defense. If you practice it each week and have sound fundamentals, then I think you too can win with your goal line defense.

39
Defensive Line Play versus the Passing Game

(From 1976 Summer Manual of the AFCA)

GIB ROMAINE Assistant Coach, University of Maryland

When pass defense is being discussed among coaches, it is commonly understood that the best type of pass defense is a good pass rush. As defensive line coaches, we place great emphasis on stopping the running game. By doing this, however, we sometimes unconsciously neglect the passing game. The importance of defending the passing game is obvious when checking defensive breakdowns—which usually occur in the passing game. The quickest way for an offense to score and get back into the game is by way of the pass.

At the University of Maryland, we feel it is very important that our players have football intelligence. A player can be coached in this area just as with the other techniques and skills. A part of this area on which we place a great deal of emphasis is the down-and-distance situation. It is surprising how many times a player will be in the heat of battle and have no idea what the down is and especially what the distance is. By being aware of this, it will help the players to react to what the offense may do.

The same defense may be called in a short-yardage situation, as we would have when we expect a pass to be thrown. The way the defensive player will carry out his assignment will vary according to these situations. In short-yardage situations, the player will stay lower than when a pass is expected. In a passing situation they will move at a height that will place them in a position to rush the passer.

To keep our players alert of down and distances, we have one of our linebackers call the down and distance before each defense is called in the huddle. To reinforce this, our coaches often quiz our players in practice when breaking the huddle to make certain that they are alert of the situations.

Besides the down and distance, it is important that your players know the position of the ball on the field. They should be aware of what the offense will do when they are backed up, being aware that they will usually be more conservative in their play selection, and know that the offense will be more free wheeling when in the four-down zone.

It is important, especially for the rushers with contain responsibilities, that they be aware of whether the ball is on the hash or in the middle of the field. If the ball is on the hash, the contain rusher to the short side has less field to protect, so he can be more aggressive with his rush. The contain rusher to the wide side has more ground to protect, causing him to be more conscious of containment. If a quarterback is going to scramble or sprint out, it is usually to the wide side.

We encourage our players to study as much film of our opponents as possible. It gives them a chance to study the movements of the offensive man they will be lining up against. They must be aware of their blocking techniques, possible weaknesses, and any tips they may be giving. It is surprising how often a blocker will change his stance or sit back in his stance. If it is picked up in film study, it can be of great advantage to the defense. They should be aware of the depth that the quarterback sets, so that they can adjust their rushes accordingly.

We are basically like everyone else when playing our reading defense. We react on the movement of the offense. There is one exception to this rule: When we face a long-yardage situation and expect a pass, our linemen will move up and crowd the football, keying the football and moving on its movement, trying to get to and by the blocker before he has a chance to get set. In these situations our linemen will adjust their stance, similar to that of a sprinter, staggering feet and narrowing the base. This will aid us in getting a good jump on the ball.

SAC Chart

To emphasize the importance, and as an incentive to our linemen, we have a SAC club. A chart is kept listing our individual game leaders and our overall leaders. At our team meetings on Sunday afternoons, Coach Jerry Claiborne goes over this chart along with other charts. This adds some competitiveness among our linemen to be the best, and it helps them to realize the importance of stopping the passing game.

Pass-rush Guidelines

1. If a pass is anticipated, have in mind a technique to use before the ball is snapped.

2. Once the rusher recognizes the pass, he must yell, "pass!"—if someone is getting a run read, this call will alert them, so that they can start working up the field toward the quarterback.

3. Don't raise up when the blocker shows pass, get the proper body lean, and get to the blocker as quickly as possible. Quick reaction time is important in cutting down the time needed to get to the quarterback.

4. Keep body lean and hands in front of body to protect against the cut block.

5. Do not stop, keep momentum toward the quarterback, and take short quick steps, which will help to keep constant pressure on the blocker and help in any type of redirection.

6. Stay in rush lane and sprint to the quarterback. If knocked out of lane, fight to get back. Many big offensive plays are the result of a lineman rushing out of his lane.

7. Adjust the rush lanes to where the ball goes. Keep the quarterback in front of you.

8. When the quarterback cocks his arm to throw, if you see his eyes, get your hands up. If you can't see his eyes, keep your hands down and run through him. There is no sense in getting your hands up, which slows down your rush, when the quarterback is throwing in a different direction. You may get to him if he has to hesitate with his throw.

9. Tackle the quarterback high and press his arms to his side. This will hamper the throwing motion, plus the threat of the ball being thrown with the tackler hanging on to his legs will be gone.

10. Contain rushers should not leave their feet. They must keep their feet on the ground and be in a position to contain the quarterback.

11. When the ball is thrown, the rushers' job isn't over. They should turn and break on the ball because the play isn't over until the whistle blows.

12. If there is an interception, it is the responsibility of the contain rusher opposite from where the ball is thrown, to block the quarterback. He is the player who usually makes the touchdown-saving tackle.

Pass-rush Techniques

Grab and Shoulder Turn

This is a good technique for an inside or outside pass rusher. When pass shows, come hard and low into the blocker with arms extended, grabbing hold of the blocker. As the blocker fights the constant pressure being put on him, pull and turn one of his shoulders forward. In a coordinating move, take away the blocking surface by turning your shoulders and throwing the opposite arm over the blocker's head. It is important to be moving toward the quarterback at all times. Try to step directly behind the blocker as you go by him. If a lateral step is taken, it gives the blocker a chance to recover.

Shoulder Scoop

This can be used best by outside rushers. It is an excellent technique to use when it is a long-yardage situation and a pass is expected. As the blocker shows pass, drive hard to his outside, concentrating on the outside half of his body. At the point of contact, dip the inside shoulder with a scooping movement of the inside arm and attempt to sprint to the quarterback. Be sure to come right at the blocker. A common fault is that the rusher will loop or round off the angle. The blocker must think that you are going to attempt to run over him.

Shoulder Club

This can be an excellent rush when playing someone who likes to run his man by the quarterback. It is a good technique for an outside rusher. Drive through the outside shoulder of the blocker, getting the inside arm on his inside when contact is made. Drive hard up the field, bringing the blocker with you. When at a depth close to that of the quarterback, use the blocker's momentum and club him up the field with the inside arm and step to the inside. If this is done by a contain rusher, it is important that it be done at a depth where he can still keep containment. A common mistake is that the rusher tries his move too early without getting the blocker moving back toward the quarterback.

Shoulder Butt

This technique is used by ends when taking on a back's block. Drive the inside shoulder and forearm through the blocker's chest, getting the outside hand on the blocker. Drive him into the quarterback. It is important that the rusher keep his feet under him and stay low enough in order to protect against being cut down.

Finesse

This is a good change-up rush. Try to avoid as much contact as possible with the blocker. Give a quick head fake one way and come back to the other side of the blocker. You see this movement many times on the basketball court. Get up the field as quickly as possible. Try to get a hand on the blocker's head to help control him.

Part Seven
Kicking

40
The Punt, Punt Return, and Block

(From 1980 Proceedings of the AFCA)

BOB BLASI Head Coach, University of Northern Colorado

Approach to the Kicking Game

At Northern Colorado, we break down our game film into offense, defense, and kicking game each week. We grade, study, and evaluate them in that manner. We find in many instances that the kicking game involves nearly 20 percent of the total game. In other words, we find that in grading the films, on the average, we are going to grade seventy-five offensive plays, possibly seventy-five defensive plays, and twenty to thirty kicking game snaps. This does indicate to us that the kicking game involves roughly 20 percent of what your offense or defense involves individually. Therefore, this dictates that we should spend a comparable amount of time on the kicking game, or, put better, place an emphasis on the kicking game that is consistent with the number of snaps involved during an actual game situation. Of course, this does not necessarily mean that we are going to spend 20 percent of our practice time on the kicking game.

Many skills required for the kicking game are carryover skills that come from certain facets or phases of the offense or the defense. For example, in the punt coverage, the tackling is consistent with tackling on defense. Blocking techniques for the punting game are very similar to those of pass blocking on offense. Normally, the kicking specialists are working at a different time or during a specialty period to place extra emphasis on that particular part of it.

We actually spend about twenty to twenty-five minutes per practice session on the kicking game. It varies a bit, depending on the time of the season. I would say during our double sessions early in the year, we spend more than that amount of time per practice. As we get it down a little better, we will spend less time on it. As we get into the actual season, our kicking game time probably averages about fifteen to twenty minutes per day.

A general thought along these lines is the fact that we break down every part of each kicking game phase and assign individual coaches responsibilities for each particular phase. For example, with the spread punt, I, as the special teams coordinator, will oversee the total coverages and individual performances. The sprinters are handled by our receiver coach, Bob Green. Our contain people are handled by our tight end coach. Our five interior linemen are assigned to Myron Smith, our offensive line coach. One of our assistant backfield coaches is assigned to the fullbacks, and our punter is assigned to our kicking coach, Buck Rollins. A total of six coaches handle the punt.

As mentioned, we teach the punting game and practically all other phases of the kicking game in a breakdown manner. In other words, when we are introducing the kicking game, we do it by first introducing the particular phase to the squad on the chalkboard, giving them their individual assignments, telling them what people are likely to be performing in certain positions, and telling them what we expect. For example, in sprinters we are looking for a very quick and tenacious individual with speed—not only speed, but the desire to get down and cover the football. Our sprinter people are generally defensive halfback types or wide receiver types, sometimes offensive halfbacks.

As contain people, we very often use defensive ends, linebackers, or tight end types. In the interior, of course, we are looking for people who have not only coverage speed, but also blocking ability. We do not, in our particular scheme of things, use defensive people there very often. I know that a lot of people do and have had a great deal of success, but overall, we are looking at people who are used to blocking and who have enough speed and movement to get down and cover the ball. Of course, at the fullback position, we are looking for a blocking back type person. He normally is an offensive fullback, but on occasion, we have used linebacker types at that position.

The next thing we do in teaching a particular part of the kicking game is to assign a breakdown period on the field. Each coach, as assigned, takes his group of people and works in separate drills on those specific techniques required for that phase. The first two or three times a player is exposed to his technique on the field, he will spend sessions of approximately twenty minutes each with his position coach. This not only gives us the opportunity to teach the desired techniques, but does give each coach a chance to see several individuals repeat the skill over and over again. This helps tremendously in our selection process when we narrow it down to the two or three people we are actually going to spend time with and use in that particular position.

We think it is important to emphasize the fact that we want to work on the kicking game fairly early in the practice session. Most often we will schedule the kicking game immediately following warm-up stretchers and agilities. The reason that I like to do this is that the kicking game involves many, many individuals, and there will be some standing-around time. It is very difficult to avoid that and to gain the attention of the people. Therefore, we like to do it early in practice when our players are alert and not tired. We find that we can utilize the time in a much more effective way; and, as I have said before, we work on it every day.

We feel that we are going to win—and we really sell our squad on this—at least two to three football games every year on our kicking game alone. We know that in a ten- or eleven-game schedule we are going to be playing people who are equal to or better than us offensively and equal to or as good as us defensively; and, if we are going to gain that winning edge, we have got to gain it somewhere. We feel that at least two or three times a year that it is going to come down to who does the best job in the kicking game.

We like to limit the variations of our kicking game, but at the same time, we want to have enough variation of each phase to handle every possible situation. For example, we want more than the spread punt in our punting game package. We want to consider the quick kick, the tight punt, and what I call the "blooper" punt (short, high kick) when you are plus 35 or better, along with the out-of-bounds or directional kicks and fakes. So, again, we do not want more phases than we need, but we want to have enough to handle all situations. If there is a conflict in our minds between too much multiplicity or too much simplicity, I would probably favor the side of simplicity.

Spread Punt

We have been very fortunate over the years to have had an excellent coverage record. Our opponents since 1975 have averaged 1.3 return yards per attempted return. We feel this is very good. Our game-to-game goal is to hold our opponent under 3 yards per return. As many of you do, we give individual helmet awards after each game. Members of the punting team get a Bear Award if they held their opponent under the 3-yard goal.

I think it is important that we examine the philosophy of the spread punt before we get into the actual execution of the punt and into the individual assignments. First, the spread punt, as opposed to the tight punt, allows us much better coverage. It allows us to release our people on the line of scrimmage quicker, in that the punter is deeper and the line is spread out so that we are going to get a better lateral coverage of the football field. What it really boils down to is a time-and-distance factor. Time factors are: (1) the speed of the snap, (2) punter's speed in getting the ball away, (3) the hang time of the football, and (4) speed of the coverage people getting down under the football.

Distance factors involve the line splits (dictating distance from the ball to the outside rush) and the punter's depth. Linemen tend to vary splits from time to time; if you are too tight, you end up with a very short distance from the outside of your sprinter to the ball. Chances of getting the ball blocked from the outside are increased if these people do not take proper splits, and we pay very special attention to that as we coach it.

The depth of the punter is another important distance factor. Some people like to put him at 13 yards; some people like to get back there at 15; and, of course, that distance depends on individual preference in some cases. Sometimes it depends on the ability of the punter to get the ball off quickly, whether he is a one-and-one-half-step or two-and-one-half-step kicker or whatever.

As you can see in Diagram 1, the guard-center split is 2 feet, the guard-tackle split is 3 feet, the tackle-end split is 3 feet, and the sprinter is 4 feet. Our center will snap the ball at his own discretion. We do not use a count on the punt snap. Our fullback will give the set call, indicating that everybody is ready, and at that point, the center will look for the punter's signal that he is ready. Any time thereafter, the center is going to center the ball.

We think it is imperative that the center gets that ball back and gets it back sharply. We want him to be comfortable and center at his discretion rather than on a count. If he has a nose guard sitting right up in his face, we want to give him a chance to look up, then

Diagram 1

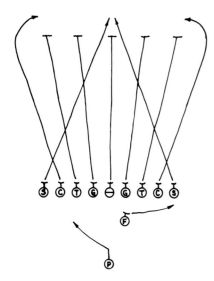

look back and make sure he is comfortable and everything is set. He is the key man in this punting situation, and it is imperative that the ball comes back correctly. Our guards, tackles, contain, and sprinters are all in a two-point stance with elbows on their knees in what we would normally term a ready position.

Let me first cover the blocking assignments of the various people up front as well as the fullback, and then we will get into their coverage assignments. The center is to block anyone covering any part of him. The guard's role is to block inside on or outside. If he has someone in his gap, he is going to call "gap" and alert the tackle that he will be blocking down. The tackle's rule is to block head on or outside, also, unless he gets the gap call. In the event he gets the gap call, then he is going to block the next man out from the guard's block regardless of where he is lined up. Contain's rule is to block head on or outside unless he gets the gap call. He will block one full count before he releases and the guard and tackle will block one and one-half counts. The reason for this is that he is farther from the ball; therefore, the threat of the block of the punt is less out there than it is inside, thus allowing him to release a half count faster.

Sprinter's rule is to block for half a count anyone covering any part of him or within 1½ feet outside of him. Of course, if he gets a gap call from contain, he is going to have to block his gap at least a full count before he can release. So, all in all, we are head on or outside unless you get the gap call, where we will just talk it out to make sure all gaps are covered.

If we get a ten-man load, then we have to give that some special attention during the week. Our general thought there is that if we have to release someone and let them go, it is going to be the very outside pressure man on the line of scrimmage. In other words, he is going to have to go the greatest distance. If we get a tremendous one-side overload, then we are going to be thinking about cutting our splits down about another foot and just using a jamming effect inside; feeling that if they cannot get a clean shot through there, our fullback will do the rest as "clean up" man.

Our fullback is spaced at exactly 7 yards behind the guard, and we insist on the 7-yard distance. We feel that this is the optimum distance to give him the best vision, and he can pick up anyone breaking through. His assignment is to pick up the most dangerous penetrator.

Now for the coverage phase. Once the fullback's block has been made and the ball is away, he is going to filter over to the right of the formation and become a safety man covering the right side of the football field. The punter, once the ball is away, is going to filter to the left side and be the safety man on the left as shown in Diagram 1. Turning to the sprinters, who are the key people in our coverage, we want to pick them for their special abilities, which are speed, tenaciousness, and, in some respect, blocking ability. However, they do not have to be super blockers if they are wide positioned. They will release after one full count after the ball is snapped and run directly to the football without any regard for special coverage or contain assignments. They are force people. Ideally, we would like to have a sprinter meet the football as it touches the returner's hand. We want them to attack the football from an outside position but not a contain position. In other words, they are our forcing attack pair We would prefer they not take a frontal position on the ball carrier, but if that is what they have to do to get to the football quickly, we would allow that. Ideally though, we want them coming from the outside in.

Our contain people block one full count and release. They will take an outside fan release locating the football as they go. About one and one-half seconds after they hear the thump, the ball should come into their line of vision. At that point, they will take a quick peek without turning their head completely up. They will locate the football and get an outside contain position on the return man.

We feel that it is very important that a contain person understands that he not only has to get outside the football, but that he has to get outside the football and up even with the football so that he has a sure contain position. Then we want him to squeeze down the alley, so to speak. In other words, it is not just good enough for him to be completely outside and leave the ball carrier a great deal of running room between him and the sprinter and saying, "Hey! Coach,

I handled my job. I turned him in." That isn't his total job. His total job is to attack from the outside in, and at the same time, squeeze the alley down and shut the ball carrier off so that he does not have a great deal of room between the sprinter and himself. Therefore, we want him to move on down toward the ball, get even with the football, and squeeze it down. If he is going to make a tackle, we never, never want him to have a frontal tackling position on the football. We tell him he is going to attack the football from the side or actually from behind as the ball carrier breaks inside of him.

Coverage for our interior people involves releasing after the block and in a fan formation. Let us take our center first. Our center is going to release directly for the football. Again, following our rule, once he has released he is going to take a peek at the football. Our punter will sound out verbally "right," "left," "short," or whatever the situation is on the punt. This will give our coverage people a clue as to where to look for the ball.

Our center is going directly down the middle to the football and will break down in a ready position 4 feet from the football. Breaking down in the hitting position, squat position, he is going to slide and keep the ball carrier in front of him. Our guards will release to the right and left respectfully in a fan. Again, when they are 4 feet from the football, they will break down into a hitting position and slide. Our tackles will do the same so that we get fan coverage as shown in Diagram 1.

Once again, I emphasize we want them to break down, slide, keep their shoulders parallel to the yard stripes rather than get their body turned so that the back can cut back. We feel that with the pressure of our sprinters, the contain of our outside people, and the fan break down, we can actually corral that ball carrier and give him no place to go.

Punt Return

We use a normal wall return as well as a middle return. I think the wall return is fairly conventional. We have used it for many years. I would have to say that it is not quite as effective as it once was when we were allowed to block below the waist, but we have averaged over 7 yards per return the last few years. This is fairly good but not fantastic compared to ten years ago when many times we were averaging 12 to 15 yards per return. I really feel that the rule forbidding blocking below the waistline on punt returns has hurt our return game. (At the same time, I feel that it is a good rule and is in the best interest of football.)

We feel we must accomplish three objectives on our punt return. In order to accomplish these, we study film and scout reports of our opponents in great detail, trying to figure out just what is the best way each week to get these things accomplished. Number one, we must contain their best coverage people. So we will vary our return from week to week. For example, if this particular tackle is one of their best people, you can bet your bottom dollar that we are going to get somebody on him, we are going to hold him up at the line of scrimmage, and we are not going to let him come off of there and get after our return people.

On the other hand, if they have somebody who has not made a tackle all year, he is sluggish and slow getting down, we are not going to expend any of our good people trying to hold him up. We are going to let him go and get one of our defensive people shifted over so that they are going to hold up one of their best people. That is not necessarily the exact way it is going to be from game to game, but it is the general idea and general execution that I am going to present.

Our second objective is that we want to force the kick to the most favorable area, or we want to get him to shank the football and get a short kick. The third objective is to force the kicker to kick on time. In other words, we want him to get that football away and get it in our hands so that we can start the runback. If he stands back there and holds the football until all his friends get down there, we are going to end up fair catching the ball or have some problems returning it because they are going to have great coverage on it. I have already mentioned how we are going to try holding up their best coverage people by putting someone on them and not letting them get out of there free.

The last two objectives are going to be accomplished by offside end and backer, who are our force people. They are going to take an alignment as shown in Diagram 2. The away end is going to be lined up $1\frac{1}{2}$ feet outside the end man on the line of scrimmage. Our backer is going to take the next gap in on the snap of the ball. They have a free rush. We will let them have the option of going for the football any time they feel they can block the ball clean.

Many times on a regular punt return, we will make the block even though we do not have the block on. Usually because of a poor snap, or mishandled football, or something like that, we want to make certain that we have people in there coming after the football. Now, our backer is going to take the inside position as diagrammed. His rule is to go in front of the personal protector. He is never to go behind the personal protector. If the personal protector backs up to block the end as he is coming in, then, of course, he may get a free shot at the football, and he is allowed that shot. Otherwise, if the ball is away normally, he

Diagram 2

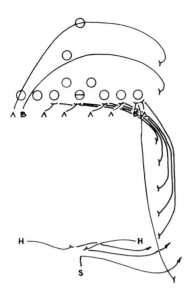

runs to the other side, and he will be the second-to-last man in the wall.

Our end, again, has a free rush. If the personal protector steps up to block our backer and he has a clean shot at the football, he is going to take it. Most normally, he will just go on around behind the punter and set up in the wall and becomes the last man in that wall. In the event of a bad snap, mishandled punt, or a fake, the end has contain responsibility on his side and the backer has help contain responsibility on the far side as shown.

Punt Return Assignments

1. Left End—Two-point stance, one foot outside widest offensive lineman. On snap, end will drive hard to keep leverage on the kicker unless you are sure you can block it. On a bad snap from center, will make tackle. If the end does not block kick, he will become clean-up blocker inside wall for ball carrier.

2. Right End—One foot outside widest man on line of scrimmage. Deliver two-hand shiver blow to the man on the end of the line of scrimmage, turn and sprint to point halfway between hash mark and sideline. (Ball on far hash mark, set up on hash mark on wide side of field.) Turn upfield and sprint to set wall 30 yards downfield. Number one man in wall block inside. Two-point stance.

3. Rip Linebacker—Outside shade of wide man on line of scrimmage in a two-point stance. Deliver a double-hand shiver to the wide man after the end releases him and then control him as long as possible. When control is lost, turn and block outside wall

downfield. Make him release inside. Do not let him release outside into wall. Turn and block out at the corner.

4. Right Tackle—Line up in second gap from outside. Stance will be four-point twelve inches off the ball. On the snap of the ball, loop step outside to a head-up position on second man from outside. Deliver a two-hand shiver to head or shoulder pads. Right tackle will be number two man in wall sprint hard to turn point. Block inside.

5. Right Guard—Twelve inches off the ball in a four-point stance. Line up in the gap between center and guard on right side of line. Execution will be the same as tackle. Loop step to head-up position on the third man in, hit and sprint to turn point. Number three in wall. Block inside.

6. Left Guard—Line up in guard and center gap on left side of line, twelve inches off the ball. Make a loop step to a head-up position on center. Deliver a two-hand shiver, release and become number four man in wall. Sprint to turn point, block back inside.

7. Left Tackle—Line up in second gap from outside on your side of line. From a four-point stance, make a loop step to the man inside you. Deliver a two-hand shiver, release and become number five man in the wall. Block inside.

8. Lew Backer—Line up first gap inside widest man. Two-point stance, twelve inches off the ball. On the snap, Lew will drive hard to a point in front of kicker to block punt. Lew has the responsibility to make the tackle in case of bad snap from center. If you do not block the kick, you become clean-up blocker inside wall.

9. Right Halfback—Line up 7 yards in front of safety. Catch and return all low and short squibb kicks. "Fair catch" short high kicks. On punts to safety, ensure the catch by blocking any player getting downfield quick. After catch, block outside any player past the wall.

10. Left Halfback—Line up 7 yards in front of safety behind the left defensive end. "Fair catch" any short high kick to your side of field. The left halfback will call the man to catch the ball. Left halfback will talk safety and right halfback on "fair catch" and closeness of tacklers to ensure the catch. On all kickers caught by safety, left halfback will get in front of runner and block first off-colored jersey.

11. Safety—Field all punts from a position deep enough to make a move. Catch the ball and break to outside, then turn upfield just inside contain. Contain man will be blocked at this point if safety has set him up good for the blocker. After cutting inside contain man, fight to get outside return wall. Give ground if necessary.

There are a couple of other coaching points that I should mention in summing up the punt return. One, it is very important that we do bring the wall to the ball. The lead tackle, of course, is responsible for that. If he comes down, and as he gets a view of the football, we want him to set the wall and then move it rapidly to the ball in order to prevent leakage at the corner. We do not want to leave a large gap between the ball and the wall so that the returner has to run laterally 15 to 20 yards before he gets to the wall. We want that lead tackle to bring that wall right on in. The other people in the wall will follow suit and squeeze the distance down again so we can shut down the elapsed time between receiving the ball and the time the runner is actually running with the ball outside the wall.

The other coaching point I want to emphasize is that we often run into very fine sprinters who are accomplished release people at the line of scrimmage. They make it difficult for us to do the kind of job we would like in holding them up. One of the most difficult things for us to handle is the extreme outside release. If he wants to drop off the line of scrimmage and come on around hard to the outside, it makes a very tough situation for us. In the event that the sprinter takes an extreme outside release on the return side, we tell our backer to run with him all the way to the corner and block him or knock him out of bounds.

We have seven people in the wall, and we want the blockers to be, under ordinary circumstances, 4½ to 5 yards apart. Therefore, our wall should cover a vertical distance of approximately 35 yards. One of the most difficult jobs we have is keeping our players from bunching up to the point where we have two people blocking the same off-colored jersey. We do not want that to happen. Of course, if they get too far apart, the opponent can penetrate the wall without anyone blocking them. That has not been nearly as much of a problem for us as our people jamming up together and creating a 15- to 20-yard wall rather than the 35-yard wall we think is necessary.

Punt Block

In blocking the punt, there are a few general principles that we try to work with. When designing a specific punt block, we try to examine the opponent's punting game very closely and try to identify some weaknesses either in personnel, alignment, or technique that would give us a good shot at the punt block.

Of course, the first thing we are going to look at is their punter. We want to know if he is a very poised punter, his number of steps, speed of delivery, and so on. Also very important in the punt block is the center

and what his abilities are; whether he has a little hitch, giving you a little bit of a jump on the ball, whether he throws a rainbow, or if he is erratic. We are much more prone to go for blocks when the center is a bit erratic or if we feel that the punter lacks poise.

The other things we are going to look at are who their sprinters are, who their contain people are, and what their specific blocking assignments are designed to do. Is there anything there that would give us some reason to believe that we have a better-than-average chance at blocking the punt? We are also going to look very carefully at line splits. If there is a tendency for some of the people to crowd up giving them a short lateral distance between the center and the end of their line, we are more prone to try to block the football from the outside.

Just a general principle: If I had my "druthers," I would not normally attempt to block a punt from inside. The main reason is that I feel that there is too great a chance of running into the kicker by a frontal attack. In order to block the punt, we are not going to aim for the punter, but we are going to aim for a spot approximately 4 yards in front of where the punter is standing plus or minus a yard, depending on whether we are looking at a one-and-one-half- or two-and-one-half-step kicker. Also, the length of the stride is to be considered. Once we identify the distance from his original spot to the point where his foot is going to meet the football, then that particular week we are going to work on getting to that spot. Of course, that spot is going to be in front of his body; and if you are attacking from a frontal position, you are going to increase your chances of running into the kicker and drawing a foul.

If there is anything I hate to have happen it is to have an opponent punting to us and then give them a first down because of a roughing call. Therefore, I would prefer to try to block the punt from outside of

Diagram 3

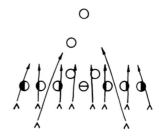

a tackle, thus lessening our chances of a roughing call. This is not to say that we will try the inside if we feel that they are going to give that to us.

Another principle is that only one man is assigned to actually block the football. Although we would rush up to ten people, he is going to be the hit man. Some people are going to be decoys, and they are going to draw the fire. In fact, we will always assign someone to draw the block of the personal protector or protectors, thus giving our hit man a clean shot at the ball. (See Diagram 3.) This is one of the typical ways in which we attempt to make the block. I think perhaps more important than the individual diagram are the basic principles of the block that we work off of. I think from game to game you have to change your exact blocking method dictated to you by the opponent's formation and any weaknesses that you may ascertain.

41
Take the "Special" Out of Special Teams

(From 1977 Summer Manual of the AFCA)

BOB ODELL Head Coach, Williams College

Each year more and more games are being decided by the kicking game. In the past, most coaches, including myself, thought of the kicking game as of just who is doing the punting or placekicking. Now the importance of snappers, punt receivers, coverage, protection, rushes, and so on, has become just as paramount in having a totally sound kicking game. Players with specific abilities for the special teams are now making the team on that merit alone.

Elements of the Successful Kicking Game

Intensity

Although intensity is essential in all areas of the kicking game, it is best observed in how you cover kicks (punts, kickoffs, and field goals). Football's true test of desire and determination is measured in covering kicks. No one will ever return a kick for a score against us unless one man fails to go all out. The first kickoff or kickoff return should set the tempo for the entire game.

Elimination of Mistakes

Most mistakes made in the kicking game are caused by a lack of concentration or a lack of belief in its importance. The result of poor concentration is poor protection, poor coverage, and careless application of the complex kicking game rules. Absolute belief in the importance of the kicking game is the key to the elimination of mistakes.

Fundamentals

A complex kicking game must be extremely sound in fundamentals. Kicking involves many precise skills.

Punters, snappers, holders, and placekickers must work many extra hours at perfecting their skills. Concentration while practicing their specialty must be total with players before, during, and after practice. Distances at which kickers and holders locate themselves, along with timing in snaps and getting kicks away, are details that must be worked at earnestly and tirelessly. These time and distance requirements are precise, and they require constant attention.

Our time elapse objectives are:
1. 14-yard punt snap   0.8 seconds
2. Punter   1.3 seconds
3. Total getaway time   2.1 seconds
4. Hang time (minimum)   4.0 seconds

Spread Punt Formation

Diagram 1

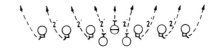

I. *Stance and Alignment*
   a. Guards, Tackles, Ends
      1. Two-point stance, feet shoulder width apart, knees slightly flexed, hands on knees, and head up.
      2. Splits on line of scrimmage will be 2′ 2′ 2′. The zone principle and a 2-foot split make

it possible for one blocker to delay two rushers over his area.

   3. Do not crowd the ball.

   b. Up Backs

     1. Three-point stance, split center-guard gap and align with head on tail of lineman.

II. *Fullback Call*

   1. Call defensive front, look for overload, check with kicker and then call "set."

III. *Assignments*

   a. Center

     1. Snap ball when you are ready (after kicker opens his hands). It is very important that snap be fast and accurate. Jerk head up, block man on, sprint to ball.

   b. Guards, Tackles, Ends

     1. Zone block principle.

     2. On snap, step out and back with outside foot and block outside area. Do not slide inside foot—keep it planted. Block high into numbers. Release in your lane to outside and sprint to ball. Ends have contain.

   c. Up Backs

     1. First responsibility is to block anyone in center-guard gap. Do not avoid a charging defensive lineman or linebacker. Sprint to ball. If you do not have someone to block, you should be first man downfield.

   d. Fullback

     1. Align 6 yards from line of scrimmage. Protect the kicking lane first. On snap assume a good balanced hit position. Search out and block the most dangerous rusher. Don't back up! Responsible for calling "load" situations. You will cover right as a safety.

   e. Kicker

     1. Align 14 yards deep. After fullback calls "set," open hands for snap. Center will snap ball when he is ready. Ball must be kicked quickly. A bad snap or slow kick are the major reasons why most punts are blocked.

IV. *Overload Adjustments*

   1. If six or more defensive men are aligned from the center's head to one side we call an overload, and change from zone to man principle. The fullback counts and yells, "Load right," or "Load left." The team will adjust as follows:

   a. Center

     1. Block man on or to load side.

     2. If a slide call is made by an up back, block man on or check to help away from load.

   b. Guard

     1. Block man on or outside.

     2. Point at man you are going to take.

   c. Tackle, End

     1. Block inside, on, outside.

     2. Point at man you expect to take.

   d. Up Backs

     1. Loadside—be big and occupy C-G gap. If more than one man attacking the gap, be ready to throw a body block with head to outside and leg whip inside. Get a piece of any defender coming through your area.

     2. Away from load—if three or less defenders are on this side, the back calls "slide" and blocks across behind the center. He will be an extra blocker and should pick up first penetration. When center hears "slide," he will block on or away from load to protect gap vacated by back. The guard-tackle-end will point to men they will block.

Diagram 2
10 Man Rush—Load Right

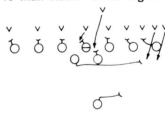

V. *Field Position Consideration*

   a. Soft Punt

     1. To stop ball inside 20-yard line.

     2. Drill on out of bounds as well as high and short.

   b. Danger Punt

     1. Any time punter cannot stand at least 13 yards from ball.

     2. Tighten splits and get ball off as quickly as possible.

   c. Punt Play

     1. Important to have a fake kick run or pass to take advantage of hard rush and keep defense honest.

   d. Taking a Safety

     1. Know when it is advisable and review on Friday before game.

VI. *Coverage*

   a. An important factor in teaching coverage lanes

is moving ball from hash to hash. Players on outside should keep ball on inside shoulder.

b. Always have a stop watch when teaching the kicking game.

Punt Defense—Blocks/Returns

I. *Criteria*

a. Thorough study and knowledge of opponent's punt formation, personnel strength and weaknesses, and evaluation of opponent's timing and technique.

b. Similarity—disguise blocks and returns.

c. Knowledge and concentration by all members of punt defense team to insure success.

d. Ultimate desire and determination to cause the big play.

e. Of all six aspects involved in the kicking game, the area of punt defense has the ability, more than any other, to change the complexion of a game. The sound of a blocked punt or the scene of a great runback can instantly change the momentum of a game and ultimately be the deciding factor in either victory or defeat.

f. We will overemphasize our ability to block punts.

II. *Numbering System*

a. Number the gaps, regardless of punt formation, from one to five counting from the center out.

Diagram 3
7 Man Pro Punt

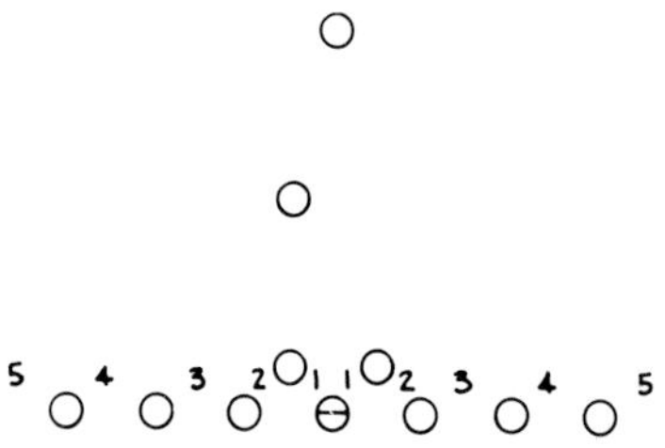

Diagram 4
9 Man Punt

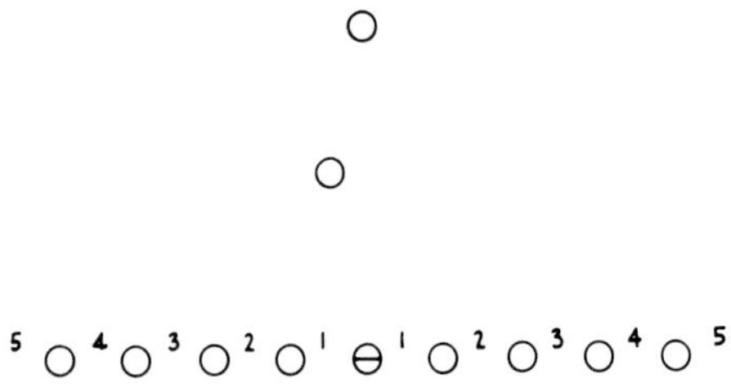

b. A double digit number designates assignments. For example: 23, 42, 15, 34, and so on.

III. *Alignment*

a. Left Linebacker, Left Tackle, Left End

1. Work as unit and align according to first digit of the call.

2. Linebacker aligns in or attacks that gap.

3. Tackle aligns inside linebacker—end outside.

Diagram 5
23 Call

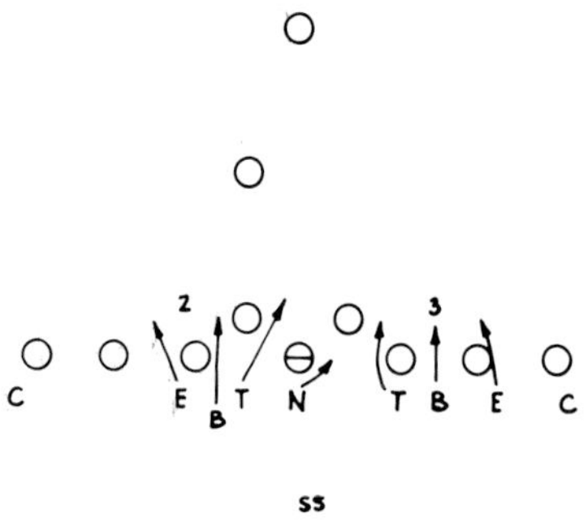

b. Right Linebacker, Right Tackle, Right End

1. Work as a unit and align according to second digit of call.

2. Linebacker aligns in or attacks that gap.

3. Tackle aligns inside—end outside.

c. Middle Guard

1. Align on head of center—rush through center or pick a side—depending on call.

d. Cornerbacks

1. Align on or outside widest man (No. 5 position) and rush or cover depending on direction of call.

2. For example: 23 Block right.
   (a) Right corner will rush.
   (b) Left corner will cover, that is, look for tricks—fake kick run or pass his way.

e. Strong Safety

1. Alignment and assignment may vary.
   (a) Block Call—line up 6 to 7 yards behind middle guard. Cover widest man as a potential receiver or check for fake kick run on the side where the corner is rushing. May also align on line of scrimmage.
   (b) Return Call—drop back to twin safety position.

f. Free Safety

1. Depth depends on kicker's ability, wind, position on field, and so on, and responsible for catching the ball—do not let it hit the ground.

2. If double safety, align on left side and control who catches the ball.

Diagram 6

34 Right

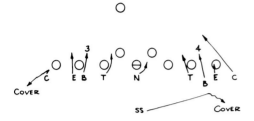

IV. *Benefits*

The benefit of the system is that you can come up with many combinations of blocks without having to draw up last minute plans on the sideline. You can take advantage of certain weaknesses by merely calling two numbers and a direction, and the players know exactly what to do without confusion or hesitation.

> **Kicking Game Dont's**
> **Do not** block below the waist.
> **Do not** be offside.
> **Do not** rough the kicker.
> **Do not** clip.
> **Do not** let ball bounce.

Field Goal

Diagram 7

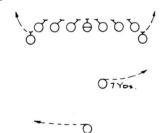

I. *Assignments*
a. Linemen
1. Three-point stance with a shoe width split.
2. Feet in normal offensive stance.
3. Normal weight on hand.
4. Step with inside foot in front of the man to your inside.
5. Keep hips and shoulders square to line of scrimmage.
6. Block inside gap or over.
7. Center snaps ball when ready—after holder opens his hands. Has blocking responsi-

bility on a man over him. Snap must be quick and accurate.
8. Coverage as important as punts or kickoff.
b. Wings
1. Three-point stance splitting outside leg of end with a one-quarter turn to outside.
2. Block first rusher outside end. This is not an aggressive block. Let him come to you.
3. Contain responsibility.
c. Holder
1. 7 yards deep.
2. Check with kicker.
3. Call "set" and open hands when ready to receive ball.
4. Must have good quick hands.
5. Safety cover right of ball.
d. Kicker
1. Concentrate
2. Safety cover left of ball and call direction.
e. Team
1. Block first.
2. Cover lane and listen for call.
3. "Bust a gut."

Extra Point

All personnel are in the same position and have the same reponsibilities as in a field goal, with the exception of coverage.

Field Goal Defense

I. *Can use same numbering system as versus punts.*
II. *Situations:*
a. Basic Field Goal Block
Has built into it the elements of rush, normal precaution against fake, and provision for a return.
b. Overload Field Goal Block
Puts stress on a heavier rush without abandoning the possibility of defensing a fake and still providing for a return.
c. All-Out Field Goal Block
Used in a positive kicking situation whereby we commit all resources to the rush with no concern for the fake or the return. This will be the same as our point-after-touchdown rush.
d. Prevent Defense Against Field Goal
We want opponent to kick, and where our main concern is guarding against the fake.

Point After Touchdown Defense

In the basic point after touchdown block, we will commit all resources to the rush with no concern for the fake.

Kickoff

I. *Coverage*

    a. Huddle for call before kickoff.

    b. All men line up facing the kicker with front foot on the 35-yard line. When kicker says "set," put hands on knees.

    c. When kicker passes your line of vision, take off in pace closely behind kicker. Don't be offside!

    d. Go down on kick as fast as possible, maintaining proper lane spacing, running under control. Be ready to react to ball. Use your hand, speed and agility.

    e. Don't stop to catch a blocker, be nifty and avoid blocker early, but get back into your lane. Whenever you are within 7 yards or less from the ballcarrier, with blocker in between, go through the blocker to make the hit, never around.

    f. Stay on your feet; if knocked down, get up immediately and get back into your lane.

    g. All men angle toward ball, move as a unit, keep in your lane. Don't crowd the man on your inside, keep spacing to your inside.

    h. Remember, once the ball goes 10 yards, it is a free ball.

II. *Returns*

    a. Most important factor, if you want consistency, is to allow enough time on the practice field. The most effective teaching method is to have members of the kickoff team cover "one at a time" at full speed. This allows the coach to observe individual techniques, and the members of the receiving team get a realistic feel for their assignment without the confusion of twenty-two players running all over the field. Hustling the first 10 yards to get to the blocking area is most important. Most blocks are missed because the kicking team out-hustles the receiving team. We do not block live in practice, just butt or grab the assigned player.

    b. We use a "wedge," return "right" or "left," and an "on side" return.

Reminder Checklist

Fair Catch Rules

1. Ball cannot be advanced after fair catch signal.
2. Only the player signaling "fair catch" is protected.
3. Protection of receiver ends when the ball touches the ground.
4. You do not have to field it, but you can't block covering men.
5. Coverage team, anticipate fair catch fumble.
6. Do not use fair catch unless necessary.
7. Cannot interfere with right to fair catch.
8. Only the man fielding the ball should signal the fair catch.

Punt Block Rules

1. Get off the ball; do not be offside.
2. Look at the ball.
3. Go to kicking area.
4. Don't rough the kicker.
5. Automatic return away.
6. Partially blocked punt crossing the line of scrimmage is as if it had not been touched.
7. Fourth-down punt not crossing the line of scrimmage will be our ball, so try to advance it. (Do not fumble.)
8. Third-down punt not crossing line of scrimmage is free ball, so get possession.
9. Field goal block and return procedures same as punt block and return procedures.
10. A blocked punt is usually good for a touchdown.

Punt Return

1. Don't be offside. End men on line call across.
2. Don't rough the punter.
3. Don't let the ball hit the ground.
4. Don't clip. Block high.
5. Call "Peter" if not handling ball. (Peter call designates to the remainder of the team to pull off blocks and stay away from ball.)
6. Generally, do not handle punts inside your 10-yard line.
7. Never go into return unless sure punting situation. Know our procedure for quick kicks and unsure kicking downs.
8. Know rule of first touch. Official downs the ball.
9. Easy way to make big yards. Each time the situation comes up, you must think this is the big play.

Punt Protection

1. Be sure you are in a legal formation!
2. Cut down splits when kicking within 3-yard line. Punter check dead line of the end zone.
3. Personal protector, check your position in relationship to punter—8 yards in front and remind punter of end line.
4. Personal protector, do not give ground and

take alignment on correct side. Get into return alley.

5. Personal protector calls when all are set, and alerts for overload. Know blocking rules and be ready for alert call.
6. Early down kicks should never be blocked.
7. Be alert for punt check-off. (Fake punt.)
8. Line may adjust splits until personal protector gives "set" command.
9. Center must wait one full second after "set" command before snap.
10. Punter alerts team to ball direction. "Right," "left," "short."
11. A punt must never be blocked on us. Have pride in your protection.

Punt Cover

1. Know our coverage.
2. Don't hold back. Run full speed. After 10 yards locate ball over inside shoulder.
3. Stay in lanes and fan out.
4. First man down, take a shot at ball carrier.
5. If you have contain, you must contain. Be aware of a reverse.
6. Don't overrun ball, balance up and take hitting position.
7. If a fair catch signal is given, always anticipate fumble.
8. Do not interfere with safety man's right to catch ball.
9. Down the ball only if it is going into end zone or bouncing toward your goal line.
10. If a fair catch signal is given on 10, anticipate fake fair catch.
11. You cannot touch ball until it touches the ground or your opponent.
12. On downing ball, do not leave it. Official stops the play.
13. Ball bouncing into end zone untouched is dead.

Kickoff Return

1. After 10 yards, it is a free ball. It must be handled.
2. Five men between 10 yards and 15 yards from ball. Make sure you have a complete team.
3. Be sure of deep kick before turning your back on ball.
4. Know approximate depth and location of ball before executing block.
5. Safety man, use judgment on handling and returning ball from end zone.

6. Safeties, know who is "call" man and direction of return.

Kickoff Coverage

1. Kicker, count your team.
2. Don't be offside.
3. Free ball after 10 yards or if touched by a receiving team player.
4. You will run past most potential blockers—if you run.
5. Keep your spacing.
6. Evade early blockers to the ball side and return to proper lane.
7. Run through blocker immediately in front of ball carrier.
8. Contain man, be alert for reverse and unusual returns.
9. Know your onside or squib kick responsibility. Know who folds as safety and contain.
10. Go after ball.

Field Goal and Extra Point Defense

1. Move into your block alignment in sure field goal range and situation.
2. Be alert for fake field goal.
3. Single safety back and be conscious of field position, time, and score.
4. Automatic return away from the block side or to wide side of field.
5. Know which is our rush side. Rush from one side only.
6. Don't be offside, but get off with the ball—blocking a field goal or extra point can win!

Field Goal and Point after Touchdown

1. Kicker will bring in play. (Possible fake.)
2. Be alert for "no huddle," if time is a factor on field goal.
3. Field goal must be covered—know your coverage.
4. Always be alert for possible run back.
5. Field goal coverage rules are the same as punt rules.
6. A placekick must never be blocked on us.

Procedure after Taking Safety

1. Kickoff coverage team puts ball in play.
2. Twenty-yard line is restraining line.
3. Line up on 15-yard line.

4. Five men on each side of kicker. Kicker is safety.
5. Any intentional safety will be a bench call and taken from punt formation.
6. Ball will be put into play either by punt or placekick.

Receiving Ball after Safety

1. Kickoff return team on field. Use normal kick-off return.

2. Move up restraining line. (10 yards from ball.)
3. A fair catch may be used in any kicking situation.
4. May also use three-deep in this situation with your punt handlers.

In kicking situations, champions keep the pressure on.

42
The Running of the Bulls

(From 1979 Summer Manual of the AFCA)

BRUCE SNYDER Head Coach, and TERRY SHEA Assistant Coach, Utah State University

They get their hands on the football before our offense ever calls a play. They move the football up-field farther than the average gain of a pass or a rushing play. And their success or failure in advancing the ball can put our offense in better position to score. They're the kickoff return unit of Utah State Aggie football, and they're aptly called the "Running of the Bulls."

In our 1978 season, our kickoff return team was ranked first in the nation (Division I) with a 26.7 return average. Two of our returns went for touchdowns and one of these scores ignited a crucial come-from-behind win early in our schedule, enabling us to move through our first five games undefeated. However, more games are lost due to kicking results than are won. Although the kicking game seems simple enough, the reverse is often the case. Kicking is an area in which the big error is more in evidence than is the brilliant execution.

A team will never have the practice time to prepare for all the kicking situations that may come up during the course of a season, but we certainly prepare our special teams to eliminate the big error. With our kickoff return unit, we set a consistent and realistic goal. Average 30 yards per return for every game. Our Running of the Bulls were able to achieve this game goal only five times this past season, but it served as a high standard of performance for a very highly motivated group of specialists.

Philosophy

Our approach in organizing the Running of the Bulls was crucial to the unit's overall success. Areas we considered vital were staff responsibilities, personnel selection, practice environment, consistency of our

return package, and a tremendous pride within the unit.

The most obvious fact about kickoffs is that the deployment of the two teams on the field is completely dissimiliar. The coverage opponent stands in a row at their own 40, while the return team is spread from their own goal line to the middle of the field. As the kickoff unfolds, the relationships become reversed. The coverage becomes dispersed and the return team recoils.

We instill in our return unit that there is no place for nifty running by returners, and the entire unit must commit itself to aggressive contact at high speed.

Staff Responsibilities

We believe there are three specialized components of a return unit. The front line, the wedge, and the returners. Therefore, we assign a coach to each group. Because we give special emphasis to our kicking game at Utah State, it is imperative to include the head coach in the staff organization. The mere fact of the head coach's involvement gives the unit a unique emphasis. So Head Coach Snyder is in charge of the front line. Coach Shea coordinates the return and coaches the wedge. By coaching the wedge, the coordinator can actually set and feel the tempo of the return during practice. Our running back coach is assigned the deep safeties. This relationship works out very well because in our program the return men are usually running backs.

Personnel Selection

The personnel are individually picked players from both the offense and defense. The players are se-

211

lected on the basis of (1) their ability to hit on the run, (2) agility, and (3) speed. We believe these criteria for selection were among the most important factors behind our success in 1978.

We found that the front line required the style of player who possessed good agility and the ability to hit on the run. These players were generally defensive backs. The wedge, who were nicknamed the Brahma Bulls, consisted of players who could certainly attack on the run as well as move in short bursts of speed. We found this type of player within our tight ends and inside linebackers, giving us some bulk at the point of attack. The two safety men were chosen for their aggressive style of running, speed, and catching ability. We want our returner to possess the courage to hit the bubble of our wedge at full speed. This style of running does not call for a nifty runner, but a runner who believes a return to the 40-yard line is a successful return.

Practice Environment

In order to make the unit really important, we decided that the players involved must feel special. We scheduled all practice time for the Running of the Bulls after daily practice to give it a special flavor. The actual on-the-field work was always held in the stadium. This change of environment, from the practice field to the stadium, gave our unit an emotional lift and it also guaranteed us gamelike conditions from a playing surface standpoint. We also found that by utilizing the stadium, we could isolate learning and avoid any after-practice distractions.

We practice kickoff return twice every week, and the personnel on the unit are released from any conditioning periods during those two practice days. Again, this small gesture of release from conditioning time gives an added importance to the unit. The players certainly maintain their conditioning standards, as the practice time devoted toward kickoff return emphasizes speed, timing, and assignments.

There is never a time when we will scrimmage our return, so a major emphasis is always placed on speed and the all-important timing between the formation of the wedge and the returner hitting up into the wedge at full speed.

Return Package

We consolidated the number of returns in order to give us the consistency we wanted and to eliminate changing our blocking patterns from game to game. We also selected our package based on the different situations we might confront during an entire season of play.

The following six returns give us a thorough, but consolidated package.

1. Wedge return
2. Side return
3. Cushion return
4. Hands team (onside kick situation)
5. Wedge team (squib kick situation)
6. Return after safety

We have found the fewer blocking patterns, the more consistent our return team has become. This consistency has also led to a higher level of productivity. We convince our unit that if we can consistently bring the ball back out 30 yards every time, then the big returns will come along.

We believe it is important that a return unit have an understanding of the playing rules that affect the overall return. We isolate eight different rules for our players to learn and couple this list with two strategy reminders.

Kickoff Return Playing Rules

1. The ball on a kickoff must travel 10 yards.
2. A kickoff that has traveled 10 yards and not yet been touched is a live ball.
3. A player on the receiving team must be given an unmolested opportunity to catch the ball.
4. If the ball goes into the end zone untouched by our receiving team, and we make no attempt to run it out, it is our ball on the 20-yard line.
5. We must block above the waist.
6. We can fair catch any kickoff or free kick.
7. Front five linemen cannot cross 45-yard line until the ball is kicked.
8. Any free kick or kickoff that travels 10 yards or more must be covered or advanced. When the ball enters the end zone:
   a. On the fly: Ball can be run out, but not necessary. If the ball is 5 yards deep into the end zone, our rule is not to run it out.
   b. On the ground untouched by receiving team: Ball is dead and does not have to be covered.
   c. Muffed by receiving team: The impetus is supplied by kicking team, ball must be covered, but not run out.
   d. Fumbled by receiving team into the end zone: The ball must be recovered and returned out of end zone.

Strategy Reminders

1. The restraining line is 10 yards from the ball. Always be alert to adjust when the kickoff is repeated—following a penalty. Center is re-

sponsible for making all alignment adjustments.

2. Anticipate an onside kick if a 15-yard penalty is assessed against the receiving team.

Pride

The pride of any group is most times established by the success that group is experiencing. In the case of our kickoff return unit we gave them an identity with the name "Running of the Bulls." Since Utah State are the Aggies this special identity was a natural—in fact, we call our kickoff coverage team the Bleedin' Bulls. We find this type of recognition gives each unit its own identity, and our players really believe it is an honor to play on one of these units. When you reach this level of peer group recognition, your special team play is really special.

Another element we attempt to cultivate within our kicking units is leadership. We select a captain for each kicking unit and the captain is responsible for the morale of his unit. Usually we choose a senior for this role and again this fits into our program's overall principle of promoting senior leadership.

We take the leadership feature one step further with our kicking teams by choosing an honorary game captain from week to week based on performance within the special teams. So every member of the Running of the Bulls knows he has a chance to be chosen a game captain and represent the special teams the following week alongside our seasonal captains.

Wedge Return

This return is our primary call. From this return we expect to bring the ball out to at least the 40-yard line. We consider this a successful return and any additional yardage is a bonus.

The wedge (Brahma Bulls) can be adjusted to all types of kicks. The most important feature is that it gets the ball started straight up the field no matter where the kick lands.

The four players on kickoffs with the most critical blocking assignments are called the wedge. At Utah State we call them the Brahma Bulls.

The wedge sets themselves ten to twelve yards ahead of the point where the ball is caught by the returner. The higher the kick, the closer the wedge sets to the returner. On the captain's "Go!" command, the wedge launches their assault on the coverage team. Their instructions are, "Don't stop to block; run over the coverage men."

Alignment

Center—Two-point stance, hands on knees, face in at a 45-degree angle. Line up on 46-yard line, split the difference between the hash marks, but do not line up directly in front of the kicker.

Guards—Two-point stance, hands on knees, face in at a 45-degree angle, line up on 46-yard line, approximately 2 yards from the hash mark.

Tackles—Two-point stance, hands on knees, face in at a 45-degree angle, line up on 46-yard line, split the difference between hash and sideline.

Ends—Two-point stance, hands on knees, face in at a 45-degree angle, line up on 30-yard line, halfway between sideline and hash.

Fullbacks—Two-point stance, hands on knees, line up on 20-yard line, five yards inside the hash.

Safeties—Two-point stance, line up at goal line on the hash. Adjust depth according to wind, kicker, and so on. Against a soccer-style kicker (right footed), left safety, aligns 5 yards upfield to account for leg swing of kicker and a lesser depth of kick.

Assignments

Center—Make certain ball is not kicked onside. Block most dangerous No. 1 man. Pick man up at 40-yard line with objective to block him out of coverage lane.

Guards—Prior to kick, make cross or base call. "Cross call" made when ball is kicked from middle. "Base call" made when ball is kicked from hash. Make certain ball is not kicked onside. Block no. 2 man. Pick up assigned men at 30-yard line. Block to outside (toward boundary) forcing men out of coverage lane. If cross blocking, point of aim is 25-yard line.

Tackles—Make certain ball is not kicked onside. Block no. 3 man at 30-yard line. Position yourself inside-out and block toward boundary.

Ends—Make certain ball is not kicked short before retreating to wedge. Form wedge at established point with fullbacks. You are the end men on the wedge (wings). If ball is kicked outside the hash mark the wedge will be set on corresponding hash. Keep eyes upfield and listen for "go" call from fullbacks. Accelerate upfield and block with outside shoulder the most dangerous color who threatens the wing of the wedge.

Fullbacks—Field any short kicks and return ball straight upfield. Once ball clears head, set wedge 10–12 yards from point of catch. Wedge is set on hash if ball is kicked .on or outside of hash. Form the apex (point) of wedge and accelerate upfield. Turn to an inside 45-degree angle once ball is fielded by safety, make "go" call, begin drive upfield. Block with outside shoulder the most dangerous color threatening middle of wedge. Drive legs through block, running over top of man.

Safeties—No. 1. Field ball and drive hard for wedge. Accelerate into wedge looking for the breakaway point. No. 2. Nonfielder, escort ball to wedge blocking any color who threatens ball. If no color shows, escort ball up into wedge and block first penetrator into wedge.

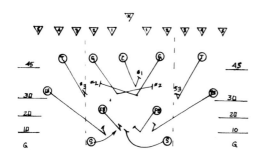

Diagram

Many of the nation's traditionally strong teams maintain their winning edge due to their emphasis on the kicking game and over the years always produce winning football teams.

All phases of the kicking game are crucial. They are pressure-packed plays. Each phase must be a success. For Utah State, the Running of the Bulls is just one of our eight special teams. We have found that these teams are actually on the field for 20 percent of the plays during an entire game. Many games are won or lost by the performance of the special teams, now more so than ever before. It is crucial to a team's success that you generate extra efforts (game-winning efforts) and be result oriented with your kicking game.

We have found success in giving each unit a constant game goal. As the season progresses these goals can be measured and the performance of your kicking game better evaluated. The following format is what we use for our weekly kicking goals.

1. Major Goal: Outperform our opponent statistically in hidden yardage.

2. Mini Goals: Kickoff cover = inside 20-yard line for every kick. Kickoff return = plus 30 yards return. Punt return = plus 10-yard return. Punt coverage = 4-yard average. Field goal/point after touchdown kick = Keep our percentage higher than our opponents.

3. Major Theme: Never have a kick blocked!

Because of our result-oriented approach to the kicking game, we established some high rankings in nearly every kicking category in 1978: kickoff return—first; net punting—third; field goals—second; and several individual player rankings. At Utah State we believe the kicking units can capture the momentum of a game.

Part Eight
Motivation and Player Relationships

43

Motivation—The Difference in Coaching

(From 1972 Proceedings of the AFCA)

LEE CORSO Head Coach, University of Louisville

I have always mentioned in all my clinic presentations that it's the duty of every coach, of every clinician, of every man, of every speaker, when he comes up to a rostrum, to honestly give his feelings, emotions, and give to you whatever he believes. These beliefs are based on my experiences at Florida State, Maryland, the United States Naval Academy, and three years at the University of Louisville. A lot of the things I'm going to tell you have worked tremendously for us. They might not work for you, but I feel it is every coach's responsibility to convey these thoughts to all his fellow coaches.

One thing I can say about the coaching profession is its members have to be the world's greatest copy cats! If one guy puts up a 5–4 defense and slants it one way, then others go back and do it. They seldom take the opportunity to stimulate their own ideas. There are so many new ideas that are introduced into the game on the field that many coaches are remiss in not taking time out to discuss, plan, and formulate their own ideas of what is the key to any successful operation—the minds of the people involved.

What I'm saying is at Louisville we coach football from the eyebrows up. We're working constantly on that mind, all the time. We work 50 percent of the meetings and 50 percent of the practices based on the mind. People think we're crazy! Well, it's just the way we've developed our theory and our feeling, and there are a lot more ideas that could be taken from this in your own way.

Another thing—don't be afraid to do exactly what you're doing now! Just because another coach says, "We do it this way," and you happen to do it that other way, don't change because maybe it fits your tackles better, or your mind, or your assistants! Do it your own way!

When you talk to football players, you'd better believe what you're talking about. They can sense it! They know that when the coach says, "I want you to do this," that he believes it. If not, they're not going to play for you, they're not going to perform for you, and most important, they're not going to respect you!

Some people are telling me, "Gosh, you guys were pretty successful last year! You did this—you did that, and so on." You know what we do the first two weeks of our spring practice, both on the field and in meetings? We work on the mind! What can we do to stimulate this young man? We have different young men every year. You've got to motivate them in different ways! I've seen guys try to motivate one football team exactly the way they do the other, and that's difficult. They're not the same! You've got to change! There's one thing I learned at the United States Naval Academy, if they taught me nothing else. I learned to "I & A"—Improvise and adjust. That's exactly what it takes in college coaching, in high school coaching, or in life.

Coaches should be ready at any moment to adjust their philosophy, if necessary. You better be ready at any moment to have rules with a little outlet. You must be ready to move quickly, to improvise, and to adjust every moment in your life when you're dealing with men fifteen to twenty years old, because they're changing! They're changing from year to year, from week to week, from day to day, and from hour to hour. Evaluate whatever you did last year to motivate your people to see if it is feasible this year. Every Sunday afternoon we look at what we're going to do to motivate our guys this week. And it changes every week. But there are some basic principles that I'd like to go over.

I continually remind myself that when you discuss

217

motivation that it is an inflammatory subject. The number one thing I feel you must do before you can motivate anyone in this world is that you must have their respect. I've heard many coaches make remarks about their way of motivating people. We, in our institution, happen to do it a little differently than most. That doesn't make us right and them wrong, or us wrong and them right; it doesn't make any difference. The question is: Are you getting the job done?

One thing that I feel very strongly about is that the coaches of the United States in grade school, high school, and college have the biggest job of any group of men in this country. And I think there's a lot more to coaching now than the X's and O's! That's not the entire answer.

Coaches have a lot more responsibility than teaching kids to run off tackle. They've got one of the most responsible jobs in the world! Sure, the X's and O's are important in winning games. It is my feeling that a coach's main responsibility to a football player is to teach him to be a better man. If it isn't, why not let him play some other sport, or let him hang around the corner, or let him go to the biology teacher? That is to me the most important responsibility of a football coach today—to take his football players and motivate them, mold them, and teach them to be better men. It's not a job either. If you stop and think about it, you can look at football coaching as basically not a job, but a privilege!

There are a lot of fathers sitting at home, playing golf, working, or flying all over who turn their sons over to the coach and ask, "Whatever you do, make them better men, because I don't have the time." When you look at it like that, it's a tremendous responsibility and privilege. And that's exactly the way we feel about coaching as a profession.

We try to instill in our players what we call the magic of believing. I'm a fanatic on this. If you can get this across to your guys, it will overwhelm them like a magic. They won't know where it came from, but they'll start reacting and they'll start being beautiful, and they'll win!

The first thing is they must believe in themselves. You're putting in their minds a little at a time the magic of believing in themselves. You see a guy, for example, walking into a room and people will say, "I don't know who that guy is, but he must be a winner." This is because he moves, looks, and acts as if he believes in himself. If you don't believe in yourself, don't ever expect any man to believe in you. They won't do it. You've got to have that inner belief first.

Never downgrade a man. You've got to have a personal inner pride. You've got to get it out of him—it's inside. How? You keep telling him he's got it there. You tell him he's got more pride than you've ever seen

in anybody! The player will end up saying, "I do have that personal pride, and the other guy doesn't, and when it gets down to the fourth quarter, I'm going to win!" You may think that won't work, but it will.

When I got the job at Louisville, in three days I spent more money on football uniforms than my predecessor did in five years. I bought the finest jerseys in the world! I changed them from cardinal, which was kind of dull, to scarlet. I also bought beautiful white helmets and white silk pants with scarlet looped belts! It was a little effeminate, but I said to the players, "Gentlemen, you now look like what we're going to be—champions. You've got the finest uniforms in the world. You look like a champion! You're going to play like a champion!!" You know what happened? They looked at each other and said, "You're right! You're damned right, we do look better! We're a lot better team than we were last year!"

In their minds, they felt like they were better! This is a very important point. Then the next thing that you do, you coach them like crazy in pregame warmup. Not only do we tell them they look like the best team in the world, we tell them that we have the world's best pregame warmup. When we come on that field, they explode! And each guy's got a spot, 3 feet from the other guy, and they run in a certain kind of pace, and they hit that goal post and they turn down that field and they break off, and they break into football position, and they look like the greatest team in the country! In our opener in 1970, we were thirty-point underdogs to Florida State, and lost only 9–7.

A coach from Georgia Tech, who was going to play Florida State the next week called me and said, "I want your pregame warmup." I said, "Don't you want any of my plays?" He said, "No, just your pregame warmup." *Sports Illustrated* mentioned it, and I got letters about our warmup from as far away as Alaska. Everybody's doing everything perfectly and the other team looks at them and says, "Boy! We're going to have a hell of a game with that team today!" It's like show business—like Broadway—you've got to get their attention in the opening number. It gives the impression we're a good team, and you've yet to snap the ball! The point was the image. You're not only dressed like a champion, you look like a champion, you move like a champion in the pregame warmup, and we honestly think it's worth a touchdown!

In phase two, we get into the huddle. We even practice ten minutes a day on breaking the huddle. They come out of that huddle and move on the line of scrimmage in perfect position. The other team says, "That's a real football team." And everybody in the stands say, "Wow! If that coach had some material, he'd be a hell of a coach!"

After you snap the ball, you can't promise anybody anything. That's when the other guy's talents come into play. But on your side of the line, you can do anything you want. And they can't hit you! Now you stop and think about that sometime. You stop and think how long you've spent on your pregame warm-up. Our guys take pride in their pregame warmup. They actually think it helps them win! They actually think it's worth a touchdown at the end! It doesn't make any difference whether it does or not—what's important is they think it does.

Another thing we've learned is that there's no use worrying about the other guy's talent. There's nothing you can do about it. You cannot control the other man's team, and 90 percent of the coaches worry too much about what the other guy's got. You can't do anything about it. Worry about what you've got, and make them the best. Motivate them and you win your share.

We run into it a lot of negative thinking in football—there's always something wrong, always something bad. We do not allow one negative phrase in our whole organization. We've got the world's worst dressing room, but it's close to the practice field. That's positive thinking. Always sell this positive attitude.

If you think things are bad, go by the cemetery. That's the philosophy we try to have. You say that doesn't have anything to do with winning, but let me tell you, it's more important than anything I can tell you about the I formation.

The next thing in this basic belief—in the magic of believing—is we believe in the basic right and dignity of every man to be different. We preach this over and over and over again, that every man has the right to be own self and to be his own man, no matter what he believes in.

We have developed two training rules. The first one is to treat every man as you want to be treated yourself. That's all we ask you to do. And you know what happens? You'll find a beautiful family starting to develop. Because when a guy starts to say something to somebody else, and he realizes, "I wouldn't want him to say that to me," it comes as a reaction because they feel it in the heart.

The second training rule is to act like a man and you'll be treated like a man. Act like a bum and people will treat you like a bum. You might say, "What does act like a man mean?" Players know! Let them use some of their imagination. You get those two basic principles across to them, and they'll play. And when they get to respecting the coach, then he can motivate them.

All coaches are looking for discipline, and no matter what anybody tells me, the first thing you've got to have in order to discipline a man is his respect of you as a person. That's number one.

We have tried a different approach to the normal rigid discipline. We have tried from the inner self; we have gone to a point where we tell these men we want them to be disciplined from the inside out, exactly the way you try to heal a wound. People get cut and they sew them up, but the real danger is underneath. You tell a guy to move and he moves. He's not always disciplined—he's on command—he's a robot!

You get those players and you regiment them, and you tell them to move, and they'll do it. When it gets down to the fourth quarter, and it's fourth and 1, they'll quit a lot of times. They'll say, "To hell with it! That guy is driving me crazy! I don't believe in that guy anyhow!" But if you get down on fourth and 1, and they're all coming together and they say, "Hey! Let's get it, let's get this one!," they'll get it!

I've discovered that the longer a man coaches, the rougher and meaner and more aggressive and the more disciplined the players are.

The first thing we talk about at our first meeting is drugs. We tell them smoking used to be against the rules, but if you partake in drugs, it's a felony. It's against the law. You're finished. We tell them that if any man ever comes in contact or has anything to do with drugs, he should never show his face around the football team ever again! He's gone! All you need is one football player to go to a party and just sit there and let some guy pull out his weed and start puffing on it, and it's marijuana, and they get you. Headlines read, "FOOTBALL PLAYER INVOLVED IN DRUG SCANDAL." So we tell them, "Look, this is serious business. This isn't like the coach catching you smoking. So, the first time you're at a party and a guy pulls out his weed, then get your butt out of there!"

Don't be afraid to talk to your squad. This is what I mean by motivation. You've got to talk to them about current problems. You can talk to them like, "Gentlemen, we're not going to have any alcoholic beverages on this team." They're going to drink anyhow. No smoking? Talk to them like men. Some people say you can't have discipline if your guys have long hair. There is no correlation between long hair and a guy being disciplined. The disciplined guy is the one who moves when we say move. The disciplined man is the one who, when its fourth and 1 will say, "We've got to get it!" and gets it! That is discipline. We didn't have a single offside in 1970. That's discipline. In 1970 we were number one in the nation in the least fumbles lost—five all year. That's discipline. What you're trying to get is the guy with the inner discipline.

This is another point. I've heard college coaches say, "Run the dead wood off!" You're not gaining anything there—you're losing a possibility. You're losing a guy who could possibly help in some way. The most important thing that you do, and I've seen it happen a thousand times is to run a guy off who's on the fourth team, and guess who his best friend is? The star! And the star says, "Someday, coach, I'm going to get you for running my best friend out of here." So, if you can, and I know it's hard, be respectful to the guy with less ability because you are usually judged by the team on the way you treat your reserves.

In your attempt to motivate players, don't ever let anyone else in the world, excluding your family, be more important than your players. Now, how do you prove that? We have what we call an open door policy. If I'm in my office talking to one or two coaches or a member of the press and there's a knock at the door and it's one of my players, I say "You guys excuse me." They get up and have to leave. My player comes in and sits down and I listen to him. Because what's not important to you is a lot more important to him, or he won't come to you unless it is.

I had a kid last year come and ask me if he could go to a high school prom before our biggest scrimmage of the year. I said, "What?" The kid said, "I've got to go home for this high school prom." I told him to go.

He came back! He's twice the football player now! You know why? It was very important to him that I understand how he felt, and we showed some consideration, some respect for his opinion.

You must believe that the most important people in the world besides your family are your players, because that's what you want them to believe about their coach. Every day, do something respectful toward a player. Some day it will come back to you. We try to do that.

In this philosophy that we have, the most important thing that I want to tell you is that this belief we have in leadership and motivation is to try to avoid the extremes if you can. Don't go all the way in one direction letting them do anything they want to, and don't go all the way in the other direction telling them they can't do anything! Try to hit, in your own way, a happy medium.

The magic of believing will work, but the coach must believe it first. The challenge coaches face is a tremendous one. They can only succeed if they continue to go over the relationships and duties with their players with the same aggressive and progressive attitude that they have on the blackboard.

44
The Winning Edge

(From 1979 Proceedings of the AFCA)

CHRIS AULT Head Coach, University of Nevada, Reno

My topic is not on the X's and O's of the game, but rather on the one thing that I have entitled the "winning edge"—to put it simply, the motivation of people. The world is full of educated derelicts, simply because they forget what it really takes to succeed outside the classroom. You alone control your own destiny, that's why I say that the greatest investment on earth pays dividends—that investment is you and the best way to get immediate returns on it is to help others along the way.

Problems

You and I are special people because we are problem solvers; it is the difference between what we have and what we want. Think about this for a minute: every problem created stems from the solution of another problem. An example of this is pollution—pollution is the solution from the horse-and-buggy days. People run offensive and defensive schemes as a result of certain solutions obtained through previous problems.

It's amazing to think how rich we are in technical and product knowledge and how poverty stricken we are in people knowledge—we as coaches have a job and that is to educate our athletes, both on and off the field. It's essential to get our athletes to believe in what we're doing. That's why we have the ability to be problem solvers. Sometimes, we find ourselves trying to solve problems in both the theory of the game and the psychological aspect without pinpointing the problem.

I strongly feel that in order to pinpoint any of your players' problems, you have to communicate with them; asking questions is a great way to provide this communication and to get player input. I think it is important to have the players feel that they are more than just a number; that you respect their opinions and thoughts. I don't think the players of today are looking for discipline as much as they are for leadership.

When our players present us with their problems, it gives us as coaches a good chance to show just how great we are. However, there is a time when all the problem solving has to be put in its place and we have to be realistic and demand the execution needed to win on the field. I know if the players feel you are behind them, willing to help when they need it, their response on the field will, in most cases, be positive.

Some years ago, Stanford did a study that showed that 12.5 percent of success was due from product knowledge and 87.5 percent was due from people knowledge. It's not how much you know, it's how you teach what you thoroughly understand.

People like to receive recognition. Everybody wants to feel good. We all want to identify with winners, because that's what makes people feel the best. My dad once told me that, as a coach, people don't want to hear about your problems, they want you to solve theirs; so don't tell people your problems, just try to understand theirs. He felt that 80 percent don't care about your problems and the other 20 percent are happy you've got some.

Solving problems is a big part of life—it's a tremendous challenge and a wonderful feeling when we help to eliminate these obstacles for others. We all need support, we all need help, so try to keep this in mind. People can refuse words, but not an attitude.

Goals

Are goals necessary? Most people have the wrong idea about setting goals. We have a saying at Nevada that goes, "Any road will take you there if you don't know where you're going."

I'm saying goals are an absolute must—we must provide our players with a target, so that they can see something worth working for. Can you imagine Sir Edmund Hillary, who was the first to scale Mount Everest, the highest mountain in the world—can you imagine someone coming up to him and saying, "Sir Edmund, how'd you climb that big ole mountain?" and him answering, "Oh, I was just walking around and thought I'd take a hike." No, I don't believe that's the way it happened. The greatest marksman in the world can't hit the target if you blindfold him and spin him around. Now, we all say that's pretty easy to figure out and that's right, so here's my question to you: How can a person hit a target he can't see? In other words, how can a person accomplish anything if he doesn't know what he's trying to accomplish?

This is where your imagination will come into play. Imagination means nothing more than image. Psychologists say there is a deep and profound tendency in human nature to become precisely like that which we habitually imagine ourselves. Create a picture, push it in your subconscious, and, once your imagination has projected the image you want, you can begin work.

Some people project a self-image that other people create. You can't be anything but yourself in our business. The youth in this day and age will see right through the phonies. We shouldn't, therefore, try to be someone we aren't. We should try to become a better person each day. Nobody is a born winner or a born loser. We are exactly what we think we are—nothing more and nothing less. Therefore, as individuals our self-image must be one full of confidence and positive thoughts, if we want to reach that goal of being a consistent winner.

Consistency

At Nevada, the most important thing we have done is to establish consistency in our program. The foundation for our philosophy has not changed in the three years we've been at the university. We have certain beliefs that we think are important for us to establish in order to win consistently.

If there are changes to be made, we will make them, but the foundation within our philosophy will not change. It's like running an offense. If you're a veer team, you will run the option, but your blocking schemes may not be the same as the next guy. However, the foundation will always remain—veer.

Our players know from the first day what we expect of them. It's not only explained in great detail, but it's also put in writing for them. When you sit down to write your philosophy, finding the words is sometimes difficult. We have found that when things are in black and white for our players to read over and over, there is usually very little disagreement when a controversy arises.

Many people say they could do more and get more done if they just had more time. Time is not the problem, but lack of direction is. As I was rewriting our team goals in 1978, I wrote that you can be what you want to be, do what you want to do, and go where you want to go. In reality, you can do just about anything if you have direction and you don't wait for things to happen. People who wait on external changes to make internal moves are going to come in second.

Man has a lot of room to grow, and if you want to make some changes within yourself, you can. Set big goals for excitement, but be specific—set long range goals, then break it down daily. Develop positive thinking because we live in a negative world. How negative is this world? Here are some examples: When your kids leave for school your wife says, "Don't get hit by a car"; overweight people say everything they eat turns to fat; others say thank God it's Friday, now everything is fine. Sometimes people around us are so negative that they almost become noncaring. You become part of what is around you.

Enthusiasm

I know the best way to be positive is through enthusiasm. Enthusiastic people are fun to be around—they put a sparkle in your eye and a bounce in your walk. It's contagious—every morning you wake up, you have a choice, are you going to be excited or be a wet blanket. Will you be enthusiastic or tear people down? Enthusiasm is a skill that can be taught just like any other skill, but to be enthusiastic, you must know in which direction you want to go and then have a thorough understanding of how you plan to attack this area. To be enthusiastic you have to feel good, and in order to feel good you have to act good.

Here's something interesting to remember—logic is not going to change any emotion, but action will. Because we preach success so much, don't be afraid to aim at the top. The real secret of success is to find a need and fill it with positive actions. Anything the mind can conceive can be achieved.

Failure

We may have lost a few games, but those are just temporary setbacks. Failure is when you stop and quit trying. It's when your commitment to accomplish your goal is not firm. It's when your self-image no longer projects that image of a positive and enthusiastic leader.

I am a firm believer that when a person experiences a temporary setback or something negative happens, it's for a reason. We don't always agree with the reason, but the important thing is to learn from your mistakes. There is always light at the end of the tunnel—of course, be positive that the light doesn't belong to a locomotive. I'm of the firm belief that if it's important enough you'll find a way to succeed. Man's greatest moment of happiness is to be tested beyond what he thought might be his breaking point—and succeed.

Coaching is the greatest profession in the world. There is no profession more challenging, demanding, and exciting. People are influenced by our thoughts, decisions, and actions. It's up to us to make sure we provide each athlete with the greatest learning system known to man—it's called trial and error, and if used properly, everyone will become a better person. I would like to leave you with this thought: "Upon the plains of hesitation, bleached the bones of countless millions who, on the threshold of victory sat to wait, and waiting they died."

45

A Philosophy of Motivating Athletes

(From 1977 Summer Manual of the AFCA)

JAMES E. COUNSILMAN Swimming Coach, Indiana University

It is pretty obvious that if a person wants to motivate another person, he must find a "motive" or a reason for making him want to do that thing.

In coaching athletics, this motive is frequently "fear" of the coach. The athlete is afraid the coach will scream at him, belittle him, humiliate him, and so on. The coach has so often been characterized as a person who motivates through fear that this has become the stereotype.

Early in my coaching career, I was told by another coach that I would never be successful and that I would never be able to gain the athletes' respect because they "weren't scared to death of me" as they were of him. He often said, "Hold them at arm's length. If they get too close to you, they won't respect you." As a result of his evaluation, I had to examine my philosophy concerning athletic motivation. I knew I could never be the type of coach who constantly chewed out his athletes or used fear to motivate. I decided that every coach had to acquire his own method of motivating athletes and that I had to develop my own style. That style had to be compatible with my philosophy and my personality.

After a period of time, and certainly after no great creative effort, I came to the conclusion that all people are motivated by the desire to fill certain needs that are basic to all humans. Although all of us have these basic needs, some individuals have a stronger desire to fill certain needs than others. For instance, we all have a need for recognition. Some people feel this need so intensely that it is the extreme; others need less recognition and can be classified at the low end of the range. All of us know coaches and athletes who represent these extremes, but most fall somewhere in between. I bring this up to emphasize the fact that all of us, coaches and athletes alike, have varying philosophies

of what is important. Consequently, we are motivated by slightly or even widely divergent means. Some coaches may be able to motivate certain types of athletes and not others.

I have said that all humans are controlled in varying degrees by their basic needs or drives. It would be easy, if this were not the case, to map out a standard approach for all coaches to follow. It would also be dull; but that is not the point I want to emphasize now. What I want to stress is that what is good for one person may be disastrous for another. The assistant of one coach I know so admired his boss that he adopted the head coach's goals and emulated him in every aspect of his coaching duties. The head coach was strongly motivated, with a high compulsion to achieve and a high tolerance for stress. The assistant coach had a lower ego drive and a lower tolerance for stress. In adopting the philosophy of the head coach, the assistant was establishing a situation incompatible with his personality and needs. After becoming a head coach in a high-stress situation, he recognized this incompatibility and settled for a coaching job in a less stressful environment.

In recognition of my needs, I sought a stressful situation, but I was largely influenced in the formation of my philosophy by my coach, the late Ernie Vornbrock, of the St. Louis Downtown YMCA swimming team. His primary obligation was to the swimmers—to see that they achieved their potential academically, athletically, and socially. In other words, he tried to conduct his program in such a manner as to help his swimmers gain self-fulfillment. That I feel the same obligation as a coach is due to his example.

I will not outline the needs that are basic to all humans, as I see them, in the context of a coach-athlete team situation. A list of twenty to thirty could be constructed, but I will confine myself to the primary ones that concern an athletic coach.

Love and Affection

A primary need is for love and affection—to like and be liked. I want the swimmers to know that I have a genuine affection for them and convey it when I can. If I see a former swimmer many years after his career with me has finished and I find that he has retained a strong tie with me and with his former teammates, I am pleased. In many cases we have established life-long friendships. I think this is one of the greatest things going for us in athletics.

I try to know every swimmer's grade-point average within a fraction of a point. I try to know their best swimming times in a meet and in a workout. I know their problems, their girls—and sometimes these two are the same. I know their goals and aspirations. This is one way I have of showing my affection and concern.

Affection is a two-way street; to receive it you first must give some of it away. Feigned affection is like flattery, it is counterfeit and eventually will be detected. If you do not genuinely like and understand young people, do not try to become a high school coach. I have always liked young adults and am, at least in this area, well adapted to coaching college-age swimmers. Some outstanding high school coaches have tried college coaching and found it distasteful, while others have done well at both levels. Some coaches find they are better suited to coaching girls than boys, or vice versa, or some coaches both equally well.

Once again, every coach should consider this factor before determining what type of job he looks for. He and those under his charge will be unhappy if he makes a wrong decision.

Security

Within all of us is a need for security—the security of knowing we will not go hungry, that we will have an opportunity for a job, and so on. Consider the average freshman student in a large school of several thousand students. He goes from class to class, seeing very few people he knows. He deals with many people whom he knows only casually. He finds himself in a new and strange environment where the leader of the group is someone he has never met. The students in his class are competing with him for grades. He may lack status in the group, he feels insecure. He goes to the gym for a workout. He walks in the door and the coach greets him with a "Hiya, Jim, how are things going?" and gives him a smile. He is in a familiar environment where he knows what to expect. He belongs

to the group and is accepted by the team members. He can predict that the coach will be enthusiastic and have a positive attitude. He also knows that the coach is an emotionally stable, mature individual. What a feeling of security these factors generate!

An athlete does not get the same feeling from a coach who is hot and cold, who is by turns unpredictably friendly or abusive. No one can feel secure in an atmosphere of worry, fear, anxiety, and resentment. A coach should be a stable person whom the athlete can count on—another example of the importance of maturity in a coach. If a person is contemplating coaching as a career but knows that he responds poorly to stress, he should face the fact that his athletes will be affected by his instability, and either learn to control his reactions or not coach. His highs and lows are too bewildering to his young athletes who haven't learned to be objective and to recognize that the moods of others may have little relation to themselves.

Status

Whether we like it or not, each of us has a certain rank order in the groups of which we are a part. These relative ranks in society make up our status. It has been said that life is a struggle for status, and I tend to agree. We are always trying to elevate our self-image and the image that we present to the world.

The swimmer is a member of his team, but he is also a member of the student body and probably of many other groups. He may have the lowest rank order on your team, but his membership on the team may raise his status in the student body. Thus he has raised his status in one group merely by being a member of another. This is especially true if the team is successful and has high prestige.

If you want to help your athletes achieve high status, give them a good program in order that they may be successful. Then make sure they receive recognition of their success in the form of publicity, awards, trips, and anything else you can think of.

An innovative and successful program is not the result of "good breaks," as many would have us believe. It is the result of hard and consistent effort to learn and the carrying out of what you have learned. An aspiring coach must decide if it is worth the work. Before he decides that it is not, he should consider the alternatives and ask himself if he will be content with the results of a half-hearted effort. Whatever he decides will strongly influence his evolving philosophy.

Achievement

Within each human resides the desire to achieve whatever he undertakes. It is the coach's responsibility to see that his program provides the athletes with a feeling of accomplishment, even of creativity. After a practice session in the pool, a workout on the practice field, or a lecture in the classroom, the athlete should feel he has made progress toward a goal. In order to ensure that the athlete will acquire this feeling of accomplishment, the coach must educate him on the theories of training. This information about the physiology of training will stimulate him to work more conscientiously than if he is merely following orders.

For example, I have heard uninformed people question the value of hard training. Such remarks as, "Why do you need to go 12,000 yards a day in order to swim 100 meters in a race?" are quite common. This is no mystery to a swimmer who knows what occurs in the muscles, the heart, the lungs, and blood vessels of an individual in training. His knowledge will make the swimmer more cooperative in workouts.

Part of the job of the coach is to set goals that are compatible with the abilities of the individual and the team in order that they may achieve this feeling of accomplishment. If he is unrealistic in the goal-setting process or if he tries to protect himself by setting goals that are too low, he will only lose the confidence of his athletes.

The coach also must help the athlete evaluate what has been achieved. This evaluation must be truthful and not only serve as an estimate of what has been achieved but also indicate what lines of action must be adopted for the future.

The Group Instinct

All of us need to be part of a group. I think every individual, if handled properly, is team oriented. Some psychologists refer to this phenomenon as the group instinct. It is the coach's job to foster team spirit, to form strong bonds among team members and between them and himself. This is mostly done by setting common goals, such as to win a certain meet. Even though humans are self-interested, they are also group oriented, and it is up to the coach to establish a program that considers both of these aspects.

Remember, however, that team spirit should be brought about through positive and not negative means. The cheapest method of instilling team spirit is through the use of hate psychology—hatred against other teams, an opposing coach, certain individual athletes, and so on. The use of hatred is the worst form of psychology, and, on a moral basis, belongs in no one's philosophy.

Another negative approach that should be avoided is to foster the impression that the team is "my" (the coach's) team rather than "our" team—the athletes', the managers', assistants', and coachs'—with the resulting guilt feelings if an athlete fails. Such shotgun tactics can be effective, and if you believe that the end justifies the means, you may employ them. However, you have then put yourself in a class with those who should not be guiding young people.

There are many positive methods by which a coach may enhance the feeling of "our team." One is to allow the athletes a voice in decision making. A lot of the things we do at Indiana have been decided by the whole team. I don't want to convey the idea that a coach should avoid his responsibilities by asking the team to vote on every issue. The result of a constant use of this kind of conduct is to risk losing authority, and there are many times when authority is needed. There are certain decisions only a coach can make.

Because I believe this latter point is important, let me diverge here to present a quote from Freud concerning the importance of authority: "A great majority of people have a strong need for authority which they can admire, to which they can submit, which dominates and sometimes even ill-treats them. . . . We have learned from psychology of the individual, whence comes this need of the masses, this longing for the father that lives in each of us from his childhood days."

All people vary somewhat in their need for authority. That is why we hear some athletes say, "Coach is too easy on us and doesn't discipline us enough," while other athletes may say just the opposite about the same coach, "He's too strict."

An authoritarian coach who permits the athletes no voice in decision making is as bad as the overly permissive coach who never disciplines and sometimes doesn't seem to care enough to rebuke bad behavior.

Recognition

Recognition is important to all individuals, but it is essential to a hard-working athlete. It satisfies the ego drive. The worst type of coach is one who displays indifference, never showing enthusiasm for an athlete's performance.

The coach's second responsibility is to obtain recognition for the athlete through the medium of the sports page, radio, or television—or just by his approval in workout or after a race. A pat on the back if he does well or a constructive kick in the pants— these are forms of recognition. If he is not trying hard enough, the athlete is probably really saying to you, "I'm here; be aware of me."

When talking to the press after a successful competition, spread the acclaim around. Never mention "me or I," but say, for example, "The boys worked hard for this victory. We want to give credit to our divers and our diving coach. Their points made the difference."

After a disappointing loss, don't be the kind of coach who always tries to protect himself and place the blame on someone else. Don't say such things as "We were disappointed in Joe's performance. We thought he'd take two firsts," or "The kids just didn't want to win badly enough." This kind of statement puts a terrible burden of guilt on the athletes and reflects badly on your own ability to accept responsibility for failure. Rather say, "Both the kids and I are going to have to work harder," or "We played well, but not quite well enough."

It is unwise to be so self-effacing as to completely submerge your ego, but you must be able to suppress it. Telling the media "how it is" immediately after a race or meet may be a great method of letting off steam or temporarily getting rid of your aggressions, but the repercussions of such behavior include diminishing the respect of your athletes and eventually losing your self-respect.

The place to wash your linen is in team meetings and individual conferences, not in front of the public and particularly not the press.

Self-Esteem

People have a strong desire for self-esteem. It's the coach's job to help the athlete form a good opinion of himself. Do not belittle, ridicule, or humiliate him. Try to make him see the best in himself, and, as the song so appropriately says, "Accentuate the positive, eliminate the negative." Do not let your team break into cliques or allow some team members to make a scapegoat of any person.

The late Maxwell Maltz, author of *Psychocybernetics,* a book all coaches and athletes should read, and popularizer of the concept of "self-image psychology," told me that after years of success as a surgeon and lecturer he continued to lack self-confidence in many situations. If this is true of such a person, think how fragile is the self-esteem of a young teenager and what harm can be done if he is not permitted to retain his dignity.

Here are some variations of Dale Carnegie's principles about how to get along with people. They are chosen to serve as guides in protecting another person's self-esteem.

1. Make every athlete, assistant coach, and manager on your team feel he is an important, contributing member. By giving praise and recognition when it is warranted, you will convey that message.
2. Be genuinely interested in the other person, know his name, his interests, and his needs.

3. Before you talk about an athlete's mistakes, allow him to rationalize them by sharing the blame with him: "John, you went out too hard in that race, and that was my fault for not telling you to control the first hundred."
4. Never prove another person wrong. Don't say to an assistant coach, "I told you we shouldn't have swum Jim on the relay. Now we've lost the meet just because you insisted he would do better than Harry."

The Role of Challenge

While it may be an overstatement to say that everyone welcomes a challenge, it is probably true that people who are attracted to athletics welcome a challenge, like to test themselves, and invite an opportunity to face new experiences.

The coach should plan his program to be dynamic and innovative. He should keep abreast of the latest training techniques, even adding to them or improving on them. While it is true that challenge places stress on an individual, most of us like to take a few chances, to gamble a little bit, to initiate a new method, or to get a thrill when we prove something. If a new technique doesn't work out, it's back to the drawing board and start over again. Even when a coach can't be creative, he can be enthusiastic, and his workouts can be interesting, not boring.

Other Factors

The eight needs outlined above are primary ones that coaches must consider in evolving a philosophy. In addition there are a number of other factors that should be mentioned, because a fledgling coach must make some decisions regarding them. If some seem too obvious to mention, let me state that I have met coaches who have disregarded them or lost sight of them along the way.

There is a place for honesty, truthfulness, and integrity in your philosophy. Most coaches, if they are admired and respected by their athletes, will serve as models for them to emulate. If you display dishonest practices, are argumentative, dispute decisions constantly, or are ill-tempered, many of your athletes will also tend to adopt these traits. When a person accepts the responsibility of becoming a coach, he must accept the obligations that go with it. He owes this not only to the athletes but to his profession and himself, as a matter of self-esteem.

Early in my coaching career, if I encountered troubles at the pool, I tended to bring them home along with a negative attitude. The whole family had to hear my complaints and problems. The results were pretty sad: My wife got upset at the children, who would soon sour toward one another, and someone would end up kicking the cat. The entire household suffered just because I had come home with a negative attitude. The same atmosphere was duplicated at the pool if I wasn't in a good mood. Then I woke up to what was happening and tried a different approach: Even if the day hadn't been the best, I came into the house and shouted, "Hey, Marge, lover boy is here! Hey, kids, the world's greatest Dad is here!" The whole family responded and I started to feel better too. Later, my wife and I might discuss problems I had had at work. You don't want to be a clown and phony, but it is amazing how a sense of humor and a positive attitude can bring a little perspective to a problem.

As a coach, you are the leader of your group, the head baboon, so to speak. It's up to you to set a positive mood. No one likes to be around a person who is sour and negative all the time, except perhaps other sour and negative people. Some of the coaches I admire the most are enthusiastic and positive. Just watch them and you can quickly see the enthusiasm, and positive attitude, and sense the affection they feel for the athletes. Everyone has a different way of showing affection and other emotions; just don't be guilty of hiding them.

Summary

The coach must adopt a game plan, a list of do's and don'ts, a set of principles that will guide his actions, a philosophy that will not subordinate the interests of the team, the assistant coaches, and so on to his own. He must develop an understanding and empathy with the athletes in his charge. He must be capable of forgiveness, but must also demonstrate firmness and the ability to discipline when that becomes necessary.

As I stated in the beginning, even though most of us have the same needs, we also have different personalities, energy levels, and goals. Therefore, it is necessary for each of us to formulate an individual coaching philosophy. I believe the guidelines I have stated, the examples of my own decisions and those of others that I have presented will help you in the formulation or evaluation of your own.

Part Nine
Recruiting

46

The Art of Successful and Satisfying Recruiting

(From 1974 Summer Manual of the AFCA)

BRON BACEVICH Head Coach, Roger Bacon High School, Cincinnati, Ohio

Recruiting talented high school student-athletes is a recognized part of intercollegiate athletic programs in the United States. Recruiting practices, however, have been so competitive and financially burdensome that they pose a problem for colleges and high schools alike. College athletic programs are hurt financially and high school athletes are annoyed by excessive recruiting, which sometimes interferes with their educational process. If properly and honestly conducted, recruiting can benefit both the college and the student-athlete. It is the purpose of this article to suggest guidelines to those who are vitally interested in keeping recruiting honorable and successful.

If recruiting is to be conducted with honesty and integrity, all those involved should be thoroughly familiar with the NCAA governing legislation. For this purpose, the National Federation of State High School Associations has published *Guide to Collegiate Recruiting*, which can help the prospective student-athlete, his parents, the high school coach, guidance counselor, and principal to protect the unfortunate prospect from both intentional and unintentional recruiting violations affecting his future collegiate athletic eligibility.

All high school personnel must insist upon conformance, not only to the letter of the rules, but also to the spirit of the rule. Colleges and universities must demand strict adherence to the legislation governing recruiting in order to maintain the integrity of the athletic program within the educational objectives of the institution. If there is a breakdown at either level, there will begin to emerge a mockery of the program at both levels. This cannot be tolerated.

In addition to this writer's many years of experience at both the high school and college levels, this article is based on personal interviews with both high school coaches and players, present college players, as well as questionnaires from both coaches and players.

Advice to Recruiters

Visiting the High School

Most high schools have definite rules pertaining to all school visitors and an additional set policy pertaining to college recruiters. It should be remembered that the high school coach very seldom has any part in formulating and establishing rules, procedures, or policy as they pertain to visitors and/or recruiters.

When you first contact the high school coach, ask what the school visiting procedures are and what the school policy is in regard to the recruiting of the student-athlete. These should be respected. It is completely out of order to ask for special considerations.

Make arrangements to visit the school in advance by card, letter, or telephone. When you do, indicate the information you want, and the boy or boys you want to talk to. Without a previous arrangement you can't expect the coach to cooperate in any way if he is otherwise occupied or committed.

Do not circumvent any rules and regulations. If the school policy is that all visitors must first report to the main or principal's office, then do just that. Be friendly and sincere when meeting any school personnel. One coach, in his reply, wrote, "Some of the schools are sending out some real creeps to do their recruiting. They are discourteous to the people in the school and a good many of them completely ignore school rules and regulations pertaining to visitors."

Another wrote, "We are really fed up with some

of the recruiters. They show a total lack of respect, courtesy, and consideration to high school personnel other than coaches. We are seriously considering denying these men the opportunity to visit our school."

The high school coach may have recruiting procedures over and above those stated in the recruiting policy of the school. The recruiter should recognize and accept the coach's right to do so, and he should, therefore, respect those as well as the rules established by the school.

Get to know the type of program a particular high school coach has. This will help in evaluating the coach's players. College coaches often assume they are experts in the evaluation of a college prospect. One coach when interviewed said, "The student-athlete's high school coach (if he is sincere and honest) needs more consideration in the evaluation. The short interview with the prospect along with a film study is not always compatible with the true picture of the prospect in the long range (four years) college plan. Oftentimes the intangibles are not explored as far as growth potentials are concerned: age, maturity, consistency, character, concern for future success, college preparations (physical and educational), and so on."

Be sincere, honest, and considerate of the high school coach, his job, his program, and his noncoaching duties and responsibilities. Make every effort to know the high school coach as a friend. Do not expect the high school coach to handle requests for information on prospects during the season.

It's not a must, but certainly a good will gesture, if you and your staff have a new, novel, or unique idea or approach to some phase of football, come prepared to share such information with the high school coach, when you visit. He is always seeking and is interested in new and different ideas concerning all aspects of football. There are some schools that mail this type of material with their annual requests for data and information on the top scholar-athletes. This is an excellent public relations approach.

Most coaches in our area have no objections to recruiters attending summer or preseason practices, workouts, or preseason scrimmages. Coaches, however, prefer to be notified in advance when a recruiter wishes to do so. Be reasonable with requests to talk with coaches or players.

A visit by a recruiter on any of the above occasions can boost the morale of the school, the coach, and the players. If the recruiter will notify the high school coach beforehand, most coaches in our area will plan a practice so the recruiter can be introduced to the squad. Many coaches will also give the recruiter an opportunity to speak to the players. However, most coaches prefer that the recruiter refrain from requesting permission to talk to any player individually.

Contacting the Student-Athlete

The most common complaint of the high school coaches is the fact that recruiters contact the student-athlete without the coach's knowledge.

Recruiters should arrange a meeting time with the student-athlete so there will be no interference with the academic program or athletic responsibility. The student-athlete should not be contacted during practice sessions or before or after a game without consent of the coach—furthermore, high school juniors and other underclassmen should not be contacted except by correspondence.

It is suggested that recruiters anticipate the questions the student-athlete (and his parents) may ask. They should be prepared to answer such questions realistically and with complete honesty and integrity. Ideally, the approach should be in terms of what is best for the boy during his years in college and for his future.

Many coaches suggest that the recruiter, wherever and whenever possible, should help the student-athlete with problems that may be unrelated to football. Further, assurance should be given to the student-athlete that the recruiter will be interested in him after he selects his school, as a person, in his total school life, as well as his football, and that the student-athlete can consider the recruiter his friend, someone he can turn to in time of need.

Also, when you ask a student-athlete to send information before or after making contact, take the time to acknowledge receipt of such information regardless of whether or not you will continue to be interested in the boy.

Student-Athlete Campus Visit

Most coaches in our area believe that requests for student-athlete visits during the season (unless the coach has no objection) should not be permitted, that a student-athlete should not be invited for a campus visit if he is not interested in the school, and that such requests should not be made if the student-athlete is competing in other sports without clearing the request beforehand with the coaches involved, and, finally, that no invitation be extended to a student-athlete unless the school is prepared to offer him a grant, scholarship, or some other form of financial aid. Student-athletes resent insistence by pressure or by inference that a visit to a campus constitutes an obligation to attend the school.

To be invited for a campus visit is the highlight of a student-athlete's recruiting experience. He looks forward to it eagerly. He will be favorably impressed if the time spent on the campus becomes for him a rich, heartwarming, and meaningful experience. Consequently, the student-athlete's host or guide should be selected carefully. He should be an individual who best represents the school and its athletic program, and who is, above all, honest, sincere, and courteous. Needless to say, he should have a positive attitude, be enthusiastic, and feel privileged to have been selected as host or guide. The modern high school boy is quick to recognize actions and comments that are "put on." It is important to caution the student guide about "bad-mouthing" other schools and other coaches. His total attitude toward the school, toward the football program, and toward the coaches will greatly influence the reaction of the student-athlete.

Punctuality is a matter of courtesy during campus visits. The recruits are very critical of having to wait to see the head coach, an important alumnus, or even the assigned guide or host.

The student-athlete wants to be treated as a person, not as just another recruit. He wants to see and meet students as well as athletes, to have the opportunity to do what other students do, to eat where other students eat, to lodge with other students. In short, he wants an opportunity to do the things a typical student-athlete does, and to become acquainted with a student's typical routine. If possible, the student-athlete's visit should be scheduled while college classes are in session. At many high schools, student-athletes in good standing are permitted to make a limited number of midweek, school-in session, visits.

The following is a typical reaction to a meaningful campus visit: "I enjoyed my visit to the campus, because it wasn't a structured visit. I was privileged to see and talk to people who weren't football players and coaches. My talk with the head coach was long enough to get answers to questions and short enough as not to become boring. The assigned athlete and I were permitted to do what we wanted to do. I had the opportunity to get a true insight of what college is really like—in the classrooms, labs, and so on."

Visiting the Home

Visiting the home of the student-athlete is one of the best means to get to know his true character and quality. The recruiter should get to know the parents of the prospective student-athlete as well as possible.

Arrangements for any such visit should be made in advance. Unexpected visits are in very poor taste, and highly resented by both the parents and the student-athlete. Be reasonable in the length of the visit, and the number of times you visit. Don't overstay your welcome.

Explain in detail to the student-athlete and his parents exactly what a scholarship, grant-in-aid, or other financial aid really is. Be clear, precise, and totally honest with them on what you are prepared to offer, so there is no misunderstanding or disillusionment later on. Be absolutely certain what you are offering meets the NCAA rules and guidelines.

Be totally honest about all information concerning your school. Withheld information is as damaging as misinformation. For example, if your school has a cooperative engineering program on paper, but has no graduates in the program, this should be made known.

Telephone Calls

Telephone calls to the student-athlete should be within reason, as to place, time, and frequency.

Most schools will not permit phone calls to students (other than from a parent for an emergency reason). On phone calls to the home, the recruiter should keep in mind that the student-athlete is a teenager who goes to school and who may also be working after school hours or evenings. He may also be involved in other school or nonschool activities and he has his school homework to do.

Calling the student-athlete at unreasonable hours, or an unreasonable number of times (one student-athlete had twelve calls during one evening), is a common complaint of both the student-athlete and his parents. It certainly is a lack of consideration for the boy's family.

Bad-mouthing

This is the most common complaint of both coaches and the recruited student-athletes. Bad-mouthing an opposing school or its coaches, especially a school within the same league or conference, is the single most often stated reason for turning down the school.

References to another school that they are guilty of "cheating" on recruiting practices and promises of illegal financial aids, that the head coach and his staff are unreasonable in their demands on the players, that racial inequalities exist, that the coaches do not take a personal interest in the student-athlete as a human being, and other such statements are typical examples of bad-mouthing that are so objectionable to student-athletes and coaches alike.

Sell your school for its own qualities, not by downgrading or degrading other institutions and coaches, in the hopes that your school will appear to be better by comparison.

Have enough pride in your school, your staff, your program, and your job to point out where, how, and why your school is best for the boy.

"Holds"

To be realistic about recruiting and the fact that every school is seeking to recruit the best possible student-athlete, the "blue-chipper," it is understandable that it may be necessary to "hold off" on a good student-athlete while trying to sign a "blue-chipper."

However, it is unreasonable and very unfair to the student-athlete who is involved, to be given false hopes as a "hold" for so long that he ends up with no place to go and no opportunities for any financial assistance.

It is important for all concerned that such a boy be informed that he is a "hold" prospect and exactly what this means. It is equally important to give him a definite date when he can expect the final decision.

The saddest and most unfair part of recruiting is the "unrecruited athlete"—the student-athlete who gets letters and phone calls from coaches and alumni, is visited personally at his high school and at his home, and is told, "We definitely are interested in you," and then all of a sudden there is no further contact or word and the student-athlete is left high and dry.

Final Decision—Student-Athlete Turned Down

When a decision has been made that the boy you have recruited is no longer desired by your staff (or head coach, if the final decision is his), it is the duty and obligation of the recruiter to advise both the high school coach and the student-athlete.

Don't just inform the coach and then ask him to convey the message to the student-athlete. If the parents were also deeply involved in the recruiting process, then the recruiter should also advise them.

Requests for Films

High school game films are important to many coaches, not only during the season, but for several weeks after the season, for various reasons.

When visiting the high school, make every effort to view the film at the school or at the motel that evening, if you are staying overnight. This is the most desirable procedure from the coach's standpoint. It is reasonable to request to take a film for the head coach or staff to look at and study. However, such requests should be made only once.

If you request a film, the high school coach assumes you will study the film. There is considerable evidence that, many times, films which have been requested have been returned without having been used.

Films should be returned as promised, both as to the promised date and the promised mailing procedures (insured if so requested and promised). Make certain the right film is returned to the proper school. The film should be returned in good condition, not broken (breaks in the film should be properly spliced, not Scotch-taped). Avoid using projectors that "burn" or "bubble" parts of the film or otherwise cause defects in the film. Make certain the films are properly rewound and placed in the proper can. It is highly unethical and a dishonest act to remove parts of a film.

Alumni as Recruiting Aids

An enthusiastic alumnus can be a tremendous asset in the total recruiting picture. However, unless the alumni are given guidelines and briefings on proper and desirable procedures in making contacts or getting information on student-athletes, more damage than good is often the result.

All rules, regulations, and procedures for recruiters for a given high school should also apply to the "bird-dogging" alumni. In addition the alumni should be familiar with the guidelines and the NCAA Code of Good Conduct for collegiate recruiting.

Some of the most common complaints about overzealous alumni are:

1. Total lack of consideration for the high school coach and his program.
2. Use of high-pressure tactics to get special consideration.
3. Contacting the student-athlete without coach's knowledge.
4. Requesting films of games during the season. Since game films are used by coaches on an exchange basis, it is completely out of order to do this.

Undesirable or Objectionable Recruiting Practices

Among the most commonly stated undesirable or objectionable recruiting practices, by coaches and student-athletes, or both, are the following:

1. Overzealousness resulting in harassment.
2. Showing only the best parts of a campus, that is, a failure to present a complete picture of what it will be like to be a student-athlete at the college.
3. Persistent calling by phone or personal visits when the student-athlete has made a positive commitment to another school or a positive indication that he is not interested in your school.
4. Promising "there will be no grade problem in

your academic area" to a student-athlete whose high school record indicates otherwise.

5. Unreasonable, undue pressure to make a decision or to sign a letter of intent, long before the deadline, by threats that the offer will be withdrawn by failure to do so.

6. Assuming that the student-athlete "belongs" to the recruiter and his school simply because the student-athlete has visited the school or has indicated an interest (without commitment) in the school.

7. Making promises that cannot or will not be kept. The most common complaint is a promise to be invited to visit the campus, then failing to do so.

8. Making verbal offers without serious intent, then, later sending the student-athlete a "Dear John" letter.

It is the belief of all high school coaches, that, if you (your head coach or his staff) have made a mistake on a recruited student-athlete, that you should admit it, then treat the student-athlete as you treat the others, and not to attempt to "run" him off.

Advice to the Student-Athlete

Every student-athlete arrives at the moment of his career when he must narrow the field of schools that he would like to attend. The task is seldom easy, and is often viewed with more than a little apprehension. If the student-athlete knows what he wants to study in college, it makes the choice of colleges a lot easier.

It is this writer's carefully considered opinion that very few high school student-athletes know how to evaluate a college scholarship, grant, or financial aid (based on need) offer.

The student-athlete's frustration is often due to pressure of overzealous alumni, a high school coach seeking to use the athlete as a stepping stone, a father who pictures the athlete as a sure "pro," or, simply, the necessity of making a decision that will affect the course of his life.

All too often the experience resolves into a hurried, high-pressured, haphazard "Alice in Wonderland" excursion, instead of a systematic evaluation based upon predetermined criteria.

It is imperative for the college to be capable of providing meaningful academic, religious, athletic, social, and cultural experiences—experiences that will enable the individual to develop his full potential.

That is why it's so essential to plan most carefully. Though it's never too early to begin thinking about suitable colleges, it's probably wise to begin establishing a general plan of action sometime during the junior year in high school. By the fall of the senior year,

at the very latest, the boy and his parents should have established some specific guidelines to govern their dealings with college recruiters.

Much of this screening can be accomplished by studying schools the same way you would study one of your high school subjects.

First, you should consult all available sources that describe college curricula and athletic programs. Second, measure your criteria and goals against the offerings of any school that you are considering. It is like shopping for a car: Know the exact features you want, and don't let a salesman talk you into settling for anything less.

Each student-athlete develops his physical and mental abilities to varying levels of excellence. If you've worked hard to develop your talents, then the selection of your school should be rewarding. There should be literally scores of schools that would be happy to have you as a member of their student bodies and their football programs.

The student-athlete must obtain a clear and realistic idea of exactly what life at the college and on the team will be like. To succeed in this, the student-athlete ought to be prepared to ask the questions that will enable him to know which school is best suited to meet his needs. To obtain answers to such questions (and thus achieve greater insight into a college and its athletic program), it is necessary for the student-athlete to do his homework. He must consult with as many individuals and groups as possible.

The preliminary work should begin with the coaches, guidance counselors, and other faculty members at his school. The young man should attempt to obtain as much specific information as possible about his ability and potential both in the classroom and on the playing field, as well as the advantages and disadvantages of attending the schools he is interested in.

He would also do well to query other students and athletes who have attended or are currently attending these colleges. This will yield an additional insight into the type of life he might expect at these schools.

Both the athlete and, if possible, his parents, should visit the schools that are seriously considered. The young man and his parents must remember that it is highly undesirable, if not downright unethical, to string along a coach or school. The prospect (and his parents) who expects to be treated honestly must be honest and frank with them. Whenever he eliminates a school, he should immediately inform the coach. He shouldn't accept any ego or pleasure trips. He is not only taking unfair advantage of the coach and school but also stealing valuable time from his studies.

It is best to narrow the field down to three to five schools. Any more than that brings on a confusing and cumbersome situation that only impedes the decision-making progress. Once the student-athlete decides on the colleges he wishes to visit, it is imperative that he make his visitations meaningful. While on the campus, he should see potential professors (especially those in his major field), the academic dean, the dean of student affairs, and even the president of the college, if the latter is available and willing to spend any time with him.

Admittedly, visitations with key personnel are often possible on the smaller campuses, but the boy should try to see such people at the larger schools as well.

The student-athlete should take advantage of the opportunity to eat on campus and stay in one of the residence halls overnight. This will give him an excellent opportunity to converse with a good cross section of the student body. Ask to stay overnight with a scholarship athlete. You can learn a lot about the school, its team, and the school's treatment of scholarship athletes by living as one for a night.

Without doubt these visitations are valuable learning experiences that the individual should take advantage of. What better way is there of obtaining a realistic concept of what is in store for him than by soliciting information, viewpoints, and opinions from the individuals and groups currently involved with either the college and the team?

It is important for the student-athlete and his parents to realize that recruiting is a two-way street. They should be aware that the recruiter has a job to do, that he is "selling" his school, his program, and himself, and that he is bound by rules and regulations established by his school as well as rules and regulations laid down by the NCAA. It will be most beneficial to all concerned if there is mutual honesty, sincerity, and a spirit of cooperation between the recruiter, the student-athlete, and his parents.

You and your parents must be cognizant of many general areas of concern about recruiting. The answers to the following questions should provide a frame of reference within which the student-athlete and his parents may compare various colleges and their athletic programs.

Accreditation

One of the first things you should check about a prospective school is the accreditation. Is the school fully accredited and highly rated academically? The NCAA will not accept a school that is not accredited. And neither should you, if you want to play in a NCAA-sponsored game or event. Also, if the school you choose is not accredited, you may find it very difficult getting into graduate school or a professional school.

Reputation of the School

What is the reputation of the college? What is the reputation and status of the department in which you intend to major? Is the school progressive and innovative in its approach to higher education?

Is it the rule or exception for athletes in this school to obtain their degrees within the usual four years?

What are the opportunities for obtaining individual attention and assistance from faculty, administrators, and counselors?

Academic Curriculum

Is education your prime concern—to grow as a person while achieving competence in your chosen areas, thereby preparing for your life's work? What type of academic discipline are you interested in pursuing?

NCAA statistics show that only 3 percent of all college athletes enter professional sports upon graduation. What happens to the other 97 percent? Like their nonathletic classmates, they enter the business world, government service, or pursue other vocational careers.

You see how important it is to choose a school that will prepare you for the time when you must enter the work force.

Examine your prospective school's curriculum carefully. Be certain that it offers you a solid program of instruction in your field of interest. If you feel unqualified to rate a school's listing of courses in the catalog, seek out a professional or a teacher to help you evaluate the school's courses.

Some schools prescribe rigid, traditional courses for their students. Others offer a student the freedom to select more of his courses. You know your capabilities; if you feel responsible enough to guide your own course selection, choose the school that offers this alternative.

Do you possess the necessary skills and abilities to achieve with hard work, some level of success in your proposed field? What does your counselor think about the school with respect to your academic ability and the major you plan to pursue? Avoid selecting a school where you will have to struggle to pass your course.

Make sure you will be able to enroll in a course that you are required to have to meet graduation requirements. (Sometimes, laboratory classes in a particular course conflict with team practices, as both are often scheduled in late afternoon.) Ask to talk with a student-athlete who is pursuing the course you plan to study; he will be able to answer many of these questions concerning curriculum and football.

Role of Athletics

Colleges are both for learning and playing. The college you select should be one where the emphasis is to recruit student-athletes with a desire to excel in college work, academically and athletically.

What is the role of athletics in this school? What is the attitude of the administration, faculty, and students toward athletics and football in particular? Are athletics and football supported by the alumni and the community?

Is the purpose of athletics in this school to serve as a farm system for professional leagues, or to attract national attention to the school, or is it to provide each student with the opportunity to develop his talents and enjoy his participation, with the end result a full, rich, meaningful, and enjoyable experience.

Caliber of Competition

What is the caliber of competition? Can you successfully compete at this level of competition? Are you as big, fast, quick, agile, and as strong as the players now playing the position you desire to play? Do your abilities and skills fit their style of play?

The best place to start in assessing your athletic skills and potential is with your high school coach. Rely on his experience and judgment to match your athletic potential with a college's level of competition. He knows your skills and potential the best. If you know a student-athlete attending the school of your choice, ask him what he thinks of your chances of playing.

Talk to the coach of the school you are interested in, and ask him how he feels you will fit into the team picture, should you decide to attend the school. Ask him how many scholarship athletes will be recruited for the team in your class. Find out if this school recruits junior college athletes, and if the school follows the practice of redshirting.

If you do possess big-time potential, is it wise to be a big fish in a small pond or a small fish in a big pond? What are your chances of playing varsity ball during your four years? Have you been promised a starting berth? How many other prospects have been told this by their coaching staff? How many outstanding athletes will be ahead of you or competing with you for a specific position? How many freshmen are actually recruited each year? How many are being or will be recruited in your position?

Does the team compete in a strong league? What is the likelihood of postseason competition? Would a team have to win the conference or just finish in the top two to win a postseason bid?

Try to determine the amount and quality of esprit of the players on the team. Are they working hard and having fun also? Or are most practices a "chewing-out" session?

Find out how much daily time is devoted to team practice. Find out if night practices are held and how often.

Are the players the kind you want to be associated with?

Scholarships, Grants-in-Aid, and Financial Aid

The NCAA defines financial aid as "all institutional funds, such as scholarships, grants, loans, work-study programs assistance, on-campus employment, and aid from government or private sources." The means of awarding financial aid is varied. Criteria for awarding financial aid can vary from outright recognition of an athlete's superior athletic ability to acknowledgement of his family's inability to meet college expenses.

The three major criteria for awarding financial aid are: (1) athletic ability, (2) academic potential, and (3) financial need. Blue-chip athletes—those students who demonstrate superior skills—stand the best chance of winning athletic aid. Lesser-skilled athletes are not overlooked completely, but it's a fact that most college team rosters are made up of good athletes. It is this group of "good athletes" that is welcomed at most schools. In fact, a good athlete with superior academic potential can often qualify for aid where a blue-chip athlete with average or poor academic potential cannot. Athletic aid is rarely awarded to average athletes, just as scholarships for excellence are rarely awarded to average students.

The following questions can be of help to the student-athlete in appraising the various offers of financial aid.

1. If I am promised or if I qualify for financial assistance—grant, scholarship, or other financial aid—what exactly does such assistance provide? How should I evaluate and compare financial assistance among various schools?

2. If I am to receive financial assistance, will it be continued if I am injured and cannot participate anymore? Is the financial assistance guaranteed for one year, two, three, or four years?

3. If I am unable to earn the degree in four years, will I continue getting financial assistance in my fifth year?

4. If financial aid is based on need, how is "need" determined? (Need is the difference between what college will cost and what you and your family can and should pay toward the cost.)

5. Under what circumstances may the financial

assistance be rescinded or reduced? What criteria does the college use for renewing aid, and what criteria does it use for canceling aid? Ask the athletic director or coach to review the rules that govern loss of scholarship.

6. Are you permitted to stay on and finish your education at the expense of the school? Find out if the school allows athletes to attend summer school at the school's expense. Ask if the athletic department supplies tutorial help if requested.

Player-Coach Relationships

The relationships a coach has with his players are most important if the college football playing experience is to be a meaningful and enjoyable experience. The student-athlete should ask the following questions.

1. Are the coach and his staff interested in me as an individual or as merely a "tool" with which to win ball games? Does the staff recognize that the primary purpose of attending college is to earn a degree?

2. Do the head coach and his staff have a reputation for competency, honesty, and integrity in all matters?

3. What are the team rules with respect to dress, grooming, hours, training, and so on? Are the current rules compatible with my personal philosophy and life-style? Has the college or coaching staff earned a reputation for mistreating or being dishonest with athletes?

4. If I am a member of a minority, would I be comfortable in a situation where there are few or no minority students, faculty members, or coaches? Is the institution cognizant of the needs of minority students? Are such needs being met?

5. Is there harmony between the current squad members and the coaching staff? How many athletes have quit the team during the past two or three years? Why? How many have been dismissed from the team within the same time period? Why?

6. Is there stability in the football program? Or has there been a great turnover of head and assistant coaches?

7. Would I like to play for the head coach or coach who will coach me?

Location

The location of the college should be examined closely.

How far away from home do you wish to go? How important is the distance factor? Can you afford to travel home during vacation periods and can your parents afford to travel to the school to see you play as often as they wish?

In what kind of town or city is the college located? Is it a metropolitan area with thousands of residents and all the ills that accompany a densely populated area? Or is it a smaller community? How close to a major metropolitan area is the school?

If you want a school with a classic campus—lots of trees and lawns—then you might consider a university or college in a small town. On the other hand, a school in a major urban setting offers many unique advantages to offset its lack of open spaces. Cities usually offer large museums, concert halls and theaters, and major professional sports facilities. Also, a large city environment provides the anonymity that many students prefer and a faster pace of life.

Schools in major urban settings often command the attention of national media. National media exposure is a quick ticket to national prominence and recognition, and, sometimes, a good way to increase the interest of pro scouts who might increase their interest in you, once having seen you perform well against the top competition in the nation.

What are the opportunities of playing before TV exposure?

Size and Type of School

The size of the school is important. As a rule of thumb, if you are considered a blue-chip athlete, you might well consider attending one of the NCAA University Division schools, because the overall competition will be superior. This is not to say that a blue-chip athlete should completely rule out a College Division school if he finds that school offers something he values, such as outstanding coaching, curriculum, facilities, or climate.

For example, some schools offer more opportunity for individual growth and recognition. In a sense, you can live the college life of a "big fish in a small pond."

What type and size of school are you seeking? Would you be happy in a large university with 25,000 or so students? A medium-size university in the 8,000–12,000 range? Or would you be more comfortable in a smaller liberal arts college with an enrollment of 1,000 to 2,000? There are advantages and disadvantages to each and the student-athlete should be aware of them.

Do you desire a public or a private college? If the latter, would you prefer a school that is religiously affiliated or secular in nature?

Would you prefer a coeducational school to one for men only? If you prefer the latter, is there any nearby college with women students?

Facilities, Equipment, and Medical Care

What type of facilities and equipment are available for academic, athletic, and recreational pursuits? Are the facilities and equipment indicative of a first-class or a "bush league" athletic program?

Is an athletic trainer available for the athletic squads? Is there a first-class training room?

What type of medical care is available to athletes? What type of insurance program is provided? Who pays for the insurance program—the athlete or the school?

Food and Lodging

What type of food service is available to the student body? Is it a smorgasbord arrangement, or are the students limited as to the amount and variety of food? Is there a training table for the football players? What restrictions are there, if any?

What about the residence hall situation? Are there rules (and are they enforced) governing quiet hours so that students attempting to study are not disturbed? Are all students required to live in campus facilities, or are they allowed to live off campus? Are apartment-style accommodations available to students, or are students limited to the more traditional dormitory-style structures?

Spiritual, Cultural, Social, and Recreational Opportunities

Social life and religious affiliation are two areas of personal preference. You should investigate each of these areas to determine if their status or role in everyday school life is what appeals to you.

You may want the freedom to live off campus, or join a fraternity. Will you have the freedom to live off campus or join a fraternity? Do scholarship athletes have this opportunity?

What spiritual, cultural, social, and recreational opportunities are available within the college? In the community? How many of such activities are within driving distance of the school? Will you have the opportunity for a balance of spiritual, academic, social, athletic, and recreational activities?

Look for clues to the school's social atmosphere by examining its rules on smoking, dancing, drinking, card-playing, and student's rights to visit members of the opposite sex in their rooms.

By eliminating those schools that do not meet your expectations, you will narrow the field of possibilities considerably.

Conclusion

If recruiting is conducted with honesty and integrity, in accordance with the governing legislation of the NCAA, and in conformance not only to the letter of the rule, but also the spirit of the rule, all those involved will enjoy mutual benefits, and recruiting will be accepted as a highly regarded activity and not "demeaning," as one top college football coach has stated; nor need it be, as one sports writer put it, "the commercial, bloodless, to-the-death match called the 'Recruiting Game'."

If the college, the college football program, the football coach, the recruiter, the high school coach, the parents, and the student-athlete are to enjoy mutual benefits, it is imperative that there exist mutual honesty, integrity, and cooperation. No longer will it be said, "Recruiting is getting out of hand. You're out there trying to sell yourself and the facts about your school and the kid ain't hearing a word you're saying. All he's wondering is when you're going to start talking about money."

Part Ten
The Coaching Career and Responsibilities

47

Blueprinting Your Coaching Career

(From 1979 Summer Manual of the AFCA)

DONALD E. FUOSS Professor, California State University, Sacramento

A syndicated article by a nationally known columnist once appeared in the newspapers throughout the country that included a letter from a woman seeking advice on how to deal with her physician-husband who did not follow the good advice that he gave to his own patients. The humanistic physician, genuinely concerned about the health and well-being of his patients, prescribed specific corrective plans of action when they were overweight, consumed alcohol and tobacco beyond moderation, did not get sufficient sleep or physical exercise, and had poor dietary habits. The physician's response to his wife for not personally practicing what he preached to his patients was that he was too busy taking care of them to be overly concerned about himself and his well-being.

An analogous situation exists among many football coaches who find themselves so busy handling the myriad details and problems of coaching, including nurturing the careers of their players, that they actually spend little time constructively planning and monitoring their own careers. Probably most have a specific goal in mind, but probably few have a specific plan for achieving that career goal. Fewer still have alternate plans in the event their career expectations do not become realizations.

The psychic rewards of coaching football can easily lull a coach into relying on the "slot machine approach" to career planning—"Through luck and good fortune my number will come up and I'll get that big job (my goal)." However, if a coach does not take or make time to give his career direction and if he has no plan for his future, the probability is greater that he will not move up as rapidly as he wishes. He may even move out of coaching entirely before it is time for his retirement.

The purpose of this chapter is twofold: (1) to urge

coaches to examine their present coaching positions and to devise a career game plan, including alternatives outside of coaching; and (2) to include some forms and concepts that coaches may find beneficial in accomplishing the first purpose.

Some of the material in this article has been gleaned from one of my books, *Blueprinting Your Coaching Career* (1973), wherein I suggested ways of finding out about and applying for positions, preparing a résumé, controlling the interview process, the follow-up, and so on, and from material that has been prepared for a book by a coauthor and myself on the psychology of coaching and effective coaching methods. Also, some materials and concepts are from management sources that I have utilized and continue to use in management classes and in presenting career-planning classes, seminars, and workshops.

Reflecting on experience from the School of Hard Knocks has aided me in the preparation of this chapter, although early in my career, as a young coach in particular, I did not hear what older football coaches were saying about the pitfalls of coaching: the high turnover rate of coaches, coaching is a terminal occupation, and there are only two kinds of coaches—those who have been fired, and those who are about to be fired!

Of the four major college football coaches who made the above statements, only one is still coaching football. The other three were terminated from their positions, and they have been making their livelihoods for some time outside of the field of coaching football.

Your Future in Coaching?

Before commencing to formulate your blueprint for career success, take a couple of minutes to try to visualize your future. Pick a date in the not-too-far-distant future—perhaps five to ten years from today—and try to visualize the status of your career then. As an example, if you are now thirty-five years of age on a college staff as an assistant coach, what do you expect to be doing when you are forty to forty-five? Do you still expect to be coaching football in the same position in the same school? Do you see yourself at a different level of responsibility at the same school? Or will you have advanced in the profession to a more prestigious position? Or can you visualize that you might not be coaching at all? The last possibility may be difficult to comprehend. While some coaches may want to get out of coaching after a number of years, others can think of nothing else they want to do except coach football. What about you?

While you are trying to visualize where you might be and what you might be doing five to ten years from today, try to speculate on your income at that stage of your life. Is there evidence that it is likely to be substantially more than you are now earning, or will it be increasing slowly, hopefully keeping up with inflation and the cost of living? Will it be reduced drastically if you decide to leave the field of coaching, possibly making a midcareer change?

Your Future Out of Coaching?

In the event of the latter, you may or may not be the one to make the decision. Depending on your particular situation, you may be reassigned or phased out so that you still remain at the same institution where you have coached, but working in a capacity other than coaching football. It may be that you are able to return to full-time teaching but only if you have been granted retreat rights to some department. For the most part, when one is on the coaching track, a teaching position opportunity is not available to the ex-coach. Athletic administration, fundraising, special assignments, and a very limited number of similar opportunities are sometimes available to a former head coach so that he may remain at the same institution but not in his previous capacity of head coach. Since the very scarcity of special positions limits the number of opportunities available, almost without exception assistant coaches are precluded.

The opportunity may not even be available for a former head coach, or he may not wish to accept such a position even if offered. Depending on his age at that particular time of his life and other variables, he may be forced to seek other employment if he does not have income from other sources.

More frequently, the coach is informed that he is fired, or he may be given the opportunity to resign so that he is not fired outright. Or it may be disguised in language that does not seem quite so harsh as "you're fired." Instead, you may be "terminated," or "discharged." Or you are told they are "not extending your contract," or that "you're being 'let go'," "dismissed." Other seemingly less harsh phrases may be used. But the painful meaning is factual: You have lost your job.

Being fired always has a devastating effect, at first at least, on the individual. Psychologists have reported the following adverse effects: There is usually one to two months of trauma—severe depression, self-doubt, and a burning, gut-wrenching but unrequited anger, a perceived sense of crushing unfairness, and generally a shattering realization that the universe does not work as it should, that virtue is not necessarily rewarded. Being fired is among the most private of experiences, and it does little good to know that it has occurred to many others. It is difficult to comprehend that it can happen to you (me), but the nature of coaching is such that it happens more often to coaches than others. Should it occur to you, then it is a matter of what you are prepared and qualified to do to earn a livelihood, and possibly gathering strength from the Latin phrase, *Illegitimi non carborundum!* (don't let the bastards grind you down!).

You Hold the Key

While there are many forces, factors, and variables, especially for an assistant football coach, over which one has little or no control, there are a number of things that you can do to minimize them to permit you to have greater control over your own fate, life, and career.

A popular television program some years ago was "This Is Your Life," and a popular song from a Broadway stage hit was "You Gotta Know The Territory." Both apply to you. You should evaluate your present position, which will be explained and illustrated. (See Diagram 1.) You should also be able to evaluate other positions that you may be contemplating.

Briefly, it is possible to stay in a position too long if you have other career goals and aspirations to move up, and there have been head and assistant coaches who can be said to have "jumped from the frying pan into the fire" in changing positions. While in his existing job a coach may not realize until too late that he has remained too long, on the other hand, some coaches have realized within a week, a month, a year that they have made a mistake in accepting a new position.

You have only so many opportunities in your career or "chapters in your book of life," so that a wrong move (or failure to move) can foul up your future if your career plan was hastily conceived. You have to do your "homework" on your present job and on the positions you consider in the future. You have to have the know-how and the know-who.

Where job termination occurs, it is a waste of your time and energy to subject yourself to the self-defeating trauma reported by psychologists in your attempt to answer "Why me?" You have got to "get with it" right away to reduce the time between termination from one position to employment in another position or job, whether it is in or out of coaching, depending on your particular circumstances. Hopefully, you will have already devised a termination plan ready for activation, just as you have devised a well-conceived career plan for your advancement.

While others will aid you whether it is termination or changing positions of your own volition, you have to be able to help yourself before you can expect others to help you. The know-who then becomes important—those who can and will aid you. Some can't and others won't help and some won't be in a position to aid you. It is a waste of your time and energy to try to involve such people in helping you to accomplish what you want to do.

Give Your Career and Life Direction

Despite the fact that a football game plan may not materialize to its fullest expectations or that it may be found to be completely awry, it doesn't deter a coach from modifying his game plan or even abandoning it at some stage of a particular game. Nor should it deter the coach from making other game plans in the future. The same principles are applicable to a coach's career plans. While a coach cannot look into a crystal ball and see what the future holds for him, he can devise a career plan, monitor it closely, and, if necessary, change or modify it. The inference is not that you should spend so much time looking at positions down the road that you fail to do "the right things" in your present position. Rather, the point is that if you fail to pause from time to time to ask yourself, "Where am I going?," "When do I expect to get there?," and "What happens if I don't make it?," you are not giving direction to your career and life.

It is easy to get bogged down and locked into a situation, with the result that you merely wait "for something better to come along." Or you can become so involved in coaching that you are unaware of threats and dangers—"the fire alarms," surrounding your coaching position. Or you may charge full speed ahead, only to find that it has led to a career dead end. Your failure to give careful thought and direction to your career is not unlike an inflated ball bobbing around in the ocean at the mercy of the wind and tides. The information and materials that follow should aid you in formulating plans. But you have to do your own homework.

SWOTS Analysis

SWOTS is an acronym, the initials of which stand for strengths, weaknesses, opportunities, threats, suggestions, and which is illustrated in Diagram 1. SWOTS has many purposes other than the two described here: for listing these particular dimensions of your present position; and for comparing two positions (present with another position which you may be considering).

SWOTS ANALYSIS

Strengths—

Weaknesses—

Opportunities—

Threats—

Suggestions—

Under each category your objective is to list as many items as possible in order to get some sort of a profile of that particular dimension of your present job and situation. Examples of strengths are: As head coach you have a long-term contract; there is a winning tradition and record over the years; your remuneration or scale of compensation is greater than coaches at comparable institutions; you have major duties and responsibilities. The opposite of these you may consider as weaknesses. On the typical job there are likely to be a number of items in each of the categories that are not the opposite of each other. As an example, while a strength might be the head coach has a long-term contract, a weakness could be that your voice isn't heard in staff meetings and in planning. From the latter you may deduce other weaknesses.

Opportunities may be part of the strengths you perceive, and the lack of opportunities on your particular job may or may not be viewed as threats. As an example: If you are the freshman football coach and you are desirous of moving up to the varsity so that you can move later on to a head position, but you have been passed over twice previously for a position on the varsity staff, your opportunities would appear to be few. While your position as head freshman coach may not be threatened, your career goal of being a head coach is stifled and, despite the strengths you may have listed, your career goal is threatened. Under suggestions it would be advisable to note: "Start looking. Should move. No opportunity for advancement."

Threats are the "fire alarms" that go off and which you hope are false; but the fire may be already smoldering although you fail to recognize the job threat. Due to the nature of coaching, there are always forces and factions that feel that firing the head coach and perhaps his assistants is the way to win more games, score more points, permit fewer points to be scored on your defense, or to recruit more effectively. Also, without getting into a discussion on the necessity for loyalty and group cohesiveness, it is enough to state that these desirable attributes are not always present on every football coaching staff, and one's own ethical and moral values and behavior are one's guides.

Aside from the above threats, you may perceive the previously mentioned example of not being heard in staff meetings as a threat, or possibly your not being included in an "in" group within the staff, or being assigned minor responsibilities and not major duties as threats to your present position and future career. The politics of the job situation environment are something of which every coach should be aware. It is very easy to get so involved in coaching that one almost loses touch with the real world. It is better to be a fire preventer than a fire fighter, and this obviously means preventing the fire from occurring rather than waiting until the fire starts and then attempting to put it out. There are threats to every job, some real and others perceived. All should be checked out.

Under suggestions you analyze the other dimensions of SWOTS and record your answer. In the final analysis, this depends on your particular situation and career goal. If your job profile is heavy in strengths and opportunities, you may wish to remain or move to another position, depending on your ultimate career goal. However, if it is heavy in weaknesses and threats, your days on that staff may be numbered.

You should not delude yourself, and it is always easier to secure another position when you are employed than when you are unemployed. Almost without exception one should not resign his job without having another position already lined up.

Analyzing Two or More Jobs

In the event that you are considering another position but you could stay in your present position, SWOTS may be used to compare the two jobs. Either lay out two separate sheets so the dimensions of both jobs can be compared, or draw a line down through the middle of the table on page 245, so that the dimensions can be analyzed on a single form.

In several instances that I am aware of, individuals who have performed the prescribed SWOTS analysis of comparing what they already have in their present position with the potential of what they would get in another position have declined the latter, deducing that the grass is not always greener on the other

side of the fence. They have not only gained insightful knowledge about the interview and job-hiring processes, but they have been able to discern important and unimportant facets of jobs. Many times one benefits more by turning down a position than by accepting it, including better insight and an appreciation for his present position.

The Job Opportunity Wedge

During one's career in coaching, or if one leaves coaching for whatever reason, he will have only so many opportunities to secure positions in order to better himself financially and professionally. Limiting this discussion specifically to coaching, it is a known fact that generally the more competence or coaching expertise one has, the greater are the opportunities for upward mobility; conversely, fewer opportunities and less mobility are available if one lacks competence.

While other factors may be involved, in general coaching expertise and age cannot be considered as separate entities; both go together in obtaining positions in coaching and in attaining career goals.

The Job Opportunity Wedge, illustrated in Diagram 1, is a concept relevant to career planning and goal achievement, which every coach should understand, especially including the assistant coach who may have chosen to remain in his position for a number of years for personal reasons. Should he not be elevated to the head coaching position after a number of years' service at the same institution, his job opportunity wedge closes more quickly because of his age, whether he remains or is forced to leave his institution to seek another position in coaching. Should he not secure the latter and must then seek employment outside the field of coaching, depending on his other competencies, skills, and qualifications, he may have few opportunities for meaningful and fulfilling employment at that particular time of his life. Briefly, the more job competencies he has, the longer one can keep his job

Diagram 1

JOB OPPORTUNITY WEDGE

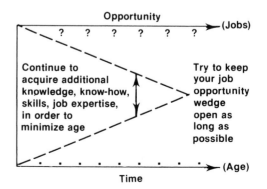

opportunity wedge open. That is why coaches should plan on acquiring other skills and competencies prior to their termination from coaching—not afterward.

Closing Horizons: Opportunity and Time (Age)

Diagram 1, illustrated by two parallel lines, symbolizes two horizons: (job) opportunity and (age) time. The theory postulated is that the longer one lives and approaches retirement, the closer these two lines come together, indicating that the closing horizons represent declining and fewer job opportunities. There are people who can commence other careers in midlife after their first retirement, and for these people the wedge closes at between age sixty-five and seventy. However, coaching is not the typical type of work, especially at the major college level of competition. Age is very much a factor in securing football coaching positions and having continuing available opportunities to coach as one gets older.

Age as a factor in coaching will be discussed in greater detail later in the chapter. What a coach should attempt to do is to keep his job-opportunity wedge open as long as possible by continually upgrading his strengths and competencies in order to minimize the age factor. In addition to presenting his qualifications as indispensable, during the interview process an older person must be alert to refute an attempt to stereotype him with all other people in his age category.

Taking Stock of Yourself: Self-Appraisal

Voluminous amounts of materials are available on goal setting, career planning, job search, résumé writing, interview techniques, time management, and related subjects, with which all coaches should be familiar, whether or not they are seeking a position presently. At some point most coaches will need to be knowledgeable of all of the above subjects, whether one is attempting to move to a better position or is being forced to seek employment other than coaching. The tips, guides, suggestions, methods, and techniques are applicable to any employable person, although the inexperienced ones may not know where or how to locate and secure such materials, and job-experienced candidates may delude themselves they are too busy or they will convince themselves that they already have all of the answers and cannot learn anything new that will benefit them. It is strongly suggested, as part of your goal setting and "blueprinting" that you make time to study in great depth any available materials.

The Other Side of the Employment Table

Anyone who has ever been involved in the employment process to any extent can probably cite a number of instances of well-qualified candidates destroying their chances of serious consideration for positions because of an ill-conceived and poorly prepared résumé or their failure to sell themselves and what they had to offer during the interview. Frequently the former prohibits the candidate from even getting his foot in the door to have an interview. The latter does not automatically mean a person will be offered the position. A candidate may garner many interviews, but preclude himself from serious consideration as the best qualified because he cannot convince prospective employers that he possesses the most and the best of what they are seeking. These two topical subjects should receive further consideration and examination.

Self-Examination

The table below illustrates a relatively simple form that may be used as a starter to answer some self-examination/self-appraisal questions pertaining to the formulation and the attainment of your career goal or objective.

SELF-EXAMINATION AND APPRAISAL

SELF-ANALYSIS
Formulating/Reaching
Your Career Goal or Objective

1. **What is your PRESENT status/position? (Where are you now?)**

2. **What is your IMMEDIATE career goal or objective? (Where are you going?)**

3. **What have you to OFFER? (What are your strengths/assets?)**

4. **What are you PREPARED TO DO TO IMPROVE the quality of what you offer? (How are you overcoming your liabilities/weaknesses?)**

5. **What is your ULTIMATE career goal or objective? (What do you want to be or do with your life?)**

6. **How/when do you INTEND TO REACH your career goal or objective? (When do you expect to get there?)**

Where Are You Now?

What is your present status/position? Making the assumption you are in coaching, you should consider the following questions in an effort to find the answer to "Where are you now?"

1. What is your age? How long have you been in coaching?
2. How long have you been in your present position?
3. What are your responsibilities? Greater or lesser than when you joined the staff? If you have had greater responsibilities previously, either on this staff or on a previous staff, why do you have lesser responsibilities presently?
4. Job-wise, are you doing all of the "right things" and "things right"? Are you producing? How is the quality of your work?
5. What is the nature of your work in terms of importance? (Some coaches have many or few details, but they may be assigned all or most of the "someone must do" and/or "go-fer" tasks.)
6. Is your opinion and judgment valued and respected? Are you heard in staff meetings and in working with other assistants?

Regardless of one's position, whether it be head coach or assistant coach, some administrator will be seeking answers to the same questions. Candidly, all administrators, which include head coaches, are looking for can-do and will-do subordinates. While this may seem like an overly simplistic statement, there are those who can do the job in that they have the necessary expertise, but they won't or they screw up, so they are undependable. Some coaches are "self-destruct" individuals, which is not necessarily characteristic only of people in the coaching profession.

Will-do individuals are ones who are eager to try anything, but they may be incapable of performing the job task correctly. Whereas the can-do person is capable, but won't or doesn't, the will-do individual tries, but can't perform the task because he does not have the necessary expertise. For effective coaching to occur, the won't or can't do individuals must be identified and upgraded, transferred or terminated, depending on the particular coaching situation (tenured or coaching track). The combined can-do and will-do person is the one who achieves the desired results, which is effective coaching. Also, he is the coach who is able to keep open his job opportunity wedge.

Where Are You Going?

It is important to set an immediate or short-term attainable career goal or objective. If you don't know where you are going, how do you know when you get there? Some coaches do not set specific career goals. They drift along from position to position, or perhaps remain in the same position often at the same level for years, maintaining blind faith in the old American work ethic that if an individual works hard and long enough at his job eventually he will be rewarded. While hard work is not likely to go unnoticed, it may go unrewarded in terms of an assistant coach on a major college staff not moving up into a head coaching position, or a small college coach not advancing upward in coaching, and so on.

Age does become a discriminatory factor, despite present laws to the contrary. There are certain more or less unofficially recognized "time plateaus" and expectations for coaches in terms of age. Generally, if a football coach has not been named to a head coaching position at a small or major college by age forty, his chances of securing such a position diminish with each succeeding year. It may be that even with former head coaching experience, no candidates beyond age forty-five will be considered. It depends on whether one is moving up from high school to collegiate coaching, or is changing positions as an assistant going from one major staff to another.

It must be kept in mind constantly that age is a tremendously important factor, especially in coaching. Therefore, you can't procrastinate or deter setting attainable goals and affixing time or target dates for the completion of immediate and short- and intermediate-range goals on the way to your ultimate long-range goal. Immediate goals may be attained in days or weeks. A short-range goal should probably be attained within a year or so at the most. Intermediate goals may be several years, depending on the span of time you affix to achieve your long-range goal. Finally, long-range goals may involve a period of many years. Focusing on the ultimate or your long-range career goal is not difficult, but determining the how and when of attaining is difficult.

While there are numerous factors involved in terms of time and attaining goals, it is important to remember that age is a critical time-constraint in coaching. The time span of the typical coach remaining in active coaching is not of the same duration as the worker in most trades, professions, and other lines of employment. The young coach in particular seldom thinks of doing anything other than coaching as his life's work, whereas there is considerable evidence to support the harsh reality that fifteen to twenty years is a long time to be active in football coaching, and many are out of the profession by then. Some may be forced out but would like to continue coaching football, and others may be glad to get out due to the pressures and stress of coaching. Probably none is looking forward to commencing a new career, especially if it is not allied in some way with what the coach has been doing for so many years. As Commissioner Fred Jacoby of the Mid-American Conference pointed out in his article, "Where Is Your Next Job?" (*1978 Summer Manual* of the AFCA): "All too often a coach doesn't stop or pause to plan a workable blueprint for his professional life and future. Very few football coaches will continue coaching until retirement at age sixty-five.... Thus, it is imperative that each coach prepare for alternate job opportunities. The critical period is between thirty-five and forty-five years of age, when a coach still has time to elect to start an alternate profession. After age forty-five you are less desirable to a potential employer." Sage comments by a person who has been connected with athletics for thirty-one years, eighteen years as a former high school and college coach and thirteen years as a conference commissioner.

What Have You to Offer? Strengths? Assets? Job Expertise?

Question 3 in Diagram 3 pertains to the job skills, attributes, assets, and expertise that you possess to do your specific job and to carry out your responsibilities and job tasks as a coach. Are you a can-do and will-do coach? It is not that you can pledge loyalty and honesty, or that you promise to work hard and long hours; or that you are dedicated and dependable, and you have other similarly desirable and highly commendable attributes. These are expected of all coaches, and while you are not likely to succeed without them, you will be hired and compensated for what you have to offer in the way of job skills or expertise. Therefore, it is important to acquire football coaching expertise, and to try to continue to improve on the quality of what you have to offer. Each individual sells thousands of hours of his time, energy, and expertise during his professional life, whether he is in or out of coaching. Therefore, the more competencies one acquires, the greater are one's chances of keeping open his job-opportunity wedge, despite the factor of age (time), which closes shut only when one is unemployable.

How Are You Overcoming Your Liabilities? Weaknesses? Shortcomings?

Where strengths and weaknesses or assets and liabilities are concerned in the self-examination/self-appraisal process, probably most people see their "looking glass" self. The latter is how we most frequently perceive ourselves, and how we wish others to perceive us. Just as a person may look at his own image in the mirror and fail to see wrinkles, gray hair, and a receding hairline, he may ignore his professional shortcomings, liabilities, and weaknesses in a like manner. One may delude himself that he possesses all strengths and assets. Some people's personalities will not permit them to acknowledge their shortcomings,

and their failure to perceive reality is to their own detriment.

In some cases, job skills and performance may be overshadowed by a lack of human skills and personality behaviors. In answering question 4, one should acknowledge both technical and human skill limitations and weaknesses and indicate how he is attempting to overcome them.

What Is Your Ultimate Career Goal or Objective?

Whatever goal you select should be realistic and attainable, and you should affix a time for reaching that goal. As an illustration, it may not be realistic for an assistant coach forty years of age to have the ultimate goal of being named head coach on the retirement of the present head coach. He is presuming that the head coach is going to retire soon, which may not be the case. A second presumption is that he has carried major responsibilities, such as offensive or defensive coordinator and/or assistant head coach. Others may rate his responsibilities lower. For whatever reasons, the long-time assistant may not be named head coach, as more than one assistant has bitterly discovered in the past. While it is impossible to get all the facts in a given situation, which means it is difficult to predict with certainty what is going to occur, by utilizing the SWOTS diagram you can record many of the facts and analyze them. Then you can set more realistic goals, possibly make more accurate presumptions, although to set goals without trying to determine the overall environment or climate is almost a meaningless exercise.

While no plan is perfect and may not materialize to your expectations, it is suggested you devote time and thought to your blueprint plan and not treat it and your career in a cursory manner. Few plans of this nature are set in concrete, so your career plan should be modified, revised, and updated from time to time so that it is current. In the meantime, let us examine briefly the person-job overlay or match-up as this deals with your present position as well as your future ones in or out of coaching.

The Person-Job Match or Overlay

The person-job match is the relationship between a person and his specific work or job. Diagram 2(A) illustrates the job requirements or the job description of all tasks, responsibilities, and expectations of that specific job. Diagram 2(B) illustrates the personal competencies, proficiencies, and specific job skills of the individual (coach).

The objective is for the person to match up with

Diagram 2

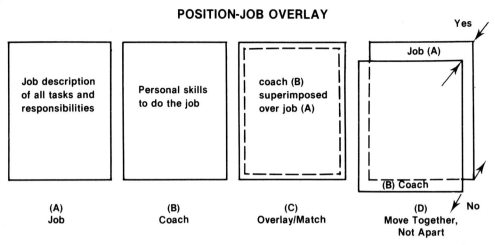

POSITION-JOB OVERLAY

(A)
Job

(B)
Coach

(C)
Overlay/Match

(D)
Move Together,
Not Apart

the job. The latter is the "standard." The perfect person-job match or overlay is illustrated in Diagram 2(C), which is the can-do and will-do performer. However, if the job or position is too big for the individual in that he simply does not have the experience and necessary expertise to handle it, then the job (A) would be superimposed over the person (B), which is not illustrated.

In most instances, however, (B) should shade (A) to some extent so that the match-up could occur in time. If (A) is shading (B), however, it is still a big job, and probably a long period of time will expire before the person masters the requirements of his job. In coaching, this could prove costly. On the other hand, the coach's expertise (B) may be far greater than his job requirements (A), so that he masters them rapidly and with ease. He is overqualified for what he is doing, and his expertise is not being utilized efficiently.

Diagram 2(D) illustrates the person and job moving closer together (top arrows), whereas the arrows at the bottom of Diagram 2(D) illustrate the person and his job moving apart. The latter can occur if the over-qualified person does not continue to find his job chal-

lenging, desires to move up but is not elevated, is no longer motivated, and so on. However, (B) and (A) can move apart, too, for the person who has not remained current and has not upgraded his skills to keep up with the demands of his job.

How do you match up with your job requirements? Just because an individual has been coaching for five years, as an illustration, this does not mean he has five times as much cumulative knowledge as he acquired his first year coaching. There are individuals on jobs in and out of coaching who may have been working for five years who have not acquired additional knowledge or expertise about their work, as they have merely repeated their first year's experience five times.

Whether we like it or not, evaluation or appraisal of our work goes on all of the time. It is far better for an individual to analyze and appraise his own job performance through self-examination and to impose self-regulatory means than it is for a superior to impose corrective means. Such corrective measures may not be an attempt to bring the subordinate up to standard by upgrading; the superior's decision may be to terminate the subordinate.

48
The Football Coach and Liability

(From 1978 Proceedings of the AFCA)

EUGENE O'CONNOR Attorney and Assistant Professor of Law, Canisius College

The law is a developing and adaptive system. As society's horizons and expectations expand, the demands on the law and courts grow.

Those who felt we could solve problems by spending money now realize that we don't have enough to continue this technique and that it doesn't always work. We have moved on to the newest idea—law and regulation will ensure each person perfect justice. Litigation to secure legal rights is a fact of life today.

Against this backdrop, the college coach and his institution cannot sit idly by and say they are exempt—that they don't deserve to be judged by the new standards applied to society.

You can no longer claim that because you assist in the maturing process of thousands of young people and are performing an invaluable community service, that you have a claim for different treatment before the bar of the law. The complaint, "It's unfair to coaches" and "It shouldn't happen" will not stop the reality of a sports injury lawsuit.

Today as a coach, trainer, or athletic director, you are going to be sued if you are careless and negligent in the carrying out of your duties and responsibilities. In recent years it would have been rare for a player to sue his coach and his college, but it is not rare today.

The coaching profession must be vigilant and protect its own interests in the area of player safety.

What Is Negligence?

Negligence is the breach of a legal duty established by law for the protection of, in this case, an athlete. Noncompliance with this "duty of care" imposes liability upon a coach and school.

The criterion for determining the extent of this "duty of care" is an objective, not a subjective, one. It is the consensus of the community as to what is proper rather than simply a single individual's judgment. Therefore, if you violate the football community's customs and usage, you will be liable if an injury occurs. Your own experience may be at variance with these norms, but you will be judged by them.

Your norms of conduct are set by three groups: the coaching profession, the American Football Coaches Association, and the NCAA. Guidance as to the norms are: (1) Your ethics code and publications of the American Football Coaches Association; and (2) Techniques established by the coaching fraternity that are recognized and accepted as sound practice by the profession and the NCAA football rules.

Your ethics code states: "The safety and welfare of his players should always be uppermost in his mind." The word "safety" is extremely significant—your program will be judged by the emphasis given to safe procedure and techniques.

It further states, "In teaching the game of football, the coach must realize that there are certain rules designed to protect the player and provide common standards for determining a winner and loser. Any attempts to beat these rules, to take unfair advantage of an opponent, or to teach deliberate unsportsmanlike conduct, have no place in the game of football."

Any talk about putting the other team's leading player out of the game or suggestive inferences to the team as to what this will accomplish can easily dynamite your career. There is a recent case where one player has sued a player on another team for deliberate and intentional infliction of injuries during a game. You can expect a "cross claim" against you if one of your players is sued for such illegal conduct and you incited or condoned it.

"The diagnosis and treatment of injuries is a medical problem and should, under no circumstances, be considered a province of the coach."

Cross the boundary from administering first aid to practicing medicine and you're asking for serious trouble.

If you violate these guidelines and injuries result therefrom, when you take the stand at a trial, plaintiff's counsel will take you apart bit by bit for a violation of these norms. "Lip service" will be of little use to you in a serious injury case.

Learn the Guidelines

Chapter 51 of this book is a reprint of "A Coach's Guide to Safe Football," published by the American Football Coaches Association. It sets forth additional guidelines for coaching football. It is extremely important that you review this chapter.

The ideas expressed in this chapter represent an emphasis on player safety. Serious injuries and litigation are not desired by insurance companies. Improvement of player safety will ensure that liability risks in football will continue to be accepted by the insurance industry. If they do not, you will no longer be a football coach. Only the major colleges would likely be able to afford the risk and costs of self-insuring football programs. Some points from that chapter should be emphasized here.

"A coach should be aware that many procedures and policies of his playing days have been found to be worthless or harmful. He owes it to his players to keep up with the latest procedures and policies recommended by medical authorities."

With respect to the latter point, can you demonstrate you are following correct procedures, particularly regarding preventing heat stroke?

With respect to disciplinary techniques, is forcing someone to run until he is in a state of exhaustion or lining up ten players 10 yards apart and having a back run the gauntlet truly related to teaching of the game? Do such procedures assist in teaching techniques? Are they safe disciplinary methods?

"A coach should not overmatch his teams physically. Neither should he overmatch his own players in practice."

Don't teach someone a "lesson" or how to do it "right" by mismatching him with a player of unusual size or skill.

"Coaches should explain and illustrate why protective and preventive measures are required for safe football. The athlete needs to know the reasons before he will follow them conscientiously."

Do you demonstrate and explain why dropping one's head or the use of the head to "spear" a player is a lethal danger in football?

"Coaches should eliminate phrases and terms which connote violence."

Make sure your spoken or written words to your players reflect adherence to this rule. Otherwise you can expect to be seriously embarrassed at a trial.

Can you seriously say you observe these suggestions—if you do, your career will not be jeopardized if litigation comes your way.

The American Medical Association disseminates much information regarding heat stroke through your own organization's literature. You had better follow it or get a doctor's written statement saying it is not good advice.

Written Procedures Important

Along this line, do you have written procedures to make sure that heat stroke is immediately dealt with?
1. Whom do you call?
2. What are you to do?
3. How soon are you to move the player?

Remember, your code of ethics charges you with responsibility for the boys' safety—parents may be unaware of the nature and seriousness of heat stroke. If they ask you to delay treatment until their doctor arrives, you may legally be in serious trouble. Work this out with the parents in memos to them before practice starts.

A recent case illustrates this problem. Parents were called by a coach to advise that their son was suffering from heat exhaustion. The initial notification of the parents occurred shortly after the end of practice. The family doctor was notified by the parents and they advised the coach the doctor would come to the school as soon as he could. The doctor arrived at approximately 7:00 P.M., hours after the onset of the heat stroke. The boy was removed to a hospital where he died. The appeals court upheld a jury verdict holding the coach negligent for the boy's death. The coach refused to allow another physician who came to pick his son up from practice to move the boy to the hospital or take proper medical measures. His refusal was based on the request of the parents to have their own family physician take care of their son. In my opinion, this case squarely faced the issue of player safety—the coach is strictly accountable when parents are not present, available, or do not comprehend the medical nature of the situation.

If a trainer services injury matters, you still must deal with the delays a lack of procedures would bring about. That the trainer made a mistake will not eliminate you as a target defendant. You will likely be sued and will have to defend your own actions.

Know Who Is Injured

To organize your program properly, I believe you must have a means of controlling the reporting of injuries.

Does one coach know if another player is injured or is recovering from injuries when he moves from coaching station to station on the field?

Is there any reason you can't have on each day's coach's practice schedule a list of the walking wounded and any limitations on their contact participation or other participation?

Request all trainers to supply written injury information and restrictions on participation and then retain it in a notebook or other form. Blackboard notices can also be used. If you don't want an overenthusiastic injured player to participate, put a plastic band, highly visible, through his face bar.

What do you do at the end of practice? Do you have a procedure to see that injuries are reported and the athlete receives treatment? What do you do about those who are afraid or hide their injury for fear of being embarrassed or being excused from the lineup?

Don't Ridicule Injured

Do you discourage by insults or abusive humor the reporting of injuries? Do you stigmatize all of those who would complain despite the frivolousness of their complaint? Either technique leads to legal trouble. You don't have to baby anyone. Listening is not a demonstration of weakness on your part. Let the trainers make the professional judgments on injuries and deal with the personalities involved.

It is important that you know what an article in the magazine of the Association of Trial Lawyers of America suggests are the responsibilities of the coaching profession. It clearly demonstrates the legal profession's knowledge of the operation of football programs and the concept of player safety.

The article, "Responsibility Is Also Part of the Game," by Samuel Langerman and Noel Fidel,* states in part:

Duties of Athletic Programs

1. To establish procedures and enforce rules concerning proper fitting of uniforms and protective gear, and safe use of equipment.

2. To structure progress with adequate review procedures to assure that participants will not move too rapidly into areas beyond their skills.

3. To select opponents with care to avoid potentially dangerous mismatching.

4. To educate concerning risks in performing

a sport when ill or injured and to establish and scrupulously enforce rules regarding reporting of illness or injury.

5. To establish check-up procedures for those who have been ill or injured to assure that illness or injury is no longer an impairing factor.

Various plaintiffs' lawyers are attempting to achieve new legal precedents governing football injury litigation. The aforesaid article suggests a definition of a warning that should be given in the area of player safety:

A warning, to be effective practically and legally, must be so disseminated, explained and enforced as to provide a realistic basis for the expectation that it will prevent the conduct against which it is directed.

The coach should have foreseen that such a warning, to be heeded, had to be repeated frequently, with clear explanation of the harm which might result from failure to comply.

Warnings Are Necessary

In product-liability cases, a key issue is the extent of the warning given by the manufacturer to the consumer as to the dangers of the product. If there was no warning given on the product, and it is dangerous in its ordinary condition and an injury results therefrom, liability is imposed on the manufacturer.

The cited "warning" is a spin-off from product-liability case legal concepts and represents an attempt to improve new affirmative duties on a coach to intensively and extensively warn a player about inherent dangers in the execution of techniques and breaking of rules.

This is a higher standard than the present negligence rule imposes, for it mandates that the coach do more than simply exercise care for the safety of his players.

Whether this concept will become case law and raise the coaches' duty of care is difficult to predict. One thing is certain, the "warning" provides a method of judging your own program in the area of player safety.

For example:

"So disseminated" equals repeated emphasis on safety admonitions.

"Explained" equals detailing of dangers from illegal or faulty execution of techniques or breach of rules.

"Enforced" equals the disciplining of players in

---

*Reprinted by permission from *Trial* magazine, January 1977, The Association of Trial Lawyers of America.

games and practices by effective disciplinary techniques for their refusal to abide by your techniques and rules.

Repeat Your Instructions

Is your information concerning player safety so repeated to gain respect for your teaching? Does your teaching have credibility that a jury would accept? If a jury looked at the number of drills to teach pass interception techniques during the season, they'd find all kinds and types used on a daily basis. Would they find the same emphasis on protection of players?

Are your teaching standards concerning player safety really standards or are they a sham?

In the law on questions of form versus substance, substance prevails.

With respect to player safety, do you teach a fumble recovery technique—how to protect oneself while recovering a fumble?

Do you warn players of the dangers of being knocked on the ground in the line of scrimmage area—do you repeatedly inform them of the dangers of being knocked off their feet?

Do you warn players about ill-fitting helmets that are damaged or in need of repair? Do you have periodic equipment inspections?

Do you warn players about the necessity of a well-developed neck in the sport and the importance of the bulled neck and "hitting position"?

Learn Legal Concepts

You should be aware of some legal concepts.

It is not essential in establishing negligence on the part of a coach to show intent to violate the rules of his profession.

The contributory negligence of a player may be an intentional and unreasonable exposure of himself to a danger created by the coaches' negligence of which danger the athlete knows or has reason to know. The player must comprehend that he is in danger and have knowledge of danger threatening through his own acts before he can be required to use care to protect himself.

Only continuous teaching techniques assure your ability to have met your "duty of care" and have demonstrated knowledge of dangers to the athlete.

A player is not required to use any extraordinary care to protect himself, and is not required to observe all danger that may exist. He will not be held guilty of contributory negligence when he failed to observe a danger that he had no reason to apprehend because of his age.

What Is Contributory Negligence?

Generally, contributory negligence of sufficient degree will result in a jury rejecting the plaintiff's claim. But in a serious injury case, the plaintiff's contributory negligence will have to be clearly established and, in my judgment, a significant factor in causing his injuries.

The assumption-of-risk doctrine provides that there is consent to injuries accidentally inflicted by an opponent upon a participant. Injuries intentionally inflicted in violation of the spirit and rules of the game may make "assumption of risk" irrelevant. Ordinary risks are the only risks assumed by an athlete.

No extraordinary risks are assumed unless voluntary consent and prior knowledge exist. Injured plaintiffs usually allege that they were subjected to an extraordinary risk and were never advised of this fact.

If there is a known danger in use of a technique it must be disclosed and evaluated before asking a player to perform it. Otherwise he has not assumed the risk unless you can demonstrate otherwise.

The Colgate University Case of 1972 involved an unsuccessful attempt by the plaintiff to establish the concept that a tackling technique taught to the plaintiff was inherently dangerous and therefore the plaintiff could never have assumed the risk in using the technique. The jury decided that the defendant, Colgate University and its coaches, were not liable.

The United States Supreme Court stated simply in one sports-injury case: "(One) is never held to 'assume the risk' of another's negligence or incompetence."

In noncomparative negligence states, assumption of risk is a complete bar to the plaintiff's lawsuit if the defense establishes facts to support the invocation of the rule.

In comparative negligence states, such as New York, the rule is that assumption of risk is no bar to plaintiff's recovery and appears to be equated with contributory negligence. Thus, in New York, if a player assumed the risk or is contributorily negligent, his damage award would be reduced accordingly. For example, a jury awards $200,000 and then finds plaintiff contributorily negligent or that he assumed the risk to the extent of 50 percent. The verdict for plaintiff is thereby reduced by $100,000, and plaintiff receives only $100,000.

When the Colgate University Case was decided in 1972, the jurors were all middle-aged. Today eighteen-year-olds serve as jurors and possess different views of contact sports than the older generation; they will tend to be more demanding and tougher on coaches because of their social views.

Use Players' Playbooks

You should be able to demonstrate with hard evidence that you have the safety of your players in mind. You can do this by keeping books and records of your practice schedules. They should reflect your input to your assistant coaches and players and emphasize teaching safe techniques and observing guidelines of your profession. Your players' playbooks should contain admonitions and warnings regarding player safety. Do your records reflect that violators of your rules have been removed from practice or games or drills?

Can you imagine if you testify and your lawyer introduces into evidence your records kept in the ordinary course of business for the year the injury took place?

Page after page of daily practice schedules contain and emphasize to you and your assistants admonitions, warnings, and demands for enforcement of sound techniques, dangers of noncompliance, instructions to remove noncomplying players, notes as to violators, and your disposition of these cases. This as evidence goes into the jury room—need I say more?

Can your players who testify as witnesses withstand a rigorous cross exam on whether they were repeatedly taught about safe techniques, whether the violators were reprimanded, whether you demonstrated continuous and comprehensive efforts to guard against the known dangers to your players? You will be judged against this background.

Two recent court decisions illustrate the newest phenomena in sports—player-against-player personal-injury litigation. A willful, deliberate, and/or reckless violation of a player-safety rule resulting in injuries to a participant is now legal grounds for the injured player to sue the wrongdoer. You must teach and emphasize safety rules of football and avoid any direct or indirect incitement, encouragement, or approval of conduct in violation of these rules. Otherwise, you may subject yourself to legal cross claims by the wrongdoer who alleges that the coach taught or condoned this type of conduct. (*Hackbart v. Cincinnati Bengals, Inc., and Charles "Booby" Clark,* 1979, and *Nobozny v. Barnhill,* 1975.)

In conclusion—two points:

The courts look very hard at the expense or time that would have been involved in preventing a sports injury. If they find that the time or effort to prevent a serious injury was so minimal and the chance of injury severe, you will be treated harshly both by juries and the courts when a severe injury occurs.

Lastly, the high school coaches look to the college coach for innovative thinking on the tactics and strategy of football. Please do not fail them by neglecting to show them how they can be creative in the area of player safety.

49
All But Ten

(From 1975 Summer Manual of the AFCA)

CHUCK MILLS Head Coach, Wake Forest University

The football coach, losing all but one game, was asked after the season how his team fared. "We won all but ten," was his reply. This may be the only way to approach the heartaches of losing.

After a number of years of winning, things turn around. It is a traumatic experience and one that instigates much soul searching. Year after year, we hear lectures, read articles, and purchase books on the "secrets of winning." But what about losing—how do we cope with that? It may not be newsworthy, it may not be worth a book, but it is real and for some it must be lived with.

The following thoughts are just that—thoughts. It isn't an answer nor is it all-inclusive. It won't thread victory from defeat. What follows are just considerations while enduring losing.

Though the thrust of this chapter is not concerned with the "whys" of losing, only the fact that losing is taking place and must be lived with. A certain evaluation of conditions contributing to the situation must be taken into account so that positive action can be formulated.

Losing Considerations

It is important to be as objective as one can be when involved in a stress situation. The reasons for not having success are varied—some can stand by themselves, some in combination with others. Injuries can decimate a team. A team may be exceptionally young and the lack of experience deprives them of success. Then when a team is ready to win, they may be so conditioned to losing that success escapes.

It may be best to use success as a checkpoint. To win takes a number of things, not all of equal importance, but in various degrees all are involved. Winning consistently comprises scheduling (both whom and the order), athletes (capable of the competition and in sufficient numbers), resources (the finances, admissions, curriculum, and the academic uniformity to allow equitable competition), and coaching. These are the four major concerns and are listed, quite possibly, in the proper order.

Defects of Our Virtues

"Defects of our virtues" is an oft-used term and applies well to winning and losing. The things that often are given credit for victory are also given the blame for defeat. An example is the team that rarely scrimmages during the season and is successful. While winning, it will be said, "We're winning because we don't hit and are fresh on Saturday." As soon as success departs, then it is often heard, "We don't scrimmage enough." And it usually will begin with those forced to endure—the players.

One of the essential disciplines a staff must exercise is evaluation and planning as the season progresses. When things aren't going as you wish, there doing. Evaluation is in order and changes possibly should be made, but exercise caution. The changes should be based on sound conclusions and not looking for a panacea. It is easily communicated to the players when the coaches are panicky or groping.

Offense, defense, practice routines, and personnel are all part of evaluation. Change may be in order, but not for the sake of change alone.

Reinforcement

When a team isn't winning, a fundamental psychological factor prevails, and this factor permeates fans, players, and, often times, the coaches. The factor is negative reinforcement as opposed to positive reinforcement. One is compatible to winning, the other to losing. Either reinforcement makes a tangible contribution to success or failure.

When winning, it is supportive, "We are winning because . . ."; when losing it is, "We are losing because . . ." Whatever the situation, this type of reinforcement tends to perpetuate the winning or losing.

Another way to say it, win or lose, is second guessing. Second guessing, if nurtured and dwelled on, becomes reinforcement for plus or minus. Among the first to second guess are the team members themselves, closely followed by coaches. This is a difficult situation because evaluation and second guessing are related but not synonymous. What must be kept in mind is that reinforcement can affect team performance.

Enduring

In losing, many avenues of support desert the loser or are eroded. In the final judgment, people can withdraw support and ignore the losing team. But, the players and coaches must endure. They can't withdraw and ignore the team, and this is the most subtle aspect of the losing syndrome to thwart. The individual may want to escape the situation but can't. It is in the conscious thinking, but kept suppressed by the participant.

Attempting to control this is a major encounter for the coach. He must not fall victim to the "enduring syndrome," and his effort to counter it is difficult. It is difficult because the coach is expected to assume a certain stance, and this stance is considered routine. When a coach attempts sincerely to influence this attitude, it is considered "coach talk." But, the problem must be faced.

If the reinforcement and enduring factors aren't dealt with, then they will devour the team and block the data for success.

Urgency

In losing, two things seem to occur—more than the usual attrition takes place, some choosing not to endure, and there will be an increase in injuries with a slower response or return to action from treatment. There is little to be done about the former, and the latter is somewhat a mystery. The injured are seldom intentionally malingering; it would seem there are psychological effects that influence physical healing. Simply, in losing there is less desire and urgency to return to be a part of the team. Urgency is a two-edged sword. For the winning team, the urgency is on the part of the player who wants to take his place and make his contribution to victory. Down deep, he wants the team to feel it will be easier to win with him. His ego deems it important that he take his place and receive his just dues for his role in the team's success.

Urgency for a losing team is more in the coaches' thoughts. They want their best players back as soon as possible in the hope of securing a win. If not careful, in their anxiety to win, coaches may press a player into action prematurely; in their desire to avoid defeat, some players may stay out of action longer than they need for recuperation.

Individual Pressure

A most delicate balance that the coach must deal with is the pressure losing exerts on the players and coaches. The coach chooses his profession, and the most direct result of losing is manifested against the coach.

The balance of concern is between that of using the players as scapegoats for losing and the point where they cannot be entirely absolved. There is usually an element of validity to either end of the spectrum, but the extremes aren't final, and in this area, the coach must be most objective.

It is obvious that players must assume responsibilities. They are the frontline in the weekly battle; but if all the pressure of losing is transferred to team members, there will be a minimal effort to win.

A player can be reduced to a point where he won't make any effort. If defeat brings castigation from the coaches and the player's effort doesn't bring subsequent success, he soon withdraws, feeling each effort compounds the situation without reprieve.

Often, a player is told if he tries harder and gives an all-out effort, he will have success; yet he never will make the pleaded-for effort. This can be a defense mechanism on the part of the player. Success has eluded him; he is told that an all-out effort will change this; if he makes the desired effort and fails, then his ego suffers a shattering blow. However, never making such an effort protects him from possible humiliation in his mind.

Team Pressure

Team pressure is oppressive during a winning streak. Each team encountered brings the thought, "Will this be the team to defeat us?" Pressure from winning is the type that gives players motivation and confidence, improved concentration, and pride in performance.

Winning pressure seems to charge adrenaline into the system. Reactions seem acute. Quite possibly the confidence and momentum of winning, plus the fear of losing, brings a sustained effort by the team.

It seems the losing team plays in spurts and lacks

the sustaining power needed for a successful game. Often they begin with a spark, but the first encounter with adversity brings futility.

In losing, the players often look for retreat; they doubt their ability to win and this affects confidence. In a sense, they wait to lose, contrary to the winning team that strives to win, "knowing" something will happen to bring victory. Confidence makes players perform for victory; lack of confidence keeps the losing team from having the confidence to dare or doubt that daring will be successful.

The Media

The media can play a very detrimental role when a team isn't winning. They, too, want success and when it isn't available, they probe for reasons. If they choose, they will grasp any avenue to explore, explain, or exploit the situation. Two major avenues a negative reporter goes after are to get the players to comment in a negative way about the team or program and the other is to get coaches to blame players.

Though it is hoped the athlete will maintain his composure, it can be especially difficult to do so immediately after a game. There can be control on the part of the coaches in blaming players in public. Again, it seems an undue pressure and is not healthy for a young man to assume the burden of defeat in the media.

There are but a few media people who will "kick you when you are down," but they are there. All you can do is not supply them with additional armament.

The Coaches

The one group who must rally the team and themselves as well is the football coaching staff. No matter what happens, they must evaluate what is happening and why it is happening—avoid excessive second guessing and avoid a panic or frustration that spreads to the team. This is more easily said than done. Coaches are a competitive group and the strenuous, unending work can aggravate strained feelings in a difficult situation. Being aware of this won't avoid it, but it does make it more understandable for all.

When things are going wrong, many groups may want out—alumni and fans, administration and faculty, and even the players themselves. The one group that must remain constant, confident, and positive is the football coaching staff.

There are notes of encouragement to build on. They must be sought out, noted, and encouraged. They must be realistic and in perspective, but they are there and a worthy tool.

Best Coaching

Experiencing both victory and defeat, it seems the best coaching jobs are done in losing efforts. But this may well be a misnomer. The coaching in a winning situation is more pleasurable; the combinations fit and work smoothly; morale on the team is high and press, fans, and so on, reinforce the success.

The losing team has the specter of defeat associated with it. Coaches are much more sensitive and defensive. They evaluate what they are doing with a more critical eye and often pass this pressure on to the players as well as to each other.

There is little difference in the time and effort put into a program be it winning or losing. The difference is the mental outlook and psychological atmosphere surrounding each.

Player Control

When losing, the team suffers in many overt ways. For the individual player, it is more personal. His ego is deflated—maybe even attacked.

If not vigilant it can initiate behavioral patterns not in the individual's, the team's, or the program's best interests. When things aren't going right on the football field, it often manifests itself in other ways, such as a loss of interest in academic responsibilities, resulting in a poorer performance in the classroom, or an effort by the player to recapture his "threatened masculinity" by antisocial behavior.

It seems a loss of football pride erodes personal pride. The locker room isn't as neat; the players won't take proper care of their gear, and a general sloppiness exudes from the time they walk into the locker room until they leave it after practice.

Win or Quit

There are very few athletes who will "downright quit." But in the process of a lack of scoreboard achievement over an inordinate period, a different drive will often consume a team. Down deep the players relinquish the thought of winning; but in its place, they may develop a pride and drive to not quit. There is a great difference between trying to win and trying not to lose. In defeat this trait may be among the few positive reinforcements to rally around. When victory comes, and it will, this determination not to surrender can be the rallying point.

There may be alternatives, but there seems to be but two ways to stop losing. It is either to achieve victory or quit. One means to go on and persevere, the other means to cease activity and avoid the possibility of defeat—or victory.

There is one way to avoid all these pitfalls—don't lose!

50
A Coach's Code of Ethics

VINCE DOOLEY Athletic Director/Head Football Coach, University of Georgia, and Chairman of the Ethics Committee, the American Football Coaches Association

It has been said many times that a football coach lives in a fish bowl. His every action is constantly under public scrutiny. Because of this fact, it is of primary importance that the coach be aware of the proper handling of the wide variety of situations he encounters.

Football is more than a century old and over these one hundred or so years, certain standards have been established outlining the ethics of coaching. These standards are under constant review and are updated on a regular basis.

The American Football Coaches Association has a Code of Ethics that covers almost every situation to confront a coach. Its provisions should be reviewed at least once a year by every coach. Those entering the profession should learn the code thoroughly and follow it.

A football coach represents an institution, its students and alumni, his players, fellow coaches, the profession, and himself. He should be aware of this tremendous responsibility and govern all of his actions accordingly.

What follows is not the complete Code of Ethics of the American Football Coaches Association, but portions of it that state the proper way for a coach to act.

Article One

Responsibilities to Players

1. In his relationships with players under his care, the coach should always be aware of the tremendous influence he wields, for good or bad. Parents entrust their dearest possession to the coach's charge, and the coach, through his own example, must always be sure that the boys who have played under him are finer and more decent men for having done so. The coach should never place the value of a win above that of instilling the highest desirable ideals and character traits in his players. The safety and welfare of his players should always be uppermost in his mind, and they must never be sacrificed for any personal prestige or selfish glory.

2. In teaching the game of football, the coach must realize that there are certain rules designed to protect the player and provide common standards for determining a winner and loser. Any attempts to beat these rules, to take unfair advantage of an opponent, or to teach deliberate unsportsmanlike conduct, have no place in the game of football, nor has any coach guilty of such teaching any right to call himself a coach. The coach should set the example for winning without boasting and losing without bitterness. A coach who conducts himself according to these principles need have no fear of failure, for in the final analysis, the success of a coach can be measured in terms of the respect he has earned from his own players and from his opponents.

3. The diagnosis and treatment of injuries is a medical problem and should, under no circumstances, be considered a province of the coach. A coach's responsibility is to see that injured players are given prompt and competent medical attention and that the most minute detail of a physician's orders is carried out.

4. Under no circumstances should a coach authorize the use of drugs. Medicants, stimulants, or drugs should be used only when authorized and supervised by a physician.

5. A player's future should not be jeopardized by any circumvention of eligibility rules.

6. A coach should not make demands on his players that will interfere with the player's opportunities for achieving academic success.

Article Two

Responsibility to the Institution

1. The function of the coach is to educate students through participation in the game of football. This primary and basic function must never be disregarded.

2. A coach shall conduct himself so as to maintain the principles, integrity, and dignity of his institution.

3. A coach should not exert pressure on faculty members to give players consideration they do not deserve.

4. A coach should not exert pressure on admissions office to admit players not qualified.

5. A coach should discuss his problems with his athletic director and/or faculty chairman in a friendly manner and then accept and support the decisions that have been reached.

6. Official student records and transcripts should never pass through the coach's office.

7. The coach should constantly be alert to see his program is being conducted and promoted properly. The coach should lend his experience and training to the governing body of the school's athletic program in the solution of football problems. Where differences of opinion arise, and the council overrides the coach's judgment, discretion should be exercised in airing such differences outside the council meeting.

8. It is highly important that a coach support the administration in all policies, rules, and regulations regarding football.

9. A coach's immediate superior, or superiors, should be notified immediately of a possible position transfer.

Article Three

Rules of the Game

1. The Football Code which appears in the Official Football Rule Book shall be considered an integral part of this Code of Ethics and should be carefully read and observed.

2. Each coach should be acquainted thoroughly with the rules of the game. He is responsible for having the rules taught and interpreted for his players.

3. Both the letter and the spirit of the rules must be adhered to by the coaches.

4. To gain an advantage by circumvention or disregard for the rules brands a coach or player as unfit to be associated with football.

5. A coach is responsible for flagrant roughing tactics. He is responsible for illegal substitutions. He shall not permit faking of injuries in order to stop the clock. He shall not permit an illegal shift with the intent of drawing an opponent offside.

6. A coach must remember always that IT IS NOT the purpose of football to hurt or injure an opponent by legal or illegal methods.

7. **Good Sportsmanship.** Habit formation is developed on the practice field. Where coaches permit, encourage, or condone performance which is dangerous to an opponent, they are derelict in their responsibility to teach fair play and good sportsmanship. This aspect of coaching must be attacked just as vigorously as the teaching of offense and defense, and to the players it is far more important than all the technical aspects of the game combined. Any coach who fails to stress this point, or who permits, encourages, or defends the use of unsportsmanlike tactics shall be considered guilty of the most serious breach of football coaching ethics.

Article Four

Officials

1. No competitive contest can be played satisfactorily without impartial, competent officials. Officials must have the respect and support of coaches and players. On- and off-the-record criticism of officials to players or to the public shall be considered unethical.

2. **Officials Associations.** There should be a cooperative relationship between coaches and officials associations, with frequent interchange of ideas and suggestions. Coaches should, whenever possible, accept invitations to attend officials' rules meetings. Similarly coaches should extend officials invitations to discuss rules interpretations with their squads, and on occasion to officiate at scrimmages, for mutual benefits.

3. **Treatment of Officials.** On the day of a game, officials should be. treated in a courteous manner. They should be provided with a private room in which to meet and dress for the game. Conferences between coaches and officials shall always be conducted according to procedures established by the governing Conference or Officials Association. In every respect the official Rule Book shall be followed in coach-official relationships, on the field and during and following a game. Any criticisms which the coach may have to make concerning officiating should be made in writ-

ing to the office which assigned the official to the game. For a coach to address, or permit anyone on his bench to address, uncomplimentary remarks to any official during the progress of a game, or to indulge in conduct which might incite players or spectators against the officials, is a violation of the rules of the game and must likewise be considered conduct unworthy of a member of the coaching profession.

4. Use of Movies in Checking Officials. It should be recognized that slow motion study of controversial decisions by officials is far different from on-the-spot decisions which must be made during the course of a game. To show critical plays to sportswriters, sportscasters, alumni, and the public, which may incite them to label officials as incompetents, must be considered unethical conduct.

Article Five

Public Relations

1. Members of the news media should be treated with courtesy, honesty, and respect. Derogatory and misleading statements should be avoided. Direct questions should be answered honestly or not at all. If good judgment indicates an honest answer would be prejudicial to the best interests of the game, ethical procedure demands that it not be answered. In such instances, "No comment" is justifiable.

2. Coaches should assume the responsibility of teaching their players how to conduct themselves in interviews in the best interests of football.

3. The Association recommends that the media be admitted to dressing rooms as soon as practicable after games.

4. Coaches should not stress injuries, disciplinary measures, academic difficulties, eligibility problems, and similar personal matters. Disciplinary problems should be a "family affair" to be solved between the coach and players. Scholastic eligibility is a province of the Dean's or Registrar's office. Injuries are essentially the province of the team physician or trainer. No good purpose can be served by emphasizing such matters.

5. Coaches should avoid talking in public about unethical recruiting and use of illegal formations.

6. Any statements that tend to portray football in any light other than being part of the educational process is detrimental to the future of the profession.

7. Falsifying weights is a bad educational process.

8. Coaches should not predict game winners.

9. It shall be unethical for coaches to use alumni, booster, and quarterback club organizations in an attempt to defeat or obstruct institutional athletic controls, or to encourage violation of established rules. It

shall be unethical for coaches to make demands, financial or otherwise, upon such groups which are not in keeping with the letter and spirit of existing controls or in any other manner misuse such strength and power in violation of accepted rules and regulations.

10. Accepting money or goods for endorsement of any product or commodity not in keeping with the traditions of the coaching profession is unethical. It is the coach's responsibility to be certain the wording and sense of any testimonial does not bring discredit. Endorsement, directly or indirectly, by active members of the Association, of alcoholic beverages and/or tobacco products is unethical.

11. Solution of professional problems should be within the profession and not in the press. Newspaper columns and magazine articles over the signature of a coach are his responsibility exclusively.

12. Coaches should not be associated in any way with professional gamblers and should not be present where gambling on team sports is encouraged or permitted.

Article Six

Scouting

1. It is unethical under any circumstances to scout any team, by any means whatsoever, except in regularly scheduled games. The head coach shall be held responsible for all scouting. This includes the use of motion pictures.

2. It is unethical conduct to violate conference rules on the exchange of film.

3. Direct exchange of film is urged by the Association.

Article Seven

Recruiting

1. All institutional, conference, and national regulatory body rules pertaining to recruiting shall be observed strictly.

2. It is a breach of ethics to recruit a player enrolled at another school (or to recruit a prospective freshman who has avowed his intention to enroll at another school and who has taken residence therein) for the purpose of participating in regularly organized fall practice.

3. A student-athlete should not be recruited during his participation in another sport so that he misses, or is late for, practices and games.

4. In discussing the advantages of his institution, the coach must confine his statements to an honest

and forthright presentation of the facts. He shall refrain from making derogatory statements about other institutions and their officials.

5. It is unethical for any coach to make statements to any prospective student which cannot be fulfilled.

Article Eight

Game Day and Other Responsibilities

1. It is vitally important a coach's actions and behavior at all times bring credit to himself, his institution, and the game of football.

2. Before and after game, rival coaches should meet and exchange friendly greetings.

3. During a game a coach should be as inconspicuous as possible. Coaches are encouraged to demonstrate a friendly and kindly attitude toward their players. The attitude of coaches toward officials should be controlled and undemonstrative.

4. After game, visitors should not be permitted in team dressing room until coaches have completed their postgame responsibilities, including a careful check of player injuries.

5. Coaches should use their influence to upgrade levels of sportsmanship by rooting sections by working closely with cheerleaders and leaders of card sections.

6. A coach should do all he can to prevent scalping of tickets by players.

7. A coach shall not receive compensation from professional teams for talent scouting of or negotiating for his players.

Part Eleven
Conditioning and Safety

51

A Coach's Guide to Safe Football

Edited and Prepared by BILL MURRAY, Executive Director, and DICK HERBERT, Director of Public Relations, of the American Football Coaches Association

Football is a contact sport beneficial for its participants when properly conducted. The nature of the game makes injury-free football impossible. Those who play do so at a calculated risk and in the belief that the benefits are worth the risk. The coach should stress the value of participation, which more than offsets the risk of injury. Football is a worthwhile educational experience in the spiritual, mental, and physical development of young men. Players, parents, and the public should be reminded of this by the coach at the proper opportunities.

It is the obligation of the coach to do all he can to reduce the risk factor to its minimum. He assumes a grave responsibility when parents turn over their most prized possessions to him for the period football requires. This responsibility must not be taken lightly.

There are some basic policies and procedures developed over more than a century of experience that should be known to coaches, school officials, parents, and the players. These policies and procedures minimize the risk factor and increase the benefits from participation.

This chapter serves to cover some of the basics in the proper conduct of a football program as it pertains to the physical well-being of the players. Much of the material has been supplied and endorsed by the American Medical Association through its Committee on the Medical Aspects of Sports. This committee worked for a number of years with the National Federation of State High School Associations in assembling material.

Coaches should make a point of attending clinics and seminars that give instruction in the latest developments in the recognition of injuries, first aid, and the safe conduct of football. But the coach should not invade the province of the team physician or trainer.

The American Football Coaches Association recommends that each coach seeking more detailed coverage of the problems obtain a copy of the American Medical Association's book "Comments in Sports Medicine." The AMA's address: 535 N. Dearborn Street, Chicago, Illinois 60610.

Medical History and Evaluation

A mandatory medical evaluation and a medical history of each athlete must be taken prior to each season if that athlete is to be allowed to participate in any football activity. The complete medical history and medical examination should be on file with proper school authorities where it is readily available if needed. A physician should give written permission for a player to return to practice and competition after serious injury, especially if there has been a head injury.

In the preseason physical, the American Medical Association suggests that the examining physician should be concerned with the following kinds of problems in his evaluation: absent organs, acute infections, bleeding tendencies, convulsive disorders, hypertension, physical immaturity, previous injury, previous surgery, diabetes, emphysema and asthma, enlarged liver, heart disease, renal disease, severe myopia, structural abnormalities, hernia, artificial limbs, and anemic disorders in racial groups (that is, sickle cell anemia in black athletes).

If, in the physician's judgment, the athlete should not participate in football, the parents and the coach should readily abide by his decision.

Whenever possible, a physician should be at the field of play during games and readily available or on call during practices. When this is not possible, arrangements must be made in advance to obtain a physician's immediate service should an emergency arise. Each institution should have a team trainer who is a regular member of the staff and is qualified in treating and preventing injuries.

Each institution fielding a football team must subscribe to an athletic injury insurance program. An excellent source for information on athletic injury insurance is the American Medical Association's Council on Medical Services, Chicago, Illinois. A suggested health or medical examination form also is available there.

The most desirable plan for examinations and attendance of physicians at practices and games is for local school officials to work with their local medical and dental societies and determine mutually acceptable policies and procedures.

Immunization

It is important to know and consider the immunization status of your athletes. An outbreak of any one of the communicable diseases that are preventable with adequate immunization can debilitate your team almost overnight.

The American Medical Association recommends that players be protected against poliomyelitis, tetanus, diphtheria, and advisedly against measles—German measles and possibly mumps if they have not acquired immunity from having had the disease and/or by having had preventive immunizations. Small pox, typhoid, and yellow fever immunization are important for athletes who participate or may participate in regions where these diseases remain endemic. Flu shots may be advisable.

Immunization time is crucial. It should be provided, says the AMA, for the unprotected in order to allow for development of preventive antibodies. Since the effectiveness of certain immunizations may weaken with time (for example, tetanus and diphtheria) repeated booster doses are recommended to maintain lifelong protection. A booster shot for tetanus every ten years is adequate unless there is a puncture wound and then a tetanus booster is needed only if it has been longer than ten years.

Improving Your Medical and Training Facilities and Personnel

Many high schools find it difficult to obtain recommended medical examinations, training facilities, and personnel, mostly because of finances. The coach and school administrators should explore every avenue to satisfy the needs. Assistance from a city, county, or state often is possible if sought properly.

North Carolina and Massachusetts have begun programs on a state level. Indiana is working on a similar proposal. Surveys in these states cited the drastic need for upgrading the student health care.

In North Carolina, the Sports Medicine Division was established in the State Department of Public Instruction in 1972. Al Proctor, Ph.D., formerly head trainer at North Carolina State University, was employed to head the program and began with a modest budget of $22,500. He traveled all over the state conducting workshops, which involved 130 physicians and were attended by 950 coaches and teachers. The results were so favorable that the state increased the budget to $60,000, and another prominent trainer was added to the staff.

Three medical colleges in the state are strengthening their curricula on sports medicine, two of the state universities have established undergraduate courses for trainers, and one university has a graduate curriculum.

The university television system of eight stations conducts courses for trainers, and TV spots have been used to encourage high school football players to participate in preseason conditioning. Community colleges, extension services, state and local medical societies, emergency rescue crews, and ambulance teams have been asked for their assistance.

The program believes that having a member of the faculty trained in paramedical help through these available clinics and courses is the best answer to the problem.

The Massachusetts program is a joint effort of the State Department of Public Health and Department of Education and the Berkshire Sports Medicine Institute, Inc. This program centers on training faculty personnel through a series of courses that include 120 hours a summer for three summers. The results have been very encouraging. Extensive surveys were made in Massachusetts, sponsored jointly by the Berkshire Institute and the Johnson & Johnson Company, which revealed the acute need for the program.

Facilities

It is the obligation of the coach to make certain his practice and game areas have met all basic safety requirements before he begins practice or a game.

The most important facility for safe football is the field. It should be free of all hazards, such as rocks, obstructions, holes, glass, and any equipment that could cause injury. Curbing, benches, fences, and hard surfaces should be safe distances from the playing area. Goal posts always should be padded adequately. Tables, chairs, and other obstructions should be at least fifteen feet from the sidelines.

Do not permit vehicles—bicycles, automobiles, and so on—to park within 50 feet of the playing area.

Keep spectators a safe distance from sidelines.

Make certain there are no high voltage wires or open electrical boxes close to the field or practice area. A convenient way to rid the field of rocks and other debris is to line your squad across the end zone line and march it in a line the length of the field, picking up any foreign object and calling attention to holes.

Keep dust at a minimum by lightly wetting down the field before practice. Make certain all sprinklers are removed afterward.

Make certain all dummies, sleds, and other field equipment are in workable and safe condition. Pay particular attention to any part of a sled that needs padding. Make certain all equipment is placed so it will not be a hazard.

Make certain field is marked with a nonirritating substance. Do not use unslaked lime!

Have clean, well-organized locker rooms and demand that the players keep them that way. Do not allow any horseplay. Don't lose players from locker room injuries.

Operators of down markers and 10-yard chains should be trained in how to handle equipment to avoid injuries.

Transportation and Traffic

School officials should adopt safe rules and policies for travel for athletic teams.

There also could be danger in the movement of players from dressing rooms to practice fields. Players should be cautioned about traffic hazards and how best to avoid them.

In transporting teams, commercial vehicles and adult drivers should be used whenever possible. If pupils have to be used, select only those with reputations for safe driving and cars free from defects.

Insist that members of the team go as a team and return as a team.

Do not tolerate horseplay on a team conveyance. It could lead to injury.

First Aid and Emergency Procedures

The American Football Coaches Association strongly recommends that a physician be present for all games and at practice when possible. It knows, however, this is not always possible. If a physician is not present, there should be clearcut arrangements to reach immediately a designated physician or medical facility in case of emergency.

First Aid

There should be someone on the practice field at all times, who has emergency medical training. He should also have received special lectures on specific injuries incurred in football, including recognition and treatment of heat exhaustion and sunstroke, head and knee injuries, diabetic shock, epilepsy, and moving an injured player.

Communications System

A nonpay telephone with a direct outside line should be available at all times at the field or field facility so that a physician or ambulance can be called if necessary. The use of two-way radio is advised. Local citizen bands or amateur radio receivers could be enlisted for this purpose, since the phone could be in use or out of order.

Quality Emergency Care Facilities

A definite hospital capable of handling trauma cases (not necessarily the nearest hospital) should be designated and available at all times. Notification should be by radio whenever possible.

Notification

The facility to which the injured player is being transported should be informed of the player's condition as part of the emergency care so that the necessary personnel and equipment will be available when the player arrives.

Transportation

Emergency vehicles, staffed by emergency technicians and equipped to provide all necessary life support at the scene and during transportation, should be on immediate call.

The Training Room

A training room is of little value without the proper equipment. The American Medical Association recommends the following basic items, which should be in supply at all times:

Applicators (swabs)	Felt (wool, regular, and adhesive)
Artificial airway	
Blankets	Fire extinguishers (dry powder or carbon dioxide types)
Bulletin board and blackboard	
Cleat wrenches	Gauze pads (sterile— 4″ × 4″)
Clippers or razors	
Clock	Gauze rolls (2″) for ankles and dressings
Crutches (adjustable)	
Drinking cups (disposable)	Heel cups for bruised heels
Eye patches	Ice (for cold applications)

Mouthwash
Nail cutters (toe- and fingernail)
Ointment (analgesic)
Ointment (antiglare)
Ointment (lubricating)
Powder for minor chafing
Protective pads (miscellaneous sizes)
Resin
Rubbing oil (massage)
Safety pins
Salt tables (enteric coated) and dispenser
Scales
Scalpel
Scissors (for bandage and dressing purposes)
Sink with hot and cold water
Skin adherent for taping
Slings (triangular bandages)
Soap

Spine boards (short and long)
Splints (regular and inflatable)
Stockinettes
Suction cup for removing corneal contact lenses
Tables (taping 24″ W × 72″ L × 32–34H)
Tape (adhesive, various widths and grades, including 2″)
Tape cutters
Tape removers
Thermometer (oral)
Tongue depressors
Tongue forceps
Towels (paper and cotton)
Tracheotomy tube
Water dispenser
Weight charts
Wraps (elastic and nonelastic)

In addition many training rooms have other equipment for the treatment of injuries. Such equipment as heat lamps, whirlpool baths, diathermy machines, and so on should be chosen and used with the help and advice of physicians and established trainers.

Any electrical equipment, particularly whirlpool baths, should be properly grounded before use.

Cleanliness—It Prevents Infections

To avoid infections, cleanliness should be stressed in all areas of football. Properly cleaned equipment should always be worn, especially socks, T-shirts, and athletic supporters. Players should be warned against exchanging this equipment. There should be adequate and clean showers and toilets. The training room should be cleaned daily. When equipment is not in use, it should be kept clean and properly stored.

If possible, at the end of each practice have each player put his socks, supporter, and T-shirt into a fish-net laundry bag, pin the bag so that articles will not fall out, and turn it in to the manager. The bags may be washed and dried as they are and returned to the players.

Avoid using a common towel during timeouts, and also avoid the common drinking cup. A squeeze bottle for water, with the proper dispenser, is a recommended device.

The American Medical Association says, "Foot baths or other efforts to sterilize feet, shoes, or socks

are useless and may be even harmful. This is also true of attempts to disinfect floors in and around showers with strong chemicals. The use of soap and water at frequent intervals should replace such efforts."

To avoid foot infections:
1. Dry feet thoroughly, particularly between toes.
2. In hot weather wear perforated or ventilated shoes.
3. Change socks frequently. Talcum sprinkled on feet and between toes helps to keep them dry and free of cracks and fissures that might act as a portal of entry of infection.

To avoid jockey itch:
1. Keep area dry.
2. Wear nonconstricting underclothing.
3. Use an antifungal powder.

To avoid blisters:
1. Have shoes fitted properly.
2. Have preseason issue of shoes for gradual break-in.
3. Wear two pairs of socks—sweat socks with lightweights under them.
4. Use lubricating jelly over possible friction area and cover with gauze pad.
5. Tape and wrap carefully over gauze.

Playing Equipment

There are all kinds of ideas about football equipment. It is difficult to suggest that certain equipment is safer than others. When parents and players buy the equipment, the following guidelines should be followed:
1. Deal with reputable sporting goods manufacturers and representatives.
2. Buy the best available.
3. The equipment must be fitted properly.
4. Old and worn equipment must be renovated properly or discarded. Do not use old, worn-out equipment.
5. In buying shoes, make certain the cleats conform to the standards set forth in the Rule Book. Molded soles also are recommended by many who have studied the football shoe.

Equipment should be maintained conscientiously and checked periodically for continued proper fit and absence of acquired defects. Equipment should be worn at all appropriate times, practice or games. Frequent laundering of athletic apparel will extend the life of the material and decrease the chance of infection.

All pads should incorporate shock absorbing material and cover the intended area properly. Shoulder pads should protect the clavicle and deltoid muscle. Hip pads can best protect the pelvic rim if independent from the pants, joining the sacral-coccyx portion on a one-piece belt. The fit of the pants must assure effective positioning of the thigh and knee pads.

All mouth protectors should be constructed under the supervision of dentists to insure a properly fitted protector and a complete program of education concerning its use. All protectors should be examined regularly for possible breaks. A rigid plan of hygiene concerning protectors should be taught and carried out.

Fitting the helmet and shoulder pads properly is complicated and should be done by a person who has some training.

Rules pertaining to equipment should be observed to the letter.

It should always be remembered that a helmet is for protection and not for making the head a battering ram.

All helmets bought should meet the standards that became mandatory with the 1978 season.

The coach should see to it that his players are equipped with and use proper helmets, mouth protectors, athletic supporters, shoulder pads, hip and thigh pads, knee pads, and shoes.

The mouth protector is mandatory, and the coach should stress to his players that the protectors must be worn and not merely fastened to the helmet.

To reduce the incident of injury to the shoulder girdle and upper arm, a tight jersey of porous cloth should be worn.

Basic Health Habits

A well-nourished, healthy athlete is less likely to suffer injury or illness. He also will recover from injury or illness earlier and with fewer complications.

A wholesome, well-balanced diet is necessary for the athlete and for the non-athlete. An athlete's diet should be the same as for any normal, healthy individual. Since an athlete burns more energy, he needs more calories, but it is not necessary to supplement a well-balanced diet with dietary supplements or any of the so-called "wonder fuel foods." A "more than adequate diet" is a waste at best and unhealthy at worst and does not facilitate athletic performance.

The best diet for an athlete is composed of a wide variety of good foods. There is no magic pill, wonder food, or sure-fire nutritional formula that can add anything to this optimal nutrition state.

There is no basis for the contention that excess protein aids an athlete. The body does not store protein. Therefore excess protein does not increase strength. Protein is not an efficient energy food.

A proper diet ensures enough of all vitamins. Excessive quantities of any vitamin serve no nutritional purpose and could be harmful.

During your sports season, eliminate fried foods, spiced foods, rich desserts, and heavy fats. Eat at regular times. It is best not to eat immediately before or after practice or a game.

The pregame meal traditionally is at least three hours before the kickoff. Some athletes who have difficulty eating before a game would be better off having a liquid meal.

The American Medical Association says the traditional pregame steak meal does not serve its intended purpose of providing extra energy. The reserves of energy are established by the foods eaten several days before.

Carbohydrates are the primary source of energy. If carbohydrate stores are replenished two or three days prior to an athletic performance, maximum use can be made of this nutrient to maximize performance, provided endurance activity is avoided twenty-four hours before the athletic event. But eating a candy bar just before game time is futile, since the carbohydrate cannot be assimilated in the body in such a short time.

The American Medical Association recommends four or more servings daily of enriched or restored bread or cereal; milk unless contraindicated, part of which may be replaced by cheese or ice cream; two or more servings of meat daily (beef, veal, pork, lamb, poultry), fish, eggs with dry beans, peas, and nuts as alternates; and four or more servings daily from the vegetable-fruit group (citrus fruits, other fruits and vegetables, including potatoes and at least each alternate day a deep green or deep yellow vegetable). Athletes with individual problems, such as a high cholesterol level, should use the diets prescribed by their physicians.

It is imperative that athletes abstain from alcohol, tobacco, and drugs. An athlete should make, at an early age, a firm commitment that he will not use alcohol, tobacco, or drugs if he is to improve his chances for success. If he continues to abstain, he will live longer, have fewer illnesses, feel better, and generally have a more productive and fruitful life.

"The use of amphetamines to improve athletic performance is inconsistent with the practice and ideals of sportsmanship, and since their repeated use may be associated with harmful effects, the AMA Committee on the Medical Aspects of Sports strongly condemns the prescription of these drugs for this purpose by physicians or their administration or use in athletics by coaches, trainers or participants."

Use of androgenic-anabolic steroids for the intent of gaining weight are categorically condemned for the athlete. Their hazards—although more subtle than those associated with pep pills—are as serious.

Observing habits of personal cleanliness and proper rest is necessary. Daily bathing and clean clothing will protect against germs that cause disease. Immediate attention to cuts, blisters, and bruises prevents infection. Adequate sleep is necessary for the highest level of physical and mental efficiency and allows the body to repair damaged tissue and restore the energy needed for the demands of the day.

Heat Problems

Each coach should know the latest recommended procedures for conducting practice in hot and humid weather, especially at the start of fall drills. There is no excuse for not knowing the latest recommendations of medical experts.

The American Medical Association says:

At the start of fall practice, gradual acclimation to hot weather activity is essential. Equally important is the need to adjust salt and water intake to weather conditions. This acclimation can take place over a period of a week.

As an athlete becomes accustomed to hot weather activity, he perspires more freely (thus dissipating body heat) and excretes less salt (thus conserving sodium).

The old idea of withholding water is dangerous. During exercise in heat, it is essential to replace water lost by perspiration. This could be as often as every twenty minutes, in extreme cases.

Salt must be replaced daily, especially during the acclimation period. Extra salting of food will accomplish this purpose.

It is advisable to alternate periods of strenuous exercise with periods of rest.

Symptoms of water and salt depletion may include sluggishness, headache, nausea, hallucinations, and weak and rapid pulse. The coach should watch for signs of lethargy, inattention, stupor, awkwardness, or unusual fatigue.

If illness is suspected, prompt attention to recommended emergency procedures is vital.

The AMA offers the following suggestions to help coaches prevent heat exhaustion and heat stroke during hot-weather activity:

1. Schedule workouts during cooler morning and early evening hours.

2. Acclimate athletes with carefully graduated practice schedules.

3. Provide rest periods of ten to twenty minutes during workouts of an hour or more.

4. Supply clothing that is white to reflect heat, comfortable to permit heat escape, and permeable to moisture to allow heat loss via sweat evaporation.

5. Provide water or electrolyte solution for players to use ad lib or on demand every twenty minutes. Ice can also be used freely. If adequate water is furnished on demand you will probably not have to contend with the problems of heat exhaustion or sun stroke to athletes.

6. Watch athletes carefully for signs of trouble, particularly those who lose much weight, heavy athletes, and determined athletes who may not report their discomfort.

7. Remember that temperature and humidity are the crucial factors. Measuring the relative humidity, by the use of a sling psychrometer on the field, is recommended. Heat exhaustion and heat stroke can occur in the shade.

8. Alert the hospital emergency room medical and nursing staff of the possibility of heat illness before an emergency occurs so that they are prepared to take care of a stricken athlete.

9. Know what to do in such an emergency. Be familiar with immediate first aid practices and prearranged procedures for obtaining immediate medical care, including ambulance service.

10. Outlaw the hazardous warm weather use of rubberized apparel or other dehydration devices by players.

Practice Organization

Careful planning of practice sessions is not only an efficient way to prepare for a successful season or game but will also help to prevent and reduce injuries.

The Schedule

All activities should be placed on a time basis, preferably of short duration, so that every item will be covered, including breaks for rest and replacement of liquids. The responsibility of announcing changes should be placed in the hands of a manager or trainer so that the active coach will not forget the time changes.

The Warm-up

The warm-up is very important, as a safety measure, and all practices should be preceded by a vigorous and beneficial warm-up period. Recommended exercises are described elsewhere.

Separation for Practice

All group and individual work should receive careful placement as to area of practice. Needless injuries can be prevented by seeing that group work occurs far enough from other groups so as to prevent players from accidentally colliding with each other.

Matching by Weight and Age

Although it is difficult to match players properly in football practice and games, the coach should make every effort to see that players are not severely mismatched. Injuries are more apt to occur when heavier and more mature players are matched against obviously lighter and younger opponents.

Hot and Humid

When it has been decided that unusual hot and humid conditions are a problem, reduce activity and increase rest. (See Heat Problems for details.)

Rules and Regulations

Be sure that rules for carrying on all practice activities are understood by all coaches and players and are rigidly adhered to. Your players, trainers, managers, and coaches should be so disciplined that they would never leave helmets or other unused playing equipment, water containers, first-aid kits, blankets, and so on, in an unsafe place.

Nonparticipants

Be sure that nonparticipants are clear of all practice areas and that seats and extraneous nonparticipant gear is out of the way.

Field Equipment

Never begin practice until all practice gear and any other dangerous material is removed from the practice area. This includes sleds, dummies, first-aid cases, water containers, unused equipment, such as helmets and shoulder pads.

Disability

Remove participant from practice when disability is evident.

Warm-up Exercises

A good warm-up program carries these trademarks:

1. It has active general conditioning exercises, especially for events requiring substantial strength, power, speed, and endurance.

2. It has specific exercises for events with a considerable skill component.

3. Flexibility exercises are incorporated to decrease the viscosity of the muscle.

4. The warm-up should develop gradually but be sufficiently vigorous to develop perspiration.

A number of warm-up exercises are shown. Also see Flexibility Exercises and Exercises for the Neck.

Side Straddle Hop. Stand at attention. Swing arms over head while simultaneously moving feet sideward in a single jumping motion. Then spring back to the starting position. Continue for one minute.

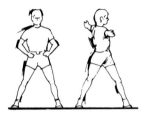

Trunk Twister. Stand with hands on hips, feet apart. Without moving your feet, twist body as far to the left and as far to the right as possible. Repeat vigorously for one minute.

Alternate Toe Touch. Stand with hands on hips, feet apart. Keeping legs straight, bend and touch right foot with left hand. Return to original position. Bend and touch left foot with right hand. Repeat for one minute.

Push-ups. Keep the hands slightly outside the shoulders, fingers pointed straight forward, arms straight, body perfectly straight. Without raising your rear end or letting the stomach sag, bend elbows and touch chest to floor. Then return to original position.

Bouncing Ball. Take push-up position. Bounce up and down. Try clapping hands together while body is in air.

Preparing for Football

Youngsters who wish to participate in football or participants who wish to be better prepared to play should be advised of measures that can improve their chances to be better players and also to make football safer for them. These drills are offered only as suggested courses of action, and the well-trained coach will have other exercises that may prove to be just as effective.

Special Neck Strengthening Exercises

A combination of isometric and isotonic exercises will add strength to your neck, safely.

Get ready by rotating your neck in half circles, alternating direction after several circles.

Use **isometric** pressure in these four positions, for six seconds each.

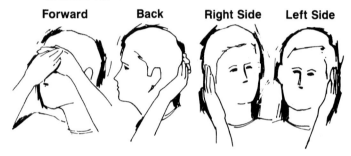

Forward   Back   Right Side   Left Side

Isometric is a static exercise where you push against your hand with complete resistance—no motion.

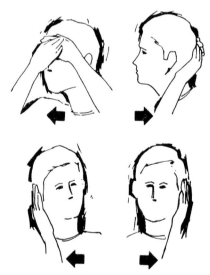

Flex your neck in half circles again and then use *isotonic* pressure in the same four positions, this time yielding to the pressure. For the forward movement, put your hands on your forehead and resist strongly while slowly letting your head move forward and back to the upright position. Use the same slow overcoming of resistance for the other three movements, each taking about six to eight seconds.

Close out your exercise by flexing your neck again in half circles.

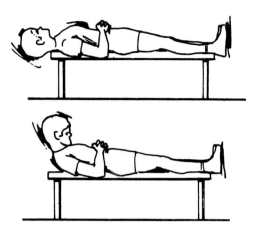

Lifting Head. Lie flat on back on table with head over end, raise head and place chin on chest, repeat twenty to fifty times. Then lie on stomach and raise head as far back as possible for same number of repetitions.

Isometric and Weight Training to Build Strength

When you are trying primarily to gain strength, isometric or "static" exercises along with calisthenics will pay big dividends.

To do static exercise, you merely push, pull, press, or lift against an object that does not move. Each exercise is done for only six seconds, but with an all-out effort!

To add stamina and strength to your body, try weight training—working out with barbells.

But! You must know what you're doing! Get the advice of someone who knows his weights. Have him recommend the weights to start with depending on your age and build.

The average teenager can start with about thirty pound of weights. Use a light weight at the start and go up, rather than begin with a heavy weight and go down. If you feel pleasantly tired rather than completely bushed at the end of your workout, you're probably using the proper weight for you.

Besides using the proper weights with the proper form, you must work out regularly to get any benefit out of weight training. That doesn't mean working out every day. The best plan is to work out on alternate days—Monday, Wednesday, and Friday. Never work out with weights two days in a row, and never work out before going out to play a game.

Before you begin your workout, loosen up your body with about 5 minutes of light exercises—sit-ups, pull-ups, stretching, bending, and the use of light weights. Before actually lifting, check that collars on bars are secure. Always have a spotter on hand for weights lifted with two hands, especially for the bench press exercises.

It is very important in weight exercising to watch your form. Work smoothly and in rhythm. Breathe deeply and naturally while performing the exercise. For most exercises, you breathe out during the stress part of the action and breathe in while returning the weight to the starting position. Do not hold breath.

Biceps Curls. Grasp barbell shoulder-width apart, with palms forward. Stand erect with elbows slightly bent. Now bend your elbows (no other motion) and bring barbell upward to shoulders. Then carry barbell back to starting position under control.

Forearm Curl. This is the same exercise except you grip barbell so palms face body. This reverse grip makes it work more on the forearms than biceps.

Squats. Stand erect with feet well apart, toes pointed forward, feet flat on ground, barbell across shoulders behind neck (use wider grip than for presses). Keeping back straight, go into a half squat, then return. Never go all the way down. You can put a chair behind you to prevent squatting too far.

Dead Lifts. Standing with feet apart, bend knees and reach down for barbell. Grasp it with ordinary hook grip about shoulder-width apart. Now straighten up to standing position and repeat. Remember, **always** bend your knees when picking up the weight or putting it down.

Toe Raiser. Take bar to rest position in front of chest. Rise on toes as high as you can, hold for an instant, then lower heels to ground. Great for the legs.

Quickness Builders

A saying often heard in modern football is, "The race is not always to the swift . . . but it is often to the quick." Flat-out speed, except by certain players in certain situations, is not the most important factor in today's game, since the majority of plays begin and end within only a 10- to 20-yard area of the field. Quickness and agility are the prime requisites needed to play modern football well. No coach will pass up a player with good foot speed, of course, but often the player who reacts instantly and correctly is the one who gets the job done. Quickness off the ball both offensively and defensively; "running to daylight" when that daylight suddenly appears; ability to recover from blocks and fakes quickly and to produce the second effort—these are some of the hallmarks of a winning player.

Here are some excellent drills a player can do to establish good habits of quickness and agility. Some you may do alone, others may be done with a partner:

1. Rope skipping. Do this frequently. Skip for one or two minutes, rest, repeat.
2. Forward Roll and Sprint. Sprint 10 yards, do a front somersault, come up running and repeat.
3. Jogging. Jog forward, backward, and sideward. Jog and break at a 45-degree angle. Jog and pivot.
4. Wave Drill (from standing position). React to another man's movements—right, left, forward, backward.
5. Wave Drill (from four-point position). Do as the above activity only follow from a four-point stance.
6. Lateral Movement. Two men face each other with a line between them. On the starting count they race each other down the line sideways.
7. Snoop. Two men from a standing position attempt to grab the back of each other's knee. One point is scored for each time one of the contestants touches the other players behind the knee. Play games to five points.
8. Shadow Drill. Two men face one another in a 5-yard area. One contestant uses evasive action to get past the other man without contact.

Improving Speed

These pointers to improve speed on the football field are not necessarily for those in the varsity sprinter class. They will help the boy whose running form (and consequently running speed) leaves something to be desired. They can especially help the bulky player who often must race downfield under kickoffs and punts, as well as other down- and cross-field coverages. All players, both the fast and the slow, may check their form against the following pointers:

1. Innate muscle fiber speed cannot be improved; however, more of the fiber can be put to work by relaxation and perfect skills in the application of force.

2. The first step in sprinting is an explosive, hard-driving step, and more force is applied on each subsequent step. The body lean at the start is forward then upward.

3. The toes are always straight ahead and the knees are lifted high with the large muscles at the front of the thighs (quadriceps).

4. Look for full drive extension of the rear leg so that there is a straight line from the hip to the toe. In order to accomplish this, you should strengthen the calf muscle through weight training and isometrics.

5. Keep the shoulders square so that the arms do not rotate the shoulders or the hips.

6. For relaxation, place the thumb over the forefinger; tight fists slow you down.

7. The arms are swung vigorously so that the hands come up as high as the chin and no farther than the hips in the back swing. This keeps the arms relaxed and creates a faster rhythm for the arms and legs.

8. The neck should remain relaxed and the eyes should be focused straight ahead. Any attempt to look over your shoulder will shorten your stride and will create loss of speed.

9. Breathing should be normal—inhaling and exhaling through the mouth.

Flexibility Exercises

Flexibility is a specific to each joint and the ligaments, tendons, and muscles.

The stretching process has to be done gradually, stretching the muscle beyond its resting length, holding the position of maximum stretch pain for several seconds, returning the muscle to resting length, and repeating the process. Don't stretch too hard or too fast. Build a daily program designed for gradual progression.

Do each exercise shown through a full range of motion to a count of 12. From 1 to 6 move smoothly from starting position to full extension. From 7 to 12 hold the position while trying to stretch even farther.

Grab Ankles. *(Hamstring—Lower Back).* Standing position—legs straight. Pull chin to knees. Place hands back of ankles.

Split *(Hamstring—Groin).* Standing position. Spread legs slowly, going out as far as possible.

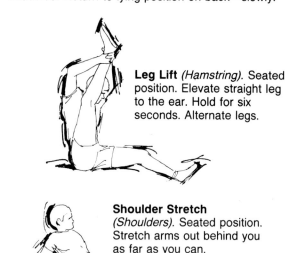

Legs-over Split *(Hips—Abdomen—Shoulders and Groin).* Lying on back—fully extended hips. Pull legs over the head and touch toes to floor. Keep legs straddled. Return to lying position on back—slowly.

Leg Lift *(Hamstring).* Seated position. Elevate straight leg to the ear. Hold for six seconds. Alternate legs.

Shoulder Stretch *(Shoulders).* Seated position. Stretch arms out behind you as far as you can.

Kneel Stretch *(Thighs).* Kneeling position. Put hands on buttocks, push hips forward and arch the back. Slowly lean back head and shoulders as far as possible.

Legs Over *(Hips—Abdomen—Shoulders).* Lying on back—fully extended hips. Pull legs over the head and touch toes to floor. Keep legs straight. Return to lying position on back—slowly.

Windmill *(Hamstring—Groin—Hips).* Lying on back. Touch toes to hand with arms extended to side. Alternate.

Leg "V" *(Hamstring—Groin—Shoulders).* Seated position. Legs straddled and straight. Place hands back of ankle. Slowly pull chin to knee. Alternate legs.

Wishbone *(Groin).* Seated position. Pull feet to crotch. Place hands on knees. Push slowly downward.

Wide Straddle *(Middle).* Seated position. Legs straddled and straight. Slowly put chin to floor.

Cradle *(Shoulders—Back—Quads—Knees).* Prone position—grasp ankles with hands—pause eight seconds and return.

Belly Rock *(Shoulders—Back—Quads).* Prone lying position. Raise both arms and legs. Rock on abdomen by lowering chest as legs are raised, then lowering legs as chest is raised. Repeat several times.

Endurance

Endurance is the ability to withstand intense exercise for a period of time, postpone fatigue, and recover quickly to a normal state. This is referred to as cardiovascular endurance, and, while muscular strength and skill are important, good performance depends primarily upon the efficient functioning of the cardiovascular system.

The relative ability to supply oxygen to the working muscles while exercising is the single most important indicator of an individual's cardiovascular endurance.

Generally, calisthenics will not develop cardiovascular endurance. But, if they are designed so that they are of a continuous nature for at least thirty minutes' duration, three times per week, an endurance effect can be achieved.

What is known as circuit training can be adapted to a certain sport. If enough sustained exercises are included, both endurance and muscular strength will result. The basic idea of this program is to compete against the clock. The athlete goes through the stations of the circuit once to familiarize himself with the various exercises. The second class, he traverses the whole circuit three times. During the third class, three laps of the circuit again are completed at maximum speed and a target is set. The target time is one half the time taken to complete the whole circuit three times. In a subsequent class when the target time is achieved, it is halved again and a new target time is set. When this new target time is achieved, the individual is ready to advance to a more difficult circuit where the whole process is repeated.

Interval training incorporates the principle of progressive overload. Four factors can be varied to achieve this result:

(1) Increasing the number of repetitions.
(2) Increasing the speed of the run.
(3) Increasing the distance to be covered.
(4) Decreasing the rest interval between runs.

From the AMA, "Jogging is probably the best way to build endurance. Bicycle riding and swimming also help. These exercises should be undertaken in the off-season period to enable the athlete to remain in good physical shape."

Short dashes or wind sprints: This is a five-day-a-week workout program designed to improve endurance. Saturdays and Sundays are rest days. This schedule should begin three weeks prior to reporting for football practice. This program is also designed to enhance an athlete's quickness.

Begin workout each day with warm-up exercises. Stretch muscles well and run 880 yards.

First Week:
10 40-yard dashes
5 30-yard dashes
5 20-yard dashes
10 10-yard dashes

Second Week:
10 40-yard dashes
5 30-yard dashes
10 20-yard dashes
10 10-yard dashes

Third Week:
10 40-yard dashes
10 30-yard dashes
10 20-yard dashes
10 10-yard dashes

Rest thirty to forty-five seconds between each dash. Obese people rest sixty to ninety seconds between each dash.

There are a number of other endurance systems, but circuit training, interval training, jogging, and short dashes are the most popular in football.

Prepractice Preparation

Although the coach in most cases is not permitted to supervise football preparation prior to regular practice, he can and should advise his players, both newcomers and veterans, as to the necessity of being in condition when the formal training season begins. You will note a suggested program for the advisement of your athletes. Although the suggested schedule shown begins in August you may wish to begin at an earlier date. (See Table 1.)

Preseason Conditioning for Football

The AMA Committee on the Medical Aspects of Sports and the National Federation of State High School Associations have recommended certain general standards of protection during spring practice, or specialized football summer camps.

1. All boys should follow faithfully a personal conditioning and acclimation program during the summer, utilizing information gained through health and physical education classes during the school year plus some specific suggestions relative to the special needs of tackle football.

2. The first day of practice should include proper fitting of protective equipment plus thorough familiarization with the importance of and procedures concerning the proper wear and care of this equipment.

Table 1
For the Athlete

August (date)	8	9	10	11	12	13	14	15	16	17	18	19	20	21	22	23–30	
Side Straddle Hop	20	20	20	20	20	20	20	25	25	25	25	25	25	25	25	50	50
Toe Toucher	20	20	20	20	20	20	20	25	25	25	25	25	25	25	25	25	30
Trunk Twister	15	15	15	15	15	15	15	20	20	20	20	20	20	20	20	25	30
Push-ups	20	20	20	20	20	20	20	25	25	25	25	25	25	25	25	25	30
Sit-ups	20	20	20	20	20	20	20	25	25	25	25	25	25	25	25	30	30
Neck Exercises	1–2 minutes								4 minutes								
1 Mile Run	1	1	1	1	1	1	1	2	2	2	2	2	2	2	2	2	2
4-way Grass Drill*	10	10	10	10	10	10	10	15	15	15	15	15	15	15	15	15	20
Forward Rolls	5	5	5	5	5	5	5	5	5	5	5	5	5	5	5	10	10

Complete the exercise period with any three exercises of your own.

INSTRUCTIONS: Circle the number of repetitions according to the respective date and exercise as you complete them.

Speed, Stamina, and Skill Drills (Perform 4 times weekly)

A. Stance and Start
1. Jog 20 yards
2. Start 5 yards
3. Walk 20 yards
4. Start 10 yards
5. Start 5 yards and cut left
6. Start 5 yards and cut right

B. Pulling out of Line
1. Right 3 times and turn left
2. Left 3 times and turn right
3. Right 8 times and turn left
4. Left 8 times and turn right

C. 4-Way Grass Reaction Drill
Football position from all fours, rise to two point, backward, lateral and forward reaction against an imaginary or real object.

Other health and safety considerations should be brought out at this time as well.

3. At least the first week of football practice should be limited to noncontact activities with emphasis on conditioning. Shorts, T-shirts, helmets, football shoes, and mouth protectors are the recommended apparel. (Early routine use of the mouthpiece promotes familiarization, acceptance, and comfort prior to the time its protective qualities become significant. Interscholastic rules require that mouth protectors and helmets be worn.) This apparel not only ensures noncontact drills while fitness and skills are improving, but also minimizes the serious hazard of heat illness. During this period, good groundwork can be laid for the diversified fundamentals of modern football, which are stressed even at the professional level.

4. The second week should be limited to controlled situations in which the coach carefully supervises appropriate contact experiences while shielding the still developing squad from unnecessary exposure to wide open play. During this period, practicing punt and kickoff plays under game conditions is strongly discouraged.

5. Practice games or game condition scrimmages should be prohibited until after a minimum of two weeks of practice.

6. A minimum of three weeks of well-planned practices should precede the first regularly scheduled interscholastic game. There is no evidence to suggest that lengthening this period beyond three weeks will bring additional benefits in health and safety.

These recommendations respect the competency and integrity of coaches, the responsibilities of school athletic administrators, and the health and welfare of the players. The governing policies of state high school associations are necessarily general as regards the period of preseason conditioning. Within this framework, however, self-enforcement of specific protective procedures by individual schools is essential.

Playing Rules and Officiating

A major objective of the American Football Coaches Association since its inception in 1922 has been the study of football playing rules so as to have a code that makes the game as safe as possible.

A set of rules, though, is not enough. Players must follow them, and coaches must teach their players how to follow them.

Every effort should be made to work with officials' groups to have the rules enforced. Mutual respect and cooperation will be most effective in bringing about a well-officiated game.

A coach should not:
1. Teach techniques that are illegal.

2. Try to motivate his players to the point where they seek to injure an opponent.

3. Encourage physical punishment of opposing players.

4. Allow his players to practice or compete after serious injury without written clearance from the team physician.

5. Harass game officials.

6. Incite the crowd against the officials.

7. Teach hate of an opponent.

Coaches should readily accept changes in the playing rules that have the objective of making the game safer.

Coaches should not seek ways to circumvent the rules. The spirit of the rules should be inviolate.

Coaches should recommend rules changes they believe will eliminate or reduce the chance of injury.

Coaches should repeatedly warn their players against spearing, piling on, clipping, slugging, and all other illegal tactics.

There can be no satisfaction from a victory achieved by illegal play.

General Observations

1. If a coach does not feel he is qualified both emotionally and technically for the many responsibilities of the coaching profession, he should leave the profession.

2. A coach must set an example for his players if he expects them to follow sound health habits and to participate in football on a high ethical plane.

3. Parents entrust their sons to the care of the coach for the hours football requires. The coach then should treat his players as he would treat his sons.

4. A coach should have a knowledge of first aid, but should not invade the province of a physician or a qualified trainer.

5. A coach should be aware that many procedures and policies of his playing days have been found to be worthless or harmful. He owes it to his players to keep up with the latest procedures and policies recommended by medical authorities.

6. A coach should not overmatch his teams physically. Neither should he overmatch his own players in practice.

7. Coaches should explain and illustrate why protective and preventive measures are required for safe football. The athlete needs to know the reasons before he will follow them conscientiously.

8. No artificial substance can elicit a greater athletic performance from an individual than he already is capable of through his own natural resources and natural ability.

9. Regular appropriate vigorous activity is bene-

ficial to everyone. The football coach should support the intramural and physical education activities at his institution. His players should be exposed to physical activities other than football because many of them soon will be ending their football playing.

10. Coaches and parents who believe swimming is not compatible with preseason football conditioning have, according to medical authorities, an incorrect view that deprives the athlete of a wonderful activity.

11. Self-medication necessarily involves self-diagnosis, and both are risky business. Remember the old medical saying, "He who treats himself has a fool for a doctor and a fool for a patient."

12. Pain-killers mask symptoms and can delay proper care until treatment is difficult.

13. According to the American Medical Association, oxygen inhalation during athletic events is impractical and expensive. Ample evidence exists that administration of oxygen prior to or after exertion has no demonstrable physiological effect either in increasing stamina or enhancing recovery.

14. Coaches should eliminate phrases and terms that connote violence. Such commands as "Kill him," "Rip his head off," and so on may get a point across but in the courtroom they are damaging. Such terms portray football as something foreign to worthwhile educational objectives and should be eliminated entirely. Do not assist the critics of the game with your use of violent language.

15. The football helmet is for the protection of the player and is not to be used as a weapon. The National Federation Football Rules specify that for safety reasons, it is illegal for a player to make the primary contact with an opponent by driving his head directly into the opponent when blocking or tackling.

The American Football Coaches Association has stated: (1) The helmet shall not be used as the primary point of contact in the teaching of blocking and tackling. (2) Self-propelled mechanical apparatus shall not be used in the teaching of blocking and tackling. (3) Greater emphasis by players, coaches, and officials should be placed on eliminating spearing.